牛津社会语言学丛书

Legal-Lay Communication

Textual Travels in the Law

法律行业内外的语言交流：

法律文本之旅

Chris Heffer, Frances Rock & John Conley 编

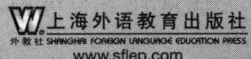上海外语教育出版社
外教社 SHANGHAI FOREIGN LANGUAGE EDUCATION PRESS
www.sflep.com

图书在版编目(CIP)数据

法律行业内外的语言交流：法律文本之旅 / （英）克里斯·海福尔(Chris Heffer)，（英）弗朗西丝·洛克（Frances Rock），（美）约翰·康利(John Conley)编.
—上海：上海外语教育出版社，2017
（牛津社会语言学丛书）
ISBN 978-7-5446-4992-6

I.①法… II.①克… ②弗… ③约… III.①法律语言学—文集—英文 IV.①D90-055

中国版本图书馆 CIP 数据核字(2017)第 209614 号

图字：09－2016－736

出版发行：上海外语教育出版社
（上海外国语大学内） 邮编：200083
电　　话：021-65425300（总机）
电子邮箱：bookinfo@sflep.com.cn
网　　址：http://www.sflep.com.cn http://www.sflep.com
责任编辑：蒋浚浚

印　　刷：上海叶大印务发展有限公司
开　　本：787×1000 1/16 印张 22 字数 575千字
版　　次：2018 年 1 月第 1 版 2018 年 1 月第 1 次印刷
印　　数：2 100 册

书　　号：ISBN 978-7-5446-4992-6 / H
定　　价：75.00 元
本版图书如有印装质量问题，可向本社调换

出版说明

社会语言学是研究语言与社会多方面关系的学科,它从社会科学的不同角度,诸如社会学、人类学、民族学、心理学、地理学和历史学等去考察语言。自20世纪60年代发端以来,社会语言学已经逐渐发展成为语言学研究中的一门重要学科,引发众多学者的关注和探究。

"牛津社会语言学丛书"由国际社会语言学研究的两位领军人物——英国卡迪夫大学语言与交际研究中心的教授 Nicolas Coupland 和 Adam Jaworski(现在中国香港大学英语学院任教)——担任主编。丛书自2004年由牛津大学出版社陆续出版以来,推出了一系列社会语言学研究的专著,可以说是汇集了这一学科研究的最新成果,代表了当今国际社会语言学研究的最高水平。

我们从中精选出九种,引进出版。所选的这些专著内容广泛,又较贴近我国学者研究的需求,涵盖了当今社会语言学的许多重要课题,如语言变体与语言变化、语言权力与文化认同、语言多元化与语言边缘化、语言与族裔、语言与立场(界位)、语言与新媒体、语用学与礼貌、语言与法律以及社会语言学视角下的话语研究等等。其中既有理论研究,又有方法创新;既有框架分析建构,又有实地考察报告;既体现本学科的前沿和纵深,又展现跨学科的交叉和互补。

相信丛书的引进出版能为从事社会语言学研究的读者带来新的启示,进一步推动我国语言学研究的发展。

LEGAL-LAY COMMUNICATION

Textual Travels in the Law

Edited by Chris Heffer, Frances Rock,

and John Conley

For Isabella, Paula, and Tom

CONTENTS

ACKNOWLEDGMENTS

The idea for this book originates from the 6th Cardiff Roundtable in Sociolinguistics, which was generously funded by the School of English, Communication and Philosophy at Cardiff University in July 2008. Adam Jaworski suggested that we might hold the Roundtable on the theme of language and law, and Gregynog Hall in the heart of the Welsh hills guaranteed that we ate and slept well. Nikolas Coupland and Adam Jaworski were very supportive during the long process of proposing the book to Oxford University Press.

The contributors to this volume have shown considerable patience while it moved toward publication. For this we are very grateful. We also thank them for their eager and constructive participation in the workshop and their fascinating resulting chapters.

We recall here the invaluable contributions of Janet Cotterill, Howard Giles, Tim Grant, Sally Nelson, Thomas Scheffer, Larry Solan, and Jenny Thomas, who were present in person, paper, or video at the Roundtable, and thus indirectly contributed to this book. We thank John Conley's assistant, Graham Ford, for his exceptional work on the production of the final manuscript. We are also grateful to Maureen Cirnitski of Newgen for guiding us so carefully and patiently through the production process. Finally we thank Hallie Stebbins at OUP for taking oversight of this project at a late stage and helping move it along.

ACKNOWLEDGEMENTS

CONTRIBUTORS

Dawn Archer is a Professor of Pragmatics and Corpus Linguistics at the University of Central Lancashire (Preston, UK). Her "forensic" research interests include: the evolution of courtroom practices over time, the role of aggression in the adversarial courtroom, and police negotiation interaction. Dawn is also well known for her pragmatics-based and/or corpus-linguistic-based research. Currently, Dawn is heading up a UCLan team of psychologists and linguists who are exploring the intersection between emotions, credibility, and deception in different private and public sector professional settings.

R. Jean Cadigan is Research Assistant Professor in the Department of Social Medicine at the University of North Carolina, Chapel Hill. She received her Ph.D. in anthropology from the University of California, Los Angeles.

John M. Conley is William Rand Kenan, Jr. Professor of Law at the University of North Carolina at Chapel Hill and an investigator in the university's Center for Genomics and Society. He received his A.B. from Harvard University and J.D. and Ph.D. (Anthropology) from Duke University. His research focuses on the linguistic and cultural aspects of law, science, and finance.

Bethan L. Davies is a Lecturer in Linguistics in the Department of Linguistics and Phonetics in the School of Modern Languages and Cultures at the University of Leeds. She has published across a number of fields including (im)politeness, Gricean pragmatics, metadiscourse and language ideologies, and critical discourse analysis. Until recently, she was co-investigator on the AHRC-funded 'BBC Voices' project at the University of Leeds. Current projects include further work on the discourses of transport and research into language ideologies associated with minority languages in the United Kingdom.

Arlene M. Davis is Research Associate Professor in the Department of Social Medicine at the University of North Carolina, Chapel Hill, core faculty in its Center for Bioethics, and Adjunct Associate Professor at the University of North Carolina School of Law. She received her J.D. from the University of Washington School of Law.

Erica L. Delgadillo is a Ph.D. candidate in the communication department at the University of Colorado at Boulder. She studies and teaches about rhetoric and argument; Delgadillo is at work on her dissertation, which is an analysis of amicus briefs in a same-sex marriage appeals case in California's Supreme Court.

Alison W. Dobson is an associate attorney at Kilpatrick Townsend & Stockton LLP in the Intellectual Property Department, Winston-Salem, NC office. She received a B.S. in applied biology from the Georgia Institute of Technology, a Ph.D. in basic medical sciences from the University of South Alabama College of Medicine, and a J.D. from the University of North Carolina School of Law.

Erin Edwards is an attorney employed in the University of North Carolina's Office of Clinical Trials. She received her J.D. from the University of North Carolina School of Law.

Susan Ehrlich is Professor of Linguistics in the Department of Languages, Literatures and Linguistics, York University, Toronto. She works in the areas of discourse analysis, language and gender, and language and the law. Her work has been published in journals such as *Language in Society, Discourse & Society*, and *Journal of Sociolinguistics* and recent books include *Representing Rape* (Routledge, 2001), *Language and Gender* (Routledge, 2008), and *'Why Do You Ask': The Function of Questions in Institutional Discourse* (Oxford, 2010), co-edited with Alice Freed.

Wendell S. Fortson received his B.S. in Biology from Tennessee State University, Ph.D. in Biomedical Sciences-Cancer Biology from Morehouse School of Medicine, and J.D. from North Carolina Central University School of Law. He completed his postdoctoral training at UNC-Chapel Hill's Center for Genomics and Society and currently works for Ethos Clinical Group.

Mark Garner is Director of the Centre for Language Assessment Research and Head of Whitelands College at the University of Roehampton in London, UK. His background is in applied linguistics, and his main areas of research are in emergency, operational, and interpersonal communication and language teaching. He has published a number of books and articles in these fields. He was co-author (with Edward Johnson) of the national standards for police radio, which are mandatory for all UK forces.

Chris Heffer is Senior Lecturer in Language and Communication in the Centre for Language and Communication Research at Cardiff University. He is author of *The Language of Jury Trial* (Palgrave, 2005) and *Rhetoric and Rights: A Theory of Forensic Discourse* (OUP, forthcoming) and has published articles in linguistic and legal journals on various theoretical and communicational aspects of the trial process and jury instruction. He has made recommendations on jury instruction to the New South Wales Law Reform Commission and to judges in England and Wales and in the United States.

Georgina Heydon is a Senior Lecturer in Criminal Justice at RMIT University (Australia). She published the first monograph to analyze the language of police interviewing in Australia from a linguistic and discourse analytic perspective. Over the last ten years, Dr. Heydon's research has contributed a new level of detail to the analysis of legal-societal issues in policing by focusing on the discursive phenomena that underlie testimonial integrity, methods of detecting deception, formality, and the right to silence.

Alison Johnson is a Lecturer in English Language in the School of English, University of Leeds, and researches in corpus-based forensic linguistics, drawing on discourse and conversational analysis, interactional sociolinguistics, and pragmatics. Formerly a police officer for six years, Dr. Johnson's doctoral research explored the use of questions in police interviews with both adults and children. Author of articles on the language of police interrogation and suspect resistance, courtroom discourse, and on plagiarism, and author of *An Introduction to Forensic Linguistics: Language in Evidence* (2007) and *The Routledge Handbook of Forensic Linguistics* (2010) with Malcolm Coulthard.

Edward Johnson, Fellow, Wolfson College, University of Cambridge, researches operational communication, constructed languages, and multimodal, multilingual, computer-mediated interaction. He has directed real-world applications including: the standard grammar for international maritime radio language (*Seaspeak*), the first controlled-language, interactive machine translation system (*Linitext*™), the police and emergency standards for the Channel Tunnel (*PoliceSpeak* and *Intacom*), and, with David Matthews, the first multilingual, email system *LinguaNet*®. The UK national police digital radio standard (*AirwaveSpeak*) was completed in 2008 and the Cabinet Office civil protection lexicon in 2010. Johnson is currently working with Columbia University, New York, on linguistic components for healthcare systems.

Martha Komter is research fellow at the Netherlands Institute for the Study of Crime and Law Enforcement (NSCR) in Amsterdam. Dr. Komter has published books and articles in national and international journals about various aspects of language use, especially in the criminal law process. Her current research concerns the ways in which police reports are drawn up during the police interrogation and the ways in which these reports are brought up in the courtroom.

Katrijn Maryns works as a postdoctoral researcher for the FWO Research Foundation Flanders and is affiliated to the Linguistics Department at Ghent University, Belgium. Her research examines discourse practices in legal-procedural contexts. She did linguistic-ethnographic work on communicative practices in asylum settings and examined issues of diversity and performance in the Belgian Assize Court. She is the author of *The Asylum Speaker: Language in the Belgian Asylum Procedure* (St. Jerome Publishing, 2006) and "Procedures without Borders: The Language-Ideological Anchorage of Administrative Procedures in Translocal Institutional Settings" (*Language in Society*, 2013).

Robert Mitchell is Associate Professor in English, Director of the Center for Interdisciplinary Studies in Science and Cultural Theory, and Faculty in the Institute for Genome Sciences and Policy at Duke University. He received his Ph.D. from the University of Washington.

Frances Rock is a Senior Lecturer in the Centre for Language and Communication Research at Cardiff University. Her research has examined language and policing in a variety of settings including the police interview and the emergency call. Recommendations following from her work have been taken up by police forces around England and Wales. Frances's publications in the area of policing include the book *Communicating Rights: The Language of Arrest and Detention* (2007). Frances is one of the editors of the *International Journal of Speech, Language and the Law.*

Karen Tracy is Professor of Communication at the University of Colorado at Boulder and a Distinguished Scholar in the National Communication Association. She is a discourse analyst who studies and teaches about institutional talk, particularly in justice, academic, and governance sites. Tracy is the author of *Colloquium: Dilemmas of Academic Discourse, Everyday Talk: Building and Reflecting Identities,* and *Challenges of Ordinary Democracy.* She is currently at work on a new book titled *Disputing Who Can Marry: Social Change through Discourses of Law-Making and Interpreting.*

Shonna Trinch is Associate Professor in the Department of Anthropology at John Jay College, City University of New York (CUNY). She received her Ph.D. in Spanish Linguistics in 1999 from the University of Pittsburgh. Her book, *Latina Women's Narratives of Domestic Abuse: Discrepant Versions of Violence* (John Benjamins, 2003) investigates how women's stories of domestic abuse and rape change and are changed, as they are cast by legal professionals from one speech genre into another. While Shonna continues to publish articles on the discourse of women who have been victimized by sexual assault and domestic violence, her current research program also incorporates discourse and sociolinguistic analyses in two new fields of inquiry, namely urban redevelopment and literacy.

Legal-Lay Communication

INTRODUCTION

CHAPTER 1
Textual Travel in Legal–Lay Communication

FRANCES ROCK, CHRIS HEFFER, AND JOHN CONLEY

While the legal process is, by its very name, a *process* that unfolds over time, analysts of discourse, including discourse in the legal arena, are methodologically inclined to start with a synchronic and apparently stable analytical unit—the immediate text—which often hides the diachronic instability of the discourse from which that text emerged. Nowhere is that instability more potent than in legal settings and in no other setting is the notion of apparently stable texts following each other along intertextual trajectories more enticing to participants.

This book has an encompassing theme—*legal–lay communication*—which it engages with critically, but it also develops a particular take on that theme—*textual travel*. This combination of themes makes it possible for the book to move beyond what would be possible with only one agenda. The chapters in the collection explore aspects of legal–lay communication, or those nodes of interaction where the legal world meets the everyday lifeworld. This may involve instances when people acting for the legal system, from police call handlers to judges, interact with people encountering the legal process in a lay role, for example, as witnesses and suspects. However, this transparent reading of "legal" and "lay" will be challenged both here and throughout the book. The book is far from being a potpourri of chapters on the theme of legal–lay communication. The theoretical nexus for the exploration in the individual chapters is the notion of textual travel, a point of departure which provides very particular insights.

We are using the portmanteau term *textual travel* as a way of bringing together a set of distinct but complementary theoretical constructs which collectively shed new light on legal–lay communication and on thinking about the ways in which texts can be transformed in social life. These include a series of concepts that are well established within linguistics, anthropology, and sociology and which have been

discussed using such terms as *delocation* and *relocation* (Bernstein 1990); *centering,*
decentering, and *recentering* (Hanks 1989); *entextualization, decontextualization,* and
recontextualization (Bauman and Briggs 1990); *intertextuality* and *interdiscursivity*
(Kristeva 1980; Fairclough 1992, 2001; Candlin and Maley 1997); *reentextualiza-*
tion and *text trajectories* (Blommaert 2005). These perspectives on textual travel
are united by a desire "to understand the 'life' of…a discourse…to identify how
it connects to other discourses in the textual chain" (Blackledge 2005: 121) or, as
it is elegantly put in Javan, "*jarwa dhosok,* taking old language (*jarwa*) and pushing
(*dhosok*) it into new contexts" (Becker 1995: 185).

Use of the travel metaphor in relation to texts is not novel. Linell, for example,
described recontextualization as arising when "discourse and discursive content
will travel across situations" (1998: 144). Blommaert too writes of texts, discourses,
and images being "shipped around" along "trajectories" with various "mappings" in
play (2005: 76) and discusses "texts that do not travel well" (2005: 78; 2008: xiv),
having cast off their original "use, value and function" (Blommaert 2008: 6). In the
legal context, Ehrlich has also talked of the "shifting" of testimony through the legal
system (Ehrlich 2007: 455). Our term *textual travel* is an effort to encapsulate these
related usages.

In short, textual travel concerns the way that texts move through and around
institutional processes and are shaped, altered, and appropriated during their journeys. In legal processes, various actors give texts context-specific linguistic lives
and send them on particular journeys. In the common law litigation process, for
example, social actors produce language, creating transient discourse. Lawyers lift
some of this language from its interactional context, or entextualize it (Bauman and
Briggs 1990), and erase the rest. Courts at each level repeat the process, resulting
in the text of texts that we call an appellate decision. Lawyers in subsequent cases
make precedential arguments by further selection, erasing this and recontextualizing that. Later courts respond by creating texts of their own, and the reconstitution
continues.

The contributors to the collection explore a wide array of processes, including
police tasking and investigation, litigation in both the civil and common law traditions, judicial metadiscourse on everyday language, oral and written communications between legal authorities and the public, and the reactions of lay participants
to legal processes. Despite this diversity of contexts, all of the chapters highlight
the "natural histories" (Silverstein and Urban 1996a) of texts and the centralities
of these histories to the respective processes under investigation. Indeed, our contributors demonstrate that the management of textual travel, including such phenomena as entextualization, and [de/re]contextualization, comprise the very core
of communication and argumentation in and around the law. The contributions
examine text (what is transferred and transformed when textual travel occurs?);
context (how much, if any, of the original context is maintained when textual travel
occurs?); voices (who or what travels and how is this manifest in the discourse?);
and discursive practices (how do speakers and writers exploit the potential for

textual travel to facilitate addition, deletion, and change?). In this introduction, we shall tease out the central concepts of legal–lay communication and textual travel in a little more detail and then show how each of the contributions develops our understanding of these concepts and our understanding of the legal processes to which they are applied.

LEGAL–LAY/LAY–LEGAL COMMUNICATION

In this age of antiessentialism, it is not possible simply to define a concept clearly from the start. At the same time, as Cameron (1998: 164) pointed out in the early 1980s with regard to feminist theory's then nebulous use of the term *language*, if we do not start with some idea of what we are talking about, then we are likely only to achieve further mystification. Tracy and Delgadillo (in their chapter here) spell out a few key questions which trouble the legal–lay distinction, such as what the terms *legal* and *lay* actually refer to and whether both *legal* and *lay* parties need to be present for legal–lay communication to take place. One question which Tracy and Delgadillo raise, about the ordering of the pair of terms, should be cleared up immediately, as far as it relates to this collection. As indicated by the subheading above, we do not, as a team, attribute any particular theoretical significance to the order of these terms. The ordering of two-part terms generally reflects the main focus of the particular users. Thus, lawyers interested in linguistic issues generally talk about the field of "law and language" (e.g., Pintore and Jori 1997), while linguists interested in legal-linguistic issues generally talk about "language and law" (e.g., Gibbons 1994). In Heffer (2005), *legal–lay discourse* was conceived as a style of legal professional discourse (see below) so it was clearly directional from legal to lay, while Conley et al. (in their chapter here) focus primarily on *lay* reactions to *legal* consent forms, so use *lay–legal*. Rock uses *lay–legal* (Rock 2007: 27) due to a concern with the needs of lay people and, beyond that, an overarching conception of the legal system as being "for" its lay users (i.e., for society). The contributions as a whole show a mixed focus on the legal and the lay with some chapters perhaps focusing more on the legal and others on the lay side of the pair.

Beyond this terminological question, Tracy and Delgadillo's chapter also presents questions which effectively identify three quite different approaches to the lay–legal distinction, and it is worth teasing these out a little here.

(1) Legal–Lay as Categories of Participant

In the first place, *legal–lay* can be construed as participant categories: *legal* participants communicating with *lay* participants. However, we then need to consider who belongs within those categories. One could restrict *legal* to those with a law degree and a professional legal qualification that allows them to practice in the profession. This has the advantage of restricting the scope to a particular community of practice with a broadly shared (and, particularly, mind-shaping) education (Mertz 2007). Observing the interaction between legal professionals (lawyers and judges) and police officers in court, for example, it is quite clear that they do not belong to the same community of practice nor share the same education, training, or interactional style.

At the same time, those working in professions relating to the law are heavily influenced by the law in their interactional practice. For example, Heydon shows in her chapter how police interviews are dictated by categories provided in advance by the law and Johnson in hers shows how interviews anticipate courtroom interaction between lawyers and witnesses. To exclude interaction not involving formally trained and qualified legal professionals would, then, miss much of what is interesting about legal–lay communication. However, this does tend to take the term *legal* beyond the professional category.

The *lay* category is also not entirely straightforward. Traditionally, *lay* (from Greek *laos* "people") has always been defined explicitly or implicitly in opposition to the particular profession (initially the clergy but then extended to other professions) that is producing, or is the focus of, the discourse. In this sense, *lay* in *legal–lay* refers (as a category of person) to anyone not belonging to the legal profession or to professions related to the law. Used in this way, *lay* will include not only nonprofessional people but also other professionals (e.g., doctors, clergy, academics) who are not *legal*. In many contexts, though, this is clearly reductive. Analysts of courtroom discourse, for example, have minimally felt the need to distinguish between (proper) *lay* and (lay) *expert* witnesses. Furthermore, police officers in court are very different interactionally from either legal professionals or other lay witnesses. *Defendants* seem to form an interactional category of their own, and Rock (2007) even divides them according to their relative experience of detention and resulting orientation. Of particular relevance here, her "expert" detainee category contains members who read particular legal texts—largely books aimed at an audience of solicitors—outside custody, yet saw themselves as too proficient to engage with informative legal texts in custody when those were provided specifically for detainees (2007: 112–13). Sarangi (2001: 4) similarly recognizes the expert dimension of those lay people who enter medical encounters with self-diagnoses and medical categorizations in mind and Matoesian (2001: 178–88) shows how a medically trained defendant can shift his testimonial status from "lay" to "expert."

Outside specific professional contexts, though, *lay* is also used to mean "nonprofessional" in general. For example, Linell (1998: 143) distinguishes between three types of institutional discourse: *intraprofessional* (e.g., among legal professionals), *interprofessional* (e.g., between legal and medical professionals), and *professional-lay* (i.e., "when professionals meet and interact with, speak with or write for, lay people"). Of this last category, Linell names, amongst other examples, "court trials." Yet trials clearly include all three types of interaction: legal submissions (intraprofessional), examination of professional expert witnesses (interprofessional), and examination of nonprofessionals (professional-lay). And what is one to make, then, of communication with the jury? In many common law jurisdictions today, where even legal professionals cannot be exempted by right, the jury is likely to be a mix of professional and nonprofessional people.

(2) Legal–Lay as Institutional Interaction

One way of avoiding the problem of categorizing the participants themselves is to see *legal–lay* as referring to institutional interaction. Drew and Heritage (1992: 3–4) argue that "interaction is institutional insofar as participants' institutional or professional identities are somehow made relevant to the work activities in which they are engaged." In this sense, *legal–lay communication* refers to the way that people acting for legal institutions, from police call handlers to judges, interact with people encountering the legal process in a noninstitutional (or *lay* in this sense) role, such as witnesses, suspects, and those with evidential expertise. The key difference between *legal* and *lay* in this conception is the extent to which participants are aware of the goal orientations, special interactional constraints, and inferential frameworks that are specific to the given institutional context (Drew and Heritage 1992: 22–25). For example, a lay witness might not understand what the "friendly" lawyer is doing when she questions him about issues he would rather not reveal, or why he cannot report what his friend was thinking, or why answering a question in a certain way presupposes an incriminating point. However, again the lines are not clearly drawn. For example, does an expert witness acting for the prosecution (the state) in a criminal case have an institutional role or a lay one? And does it matter how experienced that expert witness is, and therefore how well she is aware of the institutional goals, constraints, and inferential frameworks?

(3) Legal–Lay as Cognitive or Discursive Styles

A third approach to the *legal–lay* distinction is to see the *legal* and the *lay* as cognitive or discursive *styles* of discourse rather than categories of participant or institutional talk. As styles, *legal* and *lay* needn't necessarily be attached to particular speakers. Conley and O'Barr (1990), for example, have shown that lay litigants in small claims courts can orient to their testimony in terms of "rules" or "relationships" and that a rule-orientation is more typical of legal discourse than a relational orientation. However, some nonlegal speakers show a rule-orientation while others are clearly relational. Here a key question might be whether they are accommodating to the legal discourse context or simply following their "normal" orientation to the world. Heffer (2005), drawing on Bruner (1986), tries to tease out some discursive manifestations of a "paradigmatic" cognitive style that is typical of the law and a "narrative" cognitive style that is typical of lay orientations to the world. He then posits a hybrid style of discourse—"legal–lay discourse"—which arises when legal professionals, who are trained to think about legal cases in a paradigmatic, or rule-based, fashion, attempt to persuade lay fact-finders, who are used to reasoning about crime stories in a narrative fashion, of the guilt or innocence of the defendant.

As Tracy and Delgadillo point out in their discussion of "discourse categorization systems," the particular categorization of discourse one adopts is very much dependent on the type of empirical context one has studied in detail. For example, sociologists of science focus on the distinction between *expert* and *lay* rather than *professional* and *lay*, and Collins and Evans (2007) distinguish between *interactional* expertise (what the legal-linguistic researcher has) and *contributory* expertise (what the practicing lawyer has). However, this emphasis on the ability to walk the walk rather than just talk the talk is more applicable to science than to law, which is fundamentally predicated on language. Similarly, Heffer's notion of "legal–lay discourse" was developed through analysis of, and specifically confined to, "a type of discourse found in jury trials" (2005: 3). However, the use of *legal–lay* to describe such a specific style of discourse is possibly misleading.

Viewing *legal–lay* as a question of cognitive or discursive style can help explain how it is possible to talk of legal–lay communication when one or more participants in the communication are neither *legal* nor *lay*. For example, Conley et al. argue in their chapter that the entire process of consent-taking in medical encounters is conceived and structured from a legal perspective even if the interaction itself involves medical personnel and lay informants.

Another way of explaining legal–lay discourse beyond the presence of either legal or lay participants, though, is in terms of the presence of other voices within a given discourse. For example, Tracy and Delgadillo argue that lawyers' written briefs and oral arguments to Supreme Court justices count as legal–lay communication, rather than simply legal discourse, because the lawyers are conveying the voices of their lay clients. It is this idea of voices within voices, and of voices travelling through the legal process, that leads to our main take on legal–lay communication: that it needs to be seen not in terms of fixed categories but of fluid and ever-changing forms travelling through time and space.

TEXTUAL TRAVEL

If we can talk of texts metaphorically "travelling," it is because the notion of text has become released from its folk linguistic roots as a stable, autonomous, and bounded entity. The origins of such a move might be found in Bakhtin's challenge to Saussure's construction of the science of language as the study of *langue*, a synchronic and autonomous entity that existed outside sociohistorical processes (Saussure [1916] 1983). For Bakhtin, language was immersed in and inseparable from the sociohistorical and ideological processes in which it emerged: "Each word tastes of the context and contexts in which it has lived its socially charged life" ([1935] 1981: 293). Words thus travelled through time, as had been made all too evident by the etymological work of the nineteenth-century philologists against whom Saussure was reacting. But Bakhtin went one step further and argued that all texts are in dialogue both with previous texts and with future texts. This *dialogical principle* means that text is constrained by emerging historical patterns of text production (*genre*) but also that it can "play" with multiple, historically grounded voices (*heteroglossia*).

In introducing Bakhtin's work to the West, Kristeva (1980) coined the term *intertextuality* to account for the inevitable connections *between* texts: no text can stand on its own but must inevitably, and often unwittingly, quote and refer to other previous texts. Foucault went so far as to say that "there can be no statement that in one way or another does not reactualise others" (1972: 98) while Derrida, more radically, described text as nothing more than a fabric woven from other texts: "This interweaving, this textile, is the *text* produced only in the transformation of another text" (Derrida [1972] 1981: 26).

Intertextuality, in short, is "the property texts have of being full of snatches of other texts which may be explicitly demarcated or merged in, and which the text may assimilate, contradict, ironically echo, and so forth" (Fairclough 1992: 84). To the extent that intertextuality is a "property" of text, it might suggest a destination (the text has travelled to reach its current location), but it might also refer to the transformations that texts undergo as they move along chains and are embedded within subsequent texts. We are thus moving from echoes of past voices *in* a text to a sense of texts being linked together in a historical chain. Texts might then be seen to pass dynamically along that chain, as when Bauman talks of intertextual resonances extending "across time and space, linking discursive moments separated by a single speaker change or many decades. A few feet of interpersonal space or hundreds of miles" (2004: 128).

While literary and critical theorists were disputing the historical autonomy of the text, anthropological linguists were challenging the very notion that text and context can be separated. The perception of text in anthropological linguistic work underwent a radical transformation over the course of the twentieth-century from static artifact to dynamic process. First, text began to be viewed as "surrounded by" a situational context and linguistic cotext which determined its meaning beyond the linguistic semantics (e.g., Malinowski 1923; Firth 1957). Then analysts pointed out that the context itself was dynamic rather than static: speakers actively constructed relevant context as they spoke (e.g., Gumperz 1982; Auer and Di Luzio 1992). Thus, static *context* became dynamic *contextualization*. "Contextualization cues" such as discourse markers, intonation, raised eyebrows, and gaze could actively signal to others how aspects of what they were saying should be heard (Gumperz 1982).

Finally, in the 1980s, a group of anthropological linguists (e.g., Hanks 1989; Bauman and Briggs 1990; Silverstein and Urban 1996b) argued that not only was context not given, but text itself had to be constructed *as text* through discourse. In other words, *text* needed to be *en-textual-ized*. Bauman and Briggs defined *entextualization* as "the process of rendering discourse extractable, of making a stretch of linguistic production into a unit—a text—that can be lifted out of its interactional setting" (1990: 73). They noted that entextualization depends on the reflexive capacity of discourse, its ability to refer to itself, which is manifested most clearly in the metalingual and poetic functions of language (Jakobson 1960). Text is shaped by metadiscourse (what it says, or indexes, about itself, including the fact that it should be read as "text") and by performance, a "mode of communicative display, in which the performer signals to an audience, in effect, 'hey look at me! I'm on! watch how skilfully and effectively I express myself'" (Bauman 2004: 9).

Once text has been extracted from its interactional setting, it necessarily becomes *decontextualized*. At this point it can appear to take on autonomous meaning, even if the resultant text will tend to retain textual "sediment" from the original interaction(s) (Silverstein and Urban 1996b). Furthermore, uprooted from its original context, it can now be replanted in a new setting, that is, it can be *recontextualized*. And this can start a long chain of successive recontextualizations. Thus, while, broadly speaking, studies of intertextuality tend to focus on the textual product and its dialogue with other texts (particularly in the Critical Discourse Analysis tradition), studies of entextualization or recontextualization (different authors use either one or the other term to refer to the entire process of entextualization, decontextualization, and recontextualization) tend to focus on the diachronic process of text creation and re-creation and how texts are transformed in the process.

A third way of conceiving textual travel, which derives primarily from studies of literacy rather than speech, is to see it as processes of mediation. From this perspective, the travel itself, and particularly the mode of travel and its side effects, take on great importance as the transformation of texts is seen to be constrained by the cultural practices or "mediational means" (Wertsch 1998) available to construct those texts. These means include not only the speech organs themselves, but also modes such as writing and signing, and media such as newspapers or television. Different mediational tools, such as pen and paper or a computer, have different effects on writing activities and outputs. For example, the former facilitates drawing but hinders editing while the latter facilitates cutting and pasting but hinders simple graphic representation and can restrict the physical orientations of one or more interactants.

Neither pen and paper nor a computer, of course, facilitates the representation of speech. Furthermore even dictation can end up being very different if taken down using pen and paper, typed on a computer, or recorded on tape or video, as can its situation of production. These effects are not simply practical but are also cultural; indeed, they are potentially ideological (Johnstone 2002: 180–81). The study of mediational means and their effects (Wertsch 1993, 1994, 1998) can contribute to examinations of transformational processes by showing how "mediational means support or undermine the purposes of the participants within their communities of practice.... and how those media bring into the situation the historical, cultural or social practices of the larger society in which these mediated actions...take place" (Scollon 1998: 7).

To talk of texts "travelling" is to assume both that there is a stable element to texts (something must be doing the travelling) and that there is some fluid element (some form of transformation must take place or we should simply talk of "repetition"). However, what is stable and what is fluid is not given. Both the stable and fluid elements of text might be in the form, the propositional content, the function, the intended meaning, or the interpretation. Thus, the linguistic form of a text might remain stable while its interpretation is transformed before a new audience.

For example, when Blommaert (2005: 78–83; 2008: xiv) talks of "texts that do not travel well," he is referring specifically to texts written in third world countries which are then read in first world countries but with a far less favorable interpretation, while Heffer (this volume) shows how a linguistically stable textual formula like "beyond reasonable doubt" can be transformed in meaning, function, and interpretation over time and across communities of practice. On the other hand, the basic propositional content of, for example, a narrative text might remain fairly stable while the form, meanings, and interpretation are radically transformed. Blommaert (2005: 255) defines his notion of "text trajectories" as "patterns of shifting and transferring bits of discourse through series of entextualisations" and gives the example of a patient's oral narrative that is first scribbled down in note form by the consultant, then discussed with other colleagues, who in turn take notes and subsequently include elements of the narrative in an academic publication. Similarly, in this collection, Komter illustrates how one category of text—the suspect's statement to the police—travels through the Dutch criminal prosecution process while undergoing radical formal transformation.

Recontextualization, through transformation, can "comment on, legitimate or otherwise evaluate" text (Blackledge 2006: 144). For example, it may involve a change in *framing* (Goffman 1974), "the (re)indexing of a language user's relationships with both message and coparticipants, including potential authorships and addressees" (Sarangi 1998: 306), or a change in *footing* (Goffman 1981), the display of various alignments to what is being said. Indeed, the processes of textual travel are fundamentally ideological. Bourdieu (1990) would claim that textual travel is constrained by the normalized patterns of behavior represented by the *habitus* and the configuration of social roles, agent positions, and structures that is the *field*. Similarly, for Foucault (1972), the formation and transformation of text, both as process and artifactual product, is regulated by the *archive*, or the totality of a society's normatively imposed discursive practice.

The set of concepts we have brought together under the term "textual travel" is particularly useful in the study of legal–lay communication, where we find extensive textual movement both from legal sources (legislation, common law, regulations) to lay audiences (defendants, witnesses, juries) and from lay producers (eyewitnesses, clients, lay litigants) to legal addressees (interviewing officers, lawyers, judges). With regard to movement from the institutional to the noninstitutional, Bernstein (1990:

192) notes, in the field of education, how a "recontextualizing context" regulates the movement of texts and practices from university research (the "primary context of discursive production") to schools (the "secondary context of discursive reproduction"). Texts are appropriated by powerful "recontextualizing agents" in the form of government departments who regulate the movement of texts between these two contexts and control the sorts of transformation those texts undergo. Similarly, we might talk of the production of legal discourse through the primary context of legislation and the reproduction of that discourse in the secondary context of the police interview room or courtroom, with the movement of texts regulated by the powerful recontextualizing agents of legal authorities, legal education, and police trainers.

Recontextualization in such institutionally driven contexts then demands degrees of transformation to "accommodate" (Giles and Powesland 1975) the new lay audience. For example, Cotterill (2000), Rock (2007), and Heydon (this volume) have examined the processes which come into play when institutional actors must communicate to defendants the legal-institutional formulations of their rights: the police "caution" (UK and Australia) or "Miranda warning" (US). Halldorsdottir (2006) has examined the way that laws, legal codes, and guidelines influence lawyers' interactions with their clients and the way they influence the texts that result from those interactions, which are themselves taken up later in the process of criminal defense work. Similarly, Heffer (2005: 175–80) has shown how the statutory language of an offence definition is recontextualized in jury instruction first by transforming it into plainer formal English and then by setting it into the context of a hypothetical narrative.

Recontextualization also occurs from lay to legal contexts. Jönsson and Linell (1991) traced the differences between 30 police interviews in Sweden and the written police statements which were derived from those interviews, finding that recontextualization brought changes in narrative structure, perspective, and the degree of legal relevance, as well as increased precision, coherence, objectivity, and chronology. Gibbons (2001) adduced similar findings working with Spanish data from a Chilean hearing and Trinch (2003) shows how Latina women's oral stories of domestic abuse change when cast as reports in affidavits in their applications for orders of protection. Rock (2001) carefully charted the process through which witnesses' reports are recontextualized within interview talk and found that even with such "merely" referential (though probatively crucial) matters as time and duration, we see a movement from vagueness and uncertainty in the witness's report to apparent precision in the final written statement.

A special edition of the journal *Research on Language and Social Interaction* (39: 3) traced transformational processes exposed in the subset of legal activities which transform "talk to text" in the legal system (Komter 2006; Martinez 2006). One of the most meticulous of these papers is Scheffer's (2006) ethnographic study of a day in the life of a defense barrister (trial lawyer) in an English Crown Court as he follows a case from receipt of the solicitor's brief on the very morning of the trial to his closing argument to the jury. Scheffer follows the process of textual "microformation" (2006: 303) that takes place as the barrister rapidly evolves a theory of the case and works out how he will present it discursively through "marks, notes, a map, lists [and] drafts" that come together to "bind the present performance to the archival past" (2006: 337). Accommodation to legal discourse does not always take place via legal media- tors. Conley and O'Barr (1990) demonstrated that some lay litigants converge with the discourse preferences of legal actors and consequently appear more persuasive, and Hall (2009) has recently shown how formulaic utterances typical of policespeak travel into the talk of those who are not police officers through processes of accom- modation. Trinch (2005) shows how Latina women, when applying for protective orders, adopt legal language and incorporate it into their oral narratives of abuse.

For those working under the "textual travel" umbrella, repetition must be ana- lytically illusory, since context, and thus discourse, is actively constructed with each new interaction (Toolan 1996). Research on verbal recall (e.g., Baddeley 1990) has demonstrated that we are very poor indeed at remembering verbatim what some- one said even a moment earlier and if what someone said is recorded, it is necessar- ily mediated, decontextualized, and recontextualized. The notion of textual travel, then, is diametrically opposed to the notion of literal repetition. However, literal repetition over time remains both a powerful folk-linguistic category and an even more powerful legal category. As a folk-linguistic category, Berk-Seligson (2009) argues that repetition, when used by a defendant, can function as a "stalling device" designed to deny and resist interrogators' efforts to implicate him. She concludes that "such repetitions can empower a detainee with a strategy for self-defense in the face of a situation of asymmetrical power relationships" (Berk-Seligson 2009: 92). That repetition remains a powerful legal category, on the other hand, is evidenced in the recent work of Andrus (2009a, b), who has examined the "excited utterance" exception to hearsay in the US law of evidence. That exception allows testimony in court which reports an utterance made by someone in the heat of an unexpected or disturbing moment. However, this reduces spoken discourse to a textual artifact that can be passed around unproblematically and produces a legal fiction about the trustworthiness of utterances produced in various circumstances (Andrus 2009a).

Some parts of the legal system attempt to reconstruct interactional contexts or reprise aspects of those contexts. Seminal work by Matoesian (1993, 1995, 2001) and Ehrlich (2001, 2007) has focused on how the structures of domination inher- ent in rape are reproduced or reconstructed in the courtroom. Matoesian shows how trial talk transforms rape into consensual sex, and later shows how the expe- rience of rape can be re-experienced in the courtroom, particularly in the hostile environment of cross-examination, as "rape of the second kind" (Matoesian 1995: 676). Ehrlich, on the other hand, shows how gendered identities "filter" through the court's ideological frameworks (2001: 2). For example, she shows how wom- en's signs of acts of resistance and lack of consent to sexual activity can be recon- textualized as indicators of consensual sex (2001: 144), a form of legal-institutional recontextualization which she explores in detail in her chapter here.

A common theme in work effectively exploring what we are describing as textual travel is the loss or distortion of the lay voice as it travels through the legal system.

Ehrlich's rape victim's "strategies of resistance," for example, are "heard" as indicators of legal consent. Eades (2008) shows in a meticulous study how the voices of three Aboriginal boys, who were effectively kidnapped by six police officers, become suppressed and replaced by the voices of law enforcement during the trial of the police officers. For example, defense counsel follow the typical cross-examination strategy of trying to impeach the boys through misleading questions that lead to answers inconsistent with those given in their police statements. Inconsistencies, which are the inevitable upshot of the transformative nature of textual travel, are thus "labelled as *lies*" (2008: 156; emphasis in original). Eades sees recontextualization, as practiced in today's courts, as involving a number of negative practices such as producing biased and incomplete summaries, distorting witnesses' evidence, ignoring social context, and misconstruing witnesses' actions (2008: 330–31).

The themes raised in this review of the literature are developed in each of the book's chapters in relation to different data and from the particular perspective of the different authors. However the chapters, organized around legal themes, can also be connected to theoretical themes as the following discussion shows.

POLICE INVESTIGATION AS TEXTUAL MEDIATION

Textual travel in lay–legal communication involves diverse processes and technologies as means of transport. These mediational processes and technologies include talk, writing, email, telephone conversation, even the Internet. These processes and technologies have a range of potentially profound socially situated effects on individuals, on activities and encounters, and on legal systems. These effects influence how mediated language inserts individuals into discursive arrangements. This insertion in turn projects particular understandings of truth, knowledge, power, and subjectivity (Maybin 2000: 202). The potential for participants in legal processes to appropriate mediational means and to transform texts through intertextual processes, in the context of this projection, makes textual travel particularly important in these settings. This is illustrated clearly in each of the papers in Part One of this volume, which examines mediation as it occurs in policing settings.

In each chapter, the legal side of the lay–legal pairing is a police officer or someone working on behalf of the police. The lay side sees considerable diversity, including people telephoning police to report crimes, as well as witnesses to and suspects of crimes, along with their differing orientations and purposes. Mediation occurs in the chapters at a variety of levels and is grounded among shifts in mode and formality; at the interface of potentially conflicting expectations, motivations, and knowledge frameworks. Specifically, Mark Garner and Edward Johnson demonstrate how mediation can influence lay people's access to police assistance, Georgina Heydon shows how mediation can determine the way that crucial legal information is delivered, and Frances Rock illustrates that mediation can influence police investigations via processes of information gathering. In these settings, we are not simply observing individuals but "individual(s)-acting-with-mediational-means" (Wertsch 1993: 12) in the form of telephones, official wordings, pens and papers, computer interfaces, and entextualized legislative frameworks.

The work of the police is underpinned by textual travel. Investigations rely on collecting, interpreting, reinterpreting, revisiting, and relaying information both within the police service and to a range of people outside the service including the public, journalists, other legal professionals (such as solicitors), other emergency services organizations (such as the Ambulance Service), and other legal agencies (such as Probation Services). The introduction to Part One will underline the key idea, developed through each chapter in that part, that recognition of the influence of textual travel on police work can illuminate that work and the concept of textual travel.

The focus on policing begins with a chapter by Garner and Johnson who examine telephone conversations through which members of the public seek help from the police. Their careful scrutiny of the journey of those messages through the police procedures which eventually supply or deny a police response shows how individuals who act for the police force, through multiple interpersonal interactions, mediate institutional responses to lay people. Next, Heydon examines messages which are embedded in the institution yet communicated interpersonally—police cautions. She shows how individuals' orientations to the mediation of those institutional messages can influence the messages and their effects. Finally, Rock turns to interviews through which police officers gather information from witnesses in order to construct statements. She examines the extent to which the interview mediates the witness' experience and the ways in which it calls on information from sources other than the witness.

Thus, the three chapters here each offer perspectives on how mediation is part of police work. Each chapter illustrates that, in very different ways, textual travel influences the conduct and outcomes of policing, recognizing that textual travel is predicated on social action through text and talk.

The chapters in Part One can be seen to respond to Scollon's (1998: 6) call to find common ground to analyze ways in which "mediational means from languages to microphones, literacy to computers, news stories to telephone calls are appropriated by participants in social scenes in undertaking mediated action," without deliberately setting out to do so nor necessarily taking Scollon's perspectives more generally. Each of the chapters here shows that mediational routines (extrapolating, explaining, and working together with texts) span "the social distance between people of differential position in political hierarchies of status and power" (Bauman 2004: 142). The call handler must move toward the caller in order to understand the situation they describe, the interviewer must move toward the interviewee to entextualize their story, and the explaining police officer's frustration and apparent confusion at not explaining successfully apparently indexes a failure to span or cross hierarchical boundaries. Each chapter also features textual transformation bringing authorization (Bakhtin [1935] 1981: 342) as texts from the lay world become the key to gaining police assistance or to potentially making a successful prosecution.

Garner and Johnson's chapter establishes a theme for those which follow by focusing on micro-communicative events which often initiate investigations and do so by mediating information from the public into the police institution. Much everyday police activity is initiated by calls from the public. The call handlers' role is thus pivotal to police work. This chapter uses an operational communication framework which views each call as part of the rich patterning of communication. As noted by Zimmerman (1992), patterning occurs "laterally" (i.e., across all calls), which tend to conform to similar discourse structures. At least as important, however, is what might be styled "longitudinal" patterning—a form of mediation. This is the totality of the patterns of linguistic interaction around any given incident: a complex communicative process that begins with the caller's dialing of the emergency number and ends—if it gets that far—with the response of officers at the scene of a reported incident. Description and analysis of longitudinal patterning includes, along with the call(s) themselves, their various transformations under the influence of the organizational, operational, and technological contexts within which call handling is carried out.

The chapter uses analysis of recorded and transcribed emergency calls supplemented by participant observation of a police communication center at work, by focus groups with call handlers, and by interviews with senior officers. Garner and Johnson contribute to a thorough understanding of the discourse event, which is of interest both theoretically, as an aspect of the study of situated language, and also operationally, as an essential basis for efforts by the police to enhance practice. They are the first to explore the transformation of event-level discourses, through mediation, in police call handling, making it an important element of this part on mediation and policing.

As with recontextualization, intertextuality and its associated concepts are fundamental to texts throughout the legal process and are very evident in the chapters here. For example, Garner and Johnson's work can be viewed through the contrast between *manifest intertextuality* and *interdiscursivity*. In their case, manifest intertextuality, or "the heterogeneous constitution of texts out of specific other texts" (Fairclough 1992: 85) is evidenced by the way in which the formulations of callers to police emergency telephone lines are incorporated into subsequent reports of their calls. Interdiscursivity, or "the heterogeneous constitution of texts out of elements (types of convention) of orders of discourse" (Fairclough 1992: 85), is evidenced in the more abstract ways in which the telephone call handlers draw on institutional conventions, norms, and expectations from their training and prior experience.

The next chapter in Part One, by Heydon, moves along through the legal process to consider more purposeful evidence collection. The investigative interview provides police officers with a unique opportunity to obtain perhaps the most important evidence in a criminal case: a first-person account of events. Officers must obtain that evidence in compliance with legislation regarding suspects' rights, such as the right to silence, in order for the evidence to be admissible in court. This legislative pressure can create a tension, Heydon claims, between using precise legal language and ensuring that the suspect understands the legal text. Thus, the text of the caution is subjected to the stresses of colliding discursive trajectories. It is caught between a legal-police discourse which presses the text to retain its original legislative form and a lay-suspect discourse which presses for changes to the text so that it adequately addresses lay communicative needs.

Heydon's chapter considers the negotiation of the caution by the participants in a police interview, asking how participants' goals influence the journey of the text from legislation to courtroom (and beyond). Thus, the chapter develops the theme of mediation and policing by showing how police officers draw on a range of mediational means to transport information via the interview. Using a Conversation Analysis approach to the close examination of clarification sequences in police interviews with Anglo-Australian suspects, Heydon demonstrates how miscommunication that can undermine the integrity of the evidence could be minimized if police officers were able to draw upon a "professional voice" (Cordella 2004) and, in Goffman's (1981) sense, take up the role of "principal" when transforming cautions during interview. In this way, the police and suspect discourse trajectories might be altered as both travel toward their respective future courtroom positions of prosecution and defense.

Having explored ways in which institutional language is mediated by policing processes, Part One closes as Rock considers how lay people's language is mediated by policing processes. Here, Rock approaches mediation as an interactional process through which meanings are negotiated in the most literal sense. She uses this approach to systematically unpack and consider all of the sources which are drawn on in the construction of just one police witness statement by scrutinizing the way that that statement is constructed through a witness interview. The sources which she uncovers as having entered the interview interaction, and ultimately the statement text, include the witness' own experience of a crime event, as we would expect, but the statement is constructed using a range of other texts including legislative documents and other statements which the interviewer has previously taken. Rock shows that even the witness statement under construction comes to influence its own further construction.

Rock positions the witness statement as a "public transcript" which provides representations that are "sanctioned and legitimized as authoritative" (Park and Bucholtz 2009: 488). It entextualizes "speech of 'private' citizens" and thus "purports to speak on behalf of a consenting public" (2009: 489), constituting that public while simultaneously authorizing institutions (2009: 488). Thus, creation of the witness statement brings things beyond the text into being. Rock ultimately examines the upshots of the rich textual tapestry, in terms of sources or origins of ideas, words, and concepts in the statement. One of her observations is that the officer operates in a richly intertextual environment which reveals "relations between language and usage" in its purposes and operational conditions (Blommaert 2005:14). But she also considers the implications for the witness and for the justice process of the "chain of speech communication" (Bakhtin [1936] 1986: 91) revealed in the interviewing officer's work and his collaborative or interactive text production with the witness.

The chapters in Part One call to mind Kell's observation that the production of text is only "one moment of codification in the ongoing meaning making process" (2006: 166). As texts travel through investigative settings they work to constitute crimes by securing a police response (Garner and Johnson), classifying events as criminal or not (Rock), and casting investigations as lawful (Heydon). The "texts" which figure in each of these settings have implicitly or explicitly travelled to reach the settings, either being worked up through the legal process or in the lay world. They also continue to travel once they have left the transient settings here—the call to the police is at least logged and quantified but may become evidence, the statements become evidence if the case proceeds, and the cautions form a backdrop to felicitous investigative work. Yet the snapshot of travel in these papers affords a view of texts "used as tools to take one or more social action" (Jones and Norris 2005: 3). The actions include seeking to secure and to consider a police response (Garner and Johnson); providing "my story," constructing empathy and marshalling an account (Rock); and providing information, following and resisting regulations and institutional norms, and making decisions (Heydon). This snapshot shows how texts and other artifacts function to "claim and impute certain social identities" (Jones and Norris 2005: 3) which are shaped, restrained, and facilitated through the constellations which Garner and Johnson observe, the discourse trajectories which Heydon notes, and the chains examined by Rock.

THE LEGAL CASE AS INTERTEXTUAL CONSTRUCTION

It would not be too much of an oversimplification to say that Western legal processes are fundamentally an exercise in intertextual construction. In both the written and oral (courtroom, interviews, etc.) aspects of the proceedings, lay and professional participants create meaning through the constant exchange of texts from a wide variety of legal and lay sources.

Consider the example of a lawyer writing a brief to a court (Mertz 2007). To paraphrase Fairclough, the writer fills the brief with snatches of other texts—typically passages from precedential cases. The brief writer then quotes the texts to the court and argues that they do or do not control an issue in the present case. In producing its opinion, the court engages in its own process of intertextual construction, assimilating some texts from the briefs and perhaps contradicting others, often adding precedential passages on its own. In some circumstances, the court may even import into its opinion texts from lay (or at least nonlegal) sources such as dictionaries (compare Heffer this volume). The relevant texts thus travel from their original sources to a new life in the court's present judgment.

A related if informal intertextuality characterizes the oral aspects of legal proceedings. In the American jury room, for example, it is now known that jurors create
authority for their position through a variety of techniques that involve intertextual
construction. A juror may "testify" in the sense used in many Protestant churches,
presenting a narrative of personal experience (Labov and Waletzky 1967) as a story
of revelation and enlightenment that other jurors are urged to emulate (Maynard
and Manzo 1993). Jurors may also support their conclusions by reference to pur-
portedly universal rules of human behavior that are presented as if/then conditionals (Conley and Conley 2009). In both instances, jurors assemble a mosaic of texts
from a variety of lay and legal sources—the evidence, their instructions from the
judge, and sources external to the jury room—to construct the text that is one of
the most powerful forms of lay–legal communication: their verdict.

The chapters in Part Two of the book present vivid examples of intertextual
construction in the criminal courtroom. All deal with the ways in which legal
professionals—lawyers and judges—construct their respective cases and decisions. This process is inherently intertextual, and often heteroglossic, in the sense
of allowing for the play of multiple, historically grounded voices (Bakhtin [1935]
1981). As reported and analyzed by the authors, it can involve either of two types
of lay–legal linguistic interaction. First, in constructing their adversarial narratives,
lawyers employ live lay witnesses and also reanimate the pretrial speech (which
may have been oral or written) of lay actors. Judges do the same in conducting
investigations (in civil law countries) and in framing their decisions. Second, lawyers and judges must communicate their respective arguments and instructions to
lay jurors.

Katrijn Maryns highlights a complex and striking form of lay–legal intertextuality: the linkages between spoken and written discourses in Belgian criminal trials. Maryns analyzes audio and video recordings of barristers' pleas (arguments,
in common law parlance) that she collected in the Belgian Assize Court. In their
pleas, barristers constantly incorporate others' voices into their own. Maryns points
to intertextual linkages between spoken and written discourses to demonstrate the
complex interplay between orality and textuality that characterizes Belgian legal
procedures. Even though Belgian police interrogations are not recorded, there are
no official rules for report writing, and verbatim representations are rare. Barristers
and judges constantly reconstruct "verbatim" oral dialogue from the written reports
and use these everyday reenactments as evidence and identity-building resources
in their legal arguments. They do the same thing with earlier trial testimony that is
likewise neither recorded nor transcribed, relying on their handwritten notes.

As these linguistically complex processes unfold, boundaries between the legal
and the lay tend to fade. Although the lawyers give the appearance of accurate and
objective reproduction of past speech, the effect is, in Maryns's words, to "animate
the voice of lay participants as a strategy to shuffle their own preferred interpretations of the facts into the legal space." The shuffling is multilayered: a legal actor
draws on a legal text (the police report or a barrister's notes) as a source for creating

a new lay text—the reconstructed words of a lay speaker—and then appropriates the voice of that lay speaker to inject a legal argument into a legal space. At the end of this extended exercise in intertextuality, the former categories of lay and legal communication have disappeared into each other.

Martha Komter's chapter is a perfect complement to Maryns's. Komter's aim is to illustrate the intertextual construction of legal cases by showing how texts travel through the criminal law process, from the police investigation through the trial. The particular text she focuses on is the suspect's statement to the police, which begins its trajectory as a lay communication to a legal authority and eventually becomes reentextualized as part of an important written legal document, the case file. Evoking Maryns's focus on orality versus textuality, Komter describes the process whereby the police produce a written version of the suspect's statement and incorporate it into the case file, and then considers the ways in which judges invoke the case file to structure the trial and to guide perception. This process (like the processes described in every chapter in this part) illustrates Kristeva's (1986) concept of vertical intertextuality: the suspects' words move "up" into the police statements that incorporate them and the case file to which those statements then contribute, in contrast to the horizontal intertextuality between one case file and another.

The case file—quite literally an intertextual construction—is, in Komter's account, a ubiquitous presence in Dutch criminal trials, a text that travels from the beginning to the end of a criminal prosecution. The case file seems to be simultaneously prop, talisman, and legal resource. Judges, prosecutors, and defense lawyers keep files and stacks of papers in front of them, which they frequently consult. It is a legal requirement that judges make reference in the trial to those pieces of evidence that they will later use as a basis for their verdict. In practice, this means that judges read or summarize from the case file those items that they expect that they may need for their ruling. Judges treat police records of the suspects' statements as genuine representations of what the suspect actually said. Indeed, police records appear to invite this interpretation, as they are written up as first-person narratives. However, Komter's comparison between what suspects say in police interrogations and what is written down shows that there are substantial differences between the talk and the writing. In addition, judges' references to the information in the case file reveal how they read the file, how they guide the attention of others to its salient features, and by implication, how they construe their professional and institutional identities. Intertextual construction thus becomes a window on legal ideology.

In the next chapter in Part Two, Alison Johnson focuses on a parallel instance of intertextual construction in an English criminal case. She analyzes how police interviews were used by barristers in the 58-day murder trial of Dr. Harold Shipman, who was convicted in 2000 of the murders of 15 of his patients. She particularly documents the ways in which the defendant's narrative, originally elicited in a series of oral police interviews, was embedded and evaluated in the prosecution's case.

Fragments from the interviews were initially merged into a written intertextual document, the police investigative report, and thereafter were selectively quoted in barristers' opening speeches and witness testimony, reenacted or "animated" in front of the jury, and then reported daily by the media. Interestingly, for the first 26 days of the trial (Shipman began his own testimony on day 27), these performances of his statements to the police, now transformed into what Johnson calls "an evidential object for scrutiny and evaluation by the jury," constituted Shipman's only voice. "Thus we have," Johnson concludes, "what Rock (2007: 36) calls a 'temporal intertextual chain' in which texts are referenced, repeated, embedded and transformed as they travel across time." As Johnson follows this chain, we see the prosecution using the power of intertextuality to further the strategic objective of constructing Shipman as guilty.

The final chapter in Part Two is Dawn Archer's study of a Victorian-era "trial of the century," the 1856 conviction of Dr. William Palmer for the financially motivated murder of his friend John Parsons Cook. Aside from a lurid, Agatha Christie-style plot that drew intense public interest (Palmer was implicated in several other suspicious deaths), the case was significant as an early implementation of the Prisoners' Counsel Act of 1836, which gave some criminal defendants the right to be represented by a lawyer. Taking full advantage of the published reports of this historically significant trial, Archer uses statistical techniques to analyze the intertextual practices that the prosecutor and defense counsel (who had not previously been allowed to address a jury directly) employed to reconstruct the person and conduct of the accused.

Archer demonstrates the ways in which texts traveled as the prosecutor wove a comprehensive intertextual narrative that accounted for virtually every aspect of the crime, including the motive of the accused, the activities of the alleged accomplices, the suffering of the victim, and the perspective of the people who cared for him. Not surprisingly, the defense counsel painted a very different picture in his own, equally intertextual narrative. The texts that he invoked included a number of letters, including some that were used by the prosecution to establish guilt, but which the defense counsel used to suggest that the accused was a loyal friend of the victim. He also captured the voices of different players in the unfolding drama, performing their speech in the first person. He even recontextualized the defendant's own response to the charge by embedding it in a statement of his own opinion: "I believe that there never was a truer word pronounced than the words which he [Palmer] pronounced when he said 'Not guilty' to the charge."

Given the historical context, Palmer's defense counsel was engaging in a novel exercise in intertextuality. Indeed, so unprecedented was this form of discourse that the Lord Chief Justice, in summing up for the jury, accused him of having "challenge[d] accepted norms of forensic morality." Significantly, Archer observes, some of the practices present in the *Palmer* case are still prominent in criminal trials.

As texts travel into and through the trial and then on to appeal, there is a gradual narrowing of focus in legal discourse. At criminal trial, stories are severely constrained by the charges on the legal indictment that determine the admissibility of evidence and by the legal rules of evidence (Part Two). The chapters by Susan Ehrlich and Chris Heffer in Part Three argue that this narrowing toward an increasingly decontextualized "legal" focus can lead to a text becoming so utterly divorced from its original contextualization that its speaker loses her "voice" (Hymes 1996) and her listeners can no longer hear what was intended. Tracy and Delgadillo, on the other hand, argue that travel through the legal process does not necessarily lead to as narrow a legal focus as Ehrlich and Heffer claim, and that the degree to which it is "lay" or "legal" in style depends as much on the speaker's argument as on the particular legal genre.

Susan Ehrlich examines how trial talk from a US "post-penetration" rape case (*Maouloud Baby v. State of Maryland*) is recontextualized and radically transformed in various judicial decisions. The testimony of the complainant in both direct and cross-examination shows that, after putting up a strong resistance to the aggressive sexual advances of the defendant and his friend, she finally allows the defendant "to take his turn" provided he stops if she says so and lets her go home afterwards. But, in its recontextualization at appeal, this single act of impelled agreement (she is taken to say "yes," though she does not actually use that agreement marker) is extracted from its interactional context—characterized by multiple instances of her saying "no"—and transformed into the "initial consent" that she then withdraws after penetration. Ehrlich identifies the problem in the "referentialist" or "textualist" linguistic ideology held by legal professionals and lay people alike (Collins 1996), or the "belief in stable, denotational and context-free meaning." It is this that enables people to believe that words, phrases, or larger textual segments can be extracted from their original context and moved to other contexts without a resulting loss in meaning. Thus, the complainant's one pragmatic "yes," extracted from the context of strategic resistance, means simply agreement or "consent," irrespective of what occurred before.

According to Ehrlich, lay people are just as likely to succumb to this textualist ideology as legal professionals. Thus, it is the jury who put the following question to the trial judge: "If a female consents to sex initially and, during the course of the sex act to which she consented, for whatever reason, she changes her mind and the man continues until climax, does the result constitute rape?" At appeal, the applicant used the jury's question to frame the case in terms of the legal issue of "post-penetration rape," and, just as in the original trial the parties are restricted to discussing issues directly related to the charges on the indictment, so in the higher courts the parties are constrained to discussing the grounds for appeal raised by the applicant. Thus, the case became part of a legal discourse about post-penetration withdrawal of consent rather than the original trial question of whether or not consent was granted in the first place.

One interesting question that Ehrlich's chapter raises is whether the jury would have been as "textualist" in a nonlegal context. Lay people do not need sociolinguistic expertise to understand, in the lay context of assigning blame rather than the legal one of defining offences, that the complainant's one pragmatic "yes" needs to be viewed in the overall context of sexual aggression. However, the jurors are instructed by the judge to view the details of the case in a very particular legal way. When the judge feels she is unable (legally) to provide an answer to the jury's question, she reiterates that they should answer the question themselves on the basis of the legal definitions of rape and consent that she has provided in her jury instructions. However, given that there was nothing in those instructions that would have dealt with the very specific issue of post-penetration withdrawal of consent (even if the jury could remember the specific instructions), the jury, to some extent, were left to their own devices, and, as such, found the defendant guilty.

Although superficially very different, a similar type of incommensurability of interpretive practice can be found in Chris Heffer's account of how a repeated act of legal–lay communication can historically cease to be communicative and become a form of magical incantation. He argues that, in conveying the criminal standard of proof—"beyond reasonable doubt"—to juries, a breakdown in communication between judge and jury is likely to result from the particular trajectory the instruction has taken in the legal metadiscourse of judgments and opinions in a given jurisdiction. At the core of that metadiscursive practice is the appeal to "authorized language," which draws its power not from being *understood* but from being recognized as *authoritative* (Bourdieu 1991). The law is quite explicit about where authority lies with respect to terms it categorizes as "legal," but claims that "ordinary language" terms are within the province of lay decision makers. However, in practice, the law also grants authority in those liminal zones where the legal fades into the lay, since it is legal authorities and not the community that decide whether a term is construed as "legal" or "lay." And since those category decisions often depend on the individual preferences (or *authorized voice*) of the most powerful judges, a single term such as "beyond reasonable doubt" can be set on quite different text trajectories in different jurisdictions: a "legal" term that must be explained to juries in some jurisdictions; "ordinary language" that is necessarily understood by jurors in others. Furthermore, as precedent is firmly established and the authorized voice becomes *authoritative discourse*, the categorization of a term as "legal" or "lay" is normalized to the point where it becomes a background assumption—part of the legal-linguistic *habitus* (Bourdieu 1990)—rather than an issue in itself. Yet where this categorization proves to be empirically wrong (there is ample evidence showing that "beyond reasonable doubt" is poorly understood by jurors) then we find an incommensurability of explanatory practice.

This thesis is illustrated through the Australian murder case of *R v. Chatzidimitriou*. In this case, the lay jurors, "doing what comes naturally" (Fish 1989), seek an explanation from the judge of a "legal" term ("beyond reasonable doubt") they do not understand, while the judge, also doing what comes naturally to him, appeals to the courts' authoritative pronouncements that this "time-honoured formula" is expressed in "ordinary language" that can be understood by jurors. When recontextualized at appeal, the justices take it as *legally* given that the phrase is *ordinary* language that cannot and must not be defined; or, in the trial judge's words, "those are very plain English words and ought to be interpreted by the jury to mean exactly what they say, namely beyond reasonable doubt." The only legally relevant issue is whether or not the judge should have provided the jury with a dictionary (presumably to discover what they supposedly already know?) when they requested one after the judge failed to answer their original question. Accordingly, as the appeal court justices analyze the communication breakdown represented by this "different practice dance" (Scollon 1997), they simply fail to hear the voice of the lay jury. Instead, they make negative imputations of the lay jurors' identity: for the justices, the jurors are not unaware of a legal term but ignorant of *the* language.

Both Ehrlich and Heffer appear to claim that judicial discourse inevitably involves recontextualization that leads to a narrower legal focus on categories and principles, with a resulting loss of narrative voice for the lay participants: the complainant's story of strategic resistance in *Baby* is lost in the legal redefinition of the case as one of post-penetration rape; the jury's simple request for clarification in *Chatzidimitriou* is lost in the legal issue of whether or not a dictionary can be provided to juries. Ehrlich and Heffer also tend to see the *legal–lay* distinction as not merely a question of participant role but also as a discourse style or cognitive approach.

Karen Tracy and Erica Delgadillo challenge these claims that as events under legal scrutiny move first into a trial context and then into appellate decisions there is, in the various recontextualizations, a clear direction of transformation from contextualized "narrative" to decontextualized legal categories. Indeed, by examining the discourse of legal and nonlegal communicators across a variety of judicial venues as participants forwarded arguments about a specific issue—whether or not same-sex marriage should be legal—they evidence the problematic character of the very distinction between lay and legal. They do not focus primarily on judicial discourse as such but the discourse addressed *to* judges and legislators, examining closely three genres of discourse in particular: the litigant briefs that the state Supreme Court justices read in *Lewis v. Harris*; the oral arguments regarding the constitutionality of the existing marriage statute that occurred between plaintiff and defense attorneys and the seven justices; and the public hearing held by the New Jersey Assembly's Judiciary Committee, which involved lay speakers and lobbying groups, and elected officials.

While legal communicators are typically framed as favoring a principle-based, "paradigmatic" style (Heffer 2005) when texts are recontextualized in judicial settings, Tracy and Delgadillo argue that the style of recontextualized text in the legal process might have less to do with whether they are a legal or lay speaker and more to do with whether a party is marginalized or mainstream. They note that in the public hearing, "many gay speakers told moving stories about the effects of not having their relationships recognized" and even those that did not tell stories as such tended to disclose "intimate personal feelings and reactions." On the other hand, antigay speakers tended not to use stories or personal disclosures but relied more on abstract moral precepts. It is "outgroups, groups whose marginality define the boundaries of the mainstream, whose voice and perspective—whose consciousness—has been suppressed, devalued and abnormalized" that tend to like stories (Delgado 1989: 2412). Storytelling, in short, becomes a useful tool for "overcoming otherness."

Furthermore, Tracy and Delgadillo argue that even where the communication is solely between legal participants, as in the Supreme Court written briefs and oral arguments, some of the oppositionists' narrative voice remains, not in the form of fully fledged Labovian personal experience narratives but in the form of "narrative seeds," or "brief remarks about persons and events that evidence a potential to flower into full-blown stories." This suggests that the lay voice is still present in what is, from a pure roles perspective, an example of legal–legal communication, and thus "troubles" the very distinction between "legal" and "lay."

CROSSING CULTURAL AND IDEOLOGICAL CATEGORIES IN LAY–LEGAL COMMUNICATION

The theme of the final part of the book is the ways in which the travels of texts can elide the cultural and ideological boundaries between categories in lay–legal communication, and even change the content of those categories. As we noted above, Bernstein (1990: 192) illustrates the ideological nature of textual travel with reference to educational discourse. He argues that recontextualization is regulated by powerful agents—typically government departments in Europe—who control the sorts of transformation that texts undergo in the movement from the primary context of university research to the secondary contexts of school.

As the chapters in Part Four illustrate, the situation is even more complex in the context of the set of practices and beliefs we call the law. Fields (Bourdieu 1990) and archives (Foucault 1972) are not simple, unified realms, but rather complex amalgams of categories that have their own cultural and ideological properties— and nowhere more so than in the legal process. Whereas Bernstein's educational texts travel in only one direction—"down"—under the cultural and ideological control of government agents, the travels of the texts that comprise lay–legal communication are far less constrained. For one thing, the law itself is created both (indeed, simultaneously) from the top down and from the bottom up. Several of the chapters in this volume deal with the context of the police interview room, for example. Mirroring the top-down educational context, one contributor (Heydon) analyzes the travels of wordings and concepts *down* from the primary context of legislation to the secondary context of the interview room. But other authors (Maryns, Komter, and Johnson, for example) analyze texts traveling *up* from the now-primary interview rooms to the courts, which are in this instance secondary contexts. Moreover, while powerful recontextualizing agents are at work here as well, they are multiple—police officers, lawyers, and judges, among others—and their cultural practices and ideological agendas are diverse. As a consequence of all these factors, the transformative effects go in multiple directions.

The first chapter in Part Four, by John Conley and several medical colleagues, addresses the travels of texts in the highly regulated domain of genetic research. They analyze interviews with persons who were asked to contribute DNA samples to a genomic biobank—a research collection of human DNA. The solicitation of informed consent from research subjects is a significant if somewhat unusual form of lay–legal communication. The lay subject's direct communication is with a representative of the scientific world, typically a research coordinator. But the requirement of informed consent, usually memorialized in a signed document, is prescribed by law. This is thus an environment where the lay, legal, and scientific worlds intersect.

The chapter focuses particularly on the way that lay subjects draw on texts from a broad range of sources—including science and law, as they understand them; popular media; conversations with friends and relatives; interior dialogs with themselves; and the interaction with the interviewer—to construct and explain what their research participation means to them. The subjects recall the ways in which the scientific representative—operating in the shadow of the law—sought their signature on a written text (the informed consent document) that has emerged from the expert discourses of law and science. Some of the prospective subjects acquiesced, while others declined. But, over time and across many subsequent discursive interactions, almost all came to appreciate and then contest the ideological implications of that document. Importing texts from multiple lay discourses about science and law, many developed a set of beliefs about the meaning of their participation in the research—such as who owns their samples, who can use them, and what rights they have as subjects—that are simply "wrong" from the expert point of view. The authors suggest that the expert research community, which has treated consent as a one-time, top-down phenomenon, might do well to recognize it as an open-ended discursive process that, like law itself, operates simultaneously in both directions.

Bethan Davies's chapter examines the UK's *Highway Code,* a unique text that continually travels back and forth between advice manual for lay drivers and legal document. In its life in the cultural and ideological world of lay drivers, the *Code* operates "as the 'rules of the road' for the British road user; it contains advice about using the road, legal requirements for road users and explanations of all road signs and markings." But it can also act as an operative document in a court of law, providing evidence of drivers' legal duties. In Bernstein's (1990) terms, it must function simultaneously in two primary contexts—advice manual and legal text.

As Davies demonstrates, *The Highway Code*'s existence straddling the lay–legal boundary is an uncomfortable one. For the book to succeed, Davies writes, its lay users would need to perform a neat intellectual, cultural, and ideological trick: they "would need to be able to both recognize its multiple purposes and understand the text as a legal document." To assess its success, she investigates the public consultation process during the most recent revision of the *Code* for evidence of lay users' understandings. She focuses on the use of modals to indicate distinctions between advisory and mandatory rules as a particular source of difficulty. Not surprisingly, she concludes that the *Code* ultimately fails: it is not, she writes, "a text that travels well." The reason for the failure is less predictable—it turns on the question of "whether it is reliably recognized as a travelling text at all." That is, do its intended readers appreciate the multiple cultural and ideological boundaries that it continually crosses? Davies's evidence is that they do not, with attendant practical and legal consequences for all concerned.

In a further development of the themes of culture and ideology in lay–legal communication, Shonna Trinch's chapter analyzes Latina women's reports of rape in interviews with legal authorities in which the women seek protective (restraining) orders against their husbands or partners. Trinch finds that, contrary to widespread stereotypes about Latina women's cultural sensibilities concerning rape, they actually showed great variation in disclosing sexual violence. Moreover, few showed "outward signs of shame, stigma, fear of speaking, or a need to suffer alone in silence." In fact, "their coming to speak about their situations in search of a solution was only ONE of the things they had on their 'to do' list for the day."

Trinch explores the ways in which the narratives of rape victims have previously traveled into the legal realm, helping to shape the relationship between the ideologically salient lay categories of "victim" and "survivor" and the legal category of rape. She finds in her data, however, a new cultural text, a largely suppressed narrative of rape as everyday violence that challenges the traditionally accepted ideology of rape. Specifically, Trinch writes, "We can see how rape narratives involve more than the idea that rape may cause its victims severe and irrevocable damage." She argues that the importation of this new text into legal discourse might help to resist rape's power to silence its victims by creating "an understanding that can dispel existing stereotypes that box women in and limit their resilience."

THE TRAVELS OF THIS TEXT

This book itself represents the outcome of an eventful textual journey that began with the invitation of a small group of researchers from a wide variety of academic backgrounds to the 6th Cardiff Roundtable in Sociolinguistics on Legal–Lay Communication, organized by Chris Heffer and Frances Rock and held in the "remote" hills of Wales in July 2008. The participants were selected by the organizers to provide a broad range of perspectives on communication between legal and lay people: their combined expertise represented the fields of linguistics, communication, anthropology, language studies, and law, and took in interaction between a wide variety of participants in a large range of legal settings. Many of the participants, though not all, have contributed to this volume.

While the primary intention of the meeting was to provide a forum for very diverse perspectives on legal–lay or lay–legal communication, and the methods and theoretical frameworks varied considerably, as the Roundtable process progressed from initial abstracts to final thoughts, a particular broad take on legal–lay communication as involving the travelling of texts began to emerge. At the Roundtable, it was striking how pervasive and productive this theme was for all speakers. Some had explicitly addressed the concept during their talks. Susan Ehrlich, for example, had talked, after Blommaert, of the "travelling of discourses across settings," and several contributors had referred to such theoretical concepts as entextualization, recontextualization, intertextuality, and mediation. Our Keynote Speaker John Conley summed up this emergent theme in the Closing Session as "the travels of texts," which we were later to draw under the umbrella of "textual travel." During the Closing Session, others felt that textual travel would offer a useful way to revisit and reframe their ideas.

The Closing Session of the Roundtable thus represented the opening for this book. At this point the editors, with the consensus of the contributors, began to introduce an explicit framing or preferred metadiscourse for contributions to the book, and some authors made very significant changes to their original contributions. At the same time, this reframing was nothing like as draconian (we hope!) as the discourse analytic workshop described by Blommaert (2005: 142–56). Indeed, although we believe that the final textual artifact provides both an exploration of the theme of legal–lay communication and develops a particular "textual travels" take on that theme, the individual contributions do still represent the rich diversity of the original group of participants.

The three editors have taken an equal role in producing this book, providing different strengths and taking the lead at different moments to keep the project moving along. Nothing should be construed from the order of names on the book or this introduction. They are not indexical orders.

By highlighting the centrality of textual travel to the otherwise extremely diverse domain of legal–lay interaction, and by asking why and how this travel is so pervasive here, we hope this book will contribute to the body of work in other settings where textual travel is salient. More immediately, though, it can enrich our understanding of the socially imperative matter of communication between legal actors and those they investigate, represent, and sentence.

CASES CITED

Lewis v. Harris, 188 N.J. 415; 908 A.2d 196 (N.J. 2006).
Maouloud Baby v. State of Maryland, Court of Special Appeals of Maryland, 2005. 172 Md. App. 588, 916 A.2d 410; 2007 Md. App. LEXIS 60.
R v. Chatzidimitriou (2000) 1 VR 493.

REFERENCES

Andrus, Jennifer. 2009a. The development of an artefactual language ideology: Utterance, event, and agency in the metadiscourse of the excited utterance exception to hearsay. *Language & Communication* 29(4): 312–27.

———. 2009b. Beyond texts in context: Recontextualization and the co-production of texts and contexts in the legal discourse, excited utterance exception to hearsay. *Discourse and Society* 22(2): 115–36.

Auer, Peter, and Aldo Di Luzio. 1992. *The Contextualization of Language*. Amsterdam: John Benjamins.

Baddeley, Alan D. 1990. *Human Memory: Theory and Practice*. London: Lawrence Erlbaum Associates.

Bakhtin, Mikhail. [1935] 1981. *The Dialogic Imagination*. Austin: University of Texas Press.

———. [1936] 1986. *Speech Genres and Other Late Essays*. Austin: University of Texas Press.

Bauman, Richard. 2004. *A World of Others' Words: Cross-cultural Perspectives on Intertextuality*. Malden, MA: Blackwell.

Bauman, Richard, and Charles L. Briggs. 1990. Poetics and performance as critical perspectives on language and social life. *Annual Review of Anthropology* 19: 59–88.

Becker, Alton L. 1995. *Beyond Translation: Essays Toward a Modern Philology*. Ann Arbor: University of Michigan Press.

Berk-Seligson, Susan. 2009. *Coerced Confessions: The Discourse of Bilingual Police Interrogations*. New York: Mouton de Gruyter.

Bernstein, Basil. 1990. *Class, Codes and Control. Vol. 4, The Structuring of Pedagogic Discourse*. London: Routledge.

Blackledge, Adrian. 2005. *Discourse and Power in a Multilingual World*. Amsterdam: John Benjamins.

———. 2006. "The men say 'They don't need it.'" Gender and the extension of language testing for British citizenship. *Studies in Language and Capitalism* 1: 143–61.

Blommaert, Jan. 2005. *Discourse*. Cambridge: Cambridge University Press.

———. 2008. *Grassroots Literacy: Writing, Identity and Voice in Central Africa*. London: Routledge.

Bourdieu, Pierre. 1990. *The Logic of Practice*. Translated by Richard Nice. Cambridge: Polity.

———. 1991. *Language and Symbolic Power*. Translated by Gino Raymond and Matthew Adamson. Cambridge: Polity Press.

Bruner, Jerome. 1986. *Actual Minds, Possible Worlds*. Cambridge, MA: Harvard University Press.

Cameron, Deborah. 1998. *The Feminist Critique of Language*. 2d ed. London: Routledge.

Candlin, Christopher N., and Yon Maley. 1997. Intertextuality and interdiscursivity in the discourse of alternative dispute resolution. In *The Construction of Professional Discourse*, ed. Britt-Louise Gunnarsson, Per Linell, and Bengt Nordberg, 201–22. London: Longman.

Collins, Harry M., and Robert Evans. 2007. *Rethinking Expertise*. Chicago: University of Chicago Press.

Collins, James. 1996. Socialisation to text: structure and contradiction in schooled literacy. In *Natural Histories of Discourse*, ed. Michael Silverstein and Greg Urban, 203–28. Chicago: University of Chicago Press.

Conley, John M., and William M. O'Barr. 1990. *Rules versus Relationships: The Ethnography of Legal Discourse*. Chicago: University of Chicago Press.

Conley, Robin, and John M. Conley. 2009. Stories from the jury room: How jurors use narrative to process evidence. *Studies in Law, Politics, and Society* 49: 25–56.

Cordella, Marisa. 2004. *The Dynamic Consultation: A Discourse Analytical Study of Doctor–Patient Communication*. Amsterdam/Philadelphia: John Benjamins Publishing.

Cotterill, Janet. 2000. Reading the rights: A cautionary tale of comprehension and comprehensibility. *Forensic Linguistics* 7(1): 4–25.

Delgado, Richard. 1989. Storytelling for oppositionists and others: A plea for narrative. *Michigan Law Review* 87: 2411–41.

Derrida, Jacques. [1972] 1981. *Positions*. London: Athlone Press.

Drew, Paul, and John Heritage. 1992. *Talk at Work*. Cambridge: Cambridge University Press.

Eades, Diana. 2008. *Courtroom Talk and Neocolonial Control*. New York: Mouton de Gruyter.

Ehrlich, Susan. 2001. *Representing Rape: Language and Sexual Consent*. London: Routledge.

———. 2007. Legal discourse and the cultural intelligibility of gendered meanings. *Journal of Sociolinguistics* 11(4): 452–77.

Fairclough, Norman. 1992. *Discourse and Social Change*. Cambridge: Polity Press.

———. 2001. *Language and Power*. 2d ed. London: Longman.

Firth, John R. 1957. *Papers in Linguistics 1934–51*. Oxford: Oxford University Press.

Fish, Stanley. 1989. *Doing What Comes Naturally: Change, Rhetoric and the Practice of Theory in Legal and Literary Studies*. Oxford: Clarendon Press.

Foucault, Michel. 1972. *The Archaeology of Knowledge*. London: Routledge.

Gibbons, John. 1994. *Language and the Law*. London: Longman.

———. 2001. Legal transformations in Spanish: An "Audencia" in Chile. *Forensic Linguistics* 8(2): 24–43.

Giles, Howard, and Peter Powesland. 1975. A social psychological model of speech diversity. In *Speech Style and Social Evaluation*, ed. Howard Giles and Peter Powesland, 154–70. New York: Harcourt, Brace.

Goffman, Erving. 1974. *Frame Analysis: An Essay on the Organization of Experience*. New York: Harper and Row.

———. 1981. *Forms of Talk*. Philadelphia: University of Pennsylvania Press.

Gumperz, John J. 1982. *Discourse Strategies*. Cambridge: Cambridge University Press.

Hall, Phil. 2009. Policespeak. In *Dimensions of Forensic Linguistics*, ed. John Gibbons and Maria Theresa Turell, 67–94. Amsterdam: John Benjamins Publishing Company.

Halldorsdottir, Iris. 2006. Orientations to law, guidelines, and codes in lawyer–client interaction. *Research on Language and Social Interaction* 39(3): 263–301.

Hanks, William. 1989. Text and textuality. *Annual Review of Anthropology* 18: 95–127.

Heffer, Chris. 2005. *The Language of Jury Trial*. Basingstoke, UK: Palgrave Macmillan.

Hymes, Dell. 1996. *Ethnography, Linguistics, Narrative Inequality: Toward an Understanding of Voice*. London: Taylor and Francis.

Jakobson, Roman. 1960. Closing statement: Linguistics and poetics. In *Style in Language*, ed. T. A. Sebeok, 350–77. New York: Wiley.

Johnstone, Barbara. 2002. *Discourse Analysis*. Oxford: Blackwell.

Jones, Rodney, and Sigrid Norris. 2005. Discourse as action/discourse in action. In *Discourse in Action: Introducing Mediated Discourse Analysis*, ed. Sigrid Norris and Rodney Jones, 3–14. Abingdon, UK: Routledge.

Jönsson, Linda, and Per Linell. 1991. Story generations: From dialogical interviews to written reports in police interrogations. *Text* 11(3): 419–40.

Kell, Cathy. 2006. Crossing the margins: Literacy, semiotics and the recontextualisation of meanings. In *Travel Notes for the New Literacy Studies: Instances of Practice*, ed. Kate Pahl and Jennifer Rowsell, 147–69. Clevedon: Multilingual Matters.

Komter, Martha L. 2006. From talk to text: The interactional construction of a police record. *Research on Language and Social interaction* 39(3): 201–28.

Kristeva, Julia. 1980. *Desire in Language*. New York: Columbia Press.

———. 1986. *The Kristeva Reader*. Edited by Toril Moi. Oxford: Blackwell.

Labov, William, and Joshua Waletzky. 1967. Narrative analysis: Oral versions of personal experience. In *Essays on the Verbal and Visual Arts: Proceedings of the 1996 Annual Spring Meeting of the American Ethnological Society*, ed. June Helm, 12–44. Seattle: University of Washington Press.

Linell, Per. 1998. Discourse across boundaries: On recontextualizations and the blending of voices in professional discourse. *Text* 18(2): 143–57.

Malinowski, Bronislaw. 1923. The problem of meaning in primitive languages. In *The Meaning of Meaning: A Study of the Influence of Language upon Thought and of the Science of Symbolism*, ed. C. K. Ogden and I. A. Richards, 296–336. London: Kegan Paul, Trench, Trubner & Co.

Martinez, Esther. 2006. The interweaving of talk and text in a French criminal pretrial hearing. *Research on Language and Social Interaction* 39(3): 229–61.

Matoesian, Gregory. 1993. *Reproducing Rape: Domination through Talk in the Courtroom*. Cambridge: Polity Press.

———. 1995. Language, law and society: Policy implications of the Kennedy Smith rape trial. *Law and Society Review* 29: 669–701.

———. 2001. *Law and the Language of Identity: Discourse in the William Kennedy Smith Rape Trial*. Oxford: Oxford University Press.

Maybin, Janet. 2000. The new literacy studies: Context, intertextuality and discourse. In *Situated Literacies: Reading and Writing in Context*, ed. David Barton, Mary Hamilton, and Roz Ivanic, 197–209. London: Routledge.

Maynard, Douglas, and John Manzo. 1993. On the sociology of justice: Theoretical notes from an actual jury deliberation. *Sociological Theory* 11(2): 171–93.

Mertz, Elizabeth. 2007. *The Language of Law School: Learning to "Think Like a Lawyer."* Oxford: Oxford University Press.

Park, Joseph Sung-Yul, and Mary Bucholtz. 2009. Public transcripts: Entextualization and linguistic representation in institutional contexts. *Text & Talk* 29(5): 485–502.

Pintore, Anna, and Mario Jori. 1997. *Law and Language: The Italian Analytical School*. Liverpool: Deborah Charles Publications.

Rock, Frances. 2001. The genesis of a witness statement. *Forensic Linguistics* 8(2): 44–47.

———. 2007. *Communicating Rights: The Language of Arrest and Detention*. Basingstoke, UK: Palgrave Macmillan.

Sarangi, Srikant. 1998. Rethinking recontextualization in professional discourse studies: An epilogue. *Text* 18(2): 301–18.

———. 2001. On demarcating the space between "lay expertise" and "expert laity." *Text* 2(1–2): 3–12.

Saussure, Ferdinand de. [1916] 1983. *Course in General Linguistics*. Translated by Roy Harris. London: Duckworth.

Scheffer, Thomas. 2006. The microformation of criminal defense: On the lawyer's notes, speech production, and a field of presence. *Research on Language and Social Interaction* 39(3): 303–42.

Scollon, Ron. 1997. Handbills, tissues and condoms: A site of engagement for the construction of identity in public discourse. *Journal of Sociolinguistics* 1(1): 39–61.

———. 1998. *Mediated Discourse as Social Interaction: A Study of News Discourse*. London: Longman.

Silverstein, Michael, and Greg Urban. 1996a. *Natural Histories of Discourse*. Chicago: University of Chicago Press.

———. 1996b. The natural history of discourse. In *Natural Histories of Discourse*, ed. Michael Silverstein and Greg Urban, 1–17. Chicago: Chicago University Press.

Toolan, Michael. 1996. *Total Speech: An Integrational Linguistic Approach to Language* Durham, NC: Duke University Press.

Trinch, Shonna. 2003. Latinas' narratives of domestic abuse: Discrepant versions of violence. Amsterdam/ Philadelphia, John Benjamins.

———. 2005. The acquisition of genre and authority: Latinas, intertextuality and violence. The International Journal of Speech, Language and the Law 12(1): 19–48.

Wertsch, James. 1993. *Voices of the Mind: A Sociocultural Approach to Mediated Action.* Cambridge, MA: Harvard University Press.

———. 1994. The primacy of mediated action in sociocultural studies. *Mind, Culture and Activity* 1: 202–8.

———. 1998. *Mind as Action.* Oxford: Oxford University Press.

Zimmerman, Don. 1992. The interactional organization of calls for emergency assistance. In *Talk at Work: Interaction in Institutional Settings,* ed. Paul Drew and John Heritage, 418–69. Cambridge: Cambridge University Press.

PART ONE

Police Investigation as Textual Mediation

CHAPTER 2

The Transformation of Discourse
in Emergency Calls to the Police

MARK GARNER AND EDWARD JOHNSON

INTRODUCTION: EMERGENCY CALL HANDLING

When members of the public in the United Kingdom want to make contact with the police by telephone, they can choose one of two methods. They can call the nationwide emergency number (999) and will be asked by an operator which emergency service they require. For non-emergency police matters, they should call a different number, which varies in different parts of the country. In many forces, calls to either number are dealt with by several teams of call handlers in a single communications center, although some forces may use more than one building. The call handler is responsible for deciding on the appropriate action, which can take a number of forms. At times it is enough to provide information or guidance, or to make contact with a local police station or another agency. At other times the caller may be advised to take no immediate action and to ring again later if the situation he or she is reporting continues to be a cause of concern. Only when the call handler judges that an incident or situation is, or has the potential to be, sufficiently serious will police officers be deployed to the scene. These last-mentioned cases are the focus of this chapter.

Call handlers have to make sense of each call and assess it in the light of procedures and current demands on resources. They set the agenda for, and act as gatekeepers to, police assistance. As the frontline interface between public and police, they also have an important role in helping to shape perceptions of and relationships with the police. Each call is audio-recorded and logged on a database with a classification according to the nature of the incident reported. The statistics of these classifications are used to inform policy and planning.

British police forces invest considerable time and resources in both the technology and the management of their communication centers. Call handling is now largely consolidated into one large, centralized center for each force or geographical area. In order to free police officers for operational activities, call handling has been "civilianized,"[1] although it is conducted under the general supervision of one or more police officers. Given the constant pressure on police time and resources, and the increasing numbers of calls being made to 999 (Barrar et al. 2001: section 3.4.6), issues of value for money, operational efficiency, and customer satisfaction are particularly salient. There is a growing awareness that this greater demand is placing a strain on police resources,[2] reflected, for example, in publicity campaigns to increase public use of the alternative number for matters other than immediate emergencies. Consequently, there has in recent years been an emphasis on maintaining and improving the standards of call handling in all forces. The first national standards for call handling (HOCD 2005) were published a few years ago.

Only a minority of all calls to the emergency line results in the dispatch of officers to a scene, but calls from the public are the impetus for a significant proportion of day-to-day police activity. The call handlers' role is thus pivotal to police work. It was described in detail, in the American context, some years ago by Antunes and Scott (1981), and notwithstanding certain cultural differences between Britain and the United States, and many subsequent changes in technology, organization, and operational procedures, their description is still largely apposite today. Antunes and Scott describe call handlers as "street-level bureaucrats"—persons who work in a bureaucratic setting, have substantial discretion in the conduct of their job, and interact constantly with citizens in significant ways. Police call handlers may work in a more strictly limited domain than many street-level bureaucrats, but nonetheless they have wide discretion in deciding on the appropriate response to a call. They have to engage with the caller, interpret what the caller is saying, assess its relationship to procedures, and rate its importance in the light of the current demands on resources. They exercise therefore considerable influence on both the day-to-day efficiency of the force and its relations with the public.

Call handlers' actions can have broad, long-term outcomes. Occasionally, such as when an inappropriate response to a call leads to grave consequences, their work attracts media attention (see, e.g., Garcia 1999). Fortunately, however, such misjudgments are rare: call handlers receive extensive pre-service and regular in-service training and monitoring, and supervisory call handlers and police officers are always on hand to provide advice or to take over a call if required. Much more influential on public perceptions is the ongoing pattern of handling calls: the calling experience. The importance of politeness in dealing with callers is obvious; equally significant is the necessity of leaving callers with a sense of confidence that the call has been taken seriously and responded to efficiently. Otherwise, they may react in ways that are detrimental to ongoing police operational activities. For example, as our corpus of calls shows, some members of the public are uncertain about ringing the emergency number at all:

Please don't think I'm bothering you erm but I'm sitting in my office at the moment and an alarm has gone off in full literally just gone off is that the sort of thing I phone 999 for?[3]

If hesitant callers such as this one are not reassured, they may in future fail to report incidents or suspicions, thus depriving the police of one of its major sources of operational intelligence. On the other hand, a caller who is dissatisfied may make a repeat call within a few minutes, taking up call handlers' valuable time. Such negative reactions may engender a lack of confidence in, even antagonism toward, the police (Antunes and Scott 1981: 175–76).

Considering the quantity of calls to the police and their considerable social significance, it is surprising that so few studies into police call handling have been published. The limited research interest has largely been concentrated on the language of calls, either as manifestations of institutional discourse (e.g., Zimmerman 1992; Watkin and Zimmerman 1999; Hester and Francis 2001; Kelly 2001), or as specific instances of communication problems (e.g., Garcia 1999; Imbens-Bailey and McCabe 2000). Despite their different emphases, these studies all focus on what Zimmerman (1992) describes as the "lateral" patterning of language in calls, which tend to manifest very similar discourse structures (although Zimmerman's configuration overstates the regularities; Garner and Johnson 2006).

At least as significant to an understanding of the full discourse, however, is what might be styled "longitudinal" patterning, which is manifested in the complex of linguistic actions and interactions (including the deployment of officers) set in train by a call. The call from a member of the public is not an isolated, fixed communicative entity; it is rather the initial construction of a dynamic and fluid text as it enters the police domain, and it is reconstructed and re-entextualized as it passes through a range of organizational, operational contexts and technological mediation. In relation to some incidents, more than one call, from one person or from various people, may be made, and each of these will occasion further re-entextualizations. The changing forms and purposes of the text within the police operational domain are the focus of the following discussion. The processes (or "textual travels") are initiated by the incoming call. Their culmination is the accomplishment (or abandonment) of the operational objective, which can be defined as making a situationally appropriate and timely response. A conversation then between a caller and a call handler is only one, evanescent, manifestation of a continuously evolving communicative discourse.

Other entextualizations and re-entextualizations that take place outside of this domain are also part, albeit less directly so, of the history of the text, but there is insufficient space to examine them in this chapter. They may occur in interactions prior to the call: for example, if the caller discusses with those around him what to say before ringing. They may occur after the operational response: for example, if the call is used as evidence in a court case or an official inquiry and is further transformed and reinterpreted in juridical domains.

THEORETICAL FRAMEWORK

This section briefly outlines the basic communication framework for our discussion. The approach is broadly communicative, rather than purely linguistic. The linguistic patterns are, of course, central, but they are manifestations of the complex of communicative interactions between a range of participants using a variety of media. Communication is the outcome of many simultaneous and mutually determining processes, only some of which are linguistic (Elias 1992: 20–21).

As with all complex systems, a truly exhaustive analysis of even the simplest interaction is in practice (and perhaps in principle) impossible. Nonetheless, interactions in an operational context like policing frequently bring about (or at least result in) quite definite, measurable, and often irreversible practical outcomes. It is incumbent upon us therefore to continue, as best we can, to try to understand communicative processes through whatever revealing indicative analyses are possible within a systematic framework.

In this chapter we analyze the discourse of calls using an extended version of the three-level approach to communicative interaction outlined in Garner (2004: 94–99):

1. The communicative **act** is a more or less discrete element of communicative behavior by one participant intended to achieve a primary, identifiable communicative purpose (usually described in linguistics as a *function*). The linguistic realizations of acts have long been the focus of traditional sentence grammars and, more recently, Speech Act Theory (Searle 1969; Tsohatzidis 1994).

2. The communicative **event** is a complex whole comprising a series of communicative acts, intended to achieve one or more identifiable communicative purpose(s). The event is realized by, but cannot be understood simply as the sum of, its constituent acts. A great number of events have culturally defined norms of linguistic patterning, which are the focus of discourse-based linguistic theories such as genre, narrative, and conversation analyses (Renkema 2004; Paltridge 2008).

3. The communicative **link** is the history of mutual understanding that has developed between two (or more) parties. Although the link may comprise a single event (i.e., there is only one instance of interaction between the participants), it becomes increasingly significant for the patterning of communication as the number of events grows. The link is an essential element of the analysis of any given event and can be usefully described in terms of the effect that previous interactions have on the patterning of communication within that event. In linguistics, the link is

occasionally mentioned in relation to isolated examples but is rarely if ever treated as a distinct level of analysis.

The boundaries between the levels are not always quite as clear as this description may suggest; they are interdependent in that each realizes, and is realized by, the others. For example, a conversation (event) is built up from a series of utterances (acts) by the speakers, and the purpose or function of each utterance is determined by the developing meaning of the conversation as a whole. They may also overlap: for example, a shouted "Look out!" (or a warning gesture) to a stranger is simultaneously act, event, and link.

The basic model is invaluable for investigating any given event, by enabling the researcher to describe variously the lower level acts and the higher level link, and their interrelationship within the interaction. Where, however, the focus is the achievement of an identifiable communicative purpose through a series of communicative interactions, the object of study is wider and more complex. An additional level of analysis is required. For example, a proper understanding and evaluation of a medical information leaflet given to a patient in relation to a surgical operation needs to take into account verbal consultations (face-to-face or by telephone) with the general practitioner, consultants, nurses, and others, as well as email exchanges, patient-initiated searches of the Internet, and others (see Garner, Ning, and Francis 2012). What renders a complex of such interactions a coherent series (by contrast, for example, with a number of disconnected conversations that take place at a social gathering) is their unifying communicative purpose. We are therefore proposing to include another level between event and link. This is the **constellation**—a concept that enables the researcher to analyze a series of interconnected communicative events involving multiple parties and multiple media over an extended period of time. A constellation is the manifestation within operational communication of the re-entextualization of discourses (communicative events) connected in a textual chain (Blackledge 2005: 121). The constellation realizes an overarching operational purpose; each of the events has a specific communicative purpose within an immediate context.

THE COMMUNICATIVE CONSTELLATION AND CALLS TO THE POLICE

The authors' interest in communicative constellations began during an early study of police operational communication by Edward Johnson's team at Wolfson College, Cambridge (Garner et al. 1993). Police officers who were working as part of the research team were asked to describe a typical communicative event initiated by a call from the public. Their description took the form of a three-stage flowchart, drawn on a whiteboard (figure 2.1)

The diagram reflects the widespread, simplistic view of how communication works (or at least should work), according to which the "essential message" is contained in language and is transmitted from one participant to another; changes

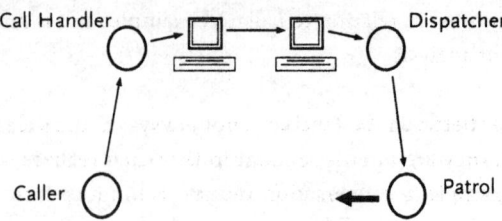

Figure 2.1
A simplistic view of the communication circuit.

in the language have no significant effect on the meaning. Readers of this book doubtless need no reminding that this "conduit metaphor" of communication (Reddy [1979] 1995) is an utterly deficient representation of the actuality. As a specific type of language-in-use, operational communication is a form of discourse characteristic of distinctive organizational contexts—in this case, a police force. Its generic forms of patterning, which make it distinct from other forms of institutional and noninstitutional discourses, are determined by such factors as policing strategies, organizational structures, and official and unofficial operational practices. The characteristics of individual texts within a given constellation are formed by the intersection of the genre patterns with local priorities, current operational demands and available resources, and by the immediate purpose, participants, and medium of expression of each constitutive communicative event. Each event, therefore, represents a transformation of the message through variant texts and mediations.

The data for the following description were gathered during a study of call handling at the invitation of a British police force. The approach was to analyze each call, not merely as an object of study in its own right, but as an instance of the overall operational communication of the force (Garner and Johnson 2006), within the basic communication framework outlined above. A corpus of recorded and transcribed calls to three lines (one of which was the emergency 999 line) was compiled (Johnson and Garner 2012). The corpus comprised 181 calls (approximately 4,000 individual speaking turns; 34,500 words), of which 32 calls (approximately 1,400 turns; 11,400 words) were to 999. These data were supplemented by participant observation of the force communication center at work, by focus groups with call handlers, and by interviews with senior call handlers and police officers. The findings of the earlier study are here reinterpreted using the extended framework, in order to describe the transformation of text at constellation level. It proved to be impracticable to make a full record of the communicative constellation around any single incident, but in any case considerations of security and confidentiality would preclude making a complete record public. The following description is, therefore, somewhat idealized, but it can reasonably be regarded as representative of the types of transformations, although not in all cases of their actual forms.

Event₁ and Text₁

The communicative constellation is initiated by Event₁: the telephone call (also referred to below as the "call," or "conversation"). Every call is predicated on the normal principles of everyday verbal interactions, as discourse analysts in general, and conversation analysts in particular, have demonstrated (e.g., Tracy and Anderson 1999; Watkin and Zimmerman 1999). There are also, however, several distinctive characteristics of a call, which are outlined below.

1. Turns by each individual speaker are short, in total averaging 8.1 words; 1.6 clauses. In every conversation, the caller's average turn (11.7 words; 1.8 clauses) was longer than that of the call handler (4.6 words; 1.3 clauses). These figures are highly consistent across all calls, regardless of participants or call length.
2. Calls are overwhelmingly oriented toward the transaction of information. This results in frequent acts of elicitation, provision, and checking, as well as a high degree of reiteration. The purposes of each communicative act were classified independently and then mutually negotiated by the researchers. The resulting percentages are shown in Table 2.1. They show that approximately three-quarters of the call handlers' acts and one-half of the caller's acts serve an information-related purpose.
3. The communicative behavior of one participant—the call handler—is governed by training and explicit guidance in the form of manuals, guides, and in particular the computer screen (discussed below). His or her behavior is also subject to continual evaluation and supervision.

Table 2.1 PERCENTAGES, BY PARTICIPANT, OF THE PURPOSES OF ACTS IN THE CORPUS

Participant	Act purpose	Percentage of total acts
CALLER	Providing information	51
	Requesting police attendance	13
	Eliciting information	9
	Interpersonal (complaining, apologizing, joking...)	9
	Stating reason for call	4
	Unclassifiable	14
CALL HANDLER	Eliciting and checking information	67
	Specifying police response	13
	Interaction management (see discussion below)	6
	Providing information	6
	Instructing to do / warning what not to do	4
	Interpersonal (calming, reassuring, rebuking...)	4

By means of these acts, one participant (in our corpus, with one exception, this is the call handler) explicitly directs the other's manner of communication. These acts arise from two distinctive characteristics of Event$_1$. First, the incident which occasioned the call is often unfolding while the caller is speaking. As a result, callers may be in a highly emotional state and need to be calmed in order to allow the necessary information to be transacted:

> Calm down a minute stop shouting so much
> Speak nearer the phone Julie please
> You're talking too fast I don't know what you're saying

The presence of other people at the scene can be a problem:

> Can you just talk to ME for a minute please?
> Move away from where the noise is so I can speak to you
> C[all] H[andler] I can't hear you your phone—
> C[aller] I know but I don't want them to hear me ringing you

In a few instances, the call handler asks the caller to take action to ascertain the required information:

> CH Okay, are you going to get out the car and see if he's all right or
> C Yeah I will do d'you want me to leave you on hold?
> CH Are you on your mobile phone?
> C Yeah I've got an earpiece in
> CH Can you take it with you at all?
> C Yeah I can yep
> CH Okay take it with you

A second distinctive feature of calls is that the call handler is engaged in two parallel communicative events at the same time: he or she is interacting with the caller and also writing a log of the call for the despatcher. This dual involvement is discussed in more detail below; here we note only that it requires the call handler to ask the caller to pause to allow time to enter the information on screen or to access a database. Approximately half of the acts classified as "interaction management" are of this kind, for example:

> Hold on a moment please
> I'll be with you in a second
> (*Each of the above is followed by a pause in the recording, in which the sound of keystrokes is audible.*)
> I'm just trying to find out where you are on the [Geographical Positioning] System just bear with me a minute

The nature of the communicative event is determined in part by the medium of transmission. In this case, the medium is a form of communications technology— the telephone—which has become so familiar that its effects are easily overlooked. Nevertheless, it should be noted that the absence of the sorts of nonlinguistic cues that are so powerful in face-to-face conversation means that interpretation must take place on the less reliable basis of the speech sounds alone, which increases the importance of information-checking acts. It also heightens the need for interaction management acts, particularly so as to reduce the effect of confounding factors, such as the speech distortions caused by speaker's emotional state and extraneous noises from the environment.

In summary, $Event_1$ is realized by a spoken text ($Text_1$), which broadly reflects the interactive and linguistic norms of everyday conversations but also has some distinctive characteristics that are determined by the caller's immediate context and by the prospective constraints imposed by the communicative constellation which it initiates. The caller's immediate environment necessitates a greater number of interaction management acts than would be expected in everyday conversation. (This is particularly noticeable in a developing incident.) The focused (concise and brief) language patterning of $Text_1$ arises from its overriding communicative function, namely, to transact information. This function is in turn determined by institutional controls on the call handler's communicative behavior, which form the frame within which $Event_2$ (see below) takes place.

Event$_2$ and Text$_2$

In $Event_2$, the call handler constructs a written text, in which he or she summarizes the main relevant points of the call, entering them into the computer by means of an interface, which consists of a highly detailed, formatted screen. (Written) $Event_2$ occurs more or less simultaneously with (spoken) $Event_1$: the call handler begins entering the data elements shortly after the beginning of the call and finishes at, or shortly after, the point at which the call is terminated. More significantly, $Event_2$ is a re-entextualization of $Event_1$, or, to put it another way, the communicative purpose of $Event_1$ is to enable $Event_2$ to occur. $Event_2$ therefore strongly influences the communicative patterns of $Event_1$, particularly its linguistic forms. This is shown in the conciseness and brevity illustrated above, and also in the nature of the information transacted, as outlined below.

$Event_2$ (entering a written text into the database) is the second major event in the constellation. In most respects, the communicative context and communicative function are very different from those of $Event_1$. In $Text_2$ the call handler acts, not in the capacity of a "street-level bureaucrat," but as an operative within the responding institution, addressing a fellow operative, the dispatcher. $Text_2$ is also, however, addressed to the institution as a whole: the written record becomes part of the documentary history of the force. As such, it is used for purposes such as compiling agglomerated statistical data and long-term planning, in addition to its rare but significant role as evidence in institutional or legal enquiries. Text$_2$ is, therefore, quite unlike Text$_1$.

The norms of speech and writing are very different, so Text$_2$ employs a new set of linguistic patterns to construct a greatly reduced and sharply focused message. Hesitations, corrections, and repetitions, for example, are excluded; a précis is made of long chunks of speech; and emotions such as anger, fear, or impatience are briefly described ("Caller seemed frightened"), or, usually, omitted altogether. The patterning of Text$_2$ is, moreover, further constrained by the screen interface. The information transacted during the telephone call has to be classified in order to enable it to be entered into specified fields, and information elements that in standard prose tend to occur together may be widely separated on screen. Some fields, such as the location of the incident, must be filled before the writer can, as it were, sign off the completed text. Certain words and phrases are prescribed (often prompted by a drop-down menu), and there are limitations on the number of characters that can be entered in most fields.

The consequences of reentextualization can be seen in Table 2.2, which shows a call handler's summary (Text$_2$) of an initial call (Text$_1$). Text$_1$, which

Table 2.2 TWO VERSIONS OF A TEXT ARISING
FROM AN EMERGENCY CALL

Text$_1$	Text$_2$
22 turns (total 145 words)	
Nature of incident:	Informant states wife's brother and father are
I've got a disturbance outside me house... my wife's	arguing with his wife.
father and her brother-in-law pissed out of their-	
causing a disturbance	
...	
Name and address of C elicited and	Mr Stainsthorpe 120 Kingsley Road,
checked by CH	Littleham, Wessex
2 turns (36 words)	
CH *With each other?*	
C *Well with my wife, but they they're going to start on*	States they are "out of their heads" and they
me that's why I'm in the house, they're out their heads	are violent
though, you don't know 'em but they're very violent	
2 turns (11 words)	
CH *Do they drink or drugs?*	They often drink and can be extremely
C *Drink they're very violent extremely violent*	violent
5 turns (43 words)	
C urges hasty response; CH asks if weapons are	No weapons seen
present	
10 turns (88 words)	
Names of involved persons elicited; C again urges	Offenders are Dave and Peter Smith
hasty response	

Text₁	Text₂
6 turns (60 words)	
CH *So what are they doing, standing in the road and arguing with your wife?*	Informant is still in house and states they are on the doorstep. Informant does not want to go out in case they start on him
...	
CH *Are you in the house now?*	
C *They're stood on the doorstep they're about to come in I know they are, if I go out there they'll start on me*	
2 turns (27 words)	
CH *And why would they be starting on you?*	
C *You don't know 'em love they're just fucking mental I've just come out of hospital I don't need this*	States they are "fucking mental"
3 turns (18 words)	
CH asks if there are children in house; C says no	No children in house
7 turns (27 words)	
CH asks what is happening now; C responds	States they are trying to get into the house
7 turns (30 words)	
Interaction management	
...	
C *Fuck they've just started on my wife* [pause] *all 5 of them*	States they have started on his wife and there are now 5 of them
2 turns (27 words)	
CH *Have you managed to get away from them?*	
C *Look can you get someone down here love they're going to start on me cars now they're fucking lunatics*	Concerned about possibility of damage being caused to his vehicles
2 turns (18 words)	
CH *Right so where are they now then?*	Offenders still outside the house
C *They're outside my house please hurry up I want them arrested*	
2 turns (14 words)	
...	
C *They're fighting with my wife they're beating her up*	States they are beating up his wife
8 turns (74 words), including 2 addressed to third party	
CH comments on poor phone reception	Informant states he has a Rottweiler dog—
C *I've got a Rottweiler with me by the way and it ain't mine*	Officer safety
11 turns (131 words)	
CH asks what is happening; CH asks for description of offenders; C responds appropriately	Offender 1—male, short, fat, white hair and beard wearing dark clothing
1 turn (23 words)	
Phone passed to Caller 2, who gives more description of one offender (*my father*)	Main offender is the father
2 turns (15 words)	
CH asks for description of other offender; C2 responds	Offender 2—Male, light coloured trousers and dark jacket

(Continued)

Text₁	Text₂
1 turn (30 words)	
C2 says why offenders have come to house	States they have come to get daughter's husband
3 turns (22 words)	Informant states he is going to let the dog loose—Officer safety
CH asks if police have arrived; C1 says yes, and he'll release the dog	
4 turns (38 words)	
Conversation terminated	

was of course spoken, is represented as a transcription. This is itself a form of re-entextualization, but this fact has had to be ignored for the purposes of our analysis of the telephone call: using the transcription as the basis of the analysis is, in effect, a convenient fudge. Furthermore, owing to limitations of space, Text₁ is presented in an abbreviated form. Some turns are omitted, and only the number of turns and words in them are stated, in order to provide a sense of the length of the call. In other places, a brief summary is made of various parts of the content and function of what was said in the call, in order to provide a sense of the communicative patterns of the whole text. Words in italics are verbatim quotations from Text₁: they are included in order to give a flavor of the whole. As in all such examples in this chapter, names and other identifying information have been changed. Note that, at one stage, caller [C1] hands the phone to another person, apparently his daughter [C2].

Event₂ influences not only the linguistic patterns and overall message construction of Text₂: it also helps to determine the contemporaneous construction of Text₁, as the majority of the call handler's communicative acts in Text₁ are directed at the construction of Text₂. Such intertextual determination often involves, in addition to the interaction management acts noted earlier, straightforward acts like checking spelling:

CH   What road's that on?
C   It's Freeburn
CH   Spell that for me
C   F-r-double e
CH   F-r-double e
C   b-u-r-n
CH   Oh right

It often also involves the eliciting of information that is not volunteered by a caller, but is critical to deciding the speed and nature of an operational response:

C   ... They're going to start [fighting] I know they are
CH   Have they got weapons on them at all?

(If weapons are present, attendance at the incident becomes urgent, and officers may need protective clothing; very serious cases may require specially armed response officers.)

In the above example, $Text_2$ is reconstructed by the call handler in approximately one-seventh of the total number of words in $Text_1$. But this is not simply a matter of omitting unnecessary words: $Text_2$ reflects different emphases. A large proportion of the turns in $Text_1$ relate to the developing violence and the caller's fear; in $Text_2$ the violence has been reduced to a few simple descriptive statements (most of which are introduced by the hedge word "states"), and the fear is mentioned once, in the unemotional sentence, "Informant does not want to go out in case they start on him." The reverse is the case with the proportions of the texts that relate to the number, identity, and physical appearance of the offenders. In $Text_1$, these topics account for approximately 8 percent of both the total number of acts and words; in $Text_2$, they account for approximately 20 percent and 25 percent, respectively of acts and words. In other words, between 2.5 and 3 times more of $Text_2$ (depending on the unit of measurement) is devoted to these topics.

These figures reflect the focus of $Text_2$ on operationally relevant information that will enable the police to deal appropriately and efficiently with the incident. The dispatcher needs to decide, on the basis of $Text_2$, how many officers to direct to the scene, in the light of the numbers of people they are likely to have to deal with. The officers who attend need to be able immediately to identify the main offenders, in order to deal with them as quickly as possible. Two further details of $Text_2$ indicate its operational orientation. The call handler has specifically ascertained, and recorded, that neither weapons nor children are involved. He also expands the text by adding (in two places) a note concerning the threat to officers' safety presented by the presence of a Rottweiler.

In this example, as in all calls, there is an absolute requirement for the call handler to make a critical decision: whether the incident is such that it is likely to warrant an operational response. If not, the automatically recorded bare details of the call (time, source, length, etc.) will suffice, perhaps supplemented by a brief summary of the outcome (e.g., "Caller told to ring local council tomorrow"). If a response is (or may be) required, the call handler will create $Text_2$ as a full, informative record, which will provide the essential information to enable two further decisions to be made by the dispatcher: the urgency and nature of the response. The call handler's selection of informative elements from $Text_1$ in creating $Text_2$ reflects his or her categorization of what is, and what is not, decision-critical.

In summary, the reentextualization of $Text_1$ as $Text_2$ is moderated by the change of medium (written vs. spoken), the new addressees, and the operational requirements of the force. The text-constructing process is guided by the computer interface, and the decision-making is guided by the call handler's experience and knowledge of strategic priorities, operational practices, and currently available resources.

At this point in the developing communicative process, two of the desired institutional outcomes have been achieved: a permanent institutional record of the call has been made, and the caller, a member of the public, has been reassured that the matter that motivated the call is being dealt with in some way by the police. If an operational response is to be set in train, however, these are not the most immediate purposes; two (and sometimes more) further communicative events and texts are required to fulfill the overriding operational purpose of taking appropriate action at the scene of the reported incident.

Event$_3$ and Text$_3$

The communicative constellation encompasses a third event, in which there is a complete reentextualization. The communicative purpose of Text$_3$ is to provide the essential information, on the basis of which the dispatcher makes the definitive decision to initiate some form of operational response, as well as the two further decisions noted above—the urgency and nature of that response. Thus, Event$_3$ is initiated by the dispatcher, on the basis of his or her interpretation of Text$_2$, and co-constructs, with the appropriate officers, Text$_3$. Like Text$_1$, Text$_3$ is spoken: but the latter is spoken over the medium of digital radio.

None of the participants in Event$_3$ was directly involved in creating either of the preceding versions of the text (Text$_1$ and Text$_2$). There is, however, a form of indirect involvement, and this is why the notion of communicative constellation is essential to the analysis. A systematic analysis of any single text depends on a sound knowledge of what occurs in other texts in the constellation. Given the requisite training, the same operative may serve, on different shifts, as either call handler or dispatcher. To illustrate from the instance we are discussing here: in the role of call handler, the operative's awareness of the role and communicative needs of the dispatcher influenced the construction of both Text$_1$ and particularly Text$_2$. In effect, the dispatcher and the call handler are at this point in the constellation jointly responsible for the operational outcome. The dispatcher, however, is one stage removed from the operational decisions, and this is reflected in all of the texts. A pragmatic (although rarely an analytical) appreciation of this mutual determination has resulted in forces' providing personnel with training and experience in both roles, which leads to greater efficiency in the communicative processes.

Since Event$_3$ is conducted verbally, the nature of the text changes once more. Having been originally spoken (Text$_1$) and then reconstructed in writing (Text$_2$), it is now reentextualized in speech. It needs hardly be stated that Text$_3$ contrasts markedly, in both communicative purpose and linguistic form, with Text$_2$; what is less self-evident is that it is also very different from Text$_1$. The communicative purpose of Event$_3$ is to deploy officers to the scene and, as far as possible, to prepare them in advance for what they are likely to encounter when they arrive. It is thus less concerned with the type of strategic decision making, evident in the preceding two events and their associated texts. All of the relevant available operational intelligence has been gleaned, and the task of the dispatcher is to make that available to the officers. In some circumstances—for example, when an incident is, or has the potential to become, sufficiently serious to require a large police presence—a number of patrols may be informed of the incident simultaneously in a "broadcast" message. For the sake of simplicity, however, we shall assume that only one patrol (one or two officers) is involved.

It is essential to ensure that the operational response is appropriate to the situation as described by the caller. The *key elements of information* transacted in Text$_3$ have, therefore, to be more or less identical to those in Text$_2$, but the patterns of expression are subject to considerable constraints, arising from the medium of communication, namely, digital radio. Communication by radio differs from that conducted by telephone in a number of respects, the main two of which are considered here, owing to limitations of space. First, radio can reach a large number of addressees at the same time, which makes it essential for a speaker to identify him- or herself and to make clear who is (or are) the particular addressee(s) for whom the message is intended. Second, whereas in a telephone conversation it is common for participants to speak at once or to interrupt each other, that is not possible over digital radio. Turn-taking is controlled by a transmission switch, so it is essential for each participant to know when the other has finished a turn. Furthermore, there is an overriding priority during operational activities to ensure that information is transacted in such a way as to maximize the efficiency of the response and to reduce the use of air-time, which has a direct financial cost to the force.

These considerations have led to the recent establishment and implementation of standards for police radio usage in the United Kingdom, known as "Airwavespeak," which were developed by the authors for the National Police Improvement Agency, and mandated for nationwide use by the peak police authorities (NPIA 2007). Airwavespeak specifies, among other things, the protocols (conversation-level procedures) and certain key vocabulary items to be used in radio interactions. Text$_3$, therefore, is characterized by highly distinctive patterning. This is shown in Text$_3$ below. It should be noted that instance we are examining occurred before the introduction of Airwavespeak. What follows is a retrospective re-entextualization, using the now mandatory radio standards. Since the authors of this chapter also wrote those standards, it may be taken to be a reliable indication of what Text$_3$ would have been had the call occurred after the national standards were introduced. (D is the dispatcher; P is the patrol, which may be on foot or in a vehicle, IP is the "informing person," or caller. Standardized phrases and prescribed constructional forms are shown in bold.)

D   **Charlie Alpha Five, Charlie Alpha Five this is Mike Whisky Over**
P   **Mike Whisky, Mike Whisky, Charlie Alpha Five Go ahead Over**
D   Are you free to attend a disturbance at Kingsley Road Littleham? **Over**
P   **Yes yes**. Can we have the details? **Over**

D	**Location** house number **one two zero** Kingsley Road. Report of two **IC1** males threatening a woman outside the house. **Over**
P	**Say again road name. Over**
D	**I say again** Kingsley: **Kilo India November Golf Sierra Lima Echo Yankee. Over**
P	**Will do**. We should be there in five minutes. **Over**
D	Offenders are given as Dave Smith and Peter Smith. One is described as short and fat, with white hair and beard and wearing dark clothing. The other has light coloured trousers and dark jacket. The daughter is in the house, with a Mr Stainsthorpe, who is the IP. **Warning**: there is reported to be a Rottweiler in the house. **Please acknowledge. Over**
P	**Warning received**. Thank you. **Over**
D	**Nothing More. Over**
P	**Charlie Alpha Five Out**

Text$_3$ is somewhat more concise, in terms of words used, than Text$_2$ (itself, as we have seen, a very compressed version of Text$_1$)—161 compared with 181, a reduction of approximately 10 percent. The ratio is reduced to approximately 65 percent if the protocols required for interaction management (e.g., call-signs such as "Charlie Alpha Five" and the end of turn marker "Over") are discounted. Text$_3$ employs approximately 40 percent fewer communicative acts than Text$_2$—15 compared with 24. A similar reduction in word usage and airtime was found in an extensive trial of standard procedures in live operational radio traffic in a British force (Johnson et al. 1993).

Our brief analysis of the transformation of the text during its "travels" is, in one sense, complete. The call to the 999 line has been reentextualized twice and condensed as far as it could be without losing essential information. These three versions represent much of the significant transformation that takes place within the communicative constellation of emergency calls. However, at least two more kinds of communicative events and their accompanying texts are relevant to our description of the constellation. Our own data relating to these events are drawn from relatively unsystematic participant observation, however, and, to judge from the research literature, they do not appear to have been studied by others, so our discussion will be in the nature of a few brief and general descriptive comments. A proper analysis of them must await further detailed research.

Event$_4$, Text$_4$, and Beyond

At the moment at which the officers arrive on the scene of the incident, the information they have about it is drawn from the interaction with the dispatcher, in the form of Text$_3$, and is highly circumscribed. They then must develop as full a picture of the actuality as possible, so as to take what they see as the appropriate action. It is not uncommon for them to find no one present. Some incidents (e.g., a faulty burglar alarm going off, reported by a passing motorist) do not involve anyone else; in others, any offenders may have fled the scene. In such cases, they make their assessment on the basis of what they can see and hear.

Often, however, as in the example examined in this chapter, people may be present, sometimes in great numbers, who may include the caller, those involved directly in the incident, and onlookers. The officers will almost invariably engage in communicative interactions with one or more of these people—which we refer to for simplicity as Event$_4$, although in practice there may be several of them. At this point, the communicative cycle initiated by the call in effect returns to its beginning. When the original caller is present, Event$_4$ is in effect a rerun of Event$_1$ (a member of the public informing the police of an incident), and Text$_4$, like Text$_1$, usually takes the form of a conversation in which the main purpose is to transact information about that incident. There are, however, differences between the two (e.g., the medium of interaction is face-to-face speech, and all participants are present at the scene), which result in somewhat different linguistic patterns. No systematic record has been made of instances of Event$_4$, but our observations show that it is often very extensive.

Text$_4$ influences other texts in the constellation both retrospectively and prospectively. On the basis of Text$_4$, a (generally brief) report (Text$_5$) is made verbally, via the radio, to the dispatcher, on the outcome of the police attendance at the incident. In certain more serious cases, there may also be a written report, compiled some time after the event (Text$_6$). Additional texts, consisting of the officers' pocket-book notes, occur within the constellation. On the basis of these texts, Text$_2$ undergoes further modifications, which may be as simple as adding a note to the effect that the incident has been satisfactorily dealt with. It can be more complex: for example, the incident may be reclassified (one instance in our corpus began with a report of gunfire, which was amended to fireworks).

Other Kinds of Events and Texts in the Constellation

Despite the relatively detailed nature of the preceding discussion, what we have presented is still a simplified picture of the communicative constellation. At several stages in the process, other events may occur, resulting in modifications to any or all of the texts we have analyzed. For example, in order to arrive at an appropriate interpretation of the call, a call handler may interact verbally with a supervisor or consult a database, either directly or through the agency of a so-called "research desk," staffed by other operatives. Similarly, it is not uncommon for the dispatcher to discuss with the call handler the meaning or salience of items in Text$_2$; we know of at least one force in which the control center was rearranged so as to place the dispatchers next to the call handlers in order to facilitate this type of interaction.

Finally, we alluded earlier to Text$_2$ as a part of what may be called the institution's memory. In this form, it has the capacity to generate further texts in the future, through the processes of intertextuality (Candlin and Maley 1997). This is most likely to occur when it is quoted for evidential purposes in inquiries or court cases, but because of the permanent nature of the record it is also a potential source for criminological, historical, and other kinds of research. Or, when key information elements are conglomerated with those from numerous other communicative constellations, it may be decontextualized into a verbal or statistical summary, for use in strategic evaluation and planning.

CONCLUSION

In this chapter, we traced the entextualization and reentextualization processes of a text at major stages in the operational processes that are set in train by a call from a member of the public to the police emergency line. An outline, indicative analysis was given of the various versions of a text, from a corpus of calls collected during a research project for a British police force. The theoretical framework for the analysis is a broad, four-level model of communication, which provides the essential setting for the more detailed analyses of the linguistic patterning of texts.

Perhaps the most important aspect of the model for the study of emergency calls—and, indeed, most communicative events in an operational context—is the constellation, which allows the researcher to track the interactions and transformations of texts which have a shared purpose or intended outcome. There are several versions of each text throughout the constellation; each version is produced in a significantly different context, under the influence of changing participants, communicative purposes, physical context, and technological medium, and mode (speech to writing and vice versa). The processes of transformation are not linear, however: each is, to some extent and directly or indirectly, determined by the others. It should be very evident from this chapter that the "information-flow" or "conduit" model (as represented in figure 2.1) entirely misrepresents the communication between the public and the police, which is, as we have shown, a particularly rich field for the study of textual travels.

NOTES

1. This term is frequently used to describe the use of other than serving officers in an ancillary police role, although strictly speaking it is inaccurate, since police officers are legally also civilians.
2. See, for example, "Why 999 Calls Take 10 Minutes to Answer," *The Times*, January 24, 2006.
3. Unless otherwise stated, all examples are taken from our own corpus of data.

REFERENCES

Antunes, G., and E. Scott. 1981. Calling the cops: Police telephone operators and citizen calls for service. *Journal of Criminal Justice* 9: 165–79.

Barrar, P., M. Wyeth, and A. Darge. 2001. Summary Report: Police call handling project—call handling performance within the police service in England and Wales. http://www.mbs.ac.uk/corporate/consultancyresearch/ documents/pchpfinal_report_000.pdf

Blackledge, Adrian. 2005. *Discourse and Power in a Multilingual World*. Amsterdam: John Benjamins.

Candlin, Christopher N., and Yon Maley. 1997. Intertextuality and interdiscursivity in the discourse of alternative dispute resolution. In *The Construction of Professional Discourse*, ed. Britt-Louise Gunnarsson, Per Linell, and Brengt Nordberg, 201–22. London: Longman.

Elias, Norbert. 1992. *The Symbol Theory*, London: Sage.

Garcia, Angela. 1999. Misplaced mistrust: The collaborative construction of doubt in 911 emergency calls. *Symbolic Interaction* 22(4): 297–324.

Garner, Mark. 2004. *Language: An Ecological View*. Oxford: Peter Lang.

Garner, Mark, and Edward Johnson. 2006. Operational communication: A paradigm for applied research into police call-handling. *Speech, Language and the Law* 13(1): 55–75.

Garner, Mark, Z. Ning, and J. Francis. 2012. A framework for evaluating the effectiveness of patient information leaflets. *Health Expectations* 15(3): 283–94.

Garner, Mark, Steve Hick, Edward Johnson, and David Matthews. 1993. *Police Communication, Language and the Channel Tunnel*. Cambridge: PoliceSpeak Publications.

Hester, Stephen, and David Francis. 2001. Is institutional talk a phenomenon? Reflections on ethnomethodology and applied conversation analysis. In *How to Analyse Talk in Institutional Settings*, ed. A. W. McHoul and Mark Rapley, 206–18. London: Continuum.

HOCD. 2005. *Call Handling Standards*. London: Home Office Communications Directorate.

Imbens-Bailey, Alison, and Allyssa McCabe. 2000. The discourse of distress: A narrative analysis of emergency calls to 911. *Language and Communication* 20: 275–96.

Johnson, Edward, and Mark Garner. 2012. Corpus analysis for operational communications. Entry in C. Chapelle (ed.), *Encyclopedia of Applied Linguistics*. Oxford: Wiley-Blackwell.

Johnson, Edward, Steve Hick, Mark Garner, and David Matthews. 1993. *PoliceSpeak in Action: Standard Radio Procedures and Phraseology for Police*, Final Report by the PoliceSpeak Research Team Cambridge for the Chief Constable of Kent (Restricted Circulation).

Kelly, Ann. 2001. Reporting a service request. In *How to Analyse Talk in Institutional Settings*, ed. A. W. McHoul and Mark Rapley, 72–85. London: Continuum.

NPIA. 2007. *AirwaveSpeak user guide*. London: National Policing Improvement Agency.

Paltridge, Brian. 2008. *Discourse Analysis*. London: Continuum.

Reddy, Margaret. [1979] 1995. The conduit metaphor—A case of frame conflict in our language about language. In *Metaphor and Thought* (2d ed. 1995), ed. Andrew Ortony, 164–201. Cambridge: Cambridge University Press.

Renkema, Jan. 2004. *Introduction to Discourse Studies*. Philadelphia: John Benjamin.

Searle, John R. 1969. *Speech Acts*. London: Cambridge University Press.

Tracy, Karen, and Donald Anderson. 1999. Relational positioning strategies in police calls: A dilemma. *Discourse Studies* 1(2): 201–25.

Tsohatzidis, Savas L. 1994. *Foundations of Speech Act Theory: Philosophical and Linguistic Perspectives*. London: Routledge.

Watkin, Michele, and Don H. Zimmerman. 1999. Reduction and specialization in emergency and directory assistance calls. *Research on Language and Social Interaction* 32(4): 409–37.

Zimmerman, Don H. 1992. The interactional organization of calls for emergency assistance. In *Talk at Work: Interaction in Institutional Settings*, ed. Paul Drew and John Heritage, 418–69. Cambridge: Cambridge University Press.

CHAPTER 3

From Legislation to the Courts

Providing Safe Passage for Legal Texts through the
Challenges of a Police Interview

GEORGINA HEYDON

INTRODUCTION

The investigative interviewing of suspects and witnesses is a "core function of policing across the world" (Walsh 1994: 152–53). The investigative interview provides
police officers with a unique opportunity to obtain a first-person account of the
events in question. As well as playing an important role in the investigation, the
accounts of witnesses and suspects are destined to become some of the most important pieces of evidence in a criminal case, should it run to trial. However, evidence
collected during a police interview can be rendered useless to the prosecution case
if the court finds that it was improperly obtained. There exists the clear risk of evidence being ruled inadmissible if the interviewing officer fails to adhere to the legislation regarding a suspect's rights, such as the right to silence, to legal advice, or
to contact a friend or relative. Given that, according to a survey by Stevenson (in
Moston, Stephenson, and Williamson 1992), 96.6 percent of cases in Australian
criminal courts included confession evidence, the protection of the suspect's rights
in relation to such evidence must have a high priority. The critical importance of
complying with legislative requirements concerning a suspect's rights and obligations during an interview can create a tension between using prescribed legal language to properly represent the legislation and actually ensuring that the suspect
understands the caution or legal text being communicated. Thus, the texts used to
communicate the suspect's rights, which have been created by a legislative process,
are subjected to the stresses of colliding discursive trajectories. On the one hand,

there is the legal-police discourse, which is realized as the police officers' contributions to the interview, and which is travelling from a legislative source toward a criminal justice goal. As will be explained in this chapter, this discourse trajectory is exerting pressure on the text to remain unchanged from its original legislative form in order to protect the police institutional interests. On the other hand, there is the lay-suspect discourse, realized as the suspect's contributions to the interview, which is travelling from a personal experiential source toward a legal defense goal. This discourse trajectory may try to introduce changes to the text so that it adequately addresses the communicative and legal needs of the lay participant. As this chapter will illustrate, suspects can and do reproduce a legal text in plain language that highlights the impact of the caution on their future actions.

This chapter describes the recontextualization of specific legal texts that occur in police interviews from this perspective of colliding trajectories. As such, this chapter will consider how the negotiation of various legal cautions and explications by the participants in a police interview is achieved, and whether the goals of the participants can be aligned to some extent so that the journey of these texts from legislation to courtroom (and beyond) is less arduous. In particular, it is proposed that the availability of a "professional police voice" might alleviate some of the communicative problems that occur during the administration of police cautions and legal explanations. In order to achieve this goal, this chapter is placed within a context of both linguistic methodologies for the analysis of institutional interviews (e.g., Drew and Heritage 1992) and police investigative interviewing training that addresses the needs of the legislative environment of interviewing.

Using tools from Interactional Sociolinguistics (Goffman 1981) within a Conversation Analysis (Sacks, Schegloff, and Jefferson 1974) approach to the close examination of clarification sequences in police interviews with Anglo-Australian suspects, I will demonstrate how miscommunication that can undermine the integrity of the evidence could be minimized if police officers were able to draw upon a "professional voice" (Cordella 2004) and, in Goffman's (1981) sense, take up the role of "principal" in relation to what they are saying. Cordella (2004) proposes that by drawing on a professional voice, institutional representatives—doctors, in her case—are better able to negotiate the occasional conflicts that arise when institutional discourse and practices must be adapted to the needs of individual lay clients. The oncologists in her study utilize their "professional voice" by drawing on their own sense of expertise to take ownership of the institutional discourse and adapt it so that it best suits the goals of the interaction with their patient. This perspective is developed further by Rock (2007), who has more recently examined the specific case of police officers delivering the caution used with suspects in England and Wales and finds that the capacity to devise an appropriate interpretation of the caution text is critical to the accurate communication of the suspect's rights. For example, Rock finds that skilled police officers are able to draw successfully on a tripartite restructuring of the text in order to make clear its meaning to the suspect (186–87).

This chapter will demonstrate that if police officers were able to draw on a professional voice in the execution of cautions and similar legal explications, the police and suspect discourse trajectories might be better managed so that both travel more successfully toward their respective future positions of prosecution and defense in the courtroom. In this respect, this chapter makes an important contribution to the current shift toward a professionalization of police interviewing (Bradley, Nixon, and Marks 2006; Clarke and Milne 2001) by adding interactional resources to the tools available to police investigative interviewers.

BACKGROUND TO THE STUDY: LINGUISTIC, INSTITUTIONAL, AND LEGISLATIVE ENVIRONMENTS OF INTERVIEWING

Legal–Lay Communication in Interviewing

In Australian jurisdictions, as well as in the United Kingdom, the United States and many other parts of the world with an adversarial justice system, a police interview with a member of the public represents the production of a text that is critical to the future of the lay participant, as well as to the functioning of the various institutions involved. The content of a police interview may lead investigators toward a particular course of action in the investigation; it may be relied upon by lawyers to construct a defense for their client; it may be used by the court to determine a person's innocence or guilt in relation to a crime; and it may influence the sentencing in the case of a guilty finding. The significance of this particular type of institutional interview for the functioning of the criminal justice system has meant that considerable effort is expended in obtaining an accurate record of the interaction and ensuring that police officers clearly communicate to civilians their rights and obligations in relation to police questioning. Without this legal protection, the court cannot be satisfied that the evidence provided by a suspect has not been distorted through coercion.

The international research supporting investigative interviewing has been dominated over the past two decades by the discipline of cognitive psychology (Bull and Milne 2004; Clarke and Milne 2001; Memon, Bull, and Smith 1995; Milne and Bull 1999; Moston et al. 1992; Pearse and Gudjonsson 1996). There can be no doubt that psychology has provided a firm foundation for the development of investigative interviewing techniques, namely the P.E.A.C.E. model (Clarke and Milne 2001: 1; Ord, Shaw, and Green 2004)[1]; however, police interview training schemes have rarely, if ever, been given the benefit of research findings emerging from any other disciplines.

This chapter is specifically concerned with the interactions between police officers and suspects relating to the suspects' rights and obligations during formal, recorded police interviews in Victoria, Australia. These interactions are critical to the outcome of the police interviews because, as explained above, they have the potential to determine admissibility of the evidence. The interactions are shaped by the legislation relating to the conduct of police interviews with suspects contained in the Crimes Act and interpreted for practice in the Police Regulations, which, at the time that these interviews were recorded, was the text that regulated professional conduct and practice for police officers in Victoria. There are three key texts that are typically read to suspects by the police interviewer. Two are delivered at the beginning of the interview following the identification of the participants: the first is the official caution which informs the suspect of his or her right not to answer questions; the second text informs the suspect of his or her right to legal advice (though not representation in the interview room itself) and to contact with a friend or relative (the "one phone call"). The third legal text being referred to in this chapter is used by Victoria Police to inform a suspect of their rights and obligations in relation to the taking of fingerprints at the end of the interview where charges have been laid.

The origins of the three legal texts presented above can be found in the Crimes Act, as mentioned. For instance, the Crimes Act 1958 states in section 464A(3):

> Before any questioning (other than a request for the person's name and address) or investigation under sub-section (2) commences, an investigating official must inform the person in custody that he or she does not have to say or do anything but that anything the person does say or do may be given in evidence.

The following excerpts demonstrate how these texts can be delivered by a police officer interviewing a suspect. The wording used here is almost identical to the wording used in all 14 interviews in this study.

In the first excerpt, the police officer demonstrates how the first two texts are typically delivered to suspects. The excerpt commences a short way into the interview (line 24 of the complete transcript) after all the people present have already confirmed their identities.

Excerpt 1: Caution given in INT4

24.[2]	pio4[3]	okay I'm now going to speak to you John about a burglary
25.		but before I do I must inform you
26.		that you are not obliged to say or do anything unless you wish to do so
27.		but anything you say or do may be given in evidence
28.		do you understand that
29.	SPT4	yeah
30.	pio4	I must also inform you of the following rights
31.		you may contact or attempt to contact a friend or relative

32.		to tell that person of your whereabouts
33.		you may contact or attempt to contact a legal practitioner
34.		do you understand those rights
35.	SPT4	yeah
36.	pio4	do you wish to exercise any of those rights before the interview proceeds
37.	SPT4	nup
38.	pio4	okay

The third, much longer text is delivered by the same police officer in the excerpt below:

Excerpt 2: Fingerprinting caution delivered in INT4

226.	pio4	John you are going to be charged with burglary and theft
227.		your fingerprints are required for the purposes of identification
228.		your fingerprints may be used in evidence in court
229.		if you refuse to give your fingerprints voluntarily
230.		a member of the police force may use reasonable force to obtain them
231.		if you are not charged with a relevant offense within six months
232.		or are so charged but the charge is not proceeded with
233.		or you are not found guilty of the offense or any other relevant offense
234.		before the end of that period
235.		the fingerprints will be destroyed
236.		do you understand all this information
237.	SPT4	yes
238.	pio4	do you wish to comment on any of the information
239.	SPT4	no
240.	pio4	do you consent to giving your fingerprints here today
241.	SPT4	don't worry me ( )
242.	pio4	okay the time is ah
243.		just on three minutes past ten
244.		do you agree
245.	SPT4	yes

This fingerprinting caution is highly complex, linguistically and conceptually, and is the cause of considerable confusion to suspects. As will be demonstrated in this chapter, the police reliance on the scripted text and unwillingness or inability to migrate the text efficiently from its legal origins to its practical application in the interaction with a suspect, results in lengthy delays and miscommunication that has the potential to undermine the admissibility of the interview evidence in the trial.

A key difference between police interviews and other forms of institutional discourse is the extent to which there exists a top-down process of recontextualization (Bernstein 1990), such that police officers act as recontextualizing agents for texts—specifically cautions and the like—that originated in a primary context of state legislation and are rearticulated in the secondary context of the interview itself. That is to say, the actual language used in the police interview is directly influenced, and in some cases, prescribed, by legislative requirements of the state, which is a situation unlike a medical consultation or classroom interaction. Indeed, the "cautioning" of suspects is even unlike other parts of the police interview. For instance, it is quite dissimilar in structure and purpose to the information gathering, where a text in the form of a narrative is produced by the suspect and becomes destined for recontextualization elsewhere as part of some future courtroom proceedings.

The precision of the opening and closing in institutional terms is safeguarded by providing police officers with training and interview aids, such as written forms that guide them through the requisite utterances and are filled out with the suspect's responses as appropriate.

This chapter draws on two forms of discourse analysis: interactional sociolinguistics, from which is drawn the participant role analysis (Goffman 1981); and Conversation Analysis (Sacks et al. 1974). The frameworks are used to examine the extent to which police interviewers, as recontextualizing agents of the legal texts, are faced with a conflict between adhering to the word of the legislation and upholding the spirit and intention of the law. The analysis and subsequent discussion will illustrate that by closely examining the path through which this seemingly simple text—the caution—must travel and observing the obstacles and conflicting forces that lie along that path, we will appreciate the complexity and delicacy of the task required of police interviewers when administering the caution. Such appreciation is critical if we are to provide appropriate training for police interviewers, from recruit to senior investigator, and avoid the damage that inadequate cautioning can inflict on the case for the prosecution, a fair trial, and the just operation of the law.

Linguistic Analysis of Interview Data—Methodology

Within the tradition of Interactional Sociolinguistics, Goffman's speaker roles provide a highly structured and reliable approach to identifying the way in which participants align themselves with the utterances produced in an interaction (Goffman 1981: 128). The analysis of speaker roles reveals the attitude or stance that a speaker takes up in relation to what s/he is saying. For instance, a speaker might occupy the role of Author if they have chosen the words they are using, which is distinct from a case where the speaker is quoting someone else's words. There are three speaker roles that are crucial to the analysis of confessional or informative talk and thus to the development of police interviewing guidelines (Heydon 2005):

- "Author" (the utterance was "written" by the participant);
- "Principal" (the participant takes responsibility for the impact or effect of the utterance); and
- "Animator" (the participant actually physically produces the utterance).

Various combinations of role alignments represent different types of talk. For instance, the combination, or "participation framework" that represents authentic confessional or informative talk is one where the suspect or witness takes up all three of these roles and "animates" an utterance that s/he has "written" and for which s/he is willing to take "responsibility." Evidence that is obtained within this "participation framework" will be more reliable in subsequent legal proceedings because the informant, whether suspect or witness, will be less able or inclined to distance themselves from their statements. If the evidence is obtained using alternative role alignments it will be less reliable. By contrast, my prior research indicates that it is common for this reliable participation framework to be eschewed when a police officer makes a claim and asks the witness or suspect to agree to it, as in the following example from an interview between a detective (pio11) and a suspect (SPT11).

Excerpt 3: Requesting confirmation where pio11 is author and animator in INT11 adapted from Heydon (2005: 142)

pio11	would this be right
	or would this be wrong
	you kept trying to persuade him to go
SPT11	not persuade
	I asked him twice

In relation to the central claim "you kept trying to persuade him to go," we can observe that the witness did not "write" the words (was not the Author), or produce the statement (was not the Animator), but is being asked to take responsibility for the effect of the words (be the Principal). The use of such a framework is shown to be risky, as the suspect will find it easier to later "disown" principalship of the utterance, potentially undermining the case for the prosecution. In the case of communicating rights, there are different concerns, and the participation frameworks that are used by police interviewers as they recontextualize the legislative texts as a "caution" in the interview will be a focus of the analysis below.

Conversation Analysis (CA) provides a method of exposing the resources used by speakers to construct a coherent conversation, or, in this case, interview. CA practitioners have identified conversational rules that participants adhere to as a way of ordering speaker turns (Sacks et al. 1974) and other rules that govern the type of contribution that will be deemed appropriate at any given time (Jefferson 1984, 1988; Michaud and Warner 1997; Moerman and Sacks 1988; Sacks 1987). While these rules can be broken or amended, they act as a baseline against which conversational norms are measured by participants and marked in the structure and content of the interaction. CA contributes to the methodology of the present research by enabling the identification of such interactional strategies as question-answer chains (Frankel 1990), topic initiations and transitions (Button and Casey 1984; Frankel 1990; Jefferson 1984), and formulations (Heritage and Watson 1979). These strategies can be aligned with the institutional goals and legislative frameworks that shape the discourse, and thus enable the linguistic analysis to be meaningfully applied to the practices of police and lay participants in actual interviews.

Legislative Framework and Institutional Parameters

As described above, all police interviews with lay participants are governed to some extent by legal requirements interpreted through police procedures. In the case of interviews with suspects, the procedures that are intended to protect suspects' rights and inform them of their legal obligations are emphasized in police training manuals and familiarity with these procedures is considered a core aspect of any officer's training and competence. In Australia, the actual legislation relating to police interviewing varies from state to state, but the essential elements are very similar. In Victoria, as mentioned earlier, suspects are informed of their right to remain silent and of their rights to contact a lawyer, a friend or relative, and, when relevant, to have an interpreter present. There are many other interactions that may take place in the course of the interview which are legally defined, such as explaining to the suspect about the tape-recording process, making a record of breaks in the interview, and making a record of the treatment of the suspect or his/her children by the police. At the end of the interview, there are formal requirements relating to charging the suspect with an offence and an exceptionally long legal text that informs the suspect of their rights relating to fingerprinting. In most of these cases, as will be discussed further below, police officers are issued with forms or cards that have statements printed on them reflecting the wording deemed most appropriate for the fulfilment of the relevant legal requirements. These statements can be read aloud by the police officer at the appropriate time in the interview and this method is generally held by police officers to be the safest approach to adhering to the legislation and protecting the integrity and admissibility of the evidence gathered in the interview.

Nonetheless, the use of these "cue cards" by police officers can backfire, as will be demonstrated in this chapter, with the potential to irreparably undermine the integrity of the interview evidence. It is at these critical moments that access to a professional police voice—that is to say, an authoritative and perhaps more discretionary approach to the presentation of legal texts in the interview—would provide officers with the level of autonomy needed to judge the extent to which a caution or legal text requires variation in order that the spirit of the law is upheld and the admissibility of the evidence protected.

Institutional Goals of the Discourse

Before we turn to the analysis of the data, a few final words need to be said about the institutional purpose and goals of police interviews. Although it is common for police to describe the purpose of an investigative interview as the elicitation of a confession (Griffiths and Milne 2006: 167), the reality is that the organizational goal of the interview is to provide an opportunity for the suspect to provide their version of events in a form that will later be admissible as evidence in court. It is not a search for "the truth" nor is it an opportunity to persuade the suspect to change his or her story to reflect some police perception of what may have happened. It is therefore of critical importance that the contributions made to the interview by the suspect are protected from any form of contamination by the police interviewers and the bulk of the legal texts used by police in the course of the interview are designed to fulfill this function. The fact that each legal text is followed by some clarification of the suspect's comprehension of the text is a testament to the importance of these texts in the legal process. It is important to emphasize this point because at the heart of this chapter lies the author's contention that, by adhering to police standardized versions of the legal requirements, individual officers run the risk of undermining the admissibility of the interview as evidence because they fail to ensure that the suspects have actually understood their rights. On the other hand, the legal texts must be delivered accurately so that they adequately address the legal requirements of the legislation. This will be discussed in detail below, but at this stage it is simply important to note the institutional importance of comprehensibility of the legal texts used in police interviews to protect the suspect's rights.

MISCOMMUNICATION OF LEGAL TEXTS IN POLICE INTERVIEWS

The legal texts used by police interviewers to fulfill legislative requirements are most commonly found at the beginning, or Opening, of the interview and at the end, or Closing, of the interview.[4] The Opening of the interview encompasses the identification of the participants, the purpose of the interview, the presentation of the right to remain silent and the right to contact a lawyer and a friend or relative.[5] In the Closing, the charges are laid and the fingerprinting caution is presented. Heydon (2005) presents an analysis of the institutional language used to construct the Opening and Closing phases of the interviews and finds that police officers displayed a reluctance to vary the wording of the legal texts, which, as mentioned above, are based on police regulations and memorized or read out from forms. This contrasts with the situation in England and Wales where officers are required to explain the caution in their own words or to have the suspects do the same if deemed necessary (Rock 2007: 186–87). Clearly there is an organizational advantage to the former approach, as it is intended to minimize the risk that the interview evidence will be ruled inadmissible due to a failure to meet the legislative requirements. However, some examples from the Closure phases of different interviews demonstrate that this inflexibility can contribute to a failure on the part of the interviewing officer to adequately explain the fingerprinting procedure despite evidence that the suspect may not understand certain aspects of the caution.

This phenomenon can be seen clearly in the following excerpt from Interview 8 (hereinafter INT8), where a lengthy clarification sequence is undertaken by the participants following the formal request for consent to obtain the suspect's fingerprints. The sequence has been reproduced in full as Excerpt 4 and provides a valuable insight into the problems associated with institutional discourse in clarification sequences.

Excerpt 4 Fingerprinting caution delivery in INT8

468.	pio8:	or you are found not *guilty* of the *offense*
469.		or any other relevant offense before the end of that *period* ⇒
470.		then the *fingerprints* will be destroyed ↓
471.		do *you* understand this *information* ↑
472.	SPT8:	so have I got a *choice* whether I get fingerprinted or *not* ↑
473.	pio8:	*do* you do you wish to *comment* o- on this information ↓
474.		do you understand what I've *said* to you ∧
475.	SPT8:	not really *no* ↓
476.	pio8:	would you like me to *read* it to you *again* ↓
477.	SPT8:	no I just *I'm* asking *you* ⇒
478.		do d- have I got a *choice*
479.		do I *have* to be fingerprinted or *don't* I ∧
480.	pio8:	you *do* you do have a *choice* ∧
481.		you can say you can *agree*-ee to have your *fingerprints* taken ⇒
482.		or you can *disagree* to have your fingerprints taken ↓
483.		(1.7) if you (2.1) *disagree* to have your *fingerprints* taken ∧
484.		then the poli- then the *police* can enter into a *certain* course of *action* ↓
485.		and that's a course of *action* I've *detailed* in this ah

486.		(0.9) in this ah (0.3) *paragraph*
487.		would you like me to *read* it to you *again* ↓
488.	SPT8:	no it's o*kay* ∧
489.	pio8:	(3.2) do you under*stand* the *information* which I've *read* out to you ↓
490.	SPT8:	yes ⇒
491.	pio8:	do you wish to *comment* on this information ↓
492.	SPT8:	(3.2) um (2.1) nah I don't want to be *fingerprinted* ∧
493.	pio8:	you *don't* want to be fingerprinted ↓
494.		oh well that's me next *question* ↓
495.		do you *consent* to giving your fingerprints ↓
496.	SPT8:	no ↓
497.	pio8:	you *don't* ↓
498.		all right ↓
499.	(sio8):	(do you wa-)
500.	pio8:	do you have any *reason* for not consenting to giving your fingerprints ↓
501.	SPT8:	I just don't *want* to ↓
502.	pio8:	okay ↓
503.		(2.3) are you *aware* (1.0) and do you *recall* me *saying* during that paragraph ⇒
504.		that if you *refuse* to give your fingerprints *voluntarily*
505.		(.) a member of the *police* force *may* use *reasonable* force to *obtain* them ↓
506.		did you *hear* me say //that* ↑
507.	SPT8:	yeah* ⇒
508.	pio8:	and are you *aware* of what *reasonable* force is ∧
509.	SPT8:	no ∧

The interaction presented in Excerpt 5 below begins with the last part of the statement of the suspect's rights and obligations regarding fingerprinting. As mentioned earlier, in the state of Victoria, the fingerprinting caution is very long and complex even by police standards and it would be reasonable to expect that suspects might not understand every aspect of it. As always, the police interviewer is required to ask the suspect if they understood the caution (as in line 471 above), a question that elicits a negative response quite regularly in the data. In the above excerpt, the suspect, SPT8, indicates that she has not fully understood the caution, by asking very directly in line 472: *so have I got a choice whether I get fingerprinted or not.* In response, we see that the police interviewer, pio8, seems unable to formulate a similarly direct clarification and the "explanation" he offers is so indirect that SPT8 believes she has a choice not to be fingerprinted which is not the case. Pio8 seems aware that a misunderstanding has occurred, but he is apparently unable to address the problem within the scope of the institutional discourse of the Closure phase. In fact, it takes another 51 lines to sort the problem out, at which point the suspect, in agreeing to the fingerprinting, states quite succinctly SPT8/560: *yeah I'm not going to be held down*—a clarification which might have occurred some five minutes earlier if the police interviewer had had access to the resources necessary to construct a more informative explanation. The way in which the particular features of police institutional discourse constrain effective interviewing will be discussed further below, but an example from another interview will demonstrate the complexity of comprehension problems in the Closure phase.

Excerpt 5: Comprehension of fingerprinting caution delivered in INT1

524.	pio1:	(0.4) then the fingerprints will be destroyed↓
525.		(0.5) do you understand that information∧
526.	SPT1:	°yes I do° ((barely audible))
527.	pio1:	do you wish to comment on any of this information∧
528.	SPT1:	no↓
529.	pio1:	do you consent to giving your fingerprints↓
530.	SPT1:	no∧
531.	pio1:	(1.5) did you understand this (.) information↑
532.	SPT1:	yep↓
533.	pio1:	(0.6) right↓ I'll just (0.4) read it to you (0.2) again slowly⇒
534.	SPT1:	°all righ°
535.	pio1	your fingerprints are required for the purpose of en- identification↓
536.		(0.4) your fingerprints may be used in evidence at court↓
537.		(0.5) if you refuse (.) to give your fingerprints voluntarily⇒
538.		(0.2) a member of the police force may use reasonable force to obtain them↓
539.	SPT1:	(0.7) oh right yeah //(that's ri-)*
540.	pio1:	you* understand that∧=
541.	SPT1:	=I understand yeah⇒
542.	pio1:	right↓ (0.4) do you consent to giving your fingerprints∧
543.	SPT1:	°no I don't°
544.	pio1:	(0.7) you understand about reasonable force to obtain them⇒
545.	SPT1:	°yeah°

546.	pio1:	(0.6) and if you're not charged within six months they get destroyed anyway∧
547.	SPT1:	right↓ (0.9) yep∧
548.	pio1:	(0.3) you understand all that↑
549.	SPT1:	yep⟹
550.	pio1:	and you still don't consent↓
551.	SPT1:	(1.0) nah⟹ I'll give 'em∧
552.	pio1:	(0.3) oh you do consent
553.	SPT1:	ye::ah∧ (.) oh∧ right↓ yeah↓ (.) no↓ look⟹ (0.2) yeah⟹ I do⟹
554.		I'll give 'em⟹ no worries⟹

Whereas in Excerpt 4 from INT8, the suspect did not understand the meaning of the caution, a different sort of problem arises in this excerpt from INT1. In Excerpt 5 above, the suspect, SPT1, indicates that he has understood the caution, but when the police interviewer, pio1, requests his consent to undertake the fingerprinting procedure, SPT1 refuses: *no* (line 530). Perhaps because this is not the preferred response (Sacks 1987), pio1 seems prepared to negotiate the matter, rather than accept the refusal and proceed to take the fingerprints by force.

In lines 538–41 we can see that pio1, like pio8, has limited resources with which to resolve the problem. As we saw in INT8, the interviewing officer relies heavily on the words and phrases used in the Police Regulations when attempting to clarify a misunderstanding, whether or not this makes grammatical sense. For instance in line 544, she asks: *you understand about reasonable force to obtain them*. In this way, she does not define any of the terms she is using, but simply checks with SPT1 that he understands them. This approach works no better for pio1 than it did for pio8, and in the end, only a chance expansion of SPT1's negative response (551/SPT1: *nah⟹ I'll give 'em∧*) clarifies the cause of the misunderstanding: SPT1 has apparently interpreted *consent* as something like *object*, and therefore responded negatively, presumably believing he was being compliant.

The clarification produced by pio1 could not have resolved the problem because it did not address the nature of the misunderstanding. Even when faced with the prospect of having to *use reasonable force to obtain* the suspect's fingerprints, pio1 does not attempt to replace the words and phrases of the legal formalities with a significantly less institutional set of terminology, despite being able to recognize that some kind of problem has occurred. In the case described here, the problem is eventually resolved. However, one can well imagine the confusion and aggravation that may have resulted had the misunderstanding not been clarified by the suspect and had the police officers proceeded to use force to obtain SPT1's fingerprints.

Another instance of misunderstanding occurs in INT1 during the process of laying criminal charges (see Excerpt 6 below). Clearly it is of critical importance to the admissibility of the evidence that the suspect knows which crimes s/he has been charged with by the police. In the excerpt below, it is unclear whether the suspect believes himself charged with criminal damage (for breaking the shop door), or he believes that he will be charged for the damage in a monetary sense.

Excerpt 6: Charging with criminal damage in INT1

497.	pio1:	(0.3) um↑ (6.7) °hm° ⟹ just going to ask you a *few* more questions ⟹
498.		you've *got* um (1.5) you're going to be *charged* with the assault on *Ian*⟹
499.	SPT1:	right∧
500.	pio1:	and you're *also* going to be *charged* with the *damage* on the door↓
501.	SPT1:	(0.6) I'll *pay* for the door↑
502.	pio1:	yeah but you //under*stand**
503.	SPT1:	I me Betty* *knows* I'll pay for *that*⟹
504.	pio1:	(0.5) but you //under*stand* * that there's *charges* pending as well⟹
505.	SPT1:	I've already (...)*
506.	pio1:	(1.0)°ri° (2.1) you're not ob*li*ged to say or do anything unless you wish to *do* so ↓
507.		but whatever you *do* say o- ↓
508.		(0.5) whatever you say or *do* may be recorded and given in *evidence* ↓
509.		you understand *that*↑
510.	SPT1:	I *do*⟹

In Excerpt 6, pio1 seems prepared to proceed to the next stage of the Closing without obtaining a clear confirmation from SPT1 that he understood the nature of the charges made against him. This is a serious failing in the interview process and one that was caused by police assumptions about the interview process which were not shared by the suspect. For instance, pio1's attempt to clarify the charge issue (504/ pio1: *(0.5) but you //understand * that there's charges pending as well⟹*) does not even use the construction *charged with* that would highlight the criminal meaning of *charge*. Therefore, line 504 can only work as a clarification of her original statement by reference to a structural rule of the interview—that information relating to events is not discussed in the Closing. This rule can be described as a type of contextualization cue (Gumperz 1982) through which the meaning of the utterance can be understood. By reference to a contextualization cue such as this rule it becomes evident that the phrase *charges pending* must relate to criminal charges and not to the financial arrangements between SPT1 and the shop owners as this latter interpretation would be introducing event information into the Closing. However, contextualization cues are not always accessible to both participants and in this case pio1 is relying on a contextualization cue for the valid interpretation of her utterance that is not available to SPT1. Without access to the appropriate cues, SPT1 is unable to correctly interpret pio1's clarification.

The discursive practices used by pio1 reveal an assumption underlying the utterance that the suspect will have access to certain institutional knowledge. SPT1, however, appears to be unaware that event information is not being discussed at this point and continues to refer only to the financial meaning of *charges*.

THE POLICE ROLE IN RESOLVING MISCOMMUNICATION

In this section the distribution of participant roles in the interview and the turn-taking structure will both be discussed in relation to the contributions they each make to the construction of the police role in addressing instances of miscommunication in the interview.

The Assignment of Roles in Communicating Rights

In a police interview, participants display changes in their orientation to a participant role framework as they move through different stages of the interview, namely the Opening, Information Gathering, and Closing (Heydon 2005). This is consistent with the variation in function of each stage. The talk in the Opening and the Closing was found by Heydon (2005) and Rock (2007: 144) to involve "form-filling" types of activities, regulated by legislative requirements, whereas the Information Gathering was found to require less formal speech that provided the suspect with more "space" to produce longer, descriptive turns.

In the excerpts above, we can observe the participation framework that typifies those parts of the interview in which the police interviewer is cast as the recontextualizing agent for critically important legislative texts: the caution and communication of the suspect's rights. The role of *animator* is obviously designated to the police interviewer—he or she always produces the talk that comprises the caution or communication of rights (cf. Rock 2007: 199–200). However, the distribution of the *principal* and *author* roles is less clear. We have already noted that the texts have an origin outside the interaction and are clearly not written by the police interviewer. Indeed, most police officers use cue cards to ensure that they faithfully reproduce the words provided by the police manual and thus assign the role of *author* to the institution. As regards the role of principal, I have argued elsewhere (Heydon 2005: 198) and maintain here that police interviewers cannot be held accountable for the consequences of uttering the caution texts, since they do not decide if or when to produce them. Rock (2007: 144) similarly finds that the role of author is taken by government drafters who write the caution texts, while the role of principal is designated to other government actors, such as the Home Office in the UK context. Police officers are compelled by legislation to undertake specific verbal tasks at preordained points in the interview, which they achieve through the recontextualization process. It could be seen that the police speakers in these parts of the interview are orienting to the presence of the tape-recorder as a third party, as argued by Russell (2000: 114), who cites Drew and Sorjonen in stating that "the tape is a strong incentive to participants to orient to their 'institutional identities.'"

In summary, therefore, the participation framework that is used by police interviewers in these data to issue cautions and communicate rights in the Openings and Closings of interviews is one where the *animator* role is assigned to the interviewer but the *author* and *principal* roles are assigned to the police institution. We can represent this alignment as PI-au/pr (Police Institution—author/principal).

To the extent that the negotiation of participant roles can be described in terms of the speaker's control over their own utterances, in the Opening and the Closing, the individual police officer conducting the interview does not have control over her or his utterances beyond controlling their physical production. This is comparable to Bakhtin's notion of "authoritative discourse" (Holquist 1981), which is discussed further by Chris Heffer in chapter 10 of this volume in terms of the normative rules that attribute a high degree of importance to the judgments of senior judges. Bakhtin describes the process through which another's discourse is appropriated and assimilated not freely, but so that it "demands our unconditional allegiance" and "permits no play with the context framing it" (Holquist 1981: 343). This is precisely the position of the police officers in the PI-au/pr framework of the Opening and Closing.

It is important to realize, however, that a lack of control over the content of utterances does not necessarily equate to a less powerful role in the interview. To further our understanding of police power as it is allocated to and exercised by individual officers, and to move toward a solution to the problem of miscommunication in communicating rights, we need to consider the allocation of interactional resources in the interviews.

Power and the Allocation of Interactional Resources

The distribution of turn types in a police interview is such that turns that constitute first pair parts of adjacency pairs are routinely allocated to police interviewers. The recurrent nature of this arrangement from one adjacency pair, typically a question-answer pair, to the next can be described as a "Q-A chain rule" (Frankel 1990). That is, first and second pair parts recognizable as questions and answers are produced by the police interviewer and the suspect respectively to form chains of such pairs across the longer sequences that make up the interview.

The effect of this arrangement on the interaction is to limit access to interactional resources by the suspect while at the same time maximizing the police interviewer's access to these resources. Thus, police interviewers have access to resources (i.e., first pair parts) that enable them to introduce, maintain, or suppress topics, whereas suspects are constrained to devices such as stepwise transitions to introduce new topics within second pair parts and have no resources available to maintain or suppress topics. This does not preclude the possibility for suspects to use strategies that enhance their position of power or control in the interview (see, for instance, Linfoot-Ham 2006; Stokoe 2010), but the interactional resources are allocated in such a way that interviewee participants do not have access to the topic management tools that can consistently shape the topic flow of the interaction.

A further dimension to this issue is added by consideration of the allocation of turn types in relation to the level of obligation placed on the recipient by a particular turn type. According to the "hierarchy of obligatingness" proposed by Thomas (1989), the turn types available to the police interviewers in the information-gathering part of the interview, which comprise mainly direct questions and direct requests, are placed at the highly obligating end of the hierarchy. The turn types allocated to suspects, on the other hand, are generally assertions about information that is known to the speaker, which are considered minimally obligating (Thomas 1989: 152–53).

In the information-gathering part of a police interview, the interactional resources used to control important aspects of the discourse are distributed in favor of the interviewing officer. The resources needed to control the topic of talk, for instance, are largely inaccessible to the suspect and those resources that are accessible, such as stepwise topic transitions, do not obligate the police interviewer to maintain the topic that has been initiated by the suspect. Resources such as first pair parts and interruptions provide the police interviewer with the potential to maintain a great deal of control over the discourse by constraining the topic and length of suspect's contributions. Therefore, the distribution of turn types and interactional resources grant the interviewers a level of power over the interaction that is unattainable by the suspect. This distribution of resources can be termed a "deference structure" (Frankel 1990), whereby the allocation of power in the form of access to interactional resources favors the police interviewer.

Police Agency in Addressing Miscommunication

To summarize the discussion so far, we have seen that the PI-au/pr distribution of participant roles in the communication of rights in the Opening and Closing of the interview provides the police interviewer with few if any opportunities to produce important utterances over which they can be said to have complete control.

However, this arrangement appears contradictory to the distribution of interactional resources that grants police interviewers a very substantial amount of control over both their own utterances and those of the suspect. In other words, within the PI-au/pr framework the police officer as an individual experiences a reduced level of power in the discourse in favor of the institution, but within the broader deference structure of the information-gathering part of the interview, the interviewing officer occupies a potentially powerful position having access to resources that control the contributions of all participants.

The key to resolving this apparent conflict is the issue of choice. Police officers as individuals can choose to align to particular participant roles just as they can choose to access interactional resources of discourse control available to them. Clearly, if police officers are to resolve the miscommunication that occurs during the caution, they need to take up a more powerful role alignment so they can clarify misunderstandings. Access to a more powerful set of interactional resources is not itself enough to achieve this as demonstrated in the excerpt from INT1. Although pio1 uses her access to first pair parts to initiate a clarification sequence when she perceives that there is a problem with SPT1's refusal to consent to the fingerprinting procedure, her strategy does not work to identify the problem. She, like the other police participants in the data, is unable take up an *author* role in relation to the caution text and simply continues to re*animate* the text as it is provided by the institution. In other words, at present, the police interviewers orient to the PI-au/pr framework in the Opening and Closing so comprehensively that they appear unable to address serious misunderstandings by the suspects. Interestingly, and perhaps not coincidentally, this situation arises at a later stage in the criminal justice process, when judges can encounter a similar difficulty in appropriately explaining their instructions to jurors, and in particular the meaning of 'beyond reasonable doubt' (see Heffer, chapter 10 of this volume).

If it were the case that simply reproducing the words of the caution accurately would ensure compliance with the legislation, then this would be a sound strategy. But the legislation requires that the suspect understands their rights, and it is clear that in this regard, the strategy of faithful reproduction will not suffice.[6] If a suspect does not understand the meaning of the caution the first time, the data show that there is a good chance he or she will not gain any enlightenment from hearing the identical phrases a second or third time. What is needed is some interpretation or explanation of the legal phrases, such as that clearly requested by the suspect in INT8—*so have I got a choice whether I get fingerprinted or not*—when faced with the ludicrous spectacle of two police officers refusing to clarify the meaning of the fingerprinting caution.

To the extent that the police officers are avoiding any rewording of the caution texts, their role as recontextualizing agents appears very limited. To address the miscommunication problems as they arise in the interview, police officers must be given a more expanded role in the process of recontextualization. Moreover, the process of recontextualization itself needs to be understood as a more complex task than simple reproduction of a set of phrases. It is not reasonable to release a text born in the regulated and static environs of the state legislature to survive in the wild and tempestuous surroundings of a police evidential interview. Police officers must be trained to recognize the signs that a legal text is failing to adapt to its new environment and provide the necessary support in the form of interpretation and explanation. It is not beyond the capabilities of experts in language and police educators to collaborate on producing guidelines for officers that will ensure both comprehension by suspects and compliance with the legislation. Indeed, there have been a number of instances of alternative approaches to this problem overseas, the most common solution being one where suspects are asked to provide their own interpretation of the legal texts and then the police interviewer offers a further clarification as required (see, for instance, Rock 2007: 258). Nonetheless, these approaches clearly introduce a more professional and autonomous role for the police interviewer than is evident in these interviews from the state of Victoria.

CONCLUSION

The product of a successful investigative interview – a first-person narrative describing the events – is a critical form of evidence in a criminal trial. A robust confession from a suspect or a detailed account from an eyewitness can greatly reduce the time and cost expended by police and prosecutors in investigating the case and preparing the brief. It is therefore unsurprising that researchers and practitioners are committed to continuous improvement in the quality of police interviewing.

In relation to the opening and closing of the interview, where the legal texts are delivered by police interviewers, the cognitive and behavioral psychology research has established some important guidelines that are relevant the present chapter. For instance, the P.E.A.C.E. model places a strong emphasis on the need to build rapport during the opening stages of the interview. Yet this would appear to conflict with the requirement (or tendency) to deliver the cautions and other legal texts using a highly stylized legal jargon and formal conversational structure that is utterly at odds with the informal and suspect-centred interactions encouraged as part of the rapport-building phase. This conflict of goals can be usefully demonstrated through the application of the linguistic analysis that is presented here such that it might contribute to the continuous improvement and development of the P.E.A.C.E. model.

It is essential that police officers from recruit level upwards are equipped with the necessary tools to address these potentially catastrophic incidents of misunderstanding, but first the problem needs to be properly understood. This chapter, by addressing the issue using the conceptual framework of textual travel, demonstrates that the problem lies with a misconception about the process of recontextualization. The analysis presented here identifies a colliding set of discourse trajectories that exert pressure on the production of legal texts within the interview. On the one hand, the police interviewers are trained to maintain the integrity of the relevant legislation contained in the Crimes Act and communicate the suspect's rights to him or her using words that closely resemble the words of the legislative text. In this sense, the legal texts are part of a discourse trajectory that originates from the legislation, travels through the police regulations to the interview, and may continue through the court trial and the evaluation of the police conduct by the police administration or state justice department. On the other hand, the suspect's interpretation of the legal texts is part of a discourse trajectory that travels from the suspect's experience of the crime event, through the descriptions elicited during the police interviews, and potentially toward the court proceedings, sentencing, corrections institutions, and eventually prison release texts. It is the confluence of these two trajectories that produces conflicting pressures on the production of the legal texts: the former trajectory exerts a pressure for the police interviewer to reproduce the texts without alteration or reinterpretation to adhere to the letter of the law; the latter trajectory introduces the necessity for the police interviewers to interpret the legal texts and make their meaning clear to the suspect. The data used in this study demonstrate that these police interviewers are inadequately equipped in their role as recontextualizing agents and that the cue card approach to communicating rights fails to account for the discoursal differences between the text's original static environment in legislation and its destination in a dynamic interview subject to all the forces and variability of human interaction.

ACKNOWLEDGMENTS

I would particularly like to acknowledge the sagacious critique provided by Frances Rock, whose invaluable assistance was critical to my developing this chapter from the original paper presented at the 6th Cardiff Roundtable in Sociolinguistics in July 2008 to a more rounded and coherent contribution in this volume. I am also very grateful to Lynn Childress for her attentive commentary on the text, and to Chris Heffer for providing insights in relation to 'authoritative voices', among other things. When an earlier version of this paper was presented at the Cardiff Roundtable, the participants were most helpful in interpreting my data in ways I had not considered, and I continue to draw on those insights in my research to this day. I am truly grateful both to the participants and to the organizers of that event.

APPENDIX: TRANSCRIPTION CONVENTIONS

The following conventions are used in the transcription of data for this chapter.

Symbol	Description
//	overlapping speech commences
*	overlapping speech ends
=	latching
(0.6)	silence measured in seconds
(.)	micro-pause of less than 0.2 seconds
°word°	softer than surrounding speech
WORD	louder than surrounding speech
word	syllables having greater stress than surrounding sounds
↑	high rise intonation
∧	low rise intonation
⇒	level intonation
↓	falling intonation
::	the sound is lengthened by one syllable for each colon
-	truncated word
h	audible outbreath
.h	audible inbreath
(h)	explosive aspiration (as in laughter)
(word)	uncertain transcription
( )	incomprehensible utterance, no transcription attempted
(( ))	transcriber's remarks, including comments on voice quality or nonverbal sounds

NOTES

1. The acronym P.E.A.C.E. is derived from the five stages of the interview taught to officers: 1. Planning and Preparation; 2. Engage and Explain; 3. Account; 4. Closure; 5. Evaluation.
2. Transcription conventions are provided in an Appendix.
3. The abbreviation 'pio' is used for the Primary Interviewing Officer, 'sio' is used for the Secondary Interviewing Officer, and the suspect is identified with the abbreviation SPT. The interview number is appended to each abbreviation to form a unique speaker code.
4. For readers familiar with the P.E.A.C.E. structure used in England and Wales, and currently being introduced in some Australian states and in New Zealand, this corresponds to the Engage and Explain phase and the Closure phase.
5. In the interviews being analyzed here the police officers are not trained to build rapport in the Opening as would be the case in jurisdictions where the P.E.A.C.E. structure is used.
6. The Crimes Act (Victoria) 1958, section 464J(b) clearly places "the onus on the prosecution to establish the voluntariness of an admission or confession made by a person suspected of having committed an offence."

REFERENCES

Bernstein, Basil. 1990. *Class, Codes and Control. Vol. 4, The Structuring of Pedagogic Discourse.* London: Routledge.

Bradley, David, Christine Nixon, and Monique Marks. 2006. What works, what doesn't work and what looks promising in police research networks. In *Fighting Crime Together: The Challenges of Policing and Security Networks*, ed. Jenny Fleming and Jennifer Wood, 170–94. Sydney: UNSW Press.

Bull, Ray, and Rebecca Milne. 2004. Attempts to improve the police interviewing of suspects. In *Interrogations, Confessions, and Entrapment*, ed. G. D. Lassiter, 181–96. New York: Kluwer Academic.

Button, Graham, and Neil Casey. 1984. Generating topic: The use of topic initial elicitors. In *Structures of Social Action: Studies in Conversation Analysis*, ed. John Maxwell Atkinson and John Heritage, 167–90. Cambridge: Cambridge University Press.

Clarke, Colin, and Rebecca Milne. 2001. *National Evaluation of the PEACE Investigative Interviewing Course.* London: Home Office.

Cordella, Marisa. 2004. *The Dynamic Consultation: A Discourse Analytical Study of Doctor–Patient Communication.* Amsterdam: John Benjamins.

Drew, Paul, and John Heritage, eds. 1992. *Talk at Work.* Cambridge: Cambridge University Press.

Frankel, Richard. 1990. Talking in interviews: A dispreference for patient-initiated questions in physician–patient encounters. In *Interaction Competence*, ed. George Psathas, 231–62. Washington, DC: University Press of America.

Goffman, Ervin. 1981. *Forms of Talk.* Philadelphia: University of Pennsylvania Press.

Griffiths, Andrew, and Rebecca Milne. 2006. Will it all end in tiers? Police interviews with suspects in Britain. In *Investigative Interviewing: Rights, Research and Regulation*, ed. Tom Williamson, 167–89. Cullompton, UK: Willan.

Gumperz, John. 1982. *Discourse Strategies.* Cambridge: Cambridge University Press.

Heritage, John, and D. R. Watson. 1979. Formulations as conversational objects. In *Everyday Language: Studies in Ethnomethodology*, ed. George Psathas, 123–62. New York: Irvington Publishers.

Heydon, Georgina. 2005. *The Language of Police Interviewing: A Critical Analysis.* New York: Palgrave Macmillan.

Holquist, Michael. 1981. *The Dialogic Imagination: Four Essays by M. M. Bakhtin.* Translated by Caryl Emerson and Michael Holquist. Austin: University of Texas Press.

Jefferson, Gail. 1984. On stepwise transition from talk about a trouble to inappropriately next-positioned matters. In *Structures of Social Action: Studies in Conversation Analysis*, ed. John Maxwell Atkinson and John Heritage, 191–222. Cambridge: Cambridge University Press.

———. 1988. On the sequential organization of troubles-talk in ordinary conversation. *Social Problems* 35(4): 418–41.

Linfoot-Ham, Kerry. 2006. Conversational maxims in encounters with law enforcement officers. *The International Journal of Speech, Language and the Law* 13(1): 23–54.

Memon, Amina, Ray Bull, and M. Smith. 1995. Improving the quality of the police interview: Can training in the use of cognitive techniques help? *Policing and Society* 5(1): 32–40.

Michaud, Shari L., and Rebecca M. Warner. 1997. Gender differences in self-reported response to troubles talk. *Sex Roles* 37(7/8): 527–40.

Milne, Rebecca, and Ray Bull. 1999. *Investigative Interviewing: Psychology and Practice.* London: Wiley.

Moerman, Michael, and Harvey Sacks. 1988. On "understanding" in the analysis of natural conversation. In *Talking Culture: Ethnography and Conversation Analysis*, ed. Michael Moerman, 180–86. Philadelphia: University of Pennsylvania Press.

Moston, Stephen, Geoffrey M. Stephenson, and Thomas M. Williamson. 1992. The effects of case characteristics on suspect behaviour during police questioning. *British Journal of Criminology* 32: 23–40.

Ord, Brian, Gary Shaw, and Tracey Green. 2004. *Investigative Interviewing Explained*. Chatswood, NSW: LexisNexis/Butterworths.

Pearse, John, and Gisli H. Gudjonsson. 1996. Police interviewing techniques at two South London police stations. *Psychology, Crime and Law* 3: 63–74.

Rock, Frances. 2007. *Communicating Rights: The Language of Arrest and Detention*. Basingstoke, UK: Palgrave Macmillan.

Russell, Sonia. 2000. "Three's a Crowd": Shifting dynamics in the interpreted interview. In *Language in the Legal Process*, ed. Janet Cotterill, 111–25. Houndsmills, UK: Palgrave Macmillan.

Sacks, Harvey. 1987. On the preferences for agreement and contiguity in sequences in conversation. In *Talk and Social Organisation*, ed. Graham Button and John Lee, 54–69. Clevedon/Philadelphia: Multilingual Matters Ltd.

Sacks, Harvey, Emanuel Schegloff, and Gail Jefferson. 1974. A simplest systematics for the organisation of turn-taking for conversation. *Language* 50(4): 696–735.

Stokoe, Elizabeth. 2010. "I'm not gonna hit a lady": Conversation analysis, membership categorization and men's denials of violence towards women. *Discourse and Society* 21(1): 59–82.

Thomas, J. A. 1989. Discourse control in confrontational interaction. In *The Pragmatics of Style*, ed. Leo Hickey, 133–56. London: Routledge.

Walsh, Michael. 1994. Interactional styles in the courtroom: An example from Northern Australia. In *Language and the Law*, ed. John Gibbons, 217–33. Harlow: Longman Group.

CHAPTER 4

"Every Link in the Chain"

The Police Interview as Textual Intersection

FRANCES ROCK

INTRODUCTION: TEXTUAL TRAVEL IN WITNESS STATEMENTS

"Communication situations...are connected in countless and subtle ways, across space and time, through artefacts (such as written texts...) and human beings who wander between situations" (Linell 1998: 144). This chapter examines such wanderings as they occur in the creation of a written police witness statement through a spoken, one-to-one interview. We will see that as a police officer and witness collaborate in text production, their activities illustrate Bakhtin's crucial idea that the utterance, here the interview, reflects "preceding links in the chain sometimes close and sometimes distant" (1986: 93). Interviews incorporate a remarkable, yet typical, range of texts.

Interviewing to gather evidence entails four forms of textual travel. Whenever we have substantial questions, we travel toward answers, be the journey straightforward, exhausting, or frustrating, by extracting, collating, and reviewing information. So it is for police investigating crimes. This is one important facet of travel in gathering evidence; the journey toward answers, right or wrong, powered by information. Further forms of travel feature in witness interviews. Witnesses might be eager storytellers or, conversely, so unwilling that they must be legally compelled to narrate. They may have clear or hazy memories. They may be comfortable with their experience or so traumatized that they can barely articulate it. Here then is a second facet of travel; information travels from witnesses according to contextual factors including willingness, memory, and certainty. Third, information from witnesses, in England and Wales, is obtained by police officers who elicit and probe, recording a version of each witness's statement, typically on paper. Such textual co-construction is an intriguing method for information-gathering. This third facet of travel, perhaps the clearest example so far of *textual* travel, involves witness and interviewer in transmodality (Pennycook 2007; Goodwin and Alim 2010). Witness interviews finally entail travel beyond the immediate interaction by invoking prior texts. This process sits uncomfortably with the expectation that witness statements represent the *witness's* experience. This chapter therefore focuses on this final form of textual travel—that into interview. Yet this travel is situated within the former three forms—the collation of evidence, the witness's circumstances vis-à-vis their story, and the co-construction of text—and so is this chapter.

Writers are readers before they can create (Still and Worton 1991: 1). For police officers writing witnesses' statements, this consumption-production relationship necessitates attending to the witness. Yet the officer inhabits a densely packed, richly textured intertextual world through which many texts, not all connected to or issuing from the witness, travel. The witness's actuality becomes, through interview, "a resource," worked on "to extract formalised and highly restricted representations" (Smith 2005: 186), but the witness's actuality does not come alone. Rather the interview becomes a point of intersection of text trajectories (Blommaert 2005: 62–64). Consider the excerpt below where a witness (W, Wanda) recounts a key moment in a crime's development to a police interviewer (P, Phil):

Excerpt 1

> 90. W I was standing by the bar and this guy's walked (.) through the back of the bar
> 91. P that's right this is what's brought it [W: yeah] towards tension wasn't it

In turn 91, the officer's *that's right* might appear to evaluate the witness's talk and his subsequent words might appear to be formulation, in Conversation Analytic terms, presenting an upshot of previous talk (Garfinkel and Sacks 1970: 343). Yet a glance at context suggests, instead, intertextuality. The officer, surrounded by papers which he has brought along, holds one up, reading and listening, as he says *that's right*. As he notes a climax *towards tension*, he points to the paper, linking it to the witness's words. Thus, the officer does not simply, or perhaps predominantly, evaluate or formulate. Rather he locates himself among intertextual chains where, at this moment, he has connected talk and text. By recognizing the interview as an intersection of textual trajectories, we see how the secondary genre of a police statement emerges from "various transformed primary genres" (Bakhtin 1986: 98–99). Moreover we see that the officers and consequently witness orient to their intertextual environment. Such activities illustrate "the magical character of replicable texts" which while "read, seen, heard, watched, and so on in particular local and observable settings," "[hook] up an individual's consciousness" into translocal relations (Smith 2006: 66). These hooks and connections draw texts into interview talk and will push them out in consequence of that talk through a "cycle of writing and talking" in which "interpretation of written knowledge" shapes talk and vice versa (Barrett 1996: 109).

KEY CONCEPTS

Travel along textual chains is captured by the theoretical notions of intertextuality and recontextualization. Intertextuality is the "relational" process (Bauman 2004: 4) by which texts relate to each other (Gee 2005: 21) when, for example, sentence structure (Renkema 1993: 89), stories (Linde 2009: 168), and text types (Fairclough 2010: 78) recall their predecessors. Recontextualization instantiates intertextuality. It involves moving text across contexts, altering in ways which inevitably comment on original and recontextualized discourse (Blackledge 2005: 12). This process of "dynamic transfer-and-transformation" (Linell 1998: 154) involves "selectivity and filtering" (Fairclough 2010: 76) in creating "new meaning" (Linell 1998: 145). These concepts entail entextualization which refers not just to textual travel "extracting discourse from its original context" (Park and Bucholtz 2009: 486) but to making a "text" (Blommaert 2005: 47) "bounded off" and "internally cohesive... and coherent" (Bauman 2004: 4). Entextualization qualifies intertextuality, "adding an important praxis-related dimension to text-context relationships" (Blommaert 2005: 48). Examining praxis, in real-time entextualization, reveals textual travel as a joint linguistic accomplishment. This is important because texts happen "in time and place" and are "integral to organised sequences of action" each being "an occurrence embedded in what is going on" entering and coordinating "sequences of action" (Smith 2006: 67). This chapter examines functions of intertextuality and recontextualization in real-time interviews.

Studies of textual travel have two main foci: first, they can focus on chains, "sequences of... texts, through which content which is in some sense the 'same'... is treated" (Linell 1998: 149); alternatively, studies examine the "mosaic of quotations" (Kristeva 1986: 37), the "multivoiced mix" (Linell 1998: 149), within individual texts. Few speech situations are more accurately described as a jangle of textual chains than witness interviews and few texts more accurately described as mosaics of quotations than resulting statements. This chapter attends to "chain relationships" (Fairclough 1992: 130) through interviews, which not only "transform" (Gibbons 2001: 28) and "textualise" (Tiersma 2001: 87) witnesses' words as they travel from the witness's lifeworld into the institutional realm but also interlink them with other textual chains.

The chain metaphor has an established heritage, notably circulated by Bakhtin's view of utterances as links "in the chain of speech communion" (1986: 93). Bakhtin describes several phenomena through this metaphor. First, language's inherent reflexivity, utterances being neither "indifferent to one another" nor "self-sufficient," such that every utterance is "a *response*" which "refutes, affirms, supplements, and relies on" prior utterances (1986: 91). The chain metaphor also implies separate, distinguishable links by stressing that an utterance has a "*definite* position" correlating with "other positions" (1986: 91). Bakhtin's further observation that particular links can be "re-accentuated" "ironically, indignantly, reverently" (1986: 91) resonates with critical scholars. Linell, for example, notes that intertextual chains "involve opportunities for manipulation and discrimination" somewhat inevitably because "not everything said" should end up "on record." He invites consideration of "when and how such discrimination amounts to misuse" (1998: 151–52). This provides a research impetus in legal settings because institutions use the past "to create a particular desired present and future" (Linde 2009) even transforming remotely "along the chain" of genres (Fairclough 2010: 76). I will consider how such discrimination figures in witness interviews.

The view presented so far of textual processes, particularly intertextuality and recontextualization, creating chains of texts through lives is clarified by Smith's notion of intertextual hierarchy. This denotes ways in which texts regulate and standardize others, "an important dimension of the textual organisation of institutional processes" (2006: 79). Within the hierarchy, texts regulate through authorization by some recognized body, involvement of particular participants and "the sequence of textually coordinated moves" (Smith 2006: 81–82). These three features make actions recognizably procedural (Smith 2006: 87). Cicourel confirms that in policing, recording "what happened" and establishing what will happen next are both accomplished within "organisational rules and practices" ([1968] 1974: 85). Thus, "the intertextual hierarchy is a two-way street": work processes "at the front-line" are governed by law's "concepts and categories" and, in turn, those processes produce institutional realities (Smith 2005: 186). These aspects of the intertextual hierarchy are crucial because they:

1. "transform the local and particular into generalized forms where they become recognisable and accountable" institution-wide;
2. allow objectified institutional realities to override individual's perspectives;
3. make "the actual actionable institutionally." (Smith 2005: 186)

These processes are explored in the textual work examined here.

Jönsson and Linell established textual travel in police interviews as a valuable focus when comparing suspects' talk to resulting written statements (1991: 423). Subsequently, textual change in police interviews has been examined in relation to syntax and vocabulary (Gibbons 2001), time representations (Rock 2001a), and suspect's voice (Komter 2006). Other legal settings have also seen attention to transformation, particularly courtrooms (e.g., Walker 1990; Eades 1996), and work has begun to trace textual travel from statement to court (Komter 2002) and right through legal systems (e.g., Eades 2008: 156). Where earlier scholars focused on the "before" of talk and "after" of writing, attention is shifting to transformative processes behind such change. Jönsson and Linell, for example, compare only the suspect's initial account and the officer's final written version because their data feature "fairly talkative" suspects accounting in "reasonably lengthy and coherent turns" with minimal officer intervention (1991: 423). Berk-Seligson, in contrast, has shown how the minutiae of an officer's reinterpretation transform a suspect's version, ultimately "putting words into the suspect's mouth" (2009: 134). Taking up this initiative, in the witness interview examined here, recontextualization resides in witness-interviewer dialogue. This permits examination of talk as a means to written text rather than comparing talk and writing as products. Transformation, accomplished invisibly in Jönsson and Linell's interviews, is then available for scrutiny here. Looking beyond the policing setting, studies including Sarangi and Brookes-Howell (2006) in medical-counseling, Mehan (1991) in education, and Slembrouck (1992) in government examine how talk is entextualized into an institutional record (case notes, reports, and Hansard records, respectively). My study steps sideways, recognizing talk which creates the institutional record itself as permeated with texts. This is possible because the interviewer here verbalizes recontextualizing processes (e.g., considering alternative formulations), practices (e.g., identifying sources), and functions (e.g., elicitation). We can therefore observe "the moment of transformation into the institutional" articulated in the flow of talk (Smith 2005: 198). Thus, I take up Barrett's trajectory "from document to interview" (1996: 111–13) rather than only "interview to document" (114–22).

Institutions are characterized by "long intertextual chains" (Linell 1998: 151; Kell 2006: 166). Witness's words exemplify an early link in chains through law's influential systems (Mertz 1996: 230; Eades 2008: 179). Police training recognizes this jangle of intertextual chains by telling officers that interviewees' accounts "may be inconsistent with evidence from other sources" including statements and forensic evidence. Training concludes that while inconsistency does not necessarily index lying it "will need exploration" (Centrex 2004: 114). The interviewer in these data himself noted the crucial importance of chains of texts in his work, saying: *we have to try and prove (.) every link in the chain (.) you know and make sure you don't break ((them)).*

INTRODUCING TEXTUAL CHAINS

This chapter, informed by examination of 25 witness interviews, uses one to illustrate functions of textual travel which reoccur across the data set. The interviewer, Phil (mid-fifties), is an experienced interview specialist. He therefore spends most of his working life interviewing and doing related administration, depositing handwritten statements for typing, for example. The witness, Wanda (early twenties), a seasoned bar worker, appeared comfortable discussing the interview topic—a disturbance in her pub involving an abusive, intimidating customer.

Throughout the excerpts, *italics* indicate Phil reading aloud, slowly, while writing. 'Single quotation marks' indicate his reading aloud text that he previously drafted. "Double quotation marks" indicate speech or thought presentation. All data are anonymized and all names are pseudonyms (Rock 2001b).

The most prominent activity which we might expect in witness interviews is the witness telling the police officer what happened, while the officer writes her words. These are A-events, concerning, for example, A's emotions, experiences in other contexts; past biography (Labov and Fanshel 1977: 100). Sure enough, much of the interview comprises such activity. Below are just two examples. In both, Wanda recounts crime-scene conversations in which she attempted to deter the accused by appearing to summons the police (excerpt 2) and summonsing them by pressing an alarm button (excerpt 3).

Excerpt 2

500.	W	Steve told me to phone the police but not to phone-the-police-phone-the-police to pre<u>tend</u> to phone the police
501.	P	yeah
502.	W	sort of to say that (.) "we're not messing about just go"
503.	P	yeah
504.	W	and (.) I did this and it didn't make any difference

Excerpt 3

620.	W	I said to Stevie "I'm putting the button //in" he said "go on then"//
621.	P	// yeh mm yeah OK // Steve was- *(.)* and you remember saying that
622.	W	yeah
623.	P	"I'm putting the button in" you remember saying that
624.	W	[nods]
625.	P	mm (.) *at this point I remember* (.) see certain things will loom large in your conscious mind

In these excerpts, Wanda's experience of situations and actions is mediated through talk; she gives her version of events. This involves prototypical intertextuality, accomplishing "a sort of switching by incorporating ('borrowing') words from another text…in the same or a different variety" (Gee 2005: 46). Talk between colleagues in an unpredictable, alarming, public situation enters an interaction between virtual strangers in relatively formalized, serene, private one. This occurs indirectly through paraphrase and thought presentation (excerpt 2) and directly as quotation (excerpt 3). The paraphrasing incorporates not only a third party's literal instructions (*Steve told me to phone*) but also his presumed pragmatic intent toward both Wanda (*to pretend to phone*) and the alleged attacker (signaling *"we're not messing about"* (turn 502)). These pragmatic matters are available to Wanda and Phil as people "in the know" (Gee 2005: 46) about strategic talk (cf. Fairclough, 2010: 81). Phil's reading-back and reading-while-writing illustrate Wanda's account being immediately recontextualized into and through writing. Wanda and Phil's activities are coordinated around the technology of writing and the activity of text production and are situated in time (Smith 2006). The interlacing of speech, repetition, suggesting text (e.g., turn 623), and reading-while-writing (e.g., turn 621) is sophisticated.

Not all textual travel was so predictable. As excerpt 4 illustrates:

Excerpt 4

425.	P	did he have a full frontal (.) that you saw
426.	W	I don't know because [P: no] I looked away from him
427.	P	no because- Pattie says not (.) all she saw was he was mooning //that's all he did//
428.	W	// yeah //
429.	P	didn't get any like (.) indecent exposure
430.	W	no ah- =
431.	P	= which- that's another offence so they didn't [W: yeah] go into that =
432.	W	= no

Here, Phil, rather than Wanda, introduces information; three prior texts, which travel into the interview and ultimately the statement. First, in turn 427, he mentions the statement of Pattie, a witness he previously interviewed, noting what *Pattie says*. Secondly, he invokes the catalogues of classifications of crimes used by legal personnel (e.g., Calligan 2009) when he introduces *indecent exposure* (turn 429) an *offence* (turn 431). Finally he invokes the Statement Control Sheet (SCS), an allegation summary written before interview. When Phil says *they didn't go into that* (turn 431) *they* are the authors of the SCS produced for this case. These are B-events, drawn from the officer's reading and background knowledge shading-off into AB-events when moving to matters "known to both A and B" (the extent of the suspect's nudity) (Labov and Fanshel 1977: 100). Doubtless these three texts (Pattie's statement, offence classifications, and the SCS) were not produced for citation in interviews but "in a different contextualisation process, at a different time, by different people and for different purposes" (Blommaert 2005: 46). Similarly,

Wanda may not have expected these texts to appear. Yet, through reentextualization (entextualization of entextualization) (Jaffe 2009: 130), they will influence the text that comes to represent Wanda. Phil's introduction of these texts cannot be dismissed as "bad practice" or, judging from the wider data set, discounted as anomaly. He uses the sources with subtlety. For example, when mentioning the SCS authors, Phil identifies events that *they didn't go into* rather than, for example, events that *they said didn't happen* thus not directly disputing Wanda's version. We tend to get absorbed in texts' content making it "difficult to envisage text" as part of, and coordinated with, ongoing activity (Smith 2006: 66). Yet here, we see the officer drawing together multiple textual chains, picking up each in tight coordination with interviewing activities.

The three sources in excerpt 4 illustrate Phil's three main types of primary text from the institutional hierarchy surrounding police interviews. First, he draws on statements and interviews, in this case, citing Pattie's statement. Statements and interviews figure in the intertextual hierarchy because *hierarchy* is "strictly a textual and conceptual relation;...not necessarily or simply related to hierarchies of position" in institutional structure (Smith 2005: 187), so a statement/interview can influence another statement/interview. The relatively numerous witnesses already interviewed about this case made this interview particularly rich in this respect. Such antecedent texts were not available for use in all interviews as statement availability is largely chance, depending on witness numbers and interview sequence (Smith 2006: 67). Very different crime-specific texts also feature. These evolved simultaneously with or because of the crime. They arise because police forces, unlike witnesses, remember systematically (cf. Linde 2009: 12). For example, police typically audio-record interactions with the public noting timings and content of telephone calls. In this interview, Phil drew on such records via an intermediary text, the SCS, and a log. The final set of primary texts are generic; regulatory frames, where "frame" denotes "the wide variety of conceptualisations, theories, policies, laws, plans, and so on that...structure the institutional action and reality" (Smith 2005: 191, 198). These frames are fully operational in police interviewing. Indeed Smith illustrates this through the work of George W. Smith (1988) on a police investigation of a Toronto bathhouse. Through a police report, sexual pleasure was "transmogrified" into criminal behavior; the actual into the institutional.

Intertextuality is not necessarily explicit. In presenting utterances as containing "reflections," "echoes," and "reverberations" of others (1986: 91), Bakhtin suggests a chain whose links are only recognizable through inference and generic familiarity. Indeed, connections can be "silently proposed," "as though the interlocutor were already well aware of them," barely acknowledged (1986: 91). Yet, given "varying degrees of reinterpretation," the opposite end of the spectrum evidences chains, introduced "directly," observable, even casually (1986: 91). Katajamäki too describes intertextuality as a continuum from the "openly mentioned" to that "beyond reach" (2009: 204) and Smith's continuum is from the obvious, like reported speech, to that "buried" in sentence structure, phrases, and terms, concealing "hybrid organization" (2006: 75). Excerpt 4 featured relatively "openly mentioned" intertextuality in isolating *what Pattie says*. Reference to the SCS in excerpt 5, below, illustrates the opposite. We join discussion of whether Wanda heard her boss being slapped:

Excerpt 5

514.	W	I heard it a couple of times but it was just like at first it was just like playful (.) //sort of//
515.	P	// yes //
516.	W	not play- you know what I mean
517.	P	mm
518.	W	and then he sort of got a bit more serious
519.	P	mm ((then)) there's *this man slapping* (.) because there's no injury fortunately (.) on this assault

Here, Phil does not explicitly flag the SCS—the witness might not even notice intertextuality. The SCS is referenced, however, in turn 519, as specifying *no injury*. This exemplifies recontextualization's "ambivalent character" as it colonizes one field with another, incorporating "external" discourses into social agents' strategies (Fairclough 2010: 233). Phil's style shift in *no injury...on this assault* evidences his access to formal lexis and legal discourses of crime typology. Thus, as well as intertextuality with a particular text, we see shades of policespeak—the distinctive "clichés and boilerplate of police language" (Hall 2008: 68, 74–84; Fox 1993)—closing an intertextual gap (Bauman 2004: 7). By confirming *no injury* Phil agrees with Wanda's claim that any slapping was on a scale from *playful* (turn 514) to *serious* (518), a scale which did not extend to *injury*, potentially scaffolding her account. His evaluation of the lack of physical injury as *fortunate* presents his orientation to events. Intertextuality, even when covert, becomes a resource for meaning-making.

Psychiatric settings see doctors approaching patients "through...case records" except in exceptional circumstances when the expression "seeing a patient blind" acknowledges the challenge created (Barrett 1996: 111–14). In police interviews too, before interviewing juvenile suspects, officers draw on witnesses and others "relevant to the case" such as teachers and parents, indeed on "whatever information" is available on the suspect. "Thus the 'picture' can be fairly complete" before interview (Cicourel [1968] 1974: 87). Given the likely paucity of information on witnesses before interview, and their particular function in investigations, officers do not gather information about them personally, but gather wide-ranging information about the case from other statements, case-specific police documents, and regulatory frames.

Having introduced Phil's recontextualization of texts not produced by Wanda and indicated the potential functionality and place of that recontextualization, the remaining analysis takes a closer look. Of course, talk is multifunctional. However, what follows examines some specific functions of intertextuality and recontextualization, asking how texts from outside an interview are incorporated into talk and appropriated, resisted, or approved.

TEXTUAL CHAINS FROM REGULATORY FRAMES

Regulatory frames are the most predictable, previously studied texts to enter institutional settings so it is with these that further analysis begins. Smith describes how regulatory frames shape forms of knowledge by governing "the selection of what will be recorded, observed, described and so on" often through categories "used at the front-line." Framing is circular because "what is assembled in this way is then interpretable by the frames that structure the selection procedures" (Smith 2005: 191). In the excerpts in this section, this circle of influence is clear. In excerpt 6 two legal sources are invoked:

Excerpt 6

751.   P   I'm just trying to think if- there's these points you have
              to prove (2.2) time distance (.) unobstructed view (1.3)
              that's about it really

Time distance and *unobstructed view* are not simply characteristics of Wanda's experience which Phil happens to deem important but "witness reliability factors" which indicate likely accuracy of identification against legally recognized measures (e.g., Bromby and Hall 2002: 147). These factors are encoded in a mnemonic acronym disseminated through police training—ADVOKATE—where D (Distance from perpetrator), O (whether Observation was impeded), T (Time since event), and A (Amount of time observing) relate to the factors mentioned in excerpt 6. Thus, Phil recontextualizes legal categorizations gleaned through training and experience and ultimately traceable back along an intertextual chain to the case which prompted ADVOKATE's development, *R v. Turnbull* [1976]. Indeed Phil draws on witness reliability factors, more or less openly (Katajamäki 2009: 204) to formulate many questions toward the interview's close, shown in figure 4.1.

A police officer in Pence's data describes writing domestic abuse case reports, saying, "I'm looking for the elements of a crime.... Was there infliction of bodily harm or the fear of bodily harm?...Was there intent?...Did the person knowingly commit the offence?" (2001: 212). Reports are designed to fit categories of domestic abuse criteria (in Smith 2005: 194). Likewise, the accounts being created in

Witness reliability factor	Recontextualised as a turn or question in the interview
D = Distance from perpetrator?	*how far away (.) from (.) you was this man (turn 699)*
O = Observation impeded?	*did you have a clear unobstructed view (turn 709)*
A = Amount of time observed?	*the whole incident lasted... from the time he walked through the bar and got (.) Stevie's attention (.) to the time (.) his girlfriend gets him out (turn 729)*
K = perpetrator Known to witness?	*had you seen him before (turn 845)* *have you seen him since (turn 847)*

Figure 4.1
ADVOKATE in interview.

excerpt 6, and through the questions in figure 4.1, are *"designed* to be subsumable by the institutional discourse" (Smith 2005: 195) creating intertextual chains between case-driven categories and interview.

The second textual antecedent mentioned in excerpt 6, also part of the regulatory frame, is *points...to prove*. These are items in summonses or charges which legally specify offences; as the name suggests, each point must be "proved" in order to prove the offence (Calligan 2009: iii). For example, the charge for indecent exposure, potentially relevant here, reads (you are charged) "that you did unlawfully, wilfully and publicly expose your naked person." This entails four points to prove. The first relates to "you" so probative talk would positively identify the suspect. The other points concern exposure being unlawful and willful (point 2), public (3), and of particular body parts, entailing that exposure occurred (4) (Calligan 2009: 134). Indeed, earlier in the interview Phil specifically queried point (4), asking *did he have a...full frontal* (turn 425) through "silently proposed" intertextuality (Bakhtin 1986: 91). Points to prove are vital intertextual resources which drive questioning as police map events and actions "into socially and legally relevant categories" which permit "inference and action" (Cicourel [1968] 1974: 86). The frameworks of ADVOKATE and points to prove thus provide felicity conditions (Austin 1962) for crime categorization. In Mehan's terms, constitutive rules (1992: 10–11) for police interviewing create constitutive institutional practices. While the legal framework stipulates what counts, the officer operationalizes that reckoning through his questioning.

Excerpts 7 and 8 also see Phil aligning Wanda's account with points to prove, in these instances, points encapsulated in the charge under section 5(1) of the Public Order Act 1986:

That you did...use threatening, abusive or insulting words or behaviour, or disorderly behaviour...within the hearing or sight of a person likely to be caused harassment, alarm or distress.

Excerpt 7 features a chain from the words "threatening," "abusive," "insulting," and "disorderly" in the charge. Phil recontextualizes these notions as *aggressive* and *mouthy* (turn 159) when asking about the suspect and his companion:

Excerpt 7

157.	P	what was their demeanour (.) were they drunk were they just giggly were they just-
158.	W	(.) they were giggly
159.	P	yeah but they weren't aggressive or mouthy or anything like that

His questions are directly informed by the entextualized points to prove. As Smith puts it, "the text of the law is a shell...the substance of which is to be found elsewhere. Giving the shell substance draws the actual into an institutional capacity to act." Phil must "produce descriptions to fill the shells" (Smith 2005: 197), as he meticulously does. Excerpt 8, much later in interview, addresses the second part of the section 5(1) charge, relating to whether the offence (1) was "within the hearing or sight of a person" and (2) likely caused "harassment, alarm or distress":

Excerpt 8

599.	P	would you say Steve's family were apprehensive
600.	W	(.) //mm//
601.	P	// his // parents
602.	W	yeah
603.	P	...was him Mum and Dad or- (.) yeah
604.	W	his Mum was upset actually (.) his Mum was (.) getting really upset

Phil's use of *apprehensive* (turn 599) directly recalls training texts on successful interviewing about this offence (Calligan 2009: 118). Wanda's selection *upset* would predictably interest Phil in relation to this charge and sure enough he incorporates it into the written statement. He judges the witness's talk piecemeal and as a whole as the teacher judges "the correctness and appropriateness of students' answers" in educational settings (Mehan 1992: 11), making decisions about individual evidential points and the general potential to witness. The need to obtain evidence on emotional responses is an intertextual imperative which Phil addressed repeatedly. Such talk, "establishing knowledge," causes interviewers to perhaps "appear to be doggedly pursuing irrelevant matters when they are in fact attempting to establish a point of evidence with the potential to make or break a case" (Hall 2008: 71). In this way, the "clarity of social facts such as 'intelligence'," and in this case, "aggressive, abusive and insulting" and "harassment, alarm and distress," is "produced from the ambiguity of everyday life" (Mehan 1996: 255). The chains from these strings respectively through "demeanour," "drunk" to "giggly" and "apprehensive" to "upset" recall chains which Barrett notes. He exemplifies shifts from the lay person's language of relationships (people "don't get on") to the doctor's typification ("conflict"), accepted by the patient through talk (Barrett 1996: 116). The interface between institutional and lay categories in excerpts 7 and 8 illustrates how the regulatory frame offers "intermediate typifications" which mediate between lay and expert knowledge and terminology (Barrett 1996: 116). They force Phil to become an "active sense maker," "choosing among alternatives in often contradictory circumstances" (Mehan 1992: 1). This is not to suggest that the regulatory frame "determines what comes next," rather it "projects" talk and text (Smith 2006: 75). The regulatory frame's functions are predictable, from previous research, guiding Phil's questions, lexical choices, and direction.

FUNCTIONS OF OTHER PARTS OF THE INTERTEXTUAL HIERARCHY

Phil's work with texts from the regulatory frame focused on organizing and achieving elicitation. We now turn to the other, perhaps more surprising, textual antecedents introduced earlier, prior interviews/statements and case-specific texts and find intertextuality serving a surprising range of functions. In excerpt 9, below, Phil marks prior knowledge, from Steve's statement, with the words *I know that*:

Excerpt 9

233.	P	so what- I know that Steve (.) had a word with him and told him just to (.) you know
		//use common sense//
234.	W	// calm down //
235.	P	and calm d- yeah OK (.) and he yeah (.) so what then (.) ignited your or excited your attention
236.	W	well I turned round and he (.) was trying to climb on the bar with his trousers down

Phil cites information from Steve, gathered beyond Wanda's experience. Intratextually, he spent much of the interview discouraging Wanda from doing the same (Rock 2012). However, his intertextual reference to Steve's evidence serves interactional functions. In turn 233, Phil initiates a question with the discourse marker *so* and interrogative *what*. This becomes a false start, giving way to summary of Steve's information. Ultimately, however, Phil repeats *so what* midway through turn 235, asking what attracted Wanda's attention, a detail which becomes crucial. Phil's recontextualization of Steve's evidence foregrounds this key moment by setting the scene. Furthermore, presenting Steve's conversation as given (Chafe 1976) prevents Wanda from speculating on that conversation. Thus intertextuality scene-sets and specifies given information which facilitates focused questioning.

The source text below is the Statement Control Sheet (SCS). Phil marks unfurling the sheet with the words *to the evidence*:

Excerpt 10

33.	P	now then (.) to the evidence [reads (5.6)] right let's see this (.) it's only half the job [reads (2.2)] I think I've been super-efficient and (.) taken the pin out (.) now (.) this occurred =
34.	W	= it was a Sunday and that's all I can //remember//
35.	P	// yes ur // I'll refresh your memory that 'it was um (.) 6pm or thereabouts' =
36.	W	= yeh =
37.	P	= 'Sunday the 12th of July' this year (.) OK so (.) at about that time- because you were finishing your shift weren't you =
38.	W	= yeh =
39.	P	= and um (.) [clicks fingers] and um Pattie was taking (.) over

Phil reads aloud from the SCS and invokes more general literacy practices (Barton 2007) in relation to it, describing his physical text processing. By presenting given information about time, date, and circumstances, and by showing Wanda how he will use text to *refresh* her *memory*, Phil elicits narrative and indicates its start-point. By *explicitly* bringing these texts into the interaction, Phil involves Wanda in recontextualization, making available potentially competing voices for consideration rather than measuring her against these sources covertly.

As well as using written texts as resources for formulating questions and eliciting narrative, recontextualization of earlier interviewed witnesses' statements co-occurs with Wanda trying to remember details:

Excerpt 11

69.	P	Pattie came in urm (.) five- (.) five forty-five she came in? earlier?
70.	W	yeah she was- I think she was ((already here when I)) [inaud. 3 syllables]
71.	P	[reaching for Pattie's statement] I think she says in her statement about that time
72.	W	yeah
73.	P	see if I've got it (.) haven't had the (.) typings come back yet (.) no what's on the original
74.	W	OK
75.	P	(3.2) [reads quietly] 'rostered to work between 6 and-' yeah she [reads-aloud] 'I arrived at 5.45pm' she says- so (.) you could say- without putting a time to it you can say just before =
76.	W	= yeah =
77.	P	= six o'clock yeh =
78.	W	= yeah =
79.	P	= your relief came yeh OK (.) *just before 6pm*

Wanda's quiet, hesitant talk suggests uncertainty about timing (turn 70) and Phil responds with the intertextual practice of cross-checking Pattie's statement (71). Establishing timing of Pattie's activities is not essential to Wanda's narrative but is ripe for inclusion in this genre (Rock 2001a). Timings ideally agree across statements. Phil's thinking-aloud about statements' travel from handwritten *original* into *typings* is essentially redundant but draws Wanda into his textual world. She is included further by hearing segments of her colleague's statement (turn 75). Such reading aloud could silence an interviewee. However, Wanda, like other witnesses, appears to embrace intertextuality, sitting attentively through cross-checking, even providing feedback (turns 72 and 74) and rapid, latched agreement markers (76 and 78). Smith notes that "disjunctures" between institutions' artificial realities and the people's actualities "are not avoidable; they are *of* the transformation" but not "necessarily malign." She exemplifies that transferring agency to an institution might benefit an individual allowing, for example, help (2005: 187). Here, we may ask whether Wanda benefits from Phil's intertextual work, in refining her story. Ultimately, Phil extrapolates from that work by suggesting, through *you could say*, a wording for Wanda's statement. This wording avoids *putting a time to it* thus recognizing her initial uncertainty and ultimately, arriving at a formulation, *just before 6 pm* (turn 79), which fits with Wanda's original assertion (turn 70).

The process of transformation means that "some aspects of lived actuality get picked out and worked up" (Smith 2005: 191) as happens with timing and duration in police interviews. The pair return to these topics much later, using a *log* (turn 735):

Excerpt 12

733.	P	four to five minutes?
734.	W	(3.2) no a bit more than that
735.	P	let's have a look what we've got in here for this bit (.) we've got a log here (.) see what it says =
736.	W	= mind you it went really (.) slowly
737.	P	mm well this bit's (1.5) the- (.) we got a message at (.) 6pm exactly
738.	W	yep
739.	P	ur (.) the bobbies were sent at- a minute later (.) and they arrived (.) at 18.04 within three minutes (.) so this had been building up obviously [W: yeah] before (.) that =
740.	W	= yeah =
741.	P	= so that =
742.	W	= he'd gone by then
743.	P	yeah //that's right//
744.	W	// yeah //
745.	P	yeah yeh
746.	W	an- yeah I would [P: mm] say about four or five minutes [P: mm] it just seemed to- (.) take a // lot longer as it does //
747.	P	// yeh yeh (.) *whole* yeh// *whole incident lasted* no more than *no more than*
748.	W	(.) mm
749.	P	yeh
750.	W	yeah
751.	P	*four to five minutes*

Phil seeks time-reference agreement with the log here, as he did with the statement above. In coordinating his actions with Wanda's he draws on the log "selectively for different purposes" (Smith 2006: 68). Wanda is once more drawn into Phil's literacy practices by his physically presenting the log, one of his "props" (Mehan 1996: 265). He involves Wanda by specifying his textual activity (*let's have a look…and see what it says*). Phil does not simply impose an external text onto Wanda's statement. His choice of *let's* when introducing the log and his reading aloud from the log in

737 and 739, raise the possibility that he sees its use as a joint activity. Furthermore Wanda does not object to the log's use. Indeed Phil initiated its use in response to Wanda's uncertainty about the incident duration (turn 734) and as he uses the log she mitigates her generous initial estimate (turns 736 and 746) thus orienting to the difficulty of assessing the passage of time. In the statement, this dialogue will be "implicit or buried" (Smith 2006: 75) as entextualization removes "common-sense understandings, which...underpinned the interview" (Barrett 1996: 117). This also removes uncertainty about timing. In recontextualizing, institutions may present subjects as making illegitimate claims that contradict the institution's authority or they may infuse original discourse with the institutional viewpoint, constructing that viewpoint as inevitable and natural. Such alteration of intertextual distance (Briggs and Bauman 1992) shows that entextualization serves power relations (Briggs 1993: 390). Certainly another form of police interview, interrogation, "is designed to confirm the officer's suspicions or firm beliefs about 'what happened' and how the particular suspect is implicated" (Cicourel [1968] 1974: 89). We could see Phil as exploiting recontextualization in these excerpts to get what is required from Wanda's talk. Yet it is alternatively possible that the exchanges in this section, rather than pressing Wanda to accept the log's timings, helped her to improve her time perspective after she herself expressed doubt.

Processes implicated in textual travel confer authority. *Recontextualization* is "inherently linked" with "fact construction" bringing "evidentiality and legitimacy" to travelling text (Sarangi 1998: 308). *Entextualization* too brings "power and authority" (Park and Bucholtz 2009: 486), Schutz and Luckmann's "objectivation" allows "subjective elements" "into the social stock of knowledge" (1973: 264). These are powerful processes, influencing lives by constructing social facts (Mehan 1996). In witness interviews, objectivation, initiated by one speaker telling another about a crime, is developed through textual travel and cemented by signing resulting texts as public confirmation of transfer of knowledge (after Bauman 2004: 150–51). Thus, police, "give official imprint to versions of reality" (Goffman 1983: 17). This can have negative effects. Recontextualization in statement-taking, for example, can simplify and constrain texts and contexts (Andrus 2009: 125); making understandings "misleadingly precise" (Linell 1998: 149) and regulated (Fairclough 2010: 78) due to indifference to the actualities of people's lives (Wilson and Pence, in Smith 2005: 188). Yet "the formalised and authorised categories to which people's actualities are fitted by those working at the front line are the only means by which those actualities can be made actionable" (Smith 2005: 188). Is the police officer, in drawing together text trajectories in interview, suppressing the witness's voice or giving voice? In making his intertextual work explicit to the witness, is he, at least, giving her some stake in transformational processes?

Smith describes how successive texts are functions of their position in sequence. She exemplifies, showing how an eyewitness's letter to a newspaper about a confrontation between street people and police received a rebuttal from officials (1999: 50–51). Once viewed in sequence, the second text, the rebuttal, provided "instructions for rereading the first." It "reconstructed" the eyewitness account as just a version

(1999: 198–99). This echoes the situation of witness statements reaching court. The court can reinterpret witnesses' original evidence as erroneous, impressionistic, fanciful, and so on. To some extent the officer who helps the witness to bond her story alongside other textual chains facilitates her contact with the legal system and helps her to legitimize her account. Thus, although recontextualization in interviews can be hegemonic, it can also empower witnesses, giving their words institutional currency. Of course, this could itself ensnare other lay participants, such as defendants.

Intertextuality was not only a resource for elicitation, questioning and ironing-out details. It also oiled the speakers' relationship:

Excerpt 13

639.	P	right? (5.2) this is a longer statement (.) than Stevie (5.3) is it you do the talking and he does the writing (.) ((never heard anybody jabber like you do)) (5.1)
640.	W	I do the talking he does the (.) playing pool
641.	P	mm yes [laughter]

In excerpt 13, Phil had been organizing papers and sharing drafting decisions with Wanda by reading her statement, here nearly complete, aloud. He breaks-off (turn 639) to note the length of Wanda's statement through intertextual comparison with a different statement. This, and his subsequent words, could be read, when merely transcribed, as folk-linguistically influenced criticism of an overly talkative woman (Kramarae 1974: 82), particularly the derogatory lexical choice *jabber*. Tellingly, Wanda orients to the turn not as criticism but as ripe for humorous expansion. Intertextuality provides for her to mischievously characterize her relationship with her boss (turn 640). Phil receives her turn positively and in-person both laughed vigorously. Here, intertextual comparison facilitates relational work. In excerpt 14, this goes further as intertextuality becomes almost gossip:

Excerpt 14

461.	P	*he sat on the bar* ur *on his bare* buttocks right? (.) I think so because urm (.) Pattie she said she had the task of wiping it all down I think she said in her statement (.) you know (.) I had to //wipe- yeh//
462.	W	// oh // oh Pattie (.) I'm sorry
463.	P	Pattie yeah (.) but somebody had to don't they you know [laughs] somebody's got a dirty old job to do got to do it so- (.) urm:: (.) // some of our but //
464.	W	//you want to see the stuff we used to pick up in the pub I used to work at//
465.	P	oh right

Not only does Phil accomplish interpersonal work by introducing the amusing image of Pattie's unsavory tasks but Wanda takes up this aside, mock apologizing to her absent colleague before both humorously note the seedier side of bar work. Wanda, too, introduces sources other than the crime event:

Excerpt 15

5.	P	OK *I am a single woman*
6.	W	single white female

Excerpt 16

79.	P	*my relief Pattie ((left)) Pattie Harper*
80.	W	Pattie darling [laughs]

These are relatively oblique references to the popular media; in excerpt 15, the film *Single White Female* and, in 16, the BBC television program *Absolutely Fabulous*, through the catchphrase *Pattie darling*. They index rapport, contributing to "an atmosphere conducive to cooperation," which is encouraged by police training and frequent in suspect interviews (Hall 2008: 87). Here, however, it is Wanda who undertakes mediated action (Scollon 1998: 6), in this case, relational work. This compliant, jovial witness frequently interjected into statement-taking—these recontextualized media phrases are undeniably "off-task" yet potentially develop her short, locally situated relationship with Phil.

ONWARD TRAVEL

As well as drawing on texts produced before interview, Phil also connects to Wanda's statement itself. This text, which he is authoring in real time while he and Wanda speak, becomes available for recontextualization piece-by-piece as soon as it is entextualized. This work also involves *intra*textuality (Linell 1998: 146–47). We return to excerpt 3, reproduced and extended below, which illustrates an intersection of intratextual and intertextual.

Excerpt 17

620.	W	I said to Stevie "I'm putting the button //in" he said "go on then"//
621.	P	// yeh mm yeah OK // Steve was- (.) you remember saying that

622.	W	yeah
623.	P	"I'm putting the button in" you remember saying that
624.	W	[nods]
625.	P	mm (.) *at this point I remember* (.) see certain things will loom large in your conscious mind won't they [W: yeah] they'll stay there because you have an active part there rather than just
626.	W	yeah
627.	P	being passive watching it (.) [reads from statement] 'I remember saying' I'm putting the (.) button in [W: nods] *I'm putting the button in* Stevie said? (.) "go on"?

In turn 627, Phil reads from the statement the words just written, *"I remember saying."* As well as intertextually connecting to the statement under construction, this intratextually links with immediately prior talk. Yet the words written and said here, *"I remember saying"* are not Wanda's words. Her formulation, back in line 620, was *I said to Stevie.* *"I remember saying"* arose from the exchange in turns 623–25 in which Phil questioned Wanda's certainty, asking *you remember saying that.* Thus, he reads from the written statement, a recontextualization of his words, not Wanda's. Having reported writing so far, Phil's next words (turn 627) *I'm putting the button in* propose upcoming writing. They indicate his plan to directly incorporate reported speech which he had queried in turn 623 and justified in 625. Following acquiescence from Wanda, he entextualizes, reading aloud as he writes the now endorsed words *I'm putting the button in.* That reading aloud triggers further elicitation. Thus chaining is extensive, with intratextual links within interview and intertextual links running from crime scene to interview and on into the statement, in turn re-entering interview.

DISCUSSION

Examining textual travel in a police interview has involved examining talk as text production, rather than only in itself. This has revealed how recontextualization and intertextuality operate in interview. Most simply, as illustrated in excerpts 2 and 3, textual travel enables witnesses to report their versions of events including reported speech and thought. Travel of the regulatory framework shapes the witness's words making them legally meaningful (excerpts 5-8). Travel from statements and crime-specific texts facilitates interview, providing for elicitation and marshaling accounts (excerpts 9-12). Travel of statements and, surprisingly, media texts achieves relational ends, involving humor, particularly (excerpts 13-16). Finally, onward travel facilitates negotiation, transforming witness's talk into evidence, through reading-while-writing and reading-back, intertwining textual chains (excerpt 17). Phil apparently drew on different parts of the textual hierarchy for different functions.

The witness and interviewer inhabit an intertextual space to which each orients and from which each appropriates. This involves skill and imagination from the officer and a degree of trust, or at least compliance, from the witness. Extending the summary above, this chapter has shown that recontextualization provides for:

- Orienting explicitly to intertextual chains (throughout);
- Pursuing agreement between texts (throughout);
- Closing intertextual gaps (throughout);
- Coordinating multiple textual chains (excerpt 4);
- Meaning-making (excerpt 5);
- Providing a verbal memory aid (excerpt 6);
- Demarcating matters of interest (excerpts 4-6);
- Foregrounding the interview's purpose (excerpt 6);
- Achieving legal ends (excerpts 6-8, figure 4.1);
- Clarifying social facts (excerpts 7-8);
- Measuring and assessing the witness (excerpt 8);
- Formulating questions and eliciting narrative (excerpts 6-9);
- Displaying given information to elicit and specify new (excerpt 9);
- Achieving tightly focused elicitation (excerpts 9 and 10);
- Working-up evidentially significant segments (excerpts 10-12);
- Involving the witness in drafting (excerpts 10-12);
- Providing support when the witness indicates uncertainty paralinguistically (excerpts 11 and 12);
- Accomplishing relational work (excerpts 5, 13-16);
- Constructing and testing text through talk (excerpt 17).

Despite these utilitarian functions, textual travel means that the witness's "final word" to the legal system, the written statement, is unlikely to contain only the witness's voice. This could have a discriminatory aspect. Eades notes that recontextualization in court indeed permits "problematic" assumptions which have serious negative effects such as distorting witnesses' evidence and misconstruing witnesses' actions (2008: 330–31). The effects of recontextualization in this chapter are ambiguous perhaps because in interview, the witness does not meet legal decision-makers face-to-face. The legal apparatus and its technologies will subordinate "individual subjectivities to institutionally generated realities" (Smith 2005: 187). Yet in making the local institutionally actionable, textual travel is instrumental in accomplishing interview and permitting the witness a place in the institutional. The "responsibility" to interview can interfere with the interviewer's "ability to *listen*" (Smith 2005: 190). Yet Phil seemingly avoids becoming ensnared by technologies of his work by sharing the intertextual hierarchy. I have argued that when Phil highlights textual processes to Wanda she is invited to slip out of a purely authorial role into a more editorial one, if not directly commenting on the intertextual terrain, at least aware of it. Of course, Phil's intertextual explicitness may simply be synthetic (Fairclough 1992), simulating close relationships in which witnesses can genuinely engage with text production without truly allowing such intervention. At the very least, explicit intertextuality initiates dialogue. Potentially it reduces discriminatory effects of recontextualization. While Wanda did not exhibit resistance to intertextuality, resistance became possible following explicit intertextuality and it features in other interviews.

This chapter has illustrated how several variables characterize each instance of textual travel in interview. Five variables have received particular attention because they highlight diversity and patterns of intertextuality and because they were particularly salient in the data, some having been identified by prior research on institutional interactions, particularly in policing. The five variables are represented along sides of a pentagon (figure 4.2), to capture the notion that they specify an intertextual space, not because they are the only variables that could, presumably, come into play. Each side is labeled to indicate the continua or discrete series they entail.

The five variables in figure 4.2 summarize the various recontextualizing resources available in interview. The figure encapsulates the usefulness of considering antecedent texts' properties (on three sides of the pentagon) in combination with properties of the recontextualization and of the speaker (one side each). Specifically, the figure combines Smith's (2006) view of texts located in time (top right side) and in an intertextual hierarchy (2005, 2006) (bottom left) with intra- and intertextuality distinction, neatly summarized by Linell (1998), (top left) and the ideas from Bakhtin (1986), Katajamäki (2009), and Smith (2006) that recontextualization can be more or less explicit (bottom right) and finally, the

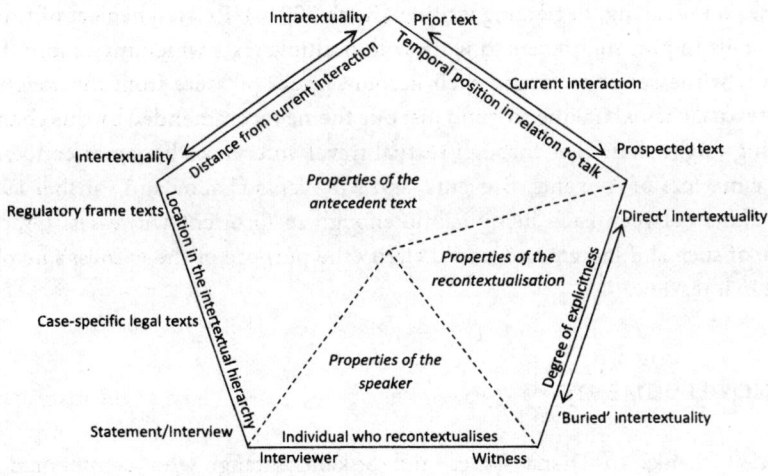

Figure 4.2
Variables of textual travel in witness interviews.

notion that texts can be introduced by different participants (bottom). Different combinations of these variables create different effects and functions as we have seen. The diagrammatic arrangement permits easy articulation of points which arise from this chapter. First, the diagram offers a visual representation, if a somewhat impoverished one, of the interview as recontextualizing space around which officer and interviewee move frequently, even within turns. Second, the diagram clarifies that particular variables might become particularly analytically useful in relation to particular excerpts. Third, the diagram makes it straightforward to isolate and combine particular variables. Finally, the diagram raises questions about which of the variables feature continua and which discrete points. This is not as straightforward as it might appear. In relation to the temporal position variable, along the top right, the officer's talk, referencing prior and prospected texts, as well as the current interaction, blurs the line between text articulated now, text under construction, and text recently written. Looking below to degree of explicitness, "buried" or "silently proposed" intertextuality appears fluid, able to change even as talk unfolds. Additionally, the line between intertextuality and intratextuality is not absolute as talk in interview becomes text simultaneously, being written and spoken at once.

Having summarized the functionality of intertextuality in interviews and illustrated how theoretical ideas combine in my perspective on textual travel, I close by evaluating the practical upshots of this work. It seems fanciful to suppose that witness statements could be produced in a textual vacuum. Interviewers will inevitably encounter prior witnesses. They will inevitably need background information from case-specific texts, as well as a sense of fit with regulatory texts. Yet it seems fanciful too, to expect police officers to negotiate the intertextual space in which they operate without training which directly addresses sources, forms, and functions of textual travel. I have earlier noted that officers' training in interview focuses on speaking, neglecting writing (Rock 2001a). Related neglect of textual travel fails to prepare officers to work with multiple texts which may cause them to sway witnesses or to record their account under pressure from the weight of intertextual chains. Calling to mind just one theme recommended by this chapter, training might show that through textual travel, interviews becomes concerned with a mixture of A-events, B-events, and AB-events (Labov and Fanshel 1977) with shifts between each being subtle enough to disorient witnesses. Officers, aware of such shifting ground, could clarify the purpose of the witness's involvement in interview.

ACKNOWLEDGMENTS

Heartfelt thanks to Diana Eades and Srikant Sarangi who commented on an earlier draft of this text but cannot be held responsible for flaws in this recontextualization.

CASES AND LEGISLATION

R v. Turnbull [1976] Cr App R 132; [1977] QB 244 (CA)
Public Order Act 1986

REFERENCES

Andrus, Jennifer. 2009. Beyond texts in context: Recontextualization and the co-production of texts and contexts in the legal discourse, excited utterance exception to hearsay. *Discourse and Society* 22(2): 115–36.

Austin, James. 1962. *How to do Things with Words: The William James Lectures Delivered at Harvard University in 1955.* Oxford: Clarendon Press.

Bakhtin, Mikhail M. 1986. *Speech Genres and Other Late Essays.* Translated by Vern W. McGee and edited by Caryl Emerson and Michael Holquist. Austin, Texas: University of Texas Press.

Barrett, R. 1996. *The Psychiatric Team and the Social Definition of Schizophrenia.* Cambridge: Cambridge University Press.

Barton, David. 2007. *Literacy: An Introduction to the Ecology of Written Language.* 2d ed. Oxford: Blackwell.

Bauman, Richard. 2004. *A World of Others' Words: Cross-cultural Perspectives on Intertextuality.* Oxford: Blackwell Publishing.

Berk-Seligson, Susan. 2009. *Coerced Confessions: The Discourse of Bilingual Police Interrogations.* New York: Mouton de Gruyter.

Blackledge, Adrian. 2005. *Discourse and Power in a Multilingual World.* Amsterdam: John Benjamins.

Blommaert, Jan. 2005. *Discourse.* Cambridge: Cambridge University Press.

Briggs, Charles. 1993. The patterning of variation in performance. In *American Dialect Research,* ed. Dennis Preston, 379–43. Amsterdam: John Benjamins.

Briggs, Charles, and Richard Bauman. 1992. Genre, intertextuality, and social power. *Journal of Linguistic Anthropology* 2(2): 131–72.

Bromby, Michael, and Maria Hall 2002. The development and rapid evaluation of the knowledge model of ADVOKATE: An advisory system to assess the credibility of eyewitness testimony. In *Legal Knowledge and Information Systems,* ed. Trevor Bench-Capon, Aspassia Daskalopulu, and Radboud Winkels, 143–52. Amsterdam: IOS Press.

Calligan, Stewart. 2009. *Points to Prove.* 7th ed. East Yorkshire: The New Police Bookshop.

Centrex. 2004. *Police Training Manual.* Bramshill, UK: Centrex.

Chafe, Wallace. 1976. Givenness, contrastiveness, definiteness, subjects, topics, and points of view. In *Subject and Topic,* ed. Charles Li. 27-55, London: Academic Press.

Cicourel, Aaron V. [1968] 1974. Police practices and official records. In *Ethnomethodology: Selected Readings,* ed. Roy Turner. Harmondsworth: Penguin Books Limited.

Eades, Diana. 1996. Verbatim courtroom transcripts and discourse analysis. In *Recent Developments in Forensic Linguistics,* ed. Hannes Kniffka, Susan Blackwell, and Malcolm Coulthard, 241–54. Frankfurt am Main: Peter Lang.

———. 2008. *Courtroom Talk and Neo-Colonial Control.* Berlin: Mouton de Gruyter.

Fairclough, Norman. 1992. *Discourse and Social Change.* Cambridge: Polity Press.

———. 2010. *Critical Discourse Analysis: The Critical Study of Language.* 2d ed. Harlow, UK: Longman.

Fox, Gwenyth. 1993. A comparison of "policespeak" and "normalspeak": A preliminary study. In *Techniques of Description: A Festschrift for Malcolm Coulthard*, ed. John M. Sinclair, Michael Hoey, and Gwenyth Fox, 183–95. London: Routledge.

Garfinkel, Harold, and Harvey Sacks. 1970. On formal structures of practical action. In *Theoretical Sociology: Perspectives and Developments*, ed. John C. McKinney and Edward A. Tiryakian, 337–66. New York: Appleton-Century-Crofts.

Gee, James. 2005. *Discourse Analysis: Theory and Method*. 2d ed. London: Routledge.

Gibbons, John. 2001. Legal transformations in Spanish: An "Audencia" in Chile. *Forensic Linguistics* 8(2): 24–43.

Goffman, Erving. 1983. The interaction order. *American Sociological Review* 48: 1–17.

Goodwin, Marjorie Harness, and H. Samy Alim. 2010. "Whatever (neck roll, eye roll, teeth suck)": The situated coproduction of social categories and identities through stancetaking and transmodal stylization. *Journal of Linguistic Anthropology* 20(1): 179–94.

Hall, Phil. 2008. Policespeak. In *Dimensions of Forensic Linguistics*, ed. John Gibbons and M. Teresa Turell, 67–94. Amsterdam: John Benjamins.

Jaffe, Alexandra. 2009. Stance in a Corsican school: Institutional and ideological orders and the production of bilingual subjects. In *Stance: Sociolinguistic Perspectives*, ed. Alexandra Jaffe, 119–45. Oxford: Oxford University Press.

Jönsson, Linda, and Per Linell. 1991. Story generations: From dialogical interviews to written reports in police interrogations. *Text* 11(3): 419–40.

Katajamäki, Heli. 2009. An editorial and its intertextual links: Case study of a Finnish business newspaper. In *Käännösteoria, ammattikielet ja monikielisyys. Vakki-symposiumi XXIX. Vaasa 13.–14.2.2009*, ed. Mona Enell-Nilsson and Niina Nissilä. *Publications of the Research Group for the Theory of Translation, LSP and Multilingualism at the University of Vaasa*. No. 36, 204–15.

Kell, Catherine. 2006. Crossing the margins: Literacy, semiotics and the recontextualisation of meanings. In *Travel Notes for the New Literacy Studies: Instances of Practice*, ed. Kate Pahl and Jennifer Roswell, 147–69. Clevedon, UK: Multilingual Matters.

Komter, Martha. 2002. The suspect's own words: The treatment of written statements in Dutch courtrooms. *Forensic Linguistics: The International Journal of Speech, Language and the Law* 9(2): 168–92.

———. 2006. From talk to text: The interactional construction of a police record. *Research on Language and Social Interaction* 39(3): 201–28.

Kramarae, Cheris. 1974. Folk linguistics: Wishy-washy mommy talk. *Psychology Today* 8: 82–85.

Kristeva, Julia. 1986. *The Kristeva Reader*. Edited by Toril Moi. Oxford: Blackwell Publishing.

Labov, William, and David Fanshel. 1977. *Therapeutic Discourse: Psychotherapy as Conversation*. New York: Academic Press.

Linde, Charlotte. 2009. *Working the Past: Narrative and Institutional Memory*. Oxford: Oxford University Press.

Linell, Per. 1998. Discourse across boundaries: On recontextualisations and the blending of voices across professional boundaries. *Text* 18(2): 143–57.

Mehan, Hugh. 1991. The school's work of sorting students. In *Talk and Social Structure*, ed. Dierdre Boden and Don H. Zimmerman, 71–90. Oxford: Polity Press.

———. 1992. Understanding inequality in schools: The contribution of interpretive studies. *Sociology of Education* 65: 1–20.

———. 1996. Beneath the skin and between the ears: A case study in the politics of representation. In *Natural Histories of Discourse*, ed. Michael Silverstein and Greg Urban, 253–76. Chicago: University of Chicago Press.

Mertz, Elizabeth. 1996. *The Language of Law School: Learning to "Think Like a Lawyer."* Oxford: Oxford University Press.

Park, Joseph Sung-Yul, and Mary Bucholtz. 2009. Public transcripts: Entextualization and linguistic representation in institutional contexts. *Talk and Text* 29(5): 485–502.

Pennycook, Alastair. 2007. *Global Englishes and Transcultural Flows*. London: Routledge.

Renkema, Jan. 1993. *Discourse Studies: An Introductory Textbook*. Amsterdam: John Benjamins.

Rock, Frances. 2001a. The genesis of a witness statement. *Forensic Linguistics* 8(2): 44–47.

———. 2001b. Policy and practice in the anonymisation of linguistic data. *International Journal of Corpus Linguistics* 6(1): 1–26.

———. 2012. "You say 'I'm sure' but you're not, are you?": Trust and distrust in police interviews. In *Discourses of Trust*, ed. Christopher Candlin and Jonathan Crichton. Basingstoke, UK: Palgrave Macmillan.

Sarangi, Sritkant. 1998. Rethinking recontextualization in professional discourse studies: An epilogue. *Text* 18(2): 301–18.

Sarangi, Srikant, and Lucy Brookes-Howell. 2006. Recontextualising the familial lifeworld in genetic counselling case notes. In *Advances in Medical Discourse Analysis: Oral and Written Contexts*, ed. Maurizio Gotti and Francoise Salagar-Meyer, 197–225. Bern: Peter Lang.

Schutz, Alfred, and Thomas Luckmann. 1973. *The Structures of the Life-World. Vol. 1*. Evanston, IL: Northwestern University Press.

Scollon, Ron. 1998. *Mediated Discourse as Social Interaction: A Study of News Discourse*. London: Longman.

Slembrouck, Stef. 1992. The parliamentary Hansard "verbatim" report: The written construction of spoken discourse. *Language and Literature* 1(2): 101–19.

Smith, Dorothy. 1999. *Writing the Social: Critique, Theory, and Investigations*. Toronto: University of Toronto Press.

———. 2005. *Institutional Ethnography: A Sociology for People*. Lanham, MD: AltaMira Press.

———. 2006. Incorporating texts into ethnographic practice. *Institutional Ethnography as Practice* 65–88. New York: Rowman and Littlefield Publishers Inc.

Smith, George. 1988. Policing the gay community: An inquiry into textually mediated relations. International Journal of Sociology and the Law 16: 163–83.

Still, Judith, and Michael Worton. 1991. Introduction. In *Intertextuality: Theories and Practices*, ed. Michael Worton and Judith Still, 1–44. Manchester: Manchester University Press.

Tiersma, Peter. 2001. Textualising the law. *Forensic Linguistics* 8(2): 73–92.

Walker, Anne. 1990. Language at work in the law: The customs, conventions, and appellate consequences of court reporting. In *Language in the Judicial Process*, ed. Judith N. Levi and Anne Walker, 203–44. New York: Plenum.

TRANSCRIPTION KEY

(.)	Short pause of less than a second
(4.2)	Timed pause of the duration stated
=	Latching on
((words))	Unclear talk
[nods]	Paralinguistic information and commentary
//words//	Overlapping talk
Italics	Reading aloud whilst writing
'single'	Reading aloud previously drafted text
"double"	Speech or thought presentation

PART TWO

The Legal Case as Intertextual Construction

CHAPTER 5

'Theatricks' in the Courtroom

The Intertextual Construction of Legal Cases

KATRIJN MARYNS

INTRODUCTION

The legal space can be analyzed as a polyphonic arena where multiple voices compete for influence and control.[1] In the extended literature on intertextuality and entextualization in the courtroom,[2] a variety of concepts are used to refer to the production of multilayered discourses in trial contexts. Mertz (1996) uses the term "legal de- and re-contextualisations" to refer to the extractability of texts and their performance from the contexts in which they are produced. Ehrlich (1998), in her study of an American rape case, focuses on the "reinterpretation" of testimony to show how talk takes on different meanings in various judicial decisions. Matoesian (1999, 2001), in his analysis of the William Kennedy Smith rape trial, argues that reported speech constitutes "the evidential infrastructure" of the court hearing as legal participants "shape evidence in testimony, project a particular social identity for themselves and for each other and naturalize their discursive authority through a complex array of linguistic resources" (1999: 73). Scheffer (2006) draws on Luhmann and Foucault to develop his notion of "discoursivization" as a mechanism of transformation by which local utterances are turned into available and binding facts.

In this chapter, I shall treat *interdiscursivity* in the courtroom as an interactional accomplishment, produced and interpreted through its ties to local and translocal forms of semiotic action, which are being entextualized and performed as seemingly objectified and iterable discourses (Bauman and Briggs 1990; Silverstein and Urban 1996). The extractability of texts—an assumption that still prevails in legal-procedural contexts—resonates with linguistic traditions that emphasize the referential meaning of language without considering its indexical functioning. In anthropological linguistic circles, however, a more dynamic conception of text and context is argued for, according to which the entextualization and the performance of discourses across interactional spaces, just like any other interdiscursive mechanism, are not merely linguistic-reflective processes but metadiscursive-constitutive processes whereby language users actively define and negotiate social meaning in their situated communicative practice (Bauman 2004; Blommaert 2005; Jacquemet 2005). Drawing on these anthropological linguistic developments, I analyze interdiscursivity as a process involving multiple revaluations of form-meaning relations, as they are delocated from one discursive space to another (Maryns 2013).

The Belgian Assize procedure is a criminal trial procedure that relies heavily on interdiscursive reconstructions of what counts as evidence. Defense counsel and prosecutors constantly incorporate tangled networks of interdiscursive linkages in their courtroom performance. What makes the Assize procedure particularly interesting for analysis is its complex interplay between orality and textuality. The Belgian legal authorities make no recordings of the interaction taking place between the institution and the individual client (police interrogations, court hearings). No matter how crucial for the further development of the legal case, the discourses produced on occasions of direct interaction between the individual and the institution are often the first to disappear from the bureaucratic processing of information: police interrogations and witness hearings, for instance, are not recorded and thus no more than the written report of the spoken interaction survives the procedure. Utterances that are locally produced in dialogic interview settings are abstracted from their discursive settings, circulated between professional knowledge structures and then inserted into new translocal settings. In this way, subjects' individual utterances become the input of a sequence of different entextualizations as these written versions of the events—now turned into a "case"—travel into and through the various stages of bureaucratic treatment (Silverstein and Urban 1996; Briggs 1997; Maryns and Blommaert 2002).

The textualist dynamics dominating the pretrial investigation, however, are in sharp contrast to the oral proceedings of the trial. The Assize Court procedure is the only procedure in Belgium in which the evidence has to be exhaustively (re) presented in front of a jury: all actors in the pretrial investigation become witnesses on trial (examining judge, police, witnesses). The jurors have to form their opinion about the case without thorough inspection of the case file.[3] Their judgment, in other words, should be motivated by the oral performance—talk-in-interaction—of the legal and lay participants (defendant, witnesses, prosecution, defense, civil parties) in the trial. Nevertheless, textuality keeps pervading the oral proceedings in the ways quotations from the written case file are mobilized, shaped, and appropriated as they travel through the legal process. The prosecution and the defense are very creative in smuggling extracts from the case file into their oral argumentation.

Probably because in many cases the trial is held several years after the date that the crime was committed, the case file is generally used as a basis for organizing the witness hearings and the debates. Quotations from the case file are then used by the courtroom speakers not only to elicit information from the witnesses but also to topicalize particular elements that they consider relevant for the evaluation of the case. But there is more. Besides quoting from expert and police reports, courtroom speakers also engage in reenacting oral dialogue on the basis of these written reports. Not only do they reconstruct translocally produced pretrial dialogue from the case file, they also use their own handwritten notes to reenact locally produced courtroom interaction. In other words, textuality is deeply implicated in oral argumentation, often in much more fundamental ways than is generally assumed and these hidden practices of entextualization form the object of my investigation.

This chapter examines the ways in which legal participants in assize trials manage the travel of spoken and written discourses produced across local and translocal stages of legal case processing. It analyzes how verbatim oral dialogue is reconstructed from written case notes and used as an evidence and identity-building resource in the construction of sociolegal realities. My approach combines linguistics with ethnography to analyze the critical role language plays in legal procedures (Conley and O' Barr 1990; Mertz 1992, 1996; Matoesian 1999; Scheffer 2006; Maryns 2006; Rock 2007; D'hondt 2009a). The everyday experience of legal and lay participants is used as a lens to examine legal institutions and their discourse practices.

Particularly interesting about this perspective is that it addresses constitutive communicative practices that tend to remain invisible in an internal legal approach. The Belgian Assize procedure leans on interdiscursive reconstructions of legal facticity. The inherently variable and therefore manipulatable nature of these intertextual linkages, however, is generally not addressed in sociolegal inquiry. The sociolegal approach assumes a more static ideology of textuality and evidentiality that takes for granted the mobility of meaning across contexts of use (Matoesian 1999; Maryns 2006). From a linguistic-ethnographic perspective, on the other hand, it is possible to move beyond a purely semantic interpretation of communicative practice to consider its indexical aspects. From this angle, language is no longer conceived as a neutral tool, but as an ideological vehicle that allows discursive evidence to be produced indexically in the courtroom.

In the next section, I begin by discussing the legal context in which I collected my data. What follows is a systematic exploration of interdiscursive devices used by the legal participants in several assize trials. My analysis of the data shows how a wide range of everyday conversational mechanisms is deployed to anticipate shared common knowledge and shuffle particular ideas and subjectivities into the legal space. For the purpose of this chapter, I zoom in on the particular interdiscursive technique of reenacting verbatim oral dialogue from written notes, both locally produced by the legal participants in the trial or translocally produced in the course of the pretrial investigation. What is particularly striking in these data is that courtroom speakers staunchly maintain objective textuality—mirrored in their marked preference for verbatim quotation—while obscuring the way they are themselves implicated in the interdiscursive process. In the discussion, I argue that the observed interdiscursivity serves as a tool to mobilize particular footings and identities that are indexically employed by the courtroom speakers to achieve well-considered rhetorical objectives.

THE BELGIAN ASSIZE COURT

The Assize Court is the highest criminal court in Belgium that deals with the most serious criminal offences. It is composed of professional judges and citizens who act as jurors. The Assize court has no permanent structure but sits on an ad hoc basis in the first instance court of each provincial capital.[4] The trial before the Assize Court is often held several years after the date that the crime was committed. Before a case goes to trial, the Public Prosecution Department ("parquet générale") has the duty to conduct a pretrial investigation. The prosecution assigns an examining judge to obtain and investigate information about the identity of the parties concerned, the circumstances under which the crime was committed and the damage caused by the offence. The examining judge is responsible for the progress of the investigation. S/he operates as the head of investigation and is entitled to coordinate the police and expert activities of analyzing the evidence and talking to the witnesses who can later be called to testify in court. Each of the parties involved in the pretrial investigation has to produce a written record of the materials obtained and analyzed. The case file of the pretrial investigation includes the official reports and records of the interrogation (on paper) and any other documents or recordings (exceptional) made in the course of the investigation.[5]

The Assize Court is composed of three judges: the *presiding judge* (a judge from the Court of Appeal) and two *assessors* (from the first instance court in the province where the trial is held). The presiding judge leads the proceedings and assists the jury members in their duties. The president has the authority to do whatever necessary to discover the truth. This is also referred to as the discretionary power of the chair. He also has the power to enforce order in the court (his police authority).

The *jury* is composed of twelve members and one or more substitute members. The jurors are selected from the population of Belgian citizens who live in the province where the trial is held, who are between 30 and 60 years old, who are able to read and write, and who enjoy full civil and political rights. The jury decides upon the question of guilt and the jurors judge solely according to their innermost conviction. It is not required from the jurors to explain their motives or reasons that led to their decision.[6] For the determination of the penalty the jurors get assistance from the three judges. The jury members are allowed to take notes and ask questions to the witnesses and the defendant.

The *public prosecution* is represented by an attorney general or his deputy, both members of the parquet générale, or by a member of the department of the "procureur du Roi." While the *counsel* is entitled to represent the interests of the defendant before the court, the public prosecutor has to defend the general interests of society and is there to ensure the application of law. The prosecutor formulates the charges in his bill of indictment and presents his position to the jury in his closing speech. The *civil parties* are the victims or the plaintiffs who claim damage for the crime committed by the defendant. In case of murder, they are usually the victim's closest relatives, assisted by a counsel. The *witnesses* (eyewitnesses, character witnesses, and expert witnesses) are interrogated by the judge in the course of the witness hearings. The jury, the civil parties, the counsel and the prosecution are entitled to collect information from the witnesses on condition that the protocol is observed: they can only indirectly address a witness, which means that all questions should be orally directed to the presiding judge who then repeats or rephrases them for the witness.[7]

I collected my data for this study in the assize courts of Ghent and Antwerp.[8] My fieldwork extended over a period of 10 months and consisted of two phases of data collection: from June to December 2006 (Ghent) and from January to October 2007 (Antwerp). I attended seven trials in total, each of which lasted for about one week. I was given permission to make audio-recordings of the witness hearings and the oral pleadings (arguments by the lawyers, the prosecution, and the civil parties) and video-recordings of the pleadings. For each case I copied the bill of indictment and the statement of defense (if any). I also conducted short field interviews with some of the prosecutors and counsels who were involved in the cases I analyzed. For the analysis I have made transcriptions of most of the debates and the pleas.

INTERDISCURSIVE DEVICES IN THE COURTROOM

In this section, I analyze the assize trial as a metacommunicative display event par excellence. My analysis in this section does not focus primarily on the meaning of legal actions, but on the discursive techniques by means of which these meanings are constituted. More specifically, I aim at an exploration of the ways textual travel is managed in the legal space through all sorts of metadiscursive devices by means of which the legal parties impose their recontextualizations of past, present, and future (hypothetical) discourses. The different modes of interdiscursivity discussed here range from instances of reported speech—direct and indirect quotation—to creative reenactments of verbal expression, body movement, and gesture. A selection of intertextual devices is traced from the data, each of which is treated under a separate heading and each of which is illustrated with transcribed extracts from my corpus.[9] I have decided to use separate headings to foreground one or another device for analytical purposes, bearing in mind, however, that they generally flow together in packages of intertextual reproduction.

Re-performing Pretrial Dialogue

As mentioned earlier in the introduction, although the Assize Court procedure is an oral procedure, the written file still leaves its mark on the proceedings. The courtroom speakers in my data corpus not only *refer to* or *quote from* expert examinations and police reports, they also *re-perform* some of the discursive input into these reports. Defense counsels frequently use this technique to offer the jury a glimpse of their clients' "off-stage" identity. In the next extract, for example, it can be seen how the defense counsel in a strangling trial re-performs a striking passage of pretrial dialogue that took place between his client and the police. Unlike most defendants in Belgium, the defendant in this case was subjected to a video interrogation. Paradoxically enough, the counsel explicitly states that he did not actually watch the video. In other words, although he did have access to the original, the counsel decides to reenact a passage from the police interview on the basis of the report from the written case file:

Excerpt 1: Defense plea (Dutch original)

1. Ze hebben een videoverhoor van hem afgenomen van 3 u (…) ik
2. zeg u (.) ik heb het nie gezien (.) maar ik heb wel de teksten
3. gelezen he (.) ge krijgt er een PUNTHOOFD van een punthoofd
4. (..) om te verstaan wat dat den Bob tegen de politie aan 't
5. vertellen is he (.) Ge KUNT NIE volgen (.) ge kunt nie volgen
6. (…) 't is 't is eigenlijk ongelofelijk (.) hij staat daar, hij staat daar
7. dus te vertellen (.) 't is gruwelijk he (.) ik excuseer mij ten
8. aanzien van de slachtoffers maar hij staat daar dan te vertellen dat
9. hij me zijn bottien boven de keel van die arme vrouw lag (..) en
10. de politie vraagt hem (.) cruciale vraag cruciaal (.) *mijnheer, wa*
11. *voeldigde toen, of wa voelde toen?* en weette wa da den diën
12. antwoordt? (…) *mijn voet voelde niks* zegt hij *mijn voet voelde*
13. *niets* (.) *JA MAAR MIJNHEER IN UWE KOP, IN UW*
14. *GEDACHTEN! (.) URM URM 'K WEET 'T NIE URM URM (..)*
15. *WAS =WAS MOEST ZE DOOD? (..) URM URM 'K WEET 'T*
16. *NIE (..) GE KUNT HET GAAN NAKIJKEN (.)* ge kunt het gaan
17. nakijken (.) ge kunt het gaan nakijken als ge mij nie gelooft (…)
18. maar 't is on 't is ongelooflijk (…)

Excerpt 1: Defense plea (my translation)

1. They have subjected him to a video interrogation of 3 hours (…) I
2. tell you (.) I haven't seen it (.) but I did read the texts he (.) it
3. drives you UP THE WALL up the wall (..) to understand what
4. Bob is telling to the police you know (.) YOU CAN'T follow (.)
5. you can't follow (..) in fact it's incredible (.) he stands there, he is
6. there talking (.) it's horrible you know (.) I apologize to the
7. victims but he is there telling that with his boot he laid on top of
8. that poor woman's throat (.) and the police asks him (.) crucial

9.   question crucial (.) *sir, what did you felt then = or what did you*
10. *feel?* And you know what that (guy) answers? (…) *my foot didn't*
11. *feel anything* he says *my foot didn't feel anything* (.) YES BUT
12. SIR, IN YOUR HEAD, IN YOUR MIND (.) URM URM I DON'T
13. KNOW URM URM (..) DID = DID SHE HAVE TO DIE? (..)
14. URM URM I DON'T KNOW (…) YOU CAN CHECK ON THIS
15. (.) you can check on this (.) you can check this if you don't
16. believe me (..) but it is incredible (…)

This seemingly verbatim quotation from the case file enables the defense counsel to manage the textual travel of particular social and indexical meanings. Through all sorts of metapragmatic signaling devices, the counsel produces a particular identity for his client:

- His use of the generic *you* (line 4: "you can't follow") to align himself with the court, the audience, and in fact, with any "reasonable" person.
- His use of extra pitch and explicit metapragmatic comments (line 5 "it is incredible," line 6 "it is horrible") to emphasize both his own indignation and the indignation of the police over the outrageous behavior of the defendant during the interrogation.
- His animation of his client as a stammering imbecile (lines 11-13).
- Dissociation from his client is also indexed grammatically in the way his client is referred to with the demonstrative "den dieën" (line 10) which expresses distance and shows disrespect.

The defense counsel's performance, although presented as a verbatim account, is actually a new chunk of spoken discourse which is constructed from a second-hand, written version of the original. The counsel, however, explicitly comments on his own performance as authentic and faithful to the written report (lines 13-14). At no point does he question the potential intertextual hiatus between reported and reporting versions of the events.

Reenacting Trial Performance: Obscuring Interactive Footing in the Reproduction of Co-narrated Events

Probably the most frequently used metadiscursive device in my corpus is the representation of utterances that have been produced earlier in the trial. As a researcher I was given permission to make recordings of both the witness hearings and the oral pleadings and this is what makes these instances of courtroom performance particularly interesting for an analysis of the way discourse travels from one stage of the trial (testimony) to the next (plea). In the following extracts, taken from a rape-murder case, it can be seen how a chunk of elicited and co-narrated discourse is reframed by the defense as active input from the witness. Excerpt 2 shows how the defense counsel (DEF), in his cross-examination of a witness (W), the grandmother of the defendant (Brian), topicalizes the rashness of his client's aggression.

Excerpt 2: Witness hearing (Dutch original)

1. DEF: als = als 'm nu op die momenten tilt sloeg = omda 'm zichzelf nog onder controle had? Of was 'm ne razende gek?
2. W: echt onder controle niet nee
3. DEF: eigenlijk (.) en dat is natuurlijk (.) ik moet mij bij mijn verdediging houden (.) maar als ik u zo hoor (.) is = is Brian bijna ne wandelende tijdbom die soms heel goe functioneerde maar als 'm ontplofte zich nie onder controle had en achteraf dee of er niks was gebeurd (.) klopt da?
4. W: ja
5. DEF: dank u

Excerpt 2: Witness hearing (my translation)

1. DEF: when = when (now) at those moments he hit the roof = because he still had himself under control? Or was he a furious madman?
2. W: not really under control no
3. DEF: in fact (.) and that is of course (.) I have to confine myself to my defense (.) but if I hear you talk like that (.) is = is Brian almost (like) a walking time bomb who at times functioned very well but when he exploded didn't have control over himself and afterwards acted as if nothing had happened (.) is that right?
4. W: yes
5. DEF: thank you

This dialogue corresponds to some of the data examples used in linguistic work on lawyers' questioning strategies during cross-examination. As Cotterill (2004) argues in her analysis of trial-by-jury interactional processes, lawyers are able to control witness testimony in the formulation of their questions, not merely in their syntactic management of question-answer structures but also in their strategic lexical choices that enable them to activate implicit interpretations of the evidence. In excerpt 2, the counsel's use of leading and closed questions considerably restricts the response potential for the witness, which is confined to a simple confirmation of a set of metaphors and synonymous expressions that emphasize the element of suddenness and lack of control in her grandson's behavior:

- the metaphor of *hitting the roof, explode, a walking time bomb*
- *a furious madman,* losing *self-control*

The multiple "lexicalizations" of the behavior of his client enable the defense counsel to produce well-considered nuances of meaning: the metaphors can be understood as what Komter (1994) described as "passivity markers," markers that stage defendants as passive spectators of their own actions. What is also noticeable from this passage is the metapragmatic comment "I have to confine myself to my defense" (turn 3), by which the counsel not only anticipates a complete dissociation from his client but also signals that this dissociation may seem inappropriate according to institutionally established participation frames.

The counsel's self-managed lexical negotiation later goes on to form a key element in his insanity plea. In excerpt 3, taken from this plea, it can be seen how the counsel re-performs a passage from his cross-examination of the grandmother as a strategically entextualized event. The grandmother is animated as both the author and the principal of what was originally a lawyer-initiated turn. The use of direct quotation gives the quoted words the status of an authentic, self-initiated witness statement.

Excerpt 3: Defense plea (Dutch original)

1. Chapeau voor de moeder en de grootmoeder (.) want de
2. grootmoeder zegt het meest gruwelijke da ge als advocaat kunt
3. horen (.) als ge denkt *ik moet toch nog voor mijne cliënt GOE*
4. *kunnen optreden* (.) maar het is één van DIE beslissing en die mee
5. me ons hebben gespeeld om te zeggen *we VRAGEN die*
6. *internering* (..) dat was een WANDELENDE TIJDBOM. *Hij was*
7. *heel rustig, kon ontploffen en dan weer rustig* (.) Jongens,
8. vrouwen, mannen, ik bedoel, dat is internering TEN VOETEN
9. UIT (.) Daarvoor is dië wet gemaakt (.) *Als hij nie zijn zin kreeg,*
10. *ontplofte hij.*

Excerpt 3: Defense plea (my translation)

1. Respect for the mother and the grandmother (.) cause the
2. grandmother says the most horrible that you can hear as lawyer
3. (.) when you think (.) *after all, I do have to act*
4. *CONSTRUCTIVELY for my client* (.) but it is one of THOSE
5. decisions that have played a role for us to say (.) we ASK this
6. internment (..) that was a WALKING TIME BOMB (.) He was
7. very calm, could explode and then calm again (.). Lads, women,

8.   men, I mean, that is internment ALL OVER (.) That's what this

9.   law is made for (.) *If he didn't get his own way, he collapsed.*

The lawyer's manipulation of interactive footing turns out to be meaningful at different levels. On the one hand, his alignment with the defendant's grandmother explicitly consolidates his insanity argument, suggesting that even the least likely to dissociate themselves from the defendant (his *own* client, her *own* grandson) have no option but to recognize his abnormality. At the same time, the way he dissociates himself from his client suggests that nothing can keep him from finding the truth, even if this would undermine the identity of his client.

Reenacting Trial Performance: The Reenactment of Body Language and Gestures

A third type of reported trial performance is the reenactment of body language and gestures. Nonverbal language, unlike verbal communication, is not accessible to everyone in the courtroom. The physical location assigned to the participants in the courtroom generates unequal access to nonverbal resources:

- The prosecutor's seat is aligned with the bench of the judges, facing the public and with a clear view of the jury box and the bench of the defense and the civil parties.
- Defendants are seated in the row behind their legal representatives—the counsels are facing the jury but have no view of their client.
- The civil parties are seated at one end of the defense bench, close to the plaintiffs, who are seated on the first row of the public bench: they face the judges' bench and have a clear view of the jury box and the defense box.

Due to the fact that they are sitting in the front row, defense counsels cannot easily observe their clients' behavior on trial. This element is strategically deployed by the civil party counsel (CP) in the next extract. In her plea, she reenacts an episode from the testimony of the legal psychiatrist. She develops her argument by drawing the jury's attention to the way in which the defense counsel urged the legal psychiatrist to confirm the defendant's inability to show emotion. She then disproves the argument of her opponent by attributing evidential value to the defendant's behavior during trial:

Excerpt 4: Plea of the civil party (Dutch original)

1.   *Maar ja (..) getuige (.) is het niet zo (.) dat Dave (.) zwaar*

2.   *getraumatiseerd is (.) dat hij misschien niet in staat is om zijn*

3.   *emoties te tonen (..) dat KAN toch? (..) en ik heb u regelmatig in*

4.   *'t oog houden, Dave, gij mij ook (.) 'k heb da gezien (.) gij mij*

5. ook (.) ik heb daar geen problem mee (..) der is één moment deze
6. week dat mij gefrappeerd heeft (...) en ik weet niet of het iemand
7. is opgevallen (......) Mandy, uw zus (..) ook nie gemakkelijk
8. voor haar hé? Ook deel uitmakend van een gezin (.) een tyraniek
9. gezin hé? Seksueel misbruikt hé? Door dië zelfde MAN he? Maar
10. ze zat hier wel hé, Dave, voor U hé? Ze heeft moeite gedaan hé
11. (.........) en dan is 't nie gemakkelijk hé Dave (.) dan zag ik
12. WEL wa vocht over uw wangen naar beneden druppelen (......)
13. En uw zus (..) ging van de getuigenstoel (.) en nam plaats
14. vanachter in de zaal (.) en ge hebt teken gedaan, Dave (.........)
15. En kijk 's naar mij (.) ik zal het u voordoen (.........) IK ((vinger
16. op borst))... HOU ((armen gekruisd voor zich)) VAN U ((vinger
17. wijzend naar voor))(...) dat hebde gij gedaan (.........) en
18. meester D. ((verdediging)) zal 't nie gezien hebben maar IKKE
19. wel (.........) IK HOU VAN U (.........) DAT is pas emotie,
20. Dave, (...) Dat is uit het BINNENSTE van uwe ziel.

Excerpt 4: Plea of the civil party (my translation)

1. *But yes (..) witness (.) is it not the case (.) that Dave (.) is*
2. *seriously traumatized (.) that maybe he is not capable of showing*
3. *his emotions (..) that is possible indeed, isn't it? (..)* And I have
4. kept an eye on you frequently, Dave, and you on me as well (.)
5. I've noticed that (.) you on me as well (.) I don't have a problem
6. with that (..) there is one moment this week that struck me (...)
7. and I don't know if anyone noticed it (......) Mandy, your sister
8. (.) not easy for her either, right? Also part of a family (.) a
9. tyrannous family, isn't it? Sexually abused, right? By that very
10. same MAN, isn't it? But she (made the effort) to be here, isn't it,
11. Dave? For YOU, isn't it? She made the effort, didn't she? (......)
12. And then it is not easy, right, Dave? Then I DID see some water
13. rolling down your cheeks (.........) And your sister (..) she stood
14. up from the witness chair (.) and took place in the back of the
15. room (.) and you gave her a sign, Dave (.........) And just look at
16. me (.) *I will show you* (.........) I ((points at her chest)) ... LOVE
17. ((arms crossed)) YOU ((pointing forwards)) (...) that's what you
18. did (.........) and barrister D. ((defense)) won't have seen it but I
19. DID (.........) I LOVE YOU (.........) THAT's real emotion,
20. Dave, (...) That comes from the deepest part of your soul.

Expert opinion on psychiatric issues—the psychiatrist's answer to the question—
doesn't even enter into the matter. What counts here is the counsel's observation of

the defendant's behavior as he was communicating with his sister from the dock. The defendant's body language is treated as evidence here and the way the civil party counsel directly addresses him reveals some meaningful footing patterns:

- The CP counsel stages herself as a member of the defendant's target group of young women and in this way she creates an atmosphere of immediate threat in the courtroom, which sustains her representation of the defendant as a very dangerous criminal (lines 3–6).
- The CP counsel aligns the defendant with his sister and this is used as an argument against him: they suffered the same trauma, but developed a different reaction to it. Not only does his performance in court demonstrate his ability to express emotions, but it also shows that he *did* have a choice to react differently to his trauma, just like his sister did. His trauma, in other words, cannot be used as an argument against mitigation (lines 7–10).

Preemptively Enacting Future Trial Discourse

A final metadiscursive device concerns the preemptive enactment of assumptive trial discourse. The institutionally established pleading order is not insignificant here: the civil parties plead first, followed by the prosecutor and the defense. Opening the plea has pros and cons: although it rules out the possibility of refuting the opponents' previous arguments, starting from pole position offers the opportunity to develop particular scenarios in anticipation of possible defense strategies. In terms of footing, this implies some sort of "virtual bargaining" (Komter 1994), where dialogic negotiation enters monological speech. In the data extract, it is the civil party counsel (CP) who preemptively invalidates a possible argument for insanity.

Excerpt 5: Plea of the civil party (Dutch original)

1. 't Water staat hem nu aan de lippen en dit is zijn enige = zijn
2. enige mogelijkheid om nog 't ontsnappen aan (.) een gewone
3. straf (.) da's nu pleiten van *ja maar kijk (.) eigenlijk = uhm was*
4. *er me mijn geestestoestand iets (.) nie in orde en zelfs zo zeer (.)*
5. *dat ik nie meer = dat ik geen controle meer had over mijn eigen*
6. *daden* (..) da's een vraag die hier zal zal gesteld worden.

Excerpt 5: Plea of the civil party (my translation)

1. He is up to his neck now and this is his only = his only possibility
2. right now to escape from (.) a normal sentence (.) that is pleading

3.   now *yes but see (.) in fact = uhm there was something with my*
4.   *state of mind (.) not quite right and even in such a way (.) that I*
5.   *no longer = that I no longer had any control over my own actions*
6.   (..) that is a question that will be asked here.

The civil party counsel's dismissal of the insanity argument lies at the very heart of his animation. What we get is the reported version of a hypothetical utterance in the first person that is attributed to the defendant. The counsel adopts the stance of the defendant displaying legal-medical expert knowledge. By means of strategic shifts in footing between impersonal-passive constructions (line 2: "that is pleading now," line 6: "a question that will be asked") and first-person constructions (line 4: "*my* state of mind, line 5: *I* no longer had control"), the CP counsel encourages the jurors to see through the defense argument of insanity. In terms of participant orientation (Goffman 1981), this instance of "self-othering" discourse, where the defendant is positioned as the principal of his own insanity declaration, makes little sense for successful "othering" requires the expertise of a third party (in this case the psychiatrist or the defense counsel)—see also D'hondt (2009a) on how this strategy is used for the cultural othering of minority participants in first instance criminal trials. In other words, if the defendant were really a mental patient, he would never be able to analyze his own mental condition: true mental illness is incompatible with self-reflection.

DISCUSSION

In the data discussed in this chapter, the courtroom participants deploy all sorts of interdiscursive devices to impose their preferred interpretations on locally and translocally produced discourses. Their trial performance gives evidence of a marked preference for everyday conversational mechanisms that serve persuasive purposes. Their use of direct speech, for instance, not only creates an illusion of objective animation of others' voices, but also, it enables the speakers to express the events with a certain instancy and explicitness that brings the original events to life in the courtroom. These highly accessible mundane conversational mechanisms, however, conceal deep-rooted tensions between lay and legal realms of discourse production and interpretation.

Complex legal–lay dynamics enter into the analysis of trial performance (a) at the level of discourse representation, articulated in the strategic interplay between orality and textuality that permeates the proceedings and (b) at the level of legal argumentation, reflected in the tension between commonsense and juridical categorizations of events and identities.

First, seemingly obvious patterns of interdiscursivity are rooted in intricate tensions between orality and textuality. Unlike many other western countries, police interviews and trial testimony in Belgium are usually not recorded nor transcribed. In the pretrial phase of investigation, oral declarations are reported in official written statements (procès-verbal) drawn up by police officers authorized by law. These statements are treated as "authentic acts" that have a legal effect of formality. Apart from the fact that the term *Pro Justitia* must appear, there are no legal regulations on how these written statements should be drawn up (Declercq 2007). General instructions for report writing that circulate among police departments may serve as a guiding principle but do not formally regulate the record-keeping process. Everyday practice allows great flexiblity in drawing up the procès-verbal. It should be noted though, that in the beginning of their police interrogation, public officials must inform declarants (witnesses and defendants) that according to the law, declarants do have the right to ask for a verbatim rendering of the hearing (the Franchimont Act 1998; Delmas-Marty and Spencer 2002). In practice, however, declarants rarely insist on a word-for-word transcription of the interrogation. Public officers are free to develop their own report writing style, which ranges from reports in dialogue form to a more summarizing style and reports taking the shape of continuous text. In the end, whatever its format, the court presumes the procès-verbal to be an objective rendition of the declarant's oral statements that has been submitted for approval.

Given this textualist treatment of oral evidence in the legal investigation, it is remarkable that although they do not have the necessary resources available (audio-recordings, verbatim reports) to produce a truly authentic version of pretrial dialogue, the courtroom participants in my corpus draw quite substantially on *seemingly* verbatim representations of oral statements. The way in which they reconstruct orality from the textual files implies a triangular travel of discourse across spaces of legal case-making: pretrial oral dialogue is first entextualized (summarized and recontextualized) in the procès-verbal on the basis of which it is then orally reconstructed in the courtroom. What the jury actually gets to see, however, is an intricate web of performances that directly links *oral pretrial dialogue* (between witness and police/legal expert) with *oral trial performance* (the oral representation of these pretrial dialogues in the trial). The fundamental textual link between these two oral phases of discourse production—the written reflection of the interrogations in police records and expert reports—escapes trial performance.

In other words, what is presented as a first-hand account of the interaction is in fact no more than a residue of laminated entextualization processes involving the active input of several participants: (a) the police officer who draws up the procès-verbal, (b) the examining judge who compiles the case file, and (c) the barrister who selects utterances from the case file to construct his version of these discourses in his plea. The barrister's filtered version of the interaction between the police officer and the witness, although presented as directly obtained from the original source, actually involves several sources of noise. In this way, seemingly transparent lay representations of pretrial discourses in the courtroom conceal the indirect, mediated, and therefore inevitably creative nature of the legal-bureaucratic textual trajectories these discourses have actually gone through.

In their trial performance, the courtroom speakers not only reproduce pretrial dialogue from the case file, but they strategically reenact courtroom dialogue on the basis of their own handwritten notes taken during the course of the debates. The same triangular dynamics can be observed here: passages from the witness hearings are first entextualized in the barrister's written notes, which are then used as the sole basis for reconstructing the courtroom dialogues in his plea. A form of interdiscursivity is preferred that masks its constitutive effects and creates an illusion of objective representation. But my data examples confirm that reported speech is rarely, if ever, a neutral representation of the original. These extracts demonstrate that the orally reported utterances are far from objective representations of what the witness had actually stated on the witness chair. Quite the contrary, the way in which their semi-authentic representations are metapragmatically framed adds significant meaning to the witness statements.

By means of his skillful manipulation of interactive footings, the defense counsel presents his preferred lexicalizations of the events through the voice of one of the key witnesses in the case. In this way, although the witnesses—both legal and lay -are given the opportunity to perform in court, in the end their utterances may be appropriated or even manipulated by the legal participants and subtly reenacted on their behalf. Interestingly in jury trials, the way in which these interdiscursive processes are openly played out in front of the jury, reveals the potential for intertextual gaps and inconsistencies that characterize the realm of "backstage" discourses (Goffman 1981) that are produced in the larger context of legal cases.

So far, I have analyzed the interdiscursive mechanisms that permeate the assize court proceedings as triangular processes of discourse representation that minimize the intertextual gap (Briggs and Bauman 1992) between reported dialogue and reporting monologue. The key question is *why* the legal actors in the data examples prefer to present their opinions through the voice of lay participants. According to Goffman, speakers rarely speak purely for themselves. In his essay on footing, Goffman (1981) explains how in everyday conversation, speakers constantly adopt different production roles (animator, author, and principal). The way in which they smoothly switch between speaker roles enables speakers to manage shifts in interactional footing: by staging themselves as mere animators of the information conveyed, they obscure the way in which they are themselves deeply implicated in the meaning-making process. In this way, their animation of other people's voices offers them the opportunity to ventilate particular ideas and subjectivities without necessarily taking the responsibility (authorship) for these ideas and subjectivities.

My analysis of courtroom interaction shows how legal actors animate the voice of lay participants as a strategy to shuffle their own preferred interpretations of the facts into the legal space. In each of the data examples analyzed in this chapter, these ventilated opinions have to do with issues of moral responsibility. Although Belgian criminal law provides the abstract-doctrinal setting for some core judicial concepts related to issues of moral responsibility, the actual implementation of these categories is at the discretion of the court (Declercq 2007). According to

Article 71 of the Belgian criminal law, for instance, "there is no indictable offence when the accused or the defendant was in a state of insanity at the time of committing the act or when he was forced by a power that he could not resist" (my translation). The legal concept of *insanity* itself, however, is not clearly specified in the law and is therefore open to several interpretations by the decision makers, who have but a limited number of instructions, such as the precondition that the mental state needs to be permanent both at the time of committing the act as at the time of judgment.

Probably because of this indeterminacy, prosecutors, defense, and civil party counsels feel the need to inform the jury and fill in assumed gaps in their legal pre-knowledge. The data show that the ambiguity in the Belgian criminal law of legal concepts related to moral responsibility opens up enormous potential for multiple interpretations and redefinitions of these concepts. On the basis of the data extracts it is reasonable to suggest that not only are the defense counsels inclined to downplay the need for psychiatric expertise on the issue, proclaiming their faith in lay opinion and commonsense reasoning, but that they also entitle themselves to challenge legal-psychiatric expertise. Their use of everyday conversational mechanisms serves them well in developing a lay perspective on the issue of insanity. Particularly striking is how they manage interactive footings in ways that challenge institutionally established footing patterns (D'hondt 2009a, b). This is reflected in the way they explicitly dissociate themselves from their own client, whose rashness and insanity is topicalized as a central theme in the debates. The legal actors appropriate and even manipulate lay ways of speaking and reasoning to indexically project a particular mental identity for their client. Moreover, the ways in which they voice their legal opinions through lay participants suggests their alignment with the jury and, in fact, with any "reasonable" citizen "tout court." In other words, their interdiscursive play adds force to their argument: not only are their own interpretations upgraded to shared commonsense ideas, their positioning work suggests an analogy between lay and expert capacities for character evaluation and in this way enables them to juxtapose or even challenge legal expert opinions with lay interpretations of evidence.

CONCLUSION

The analysis has demonstrated that even in the most formal juridical contexts, mundane conversational resources are mobilized to achieve legal-argumentative goals. The presence of both professional and lay decision makers in the Belgian assize court clearly challenged the legal actors (prosecution, defense, and civil parties) to balance between juridical and everyday forms of speaking and reasoning. First, it could be seen how seemingly authentic lay representations of trial and pretrial discourses concealed the textual, legal-bureaucratic trajectories these discourses had travelled along. The legal actors reconstructed orality from text, staunchly maintaining an illusion of objective representation—mirrored in their marked preference for verbatim quotation—while obscuring the way they were themselves deeply implicated in the interdiscursive process. This technique of seemingly verbatim enactment offered them full scope to manipulate interactive footing patterns and exploit particular meanings in their representations. Things which were not openly "sayable" in court, such as making subjective statements or deconstructing legal expert opinion, were indexically produced in reported utterances, all of which enabled the legal actors to air their preferred interpretations of the evidence without taking responsibility for what they said and how they said it. Second, seemingly transparent forms of commonsense reasoning obscured well-considered juridical categorizations of events and identities. In the data it could be seen how in their trial performance, the legal actors oriented to what was implied in their reenacted voices rather than to that which was explicitly spelled out. They could be seen to colonize commonsense opinion to selectively impose their preferred interpretations on the ambiguity of legal expert notions related to moral responsibility. This interdiscursive veil is very likely to have a powerful effect on the jury in that it enables the legal actors to topicalize transparent, commonsense scenarios of the events, but at the same time remains sufficiently implicit, so that the jury can still be attributed an active role in interpreting the facts and drawing conclusions from implicit arguments.

In other words, traditional distinctions between strictly legal and lay discursive devices, interactive footings and forms of reasoning have a tendency to fade in the Belgian Assize Court and this may have important implications for the adjudication process. Arguably, if legal actors prefer to organize their trial performance on the basis of lay analyses of the evidence and use commonsense opinion as a criterion to judge deviant social conduct, this may become problematic in multilingual and multicultural situations where the commonsense ideas of the different participants in the process diverge.

In the course of my fieldwork period, I heard many voices, including judges and prosecutors, calling for reform within the criminal justice procedure: they unanimously argued in favor of a systematic recording of police interrogations and witness hearings. Some of them advocated an increased responsibility for the presiding judge to guard against manipulative and coercive discourse practices. Further linguistic-ethnographic research of trial-by-jury processes should therefore be encouraged for it may reveal constitutive discursive mechanisms that tend to remain implicit in other legal-bureaucratic procedures.

NOTES

1. Research for this paper was made possible by the Special Research Fund (BOF, Bijzonder Onderzoeksfonds) and was conducted at the IPrA Research Centre, Antwerp University. The formulations of the basic ideas in this paper benefited greatly from discussions with Sigurd D'hondt.

2. For an elaborate discussion of the relevance of the concepts of intertextuality (Bakhtin [1953] 1981; Kristeva 1980) and entextualization (Hanks 1989; Bauman and Briggs 1990; Silverstein and Urban 1996) to the study of legal–lay communication, I refer to chapter 1 of this book.

3. Although in theory the jurors do get access to the case file as they enter the deliberation room, this file—actually a document trolley with several cardboard boxes of paperwork and other items of evidence—is too voluminous to allow for thorough examination. Prosecutors and attorneys therefore see it as one of their main tasks to point at particular details from the case file that, according to their opinion, require further inspection in the deliberation room.

4. Assize Courts are held in the cities of Antwerp, Arlon, Bruges, Brussels, Ghent, Liège, Louvain, Mons, Namur, Nivelles, and Tongres.

5. In some cases, the examining judge directs a video interrogation to be conducted (often for analysis by the psychiatrist).

6. Many scholars and legal practitioners in Belgium these days are criticizing the unmotivated character of the judgment. It is argued that this lack of motivation is at odds with the requirements of a modern judicial system. Moreover, in January 2009, the European Court of Human Rights in Strasbourg has condemned Belgium for a lack of motivation of an Assize Court verdict. Although according to Belgian criminal law, the decisions of the Assize Court are still not motivated, the judgment of the European Court will probably speed up the debates about a revision of the assize procedure.

7. Although Assize law does not provide for cross-examination, the data give evidence of an area of tension between legal directions and sociolegal practice.

8. The data presented in this chapter were collected and analyzed in the context of a research project on "Social Diversity in Legal Argumentation" (Antwerp University).

9. The strategies discussed in this chapter have been selected from a more exhaustive overview of interdiscursive devices that include both case-related and case-external sources of entextualization, involving reenactments from "crime time," as well as reports from other cases and references to the specialist literature (legal publications) and popular writings (magazines, newspapers).

REFERENCES

Bakhtin, M. [1953] 1981. *The Dialogic Imagination*. Austin: University of Texas Press.

Bauman, R. 2004. *A World of Other's Words*. London: Blackwell.

Bauman, R., and C. Briggs. 1990. Poetics and performance as critical perspectives on language and social life. *Annual Review of Anthropology* 19: 59-88.

Blommaert, J. 2005. *Discourse: A Critical Introduction*. Cambridge: Cambridge University Press.

Briggs, C. 1997. Notes on a "confession": On the construction of gender, sexuality, and violence in an infanticide case. *Pragmatics* 7(4): 519–46.

Briggs, C., and R. Bauman. 1992. Genre, intertextuality and social power. *Journal of Linguistic Anthropology* 2: 131–72.

Conley, J., and W. O' Barr. 1990. *Rules versus Relationships: The Ethnography of Legal Discourse*. Chicago: University of Chicago Press.

Cotterill, J. 2004. Collocation, connotation, and courtroom semantics: Lawyers' control of witness testimony through lexical negotiation, *Applied Linguistics* 25(4): 513–37.

Declercq, R. 2007. *Beginselen van strafrechtspleging*. Mechelen, Belgium: Kluwer.

Delmas-Marty, M., and J. R. Spencer. 2002. *European Criminal Procedures.* Cambridge: Cambridge University Press.

D'hondt, S. 2009a. Others on trial: The construction of cultural otherness in Belgian first instance criminal hearings. *Journal of Pragmatics* 41(4): 806–28.

———. 2009b. Good cops, bad cops: Intertextuality, agency, and structure in criminal trial discourse. *Research on Language & Social Interaction* 42(3): 249–75.

Ehrlich, S. 1998. The discursive reconstruction of sexual consent. *Discourse and Society* 9: 149–71.

Goffman, E. 1981. *Forms of Talk.* Oxford: Blackwell.

Hanks, W. 1989. Text and textuality. *Annual Review of Anthropology* 18: 95–127.

Jacquemet, M. 2005. Transidiomatic practices: Language and power in the age of globalization. *Language & Communication* 25: 257–77.

Komter, M. L. 1994. Accusations and defenses in courtroom interaction. *Discourse and Society* 5(2): 165–87.

Kristeva, J. 1980. *Desire in Language: A Semiotic Approach to Literature and Art.* Translated by T. Gora, A. Jardine, and L. S. Roudiez. New York: Columbia University Press.

Maryns, K. 2006. *The asylum speaker: Language in the Belgian asylum procedure.* Manchester: St. Jerome Publishing.

———. 2012. Multilingualism in legal settings. In *Routledge Handbook of Multilingualism,* ed. M. Martin-Jones, A. Blackledge, and A. Creese, 297–313. London: Routledge.

———. 2013. Procedures without borders: The language-ideological anchorage of administrative procedures in translocal institutional settings. *Language in Society* 42(1): 71–92.

Maryns, K., and J. Blommaert. 2002. Pretextuality and pretextual gaps: On de/refining linguistic inequality. *Pragmatics* 12(1): 11–30.

Matoesian, G. 1999. Intertextuality, affect, and ideology in legal discourse. *Text* 19(1): 73–109.

———. 2001. *Law and the Language of Identity: Discourse in the William Kennedy Smith Rape Trial.* Oxford: Oxford University Press.

Mertz, E. 1992. Language, law, and social meanings: Linguistic/anthropological contributions to the study of law. *Law & Society Review* 26(2): 413–45.

———. 1996. Recontextualization as socialization: Text and pragmatics in the law school classroom. In *Natural Histories of Discourse,* ed. M. Silverstein and G. Urban, 229–49. Chicago: University of Chicago Press.

Rock, F. 2007. *Communicating Rights: The Language of Arrest and Detention.* London: Palgrave Macmillan.

Scheffer, Thomas. 2006. The microformation of criminal defense: On the lawyer's notes, speech production and a field of presence. *Research and Language and Social Interaction* 39: 303–42.

Silverstein, M., and G. Urban, eds. 1996. *Natural Histories of Discourse.* Chicago: University of Chicago Press.

CHAPTER 6

Travels of a Suspect's Statement

MARTHA KOMTER

INTRODUCTION

The Dutch criminal law system is highly professionalized. Criminal cases are adjudicated by professional judges, and there are no juries (Malsch 2009). What legal–lay communication there is in the Dutch criminal law system takes place between suspects or witnesses[1] and criminal law professionals. Reports are made of many of these interactions. When a suspect is picked up and interviewed by the police or when a victim goes to the police station to press charges, their statements are written down and incorporated in what is to become the case file. These documents are subsequently dispatched to the public prosecutor, the investigating judge, the defense lawyer and the suspect, and finally to the trial judge. The public prosecutor reads these documents in order to decide on whether to prosecute. In some cases the documents are sent to the investigating judge, who is in charge of the preliminary investigations. The suspect's defense lawyer reads the case file in order to decide what line of defense to take. And finally, the trial judges read the file in order to decide how to adjudicate the case. In other words, in the process of assembling the case file, documents are drawn up and sent off to travel to many desks in different settings, to serve different ends.

The process of transformation of spoken discourse into written text has been described as *entextualization*. Entextualization refers to "the process of rendering discourse extractable, of making a stretch of linguistic production into a unit—*a text*—that can be lifted out of its interactional setting" (Bauman and Briggs 1990: 73). This entextualization involves processes of *decontextualization* and *recontextualization*. Decontextualization then refers to the extraction of a text from its original context of production; recontextualization to its subsequent insertion in a new surround through quotation, paraphrase, and so on (Bauman and Briggs 1990; Blommaert 2005).

There is a risk in describing the transportation of a text from one setting to another as if these settings "exist" independently of the activities of the participants. Such a description disregards the work the participants do in (re)creating text and context, and it undermines the analyst's ability to discern how the participants themselves exhibit which aspects of the setting are relevant (cf. Bauman and Briggs 1990; Schegloff 1987). Moreover, it has been observed that there is a reflexive relation between talk and context: people dynamically shape and reshape the contexts they are involved in, and their activities are produced and interpreted by reference to these contexts (Goodwin and Duranti 1992). Thus, the written documents produced and processed in the criminal law system provide the context for the activities they generate, but they are also products of the setting within which they operate.

In this chapter I shall analyze the process of transforming the discourse of the police interrogation into a written document that serves as "the suspect's statement" in the further criminal law process. The analysis is based on excerpts from a police interrogation and from a trial. These excerpts are selected so as to show routine features that are typical of interrogations and trials in the Netherlands.[2] The focus will be on two different stages in the process: the police interrogation and the trial, and on two different modes of production: talk and writing. I shall first describe how a suspect's statement (in a burglary case) is written down by the police to form part of the case file. I then consider the ways in which a judge draws attention to, and invokes the case file (of a robbery case) in the courtroom. The aim is to examine processes of entextualization, recontextualization, and decontextualization by showing how the relationships between talk, text, and context are managed in the interaction of professionals and suspects in the Dutch criminal law process.

THE POLICE INTERROGATION: CONSTRUCTING A DOCUMENT

In the Netherlands reports of police interrogations are drawn up contemporaneously by the interrogating officer. The interrogations are organized as talk-typing sequences, where periods of talk alternate with periods of typing. The stretches of talk consist minimally of one question-answer exchange, but usually it is a series of questions and answers that anticipates the typing (Komter 2006a). The standard style of records of police interrogations is the first-person narrative, that is, the dialogue of the interrogation has been transformed into a monologue. As the police interrogator's questions have been eliminated as questions, it becomes impossible to recognize the suspect's contributions as answers. This is the first step in the process of preparing a suspect's statement for its travels toward what is to become a legally adequate piece of evidence to be consulted and quoted in the courtroom. In the following sections I shall investigate the activities of a police interrogator and of a suspect in constructing the written text and in preparing it for its service to other professionals in later phases in the criminal law process.

Transforming Discourse into a Written Text

The interrogation discussed here is of a young man suspected of a burglary in the center of Amsterdam, during the small hours of the night. There are two participants: the police interrogator and the suspect.[3] The police interrogator starts the interview with an open question about what happened, after which the suspect states that he had been walking in the streets, cleaning his pipe, minding his own business. In the beginning the police officer listens to the suspect's story without writing anything down. After a while he starts asking more detailed questions (P is the police interrogator, S is the suspect; the bold typed text is what has been typed in the report, see note 4):

Excerpt 1

1.	P: Last night- do you remember the date?
2.	S: ((says he lost track of time))
3.	P: It's uh last <u>night</u> you were arrested,
4.	S: hm hm,
5.	P: last night it was April the 22nd, uh now too for that matter,
6.	S: ⌐Oh
7.	P: └do you remember what time it was roughly
8.	when you were walking uh in the Antoniestraat?
9.	S: U:::h no, I don't know.
10.	P: No?
11.	((types, 8 seconds))
12.	**Last night, April the 22nd 1999**[4]

The first things the police officer asks the suspect to tell him are the date (line 1) and the time (line 7) of the alleged criminal events. This excerpt shows that, as the suspect is unable or unwilling to provide the date, the police officer tells it for him (line 5) and writes it down. It is noticeable that P writes down his own words, the words he produced in response to the suspect's stated ignorance of the date.[5] One of the requirements of a police record is that it should contain the date of the events, as the public prosecutor needs to include this in the indictment to identify this particular crime. Thus, in inquiring after the suspect's memory of the date, the police interrogator anticipates his writing it down, for the benefit of future readers of the record.

After eight seconds of typing, the police officer turns his attention away from the screen to the suspect and continues:

Excerpt 2

13.	P: Uhm (3) so you came- you first went to Waterloo
14.	⌐square,
15.	S: └Well I had gone to Waterloo square
16.	P: Yes?

17. S: and then when I came back, I met that boy under under that gallery.
18. P: ((types, 17 seconds))
19. **I had been at Waterloo square.**

P resumes the interrogation after the typing by reformulating something that the suspect had told him earlier about his nocturnal activities in that area of Amsterdam. He produces it as an invitation for the suspect to continue from there. "You first went to Waterloo square" anticipates information about what the suspect did next. The suspect takes this up, first by rephrasing the police officer's suggestion (line 15), and after P's prompt "Yes?" (line 16), by telling him what happened afterwards.

If we look at the text that he writes down, it is notable that P does not write down this new information, but restricts himself to writing down the suspect's confirmation of his reformulation in line 13. As in excerpt 1, the police interrogator gets the suspect to agree on an item that needs to be included in the record: this time it is the place where the events occurred. The sentence written down now is fairly straightforward: "**Last night, April the 22nd 1999 I had been at Waterloo square.**" It is a common beginning of police records: the date is given and the stage is set for the events to be told.

The activities of the police interrogator that produced this sentence could be described as requesting information and providing the information himself when the suspect does not do so. These activities are filtered out of the written text, in that the interrogator reworks his own questions, remarks, or suggestions into the narrative.[6] It has been pointed out that there is an important difference between volunteered stories and invited stories (Watson 1990). In volunteered stories the teller controls the production of the story, whereas invited stories are to a certain extent directed at what the recipient wants, and has asked, to hear. As we have seen in the examples above, in police interrogations suspects tell invited stories. The first-person narrative style of the written statement makes it impossible for future readers of the text to reconstruct to what extent the suspect's story was volunteered or invited (cf. Jönsson and Linell 1991; Komter 2002–3).

It has been noted that questions operate conversationally as first pair parts of "adjacency pairs" that anticipate answers as their second pair parts (Schegloff and Sacks 1973); besides, they perform activities such as accusing, challenging, and so on (Atkinson and Drew 1979). Consequently, the "second pair parts" produced in response, perform the actions that go with the first pair parts, such as denying, defending, and so on. The activities discussed thus far are relatively "harmless," such as "asking for information" as first pair part, and "giving information" or "stating ignorance" as second pair part of the adjacency pair. When the interrogator resumes the talk after his writing, things change a little:

Excerpt 3

20. P: You said you had to clean your pipe?

21.	S: Yes I went to clean my pipe.
22.	P: ((types, 2 seconds))
23.	**I went**
24.	P: And what kind of pipe is that?
25.	S: Uhm
26.	P: Yes that's a silly question perhaps
27.	S: ⌐but
28.	└Well you- it's just uh it's a pipe that I bought
29.	P: ⌐in the area
30.	└yes,
31.	S: In a shop here.
32.	P: Yes
33.	S: ⌐and what do you call that pipe?
34.	└in Damstreet.

P recapitulates something that the suspect has told him earlier about clean-ing his pipe and marks that by quoting him ("you said," line 20). The suspect confirms this with a modification: "had to clean" becomes "went to clean." The police officer starts typing, but almost immediately interrupts his writing and asks for more information about the pipe (line 24). When the suspect replies with a hesitation marker "uhm" the police officer produces what looks like an apology ("silly question," line 26). Then the suspect provides a noncommit-tal answer ("just a pipe that I bought," line 28). Although this answer gradu-ally becomes more specific ("in the area," line 29; "in a shop here," line 31; "in Damstreet," line 34), it avoids addressing what the interrogator asked for. The interrogator's dissatisfaction with this answer is made clear by his rephrasing the question (line 33).

The interrogator's remark about the "silly question" can be understood when we take into account the shared knowledge of the two men. Policemen know that young men who roam the streets of Amsterdam in this area, at this time of night, are prob-ably drug users. They are also familiar with the paraphernalia of drug use (hash pipe). And drug users know that policemen have this knowledge. So the question is "silly" because both know that the police officer asks a question to which he already knows the answer. Moreover, the policeman's knowledge of the answer implies that he would not ask this question if it were not for the fact that its answer may be relevant for inclu-sion in the record. The police officer's description of the question as "silly" conveys that he distances himself from it and suggests that he is only doing his job, which is to be explicit in order to meet legal standards (cf. Stokoe and Edwards 2008).

The suspect's reluctance to be specific, and the interrogator's pursuit of the answer, may be related to the possible risks for the suspect of providing this kind of information. Although the suspect is not accused of dealing drugs, his habit may be relevant for explaining the burglary that he is accused of (and denies). The inter-rogator's second attempt to get a satisfactory answer succeeds:

Excerpt 4

32.	P: Yes
33.	⌜and what do you call that pipe?
34.	S: ⌞in Damstreet.
35.	Uhm hash pipe.
36.	P: ((with an Amsterdam accent)) Hash pipey yes.
37.	((laughs))
38.	S: ((laughs))
39.	P: Yes
40.	((types, 4 seconds))
41.	**to clean my hash pipe.**

In rephrasing the suspect's answer as a diminutive[7] with an Amsterdam accent (line 36), the interrogator indicates that he is as streetwise as the suspect. His laughter adds a note of alignment and mutuality, and defuses some of the potential tension involved in the admission to smoking drugs. The suspect honors this by joining in with the laughter.

Excerpts 3 and 4 illustrate another consequence of the deletion of the interviewer's questions in the record: it conceals the kind of activities that the questions and answers performed. The recorded sentence: "**I went to clean my hash pipe**" gives no information at all about the work the policeman put into the interrogation to prompt the answer or about the suspect's evasiveness. Thus, the professionals who get to read this sentence in the record remain ignorant not only of the questions and answers that produced this sentence but also of the insistence with which the police officer overcame the suspect's reluctance to answer.

The interrogation continues:

Excerpt 5

42.	P: Okay. U:::hm
43.	((reads from screen))
44.	"Last night, April the 22nd 1999. I was at Waterloo square. I went to clean my hash pipe."
45.	You didn't remember what time it was right?
46.	S: (No I don't)
47.	P: ((types, 8 seconds))
48.	**What it was I don't remember.**

P reads to the suspect what he has written down thus far about the date, the place, and the suspect's activities. This text is then used as a "stepping-stone" for asking the next question (cf. Komter 2006a).[8] This question (line 45) picks up on an exchange they had earlier (see excerpt 1, lines 7–10) about the time of the events. This, again, points to the fact that the record is drawn up with a view to its future readers. It can be noted that, when recording the exchange, the police interrogator forgets to write the word "time" in "what it was I don't remember." This will be looked into in the next section.

Printing and Correcting the Text

Until now, the "document under construction" has been a "virtual" reality, a growing text on the screen, visible only to the police interrogator. A sign that the interrogation is finished is the police officer's announcement that he is going to print the text:

Excerpt 6

1.   P: I'm going to print it,
2.   S: Yes that's okay.
3.   P: Then you can just read it through,
4.   then I'll just go through the report to see if there are any mistakes.
5.   ((walks away, comes back with two sheets of paper))
6.   P: Just read it through, if it's all right just tell me, (3)
7.   then I'll print it out correctly.
8.   S: ((reads, 18 seconds))

Before going away to fetch the printed report, the police officer announces that the suspect can "just read it through" (line 3), and expresses his intention to "see if there are any mistakes" (line 4). He specifies the conditions for how the text should be understood (Blommaert 2008), by prospectively defining the printed document as something that may contain mistakes. When he comes back with the two pages of printed text, he again invites the suspect to "just read it through" and asks the suspect to tell him "if it's all right" (line 6). Thus, besides inviting the suspect to read the report, he also indicates that the report should be read for its accuracy and correctness. As it happens, the suspect spots a mistake:

Excerpt 7

9.   S: What do you mean (here with) uh
10.   "I went to clean my hash pipe. What it was I don't remember."
11.   P: That is one of the mistakes.
12.   What <u>time</u> it was.
13.   I'm going to ⌜change it now.
14.   S: ⌞Oh what time it was yes ((laughs)) (2)
15.   P: I'm going to do it now.
16.   ((types))

After P has printed the corrected version, he gives it to the suspect and asks him again to read it. He also announces that he has added some details about the location of the criminal events to prevent misunderstandings. S takes a cursory look at the report and says it is all right.

The printing of the police record retrospectively identifies the suspect's statement as "complete" and the interrogation as concluded. It transforms the text-under-construction into a material object and "fixes" the document as a completed piece of evidence. The "reading instructions" that the police officer gives the suspect focus the attention on the correctness and accuracy of the document. As the printing of the document changes a virtual text into a material object, it becomes physically "detachable" from its setting (Bauman and Briggs 1990). This prospectively enables the police officer, and other professionals of the criminal law process, to ship it off to other desks and other places.

Signing the Text

After the suspect has professed his agreement with the text of the record, the police officer asks him to sign it:

Excerpt 8

1.   P: Okay.
2.   If you could then (2) uh put your initials or sign here,
3.   and sign <u>there</u>.
4.   Yes?
5.   S: ((signs))

The document consists of two pages. The suspect has to sign or put initials on the first page, and sign his name at the bottom of the second page, underneath the following sentence:

"After the suspect read his statement, he persisted in it and signed it."

This is a standard text, already written down in the record. Its counterpart is the opening sentence of the record: "After I informed the suspect that he was not obliged to answer questions and about what I wished to hear him, he stated to me the following." These sentences frame the suspect's statement, in that they are formulated from the perspective of the policeman, so that the "I" refers to the police officer, and the "he" to the suspect. The suspect's statement is told as a first-person narrative within this frame (a story-within-a-story). In this last sentence the suspect is again described in the third person. Thus, the end of the suspect's statement is marked by the police officer resuming "authorship" of the text by abandoning the first-person narrative style.

When we compare this last sentence with the events in the interrogation, it is clear that it is not a description of what actually happened. If that were the case, the text would have said: "After the suspect read his statement, he corrected a mistake and signed it." The phrase "he persisted in it" suggests interaction because people only persist in their position after it has been challenged. It reveals two possible readings of the document: first it casts the suspect's statement as potentially contestable, and second, it makes the suspect accountable for this text, instead of the police officer. In signing the document, the suspect takes responsibility for his statement: he assumes authorship of the first-person monologue in that, from now on, the "I" of the suspect's statement, for all practical purposes, becomes his voice.

The Text and the Talk

In order to get an overview of the differences between what was said and what was written down, let us compare the two. The left column is what the police interrogator said, the right column shows what the suspect said in response to that, and underneath is the text of the record:

Excerpt 9

P: Last night- do you remember the date?   S: ((says he lost track of time))
   It's uh last <u>night</u> you were arrested,   hm hm,
   Last night it was April the 22nd,
   uh now too for that matter,   Oh
   do you remember what time it was roughly
   when you were walking uh in the Antoniestraat?   U:::h no, I don't know
   No?
   Uhm (3) so you came-
   you first went to Waterloo square   Well I had gone to Waterloo
                                                       square
   Yes?   And then when I came back,
                                                       I met that boy under under
                                                       that gallery

   You said you had to clean your pipe?   Yes I went to clean my pipe
   And what kind of pipe is that?   Uhm
   Yes that's a silly question perhaps but   Well you- it's just uh it's a pipe
                                                       that I bought in the area.
   yes,   In a shop here.
   Yes   In Damstreet.
   and what do you call that pipe?   Uhm hash pipe.
   Hash pipey yes. ((laughs))   ((laughs))
   Yes.

Okay. U::::hm
"Last night, April the 22nd 1999 I had been
at Waterloo square. I went to clean my hash pipe"
You didn't remember what time it was right?   (No I don't)

Last night, April the 22nd I had been at Waterloo square. I went to clean my hash pipe. What time it was I don't remember.

Processes of de- and recontextualization can here be seen at a glance, especially when comparing the suspect's talk with the written record. The interactional organization of the interrogation has been removed from the written text. The suspect's answers and the interrogator's questions have been recast as a first-person narrative. All the information written down is told at the request of, or by the police officer, but presented as if volunteered by the suspect. The items volunteered by the suspect about meeting a boy under the gallery, and about where he bought his pipe, are not recorded.[9] These practices are routine features of Dutch police interrogations.

Summary

The talk in the police interrogation is to a large extent oriented to anticipating the recording of it in the police report, and the text of the police report anticipates its being read by the professionals in the further criminal law process. The text that the interrogator writes down in his report conceals the interactional basis of the interrogation. As a result, the suspect's statement appears to be volunteered and the activities of the police interrogator are filtered out of the text. The first-person narrative style attributes authorship of the text to the suspect, and this is confirmed by his signing of the report. The printing of the text and the signing of the document make the suspect's statement "travel-ready" to be shipped off to its various destinations. The text is prepared to function independently of the circumstances of its construction.

THE TRIAL: INVOKING THE CASE FILE

What is immediately noticeable in Dutch courtrooms is the prominent role of the case file. Judges, public prosecutors, and defense lawyers have documents and stacks of papers in front of them, which they frequently consult and refer to (cf. Komter 1998).[10] Defense lawyers inform their clients before the trial of the contents of the case file, but suspects have no copy of the documents in front of them during the trial. The management of case documents is a matter for the professionals in the courtroom.

An important legal requirement is that judges must bring up in the trial those evidentiary exhibits that they will later base their verdict on. In practice this means that judges read or summarize those items from the case file that they expect they may need for their ruling. These items are typically brought up in the course of the judge's examination of the suspect.[11] As has been shown before, judges treat police records of the suspects' statements as genuine representations of what the suspect actually told the police (Komter 2002). Indeed, the first-person narrative style of police records appears to invite this interpretation.

Part of the "recontextualization work" of bringing to life written documents in the courtroom is in introducing these documents and in showing how they are useful for the management of the trial, for directing attention to how to read them, and for exhibiting how the judges themselves have read them (cf. Goodwin 1994). In the following sections I shall point out the significance of the case file for organizing the trial and discuss how the judges bring the case file to life in the courtroom.

Organizing the Trial

The examples to be discussed here are from a case of robbery. The suspect, a drug addict, is accused of having stolen money from a woman during a drug deal. He and his accomplice allegedly grabbed the woman, unzipped her jeans, and took the money from her underpants. The suspect initially denied guilt to the police, but confessed later when he was questioned by the investigating judge. His accomplice not only continued to deny but also, when they were in custody, threatened to kill the suspect if he told on him in court.

The presiding judge (the court consists of a panel of three judges) starts the questioning of the suspect as follows:

Excerpt 10

1. J: Uhm mr Rutten,
2. the court has come across in the case file
3. of this case that has been documented, uhm (2)
4. stories and statements that (1)
5. don't always coincide.
6. Your own stories too are rather inconsistent.
7. You remember that.
8. I think it is best,
9. before going over the files with you,
10. that you yourself just tell us once more
11. what according to you happened then.

In these first moments of the examination of the suspect the judge refers to the existence and contents of the case file as a way to formulate who they (the panel of three judges) are, what they have been doing, and what kind of problems are to be solved. The case file is presented both as a source of information for the court and as an instrument for the organization of the trial. The judge indicates what kind of information it contains ("stories and statements"), what he is going to do with it ("going over the files with you"), and how he thinks it is best to proceed (first the suspect's version, then the files). In doing this, he not only describes the courtroom setting, but at the same time (re)creates it. The activities of the judge here illuminate the reflexivity of context: references to the case file explicate the setting and at the same time provide the context for activities to come.

Organizing Perception

For a more detailed analysis of the judge's activities, let us consider excerpt 10 again:

Excerpt 11

1.	J: Uhm Mr Rutten,
2.	the court has come across in the case file
3.	of this case that has been documented, uhm (2)
4.	stories and statements that (1)
5.	don't always coincide.
6.	Your own stories too are rather inconsistent.
7.	You remember that.

The presiding judge introduces himself (line 2) as spokesman of "the court" (the panel of three judges), thereby highlighting his professional and institutional identity. Through his explication of the case file as the court's source of knowledge, he underlines the official, authoritative nature of the information and, by implication, the neutrality of the court. His lexical choice "come across" (line 2) suggests that the court has not been searching the case file for specific information, but that this information just presented itself to them: the judges let the case file speak for itself. The judge continues (line 3) by mentioning things that he must take it that everybody knows (that it concerns "this case" and that it has been documented). This frames the occasion as formal and official.[12] Next, the judge identifies what it is that the court has come across in the files (stories and statements). From this it can be inferred that some pieces of the evidence (statements) are deemed more reliable than others (stories).

After a general introduction about the kind of information the court has come upon ("stories and statements," line 4), and the problems they contain ("don't always coincide," line 5), the judge comes to the point: the suspect's inconsistent statements. It is assumed, when statements "don't coincide," that some of them may be true, but they cannot all be true (Pollner 1987). When the suspect tells inconsistent stories, he is bound to be a liar on at least some issues (Shuy 1998). It is notable that in referring to the suspect's testimony the judge chooses the term "stories" rather than "statements" (line 6), which shows his doubts about the veracity of the suspect's statements. The judge concludes by referring to the suspect's memory of his inconsistent stories (line 7). It is presented as undisputed and treats the suspect as fully aware of the inconsistent positions he took in the interviews with the police and the investigating judge.

In sum, in the opening lines of his examination of the suspect (lines 1–7) the judge has identified a problem (stories and statements that don't always coincide) and narrowed this problem down as a problem of the suspect (the suspect's inconsistent stories). In highlighting or foregrounding these features of the case file, the judge displays how he has read the file and directs the perception of others toward this "professional vision" (Goodwin 1994).

The continuation shows how this is made relevant for the organization of the trial:

Excerpt 12

6. J: Your own stories too are rather inconsistent.
7.   You remember that.
8.   I think it is best,
9.   before going over the files with you,
10. that you yourself just tell us once more
11. what according to you happened then.
12. You know what it is about, from the indictment.

Up to this point the judge has been describing his problems with the case file, which now turn out to be a resource for organizing the interaction: first the suspect is given the opportunity to clear up his own inconsistencies, then they will discuss the case file. The judge's description of the activities to come ("going over the files with you," line 9) suggests that these activities consist of a sort of "co-reading" of the information to be considered. The judge shows himself to be neutral rather than adversarial, and the business to be done as a collaborative enterprise, rather than as a one-sided or adversarial affair (Komter 1998).

The judge's proposition "just tell us once more" (line 10) refers to the circumstance that suspects tell their stories many times in the course of the criminal law process and that, as the case file contains the records of these tellings, the judges already know their contents. The emphasis on "you" (line 11) illuminates the perceived subjectivity of the suspect's story. The judge does not ask to be told what happened, but what the suspect's version of it is. He invites the suspect to tell his version of the story, while showing that he knows that there are more.

"You know what it is about" (line 12) resonates with "you remember that" in line 7. The suspect's knowing and remembering is attended to. The fact that the judge explicates the source of the suspect's knowledge (the indictment) shows that he does not so much appeal to the suspect's memory and knowledge of "what happened," but rather to his memory of the statements he made and to his knowledge of the case file. The utterance shows that the judge prospectively organizes the way in which the suspect is to tell his story: as a legally relevant one, relating to the charges as written down in the indictment.[13]

The suspect responds:

Excerpt 13

> 13. S: It happened exactly as I told the invasti- investigating judge. (2)
> 14. J: Yes,
> 15. S: As for the rest I have nothing to add.

The suspect shows that he understood the judge's instructions on how to answer his question: he does not tell directly what happened, but what happened according to his statement to the investigating judge (line 13).[14] After his answer there is a two seconds' pause followed by a continuer "Yes" produced by the judge. This can be heard as an invitation to elaborate on his answer, for example, to tell the judge what he told the investigating judge. In response to this, the suspect states that he has nothing to add (perhaps because he does not want to answer questions about the identity of his accomplice). Although the suspect refers to what he told the investigating judge, the understanding is that this is identical with the written statement drawn up from the interview and included as piece of evidence in the case file.

Animating a Text

When the suspect has clarified his trial position (nothing to add to his earlier statement), the judge embarks on the next topic:

Excerpt 14

> 15. S: As for the rest I have nothing to add.
> 16. J: Shall I then read out to you a summary of that once more?
> 17. S: Yes.
> 18. J: Uh as far as it is relevant here,
> 19.   and if counsel stops having a chat with you,
> 20.   you have stated there,
> 21.   **"It is correct that on the 11th of March 1990 in Utrecht I robbed a girl together with someone else whose name I do not want to mention. I grabbed that girl and my accomplice snatched that money from her underpants"**

The judge responds to the suspect's assertion that he has nothing to add by proposing to proceed with the next item on the agenda as announced previously ("going over the files with you" excerpt 10, line 9). His proposal "Shall I then read out a summary of that" (line 16) can then be heard as a rephrasing of this earlier announcement.

What is noticeable are the deictic expressions "here" (line 18) and "there" (line 20). These illustrate in the first place the actual point of view of the judge ("here") and second, they exhibit the trajectory of a piece of text from one setting ("there") to the other ("here"). "Here" is obviously the courtroom where the judge is going to read something out of the case file that was constructed "there," in the office of the investigating judge. The judge's qualification "as far as it is relevant here" refers not just to the location (the courtroom) but also to the specific business to be conducted in the courtroom. It prospectively justifies his reading and directs the attention of the recipients to the fact that what he is about to read is legally relevant.

The judge's utterance "you have stated there" (line 20) corresponds with the suspect's earlier utterance "...I told the...investigating judge" (excerpt 13, line 13) and treats the record of the suspect's statement as straightforward representation of what he actually said in the interrogation (Eades 2008, 2010; Komter 2002; Matoesian 2000). As has been pointed out previously, the suspects' written (first-person narrative) statements are transformations of the interaction that produced the suspect's testimony and are quite different from what the suspect actually said. As the utterance "you have stated there" precedes a direct quotation from the case file, it makes no distinction between the original spoken interaction in the investigating judge's office and its written representation.

When the judge starts reading he adopts a "reading voice." Although he has announced that he is going to read a summary of the suspect's statement, the wording of his utterance reveals that he quotes literally from the text in front of him. There is no confusion as to the referent of the personal pronoun "I": it is the suspect, not the judge. The judge is merely "animating" a text whose "author" is assumed to be the suspect (Goffman 1981).[15] The suspect is treated as the "author" of this text in spite of its stilted style: "It is correct that" is not a likely beginning of a volunteered story. Yet, for all practical purposes this does not appear to matter. If we reconsider the description of the suspect signing his statement at the police station, its consequences are here revealed: the suspect has accepted that he is the author of a document drawn up and edited by someone else, and this is what he will be during the rest of the criminal law process.

Summary

In the beginning of the trial the presiding judge introduces the case file as the document around which the events will be organized. His treatment of the case file explicates the setting, that is, it reveals who the judges are, what they are doing, and what kind of business is on the agenda. In highlighting some features of the case file (inconsistencies), he structures the perception, not only of the suspect, but of all those present in the courtroom. Besides, the judge's references to the case file instruct the suspect as to what is relevant for the telling of his story. Neither the judge nor the suspect make a distinction between what the suspect told the investigating judge, and what has been recorded in the case file, that is, between the original discourse and the report of it.

DISCUSSION: ENTEXTUALIZATION PROCESSES

In this chapter processes of de- and recontextualization have been described in terms of the resources that participants draw on in interaction (cf. Pomerantz 1998). Staying with the terminology of *entextualization* discussed before (Bauman and Briggs 1990), you could say that I have examined how the police record has been extracted from its original context of production (the interaction in the police interrogating room), and then inserted in a new surround (the trial) through quotation, paraphrase, and so on. Moreover, I have also observed that the police record is indeed constructed with a view to the future settings in which it is expected to operate; and I have shown that the trial is not just a "surround" in which the police report is quoted, but that the police report is an integral part of the activities in the trial. This has revealed that the participants' actions are doubly contextual. Each action is context-shaped in that it is produced and understood by reference to the environment in which it operates; each action is context-renewing in that it forms the context on the basis of which next actions are produced and interpreted (Heritage 1984).

I have discussed how a suspect's statement to the police was elicited in interaction and reconstructed as a written document. The entextualization process involved in this transformation is not limited to the process of writing down a text on the basis of what is said, but it can be seen in the whole organization of the interrogation. The police interrogation is to a significant extent organized to be written down. The police officer asks those questions that are meant to produce "recordable" and legally relevant answers, and the record is written so as to meet the perceived needs of the professionals in the further criminal law process (Komter 2002–3; see also Haket 2007). In short, the talk anticipates the writing, and the writing anticipates its future use. The talk is transformed in such a way that the resulting text is assumed to be understandable without the contextual knowledge about the original interaction. The written text is meant to stand on its own and is constructed so as to operate independently of its construction. It is made "travel-ready" to be moved to different places, at different times, and in anticipation of different interactional constellations. Perhaps we could coin the term "precontextualization" to describe how the police officer's activities exhibit an orientation to possible future contexts of the written report.

In discussing processes of decontextualization and recontextualization I have focused on what features of the context are taken away in processes of decontextualization, and on what features of context are added in processes of recontextualization. Different types of decontextualization and recontextualization have been distinguished in the activities in the police interrogating room. I have shown how a text is decontextualized by filtering out the interrogator's questions, comments, or suggestions, and how this blurs the distinction between the suspect's volunteered contributions and his responses. A consequence of this is the disappearance from the written text of the actions that the police interrogator and the suspect performed with their questions and answers, such as challenges and evasions. This decontextualization entails a recontextualization in that the interrogator transforms the talk into writing and fashions the interaction as a coherent story. He transforms the interaction into a first-person narrative and incorporates his original questions in the text as part of the suspect's story. The suspect is presented as producing complete sentences put together as a legally relevant story. The first-person narrative reads as if the suspect has volunteered the story, casting the suspect as an active person who decides what to tell and how to tell it. Without the knowledge of the interaction lying behind the written text, this can engender inferences of communicativeness and, to some extent, cooperation of the suspect. These types of de- and recontextualizations are associated with the isolation of the talk from its interactional embedding and with the introduction of narrative coherence and legal relevance into the report.

The final activities in the interrogation show another kind of recontextualization of the written report. These activities exhibit subtle ways of reorganizing the suspect's involvement in his case as a witness to and an accomplice in the construction of his statement. The suspect is offered a document for "correction," that is, he gets the opportunity to put forward corrections or alterations, thus characterizing the document as something of which "correctness" is important, and that can be "repaired" accordingly. He is instructed on how to read his statement and implicitly informed of what is relevant for the professionals in the further criminal law process. The invitation to read and sign the document transforms the suspect from a teller of an invited story into an author of a written text, who will be accountable for this text in the further stages of the criminal law process.

Once the case file has reached the courtroom, other types of recontextualization can be observed. First, the case file is taken as a basis for organizing the trial. The dependence of the judges on the case file for their structuring activities renders their activities transparent for the other professionals in the courtroom and lends the court an air of professionalism and objectivity. Next, when reading from the case file, the judge treats the written text as a straightforward representation of what the suspect has actually said in earlier interviews. The first-person narrative style of the suspect's written statements contributes to this stance, as it camouflages the input of the interrogators in previous stages of the criminal law process.

References to the information in the case documents in the courtroom show how the judge is handling the case, how he reads the dossier, how he guides the attention of others as to the salient features of the case file, and by implication, how he construes his professional and institutional identity. Thereby the judge directs the attention to the kind of setting this is and to the kind of work that is to be done.

These activities can be taken as implicit instructions for the suspect (comparable with those of the police earlier in the criminal law process) on how to tell his story, how to read his statement, and how to equate his talk in the police interrogating room with his written statement. In this respect, in the course of his "career" in the criminal law process, the suspect is progressively "protoprofessionalized" as a more or less competent player in the field.

ACKNOWLEDGMENTS

I would like to thank Tom Koole, Marijke Malsch, Wilbert Spooren, and Hedwig Te Molder for their insightful comments on earlier versions of this chapter.

NOTES

1. In the Dutch criminal law system, there is an important difference between suspects and witnesses. Suspects cannot be expected to incriminate themselves, that is, suspects are not required to answer questions or to swear an oath that they speak the truth, whereas witnesses are.

2. The materials are taken from a corpus of 20 audio-taped police interrogations and the records made of these interrogations, and of 31 audio-taped trials. Unfortunately, the materials collected for our current research program "Intertextuality in Judicial Settings" are as yet unavailable. Eventually these are meant to follow the "career" of the suspect's utterances from the police station to the courtroom.

3. In the Netherlands the absence of a legal representative for the suspect in police interrogations is a point of discussion. At this moment there are proposals to allow suspects to bring their lawyers to the interview.

4. Transcription conventions: The transcriptions include the talk and the text that was typed at the moment in which it was typed. Although I have no video-recordings of the interrogator working on his screen, a comparison between the completed records, the transcriptions of the interrogations, and the length of the typing activities, enabled me to reconstruct what was written at what moment in the interrogation. The transcription conventions depart from the standard Jeffersonian transcript notation for reasons of readability and because the excerpts are translated from Dutch. The names have been changed. The text that is written down in the record is presented in bold typeface.

P	police interrogator
S	suspect
J	judge
full stop.	falling intonation

comma,	slightly rising intonation
question mark?	rising intonation
"quotation marks"	quotation intonation
underlining	emphasis
square brackets	overlap
(3)	pause of three seconds etc.
:::	prolongation of previous sound
(single brackets)	uncertain hearing
((double brackets))	note of transcriber

5. Whereas the law requires that the suspect's statement should contain as much as possible "the suspect's own words" (cf. Komter 2002).

6. Policemen are aware of the fact that their activities are absent from the records. In order to ensure their visibility they sometimes process their activities into the records. In doing this they maintain the routine first-person narrative style, which results in somewhat artificial constructions in the police records, which I have called: "recontextualization phrases" (Komter 2006b). An example of this can be seen in the following excerpt from a police record: "About the shoplifting I state the following. This afternoon I went to the Store in order to commit shoplifting. You tell me that that was at around 14.40 hrs. That is possible." Thus, "recontextualization phrases" in police records are descriptions of speech activities (mostly "asking" or "telling") that are phrased as part of the suspect's narrative.

7. In Dutch: Hashpijpie. Diminutives are used frequently in Dutch not just to draw attention to the small size of an object, but to add a sense of harmlessness, tenderness, or charm to the description.

8. Note that this resembles the way in which police reports are brought up by the judge in the courtroom.

9. It is obvious that the written statement does not meet with the legal injunction that it should be written down as much as possible in "the suspect's own words." It is not my intention to set up an ironic contrast between the law and the police practice. However, it has been suggested that the combination of the lack of transparency of police reports, their importance for the criminal law process, and the absence of a solicitor, makes the police interrogation a risky event (Buruma 1999).

10. The case file contains a great diversity of documents: the personal details of suspects and witnesses, the indictment, reports of police activities, written statements of suspects and witnesses to the police and to the investigating judge, reports of expert witnesses, other pieces of evidence (such as photographs, letters, situation sketches, etc.), reports of the suspect's custodial situation, psychiatric reports on the suspect's state of mind, the suspect's criminal records, and so on.

11. As witnesses are not very often summoned to appear in Dutch courts, these examinations are the most important "truthfinding" activities of Dutch judges at trial (cf. Komter and Malsch 2012).

12. It is not uncommon in openings of interaction in institutional settings that the chairperson introduces the occasion by pointing out facts and circumstances that everyone knows already (Komter 1986).

13. The influence of the indictment on the criminal law process, as the basis of the trial, had been called "the tyranny of the indictment" (Melai 1975).

14. The reports of the suspects' questioning by the investigating judge are drawn up in the same manner as those of the police, as first-person narratives

15. Speakers may draw the attention to their involvement in the events as animators, authors, and principals. The animator is the speaker who utters words and sentences; the author

is the speaker who is seen as originator of the text; and the principal is the speaker whose viewpoint or position is being expressed (Goffman 1981).

REFERENCES

Atkinson, J. M., and P. Drew. 1979. *Order in court: The organisation of verbal interaction in judicial settings*. London: Macmillan.

Bauman, R., and C. L. Briggs. 1990. Poetics and performance as critical perspectives on language and social life. *Annual Review of Anthropology* 19: 59–88.

Blommaert, J. 2005. *Discourse: Key Topics in Sociolinguistics*. Cambridge: Cambridge University Press.

———. 2008. Context is/as critique. *Critique of Anthropology* 21(1): 13–32.

Buruma, Y. 1999. Formele bevoegdheden [Formal authority]. In *Politie: Studies over haar werking en organisatie [Police: Studies on its operation and organization]*, ed. C. J. C. F. Fijnaut et al., 317–50. Alphen a/d Rijn, The Netherlands: Samson.

Eades, D. 2008. *Courtroom Talk and Neocolonial Control*. New York: Mouton de Gruyter.

———. 2010. *Sociolinguistics and the Legal Process*. Bristol: Multilingual Matters.

Goffman, E. 1981. Footing. In *Forms of Talk*, 124–59. Oxford: Basil Blackwell.

Goodwin, C. 1994. Professional vision. *American Anthropologist* 96(3): 606–33.

Goodwin, C., and A. Duranti. 1992. Rethinking context: An introduction. In *Rethinking Context: Language as an Interactive Phenomenon*, ed. Charles Goodwin and Alessandro Duranti, 1–42. Cambridge: Cambridge University Press.

Haket, V. 2007. *Veranderende verhalen in het strafrecht: De ontwikkeling van verhalen over verkrachting in het strafproces. [Changing stories in criminal law: The development of rape stories in the criminal law process]*. Dissertation, Nederlands Studiecentrum voor Criminaliteit en Rechtshandhaving.

Heritage, J. 1984. *Garfinkel and Ethnomethodology*. Cambridge: Polity Press.

Jönsson, L., and P. Linell. 1991. Story generations: From dialogical interviews to written reports in police interrogations. *Text* 11(3): 419–40.

Komter, M. L. 1986. Token up-dates: The reiteration of mutual knowledge in the opening stages of job interviews. *Human Studies: A Journal for Philosophy and the Social Sciences. Special edition: Interaction and Language Use*, 247–59.

———. 1998. *Dilemma's in the Courtroom: A Study of Trials of Violent Crime in the Netherlands*. Hillsdale, NJ: Lawrence Erlbaum Associates.

———. 2002. The suspect's own words: The treatment of written statements in Dutch courtrooms. *Forensic Linguistics: The International Journal of Speech, Language and the Law* 9(2): 168–92.

———. 2002–3. The construction of records in Dutch police interrogations. *Information Design Journal + Document Design* 11(2–3): 201–13.

———. 2006a. From talk to text: The interactional construction of a police record. *Research on Language and Social Interaction* 39(3): 201–28.

———. 2006b. The interactional antecedents of "recontextualisation phrases" in police records of suspect interrogations. Paper presented at the International Conference on Conversation Analysis (ICCA-06), Helsinki.

Komter, M. L., and M. Malsch. 2012. The language of criminal trials in an inquisitorial system: The case of the Netherlands. In *The Oxford Handbook of Language and the Law*, ed. P. Tiersma and L. Solan. Oxford: Oxford University Press.

Malsch, M. 2009. *Democracy in the Courts: Lay Participation in European Criminal Justice Systems*. Aldershot: Ashgate.

Matoesian, G. 2000. Intertextual authority in reported speech: Production media in the Kennedy Smith rape trial. *Journal of Pragmatics* 32: 879–914.

Melai, A. L. 1975. *De tyrannie van de telastlegging [The tyranny of the indictment]*. Amsterdam: Panholzer.

Pollner, M. 1987. *Mundane Reason: Reality in Everyday and Sociological Discourse*. Cambridge: Cambridge University Press.

Pomerantz, A. 1998. Multiple interpretations of context: How are they useful? *Research on Language and Social Interaction* 31(1): 123–32.

Schegloff, E. A. 1987. Between macro and micro: Contexts and other connections. In *The Micro-Macro Link*, ed. Jeffrey Alexander et al., 207–34. Berkeley: University of California Press.

Schegloff, E., and H. Sacks. 1973. Opening up closings. *Semiotica* 7: 289–327.

Shuy, R. 1998. *The Language of Confession, Interrogation and Deception*. London: Sage.

Stokoe, E., and D. Edwards. 2008. "Did you have permission to smash your neighbour's door?" Silly questions and their answers in police-suspect interrogations. *Discourse Studies* 10(1): 89–111.

Watson, D. R. 1990. Some features of the elicitation of confessions in murder interrogations. In *Interaction Competence*, ed. George Psathas, 263–95. Washington, DC: University Press of America.

CHAPTER 7

Embedding Police Interviews in the Prosecution Case in the Shipman Trial

ALISON JOHNSON

INTRODUCTION

Criminal murder trials originate in events which can be as simple as a single blow from which a man dies or as complex as a deliberate or premeditated series of murderous acts. The jury in Doctor Harold Shipman's trial in 1999 and 2000 found him guilty of the latter: killing 15 of his patients and forging the will of one of them. This chapter examines the police interview texts which arise from the physical events of these deaths, events which are situated in social time and space and which become entextualized in speech and writing within the institutional contexts of the police investigation and the trial as they become textual stories (Cotterill 2003), elicited in fragments and selectively quoted in barristers' opening speeches, read by the jury, read out and re-enacted in court, and then reported in the media via daily court reporting. Thus, we have what Rock (2007: 36) calls a "temporal intertextual chain" in which texts are referenced, repeated, embedded, and transformed as they travel across time.

In this chapter I focus on the trial of Harold Shipman (available online from: http://webarchive.nationalarchives.gov.uk/20090619142823/http://www.the-shipman-inquiry.org.uk/trialtrans.asp) looking at and examining the prosecution case and its references to a series of police interviews, chiefly: the prosecution opening speech (days 2 and 3), the appearances of the police interviewers as Crown witnesses (days 23 and 24), and the prosecution closing speech (days 40 and 41). I also refer briefly to Shipman's cross-examination (days 32 to 38), to the judge's summing-up (days 43 to 53), and to the press coverage at the time of the trial. Throughout the 26 days of the prosecution case, the defendant, Shipman, is present, but not yet a speaking participant, other than to make his plea of "not guilty" in relation to the charges, taking the witness stand only on day 27 at the beginning of the defense case. His words prior to this physical appearance are therefore embodied by others and carried into the courtroom as objects, as the transcripts, extracts from them, and an enactment of the transcripts are substituted for him in the prosecution case. The process of embedding is seen to mobilize additional resources for meaning making (Goffman 1981; Iedema 1999; Sarangi and Brookes-Howell 2006), as his words are reshaped in and by the different context.

EMBEDDING, RECONTEXTUALIZATION, AND INTERTEXTUALITY

There is some overlap between these terms and their use, so it is useful to define and separate them. I use the word "embedding" to refer to a specific activity—the insertion (Bal 1981) of text within a text—within the larger process of recontextualization. This view acknowledges Genette's (1980) theory of embedding which draws on the classical concept of narrative diegesis, proposing a level of metadiegesis or hypodiegesis where we have story about story or story embedded in story. We will examine two embedding phenomena in the trial: embedding of speech within speech (direct and indirect reported speech) largely seen in the monologic genres of opening and closing speeches and the judge's summing-up; and embedding police interviews (long stretches of dyadic interaction) within the dialogic genre of examination-in-chief and to a lesser extent in the summing-up.

Recent theorizing of text and context in institutional and professional interaction has given sustained attention to processes of recontextualization (Blackledge 2006; Hodges 2008; Iedema and Wodak 1999; Iedema 1999; Johnson 2008; Linell 1998; Sarangi 1998; Vincent and Perrin 1999; Wodak 2007). Sarangi and Brookes-Howell (2006: 6) define it briefly as "how prior talk, text and context are reproduced and transformed in dynamic, dialogic fashion with consequences for meaning making." We shall see that embedding reported speech is a highly selective and thus powerful resource of reproduction, which "favours the professional perspective" (6). Recontextualizing practices incorporate temporal and spatial aspects of context and these are signaled through the use of tense shifts and deictic expressions such as "this," "that," "these," "those," which foreground current time and space (the courtroom) against the prior time and space of the interviews, making temporal shifting integral to the process of embedding. As the interviews are embedded in courtroom interaction, text crosses the boundaries of time and space and the courtroom absorbs the interview room, adding new layers of meaning as the additional addressees (the jury) and their role (deciding on the balance of evidence whether Shipman is guilty or not guilty) become evident.

Intertextuality in institutional talk is a process that is as extensively theorized as recontextualization (e.g., Briggs and Bauman 1992 and 2009; Gordon 2006; Kozin 2008; Lauerbach 2006; Matoesian 2000; Solin 2004; Tannen 2006) and some articles use both terms as keywords, showing their interrelatedness (e.g., Hodges 2008). Separating the terms here, recontextualization relates to the "how" of reproduction, while intertextuality relates to the "what." A concept of intertextuality incorporates the notion that texts originate in prior texts and in prior times and spaces. Even where prior talk is exactly repeated from interview to courtroom the process of transfer and its new production and reception transforms its meaning. Texts rely on echoes of prior texts for their meaning and this leads to a Bakhtinian view of the "dialogicality" of texts, but also to the "intertextual gap" (Bauman and Briggs 2003: 227) between a text and its prior forms. The gap is an intertextual distance or closeness that can be "suppressed or foregrounded" (227) in a particular social setting to create intimacy or distance and thus power.

While the terms "recontextualization" and "intertextuality" occur widely across discourse linguistics, the term "embedding" is more restricted to narrative theory. Although Bal (1981) problematizes the notion of embedding, she agrees it is a semantic project and so our three terms have a central focus: semantics and meaning making. For institutional contexts this leads us to consider the ways that meanings "accrue socio-historical relevance and significance" (Iedema 1999: 63) through the selective power of embedding and recontextualizing narrative fragments in trials, creating powerful institutional meanings for the prosecution.

INTERTEXTUALITY IN THE SHIPMAN TEXTS

Before we look in detail at the trial, I start with a look at the end of the intertextual chain. The police interview and trial texts travel on as they are embedded in press coverage of the trial, making them multiply embedded, as excerpts 1 and 2 demonstrate. Excerpt 1 is from the Shipman trial transcript for day 23, and excerpt 2 is from BBC online news coverage of the trial from the same day: November 15, 1999. It condenses the entire day (149 pages of trial transcript and six re-enacted police interviews) into a short report. In excerpt 1, Sergeant Walker is in the witness box re-enacting with prosecuting counsel, Mr. Wright, the interviews carried out more than a year earlier in 1998. Mr. Wright reads the "part" of Shipman and Sergeant Walker "plays" himself (Shipman was interviewed on 15 occasions in September and October 1998). We can see how the selective process occurs; italicized portions are sites of transfer where some of the words are taken up or paraphrased in the news excerpt 2.

Excerpt 1: Trial of Harold Shipman, Transcript for Day 23, November 15, 1999

> (DS = Detective Sergeant Walker re-enacting himself from September 7, 1998, and P/Sh = Prosecuting counsel, Mr. Wright, reading Shipman's replies to questions and any turns by Shipman's solicitor, Miss Ball)
> p. 32, line 5
> DS. "OK. I've outlined broadly what the allegations are against you. Is there anything you'd like to say about them before we begin the questioning in detail?"
> P/Sh. "Not at this stage," said Miss Ball. "We will answer the questions."
> ...

p. 34, line 4

DS. "So when you left the other centre with the doctors is that—which centre is that?"

P/Sh. "That's called Donneybrook House."

DS. "Donneybrook House. And *you went to set up on your own as such.* Is that right"

P/Sh. "I did."

DS. "And that was in 19 ..."

P/Sh. "That was six years ago."

...

p. 35, line 4

P/Sh. "*I enter the record directly on to the computer.*"

...

P/Miss Ball: "But you also made manuscript notes sometimes. Can you just explain how it all works so that they get a background picture?"

P/Sh "Right. I'm a firm believer that the concept of general practice and computerisation is being held back by underdevelopment and finance and political decisions by government. That doesn't stop me computerising my practice *so I made a decision in 1992 that I would not use paper records so therefore every entry*—sorry, I'll rephrase that—*every time a patient was seen either at home or in the surgery it was recorded directly on the computer* either that day or the following day, depending on the circumstances.

...

p. 36, line 4

"So the only time I use paper records is when I'm handling a problem that might come to court, such as an assault, where a diagram of a face showing the injuries is often more useful than trying to describe it. I also use the records occasionally when I want something to act as an aide memoire to me or where I'm thinking about a patient and I'm not sure what the diagnosis is and I don't want to enter it all on the computer because my computer screen sits directly facing the patient. Obviously if I believe the patient's got a malignancy then to *write 'Cancer' as the entry alarms the patient.* To put 'Weight loss and investigations,' and then on the paper records like you thought, is obviously much more kind to the patient and is obviously much more helpful to me. If it turns out hot [*sic*] to be cancer then I've been a highly suspicious GP for no good reason."

In excerpt 2, reporting verbs are italicized, and we see that what the jury heard in court on November 15, 1999, and what Shipman had said in interviews in 1998 is reported in the simple past (rather than past and past perfective). The news blends recent past (the jury hearing the transcript re-enacted in court that day) and distant past (the police interview over a year earlier) in the same time, making it appear that the jury heard Shipman answering the police questions, showing the effect of embedding the interviews in the courtroom re-enactment.

Excerpt 2: BBC Online News for November 15, 1999

In court, Mr. Wright went through a transcript of a police interview following Dr Shipman's arrest on 7 September 1998. The jury *heard* that Dr Shipman *denied* killing Kathleen Grundy, 81. He *then told* detectives that he had kept all medical records on a computer in his surgery since he set up the solo practice in 1992. He *added* that he sometimes noted down on a piece of paper any embarrassing comments, details for future court cases, or comments that might cause alarm.

(BBC, November 15, 1999)

Five pages of the trial transcript (reduced in excerpt 1 with ellipses) are the source for only one paragraph of news coverage. An analysis of the material for the whole news story shows that the news relates to 17 pages of trial talk, but the excerpt serves to show how material is repeated and transformed as it travels over time and context. Space doesn't allow us to examine the individual transformations between excerpts 1 and 2, but it is clear to see that news transforms through paraphrase more than it directly repeats. The final passage at the end of excerpt 1 (page 36), where Shipman gives examples of occasions when he might have used paper records rather than computer entries, becomes a single noun phrase in the news: "comments that might cause alarm." Embedded in the news, Shipman is made to speak to the reading and listening public, through the media via the court, though deeply embedded in the courtroom context, making the public feel present in the court, though not there. Embedding, here, is multilayered (the interview in court in the media) and is particularly powerful if we consider that Shipman was silent at this time in court and that the interviews were further removed in time and space. The news report begins with Shipman's denial of murder, but we can see from the beginning of the re-enacted interview that there is actually no response by Shipman to the allegations. Shipman does deny the allegations within the interviews, but not at the start, or in the way the news reports it, saying he "denied," "then told detectives X," and "added." Textual fragments from interviews within the trial are embedded in a different narrative sequence in the news. We will see how textual fragments are similarly repeated and transformed over time and context between the police interviews and the trial, as they are selectively reported in the trial.

EMBEDDING THE POLICE INTERVIEWS IN THE PROSECUTION OPENING AND CLOSING SPEECHES

Prosecuting counsel, Mr. Henriques, carefully constructs the prosecution case for the jury to view by embedding fragments from the interviews in the opening speech. As text travels across time and space, it gains new meaning and significance as the police interview room and the silent tape recorder are replaced by the public courtroom and a jury of 12 people, making addressee relations far from the more usual co-present audience. While it may be assumed that Shipman in his responses to detectives during interview attempts to accommodate to some extent to his directly visible addressees, it is likely that awareness of the future invisible addressees (the court and the jury) is very limited. One of the uses of embedded interview material in the trial is to allow the jury to draw inferences from the difference between what is said in interview and what is said in court. Also present in the courtroom, as we have seen, are the press on behalf of the general public; it is even less likely that Shipman envisaged this audience as he spoke in interview.

The police interviews with Shipman (there were 15 in total) are first mentioned in the prosecution opening speech on day 2 (excerpt 3) and in doing so counsel forces the defendant to have a voice in the prosecution narrative even though he won't appear to speak until the defense case begins on day 27. He is thereby given a voice—"ventriloquated" (Bakhtin 1981) or "ventriloquized" (Tannen 2007: 22)—by the prosecution right at the start of the trial, giving his voice a salience for the jury as it is appropriated by counsel ("a ventriloquizing speaker animates another's voice in the presence of that other," Tannen 2007: 22). The jury also simultaneously sees him as a silent observer in the dock. This appropriation and embedding makes particular use of the hierarchical and institutional power of the prosecution to voice the words of the defendant. In excerpt 3, the court has just had a lunch break and is resuming for the afternoon session.

Excerpt 3: Prosecution Opening Speech Day 2, Page 14

1   MR. HENRIQUES: Members of the Jury we had reached the point
2   in the narrative where the defendant Dr. Shipman was being
3   interviewed by police officers. Perhaps the most significant thing that
4   Dr. Shipman said to the police in interview, was that *he suspected*
5   *Mrs. Kathleen Grundy was abusing drugs before her death and that she*
6   *had accidentally overdosed.* It is of course of importance that not only
7   were no morphine-based drugs found at her home, there was no
8   drug taking paraphernalia, that is syringe, raps, needles or the like.
9   Nor indeed did Mrs. Grundy's body upon examination display the
10   characteristics of long-term drug abuse. Repeated injections for
11   example, in the arm leave their mark, particularly when self-injected,
12   whilst a single injection, where a fine needle by a doctor may well not.
13   Dr. Shipman pointed to three entries in his manuscript medical notes;
14   he pointed those out to the police, in support of his contention that
15   Mrs. Grundy was in effect a drug addict. We will look now please at
16   those three entries. May I say by way of preface, the Prosecution
17   say that those are false entries deliberately made by the defendant.
18   [entries are gone through] Can you see there, the last entry on that
19   page, 12th October 1996 reads: "IBS that stands for irritable bowl [*sic*]
20   syndrome again,
21   pupils small, constipated (?) drug abuse at her age, (?)

22   codeine wait and see." See written on the printed part below.
23   The Prosecution contends that that entry has been made after
24   Mrs. Grundy's death. It is a false entry and wickedly dishonest.
25   It is manifestly crowded into the card.

The embedded indirect speech in excerpt 3 (italicized) contains an evaluatory preface ("perhaps *the most significant thing*," line 3), thereby positioning the jury to see the importance of the interview fragment at this point in the opening speech. Counsel further evaluates that narrative fragment in a matrix clause ("It is of course of importance," line 6) and then by drawing in information gathered from the police investigation outside the interview, to be given later in the witness testimonies of Mrs. Grundy's son-in-law (who cleared his mother-in-law's house after her death) and the police who searched the house. The matrix clause and its sequence emphatically deny, in multiple negation (lines 6–12), the existence of drug use and thereby dismantles the defense narrative before it is advanced. When we compare the words used by the barrister (excerpt 3, lines 1–10) with what Shipman is transcribed as saying (BBC news online, January 31, 2000) in the relevant police interview (excerpt 4), we can see how his words are transformed and given the prosecution's "lexical colouring" (Toolan 2001: 130).

Excerpt 4: Police Interview (S is Shipman and P is Police Interviewer)

1   S   If you back [sic] to the entry 12 of the 10th '96. Here I
2   commented: "IBS again, odd pupils, small, constipated, drug
3   abuse?," I have written: "At her age? Codeine?" Meaning I am
4   wondering if she is taking codeine tablets. "Wait and see." So
5   then in July, I deliberately made the comment that she is having
6   these IBS attacks every day. "Pupils small, dry mouth, possible
7   drug abuse again, denies taking any drug other than for IBS....
8   Should I do a blood test and check the urine?" I am sure
9   you are aware to do a blood test and check urine against the
10   patient's consent is not a legal event. Really difficult if she
11   denies everything. She is not really at risk. She is not an
12   intravenous user as far as I was aware. I am not sure. Still,
13   clinically, nothing of note to confirm my suspicions. "Wait and
14   see." So over that period of time, I wondered very seriously
15   whether this lady was taking drugs other than which I had
16   prescribed. And I will come back to the osteoporosis because
17   that is what I believed she was doing. I believed she was taking
18   something other than what I had prescribed for the
19   osteoporosis. I would only be guessing where she got it from?
20   ...
21   P   I have given you the cause of death. A fatal overdose of

22		morphine or diamorphine. And I have asked you to comment.
23	S	And I have commented. I have said that I had my suspicions
24		that she was abusing a narcotic of some sort, … or at least taking a
25		narcotic of some sort over a period of a year or so I am not
26		suggesting she took drugs every day. Far from it. But the sce-
27		nario was there. She did have drugs available and she may well
28		have accidentally given herself an overdose.…
29	P	I suggest to you that you have injected Mrs Grundy with a fatal
30		overdose of morphine.
31	S	[Emphatic] No. And you tell me that people in Hyde don't
32		have access to drugs. I think you should talk to your drugs squad.

(BBC News Online, January 31, 2000)

Shipman's "suspicions" (excerpt 4, lines 13 and 23), (a thing), become a process in which he is the actor through the barrister's use of an active transitive verb: "he suspected Mrs Grundy was abusing drugs." The drug abuse is referred to by Shipman much less directly in his interview—"taking drugs other than which I had prescribed" (lines 15–16) or "abusing a narcotic of some sort" (line 24). He first uses the verb "wondered" (line 14) and then the more evidential verb "believed" (line 17), rather than "suspected," suggesting that this is an honest belief, rather than as the barrister suggests, preposterous. The jury is invited to infer that such a belief is preposterous through juxtaposition of the suspicions with the repeated negative assertions of evidence of drug use prefaced by the evaluatory clause, *"it is of course of importance."*

The selective embedding of narrative in narrative allows for extradiegetic assessment that transforms meaning by introducing evaluative lexis. The first-person narrative, which is given in interview and elicited in question and answer, is embedded fragment by fragment in the prosecution case for judgment by the barrister, and then by and for the jury. This signals the value of the words said in interview as evidence, and their weight in the balance of probability that the defendant committed the crimes, forming a powerful resource of prosecution advocacy.

Over the two days of the opening speech the police interview is referred to 23 times as can be seen in the concordance (table 7.1, produced with *Wordsmith Tools*, version 5, Scott 2008). An analysis of these concordance lines reveals how the interview fragments are used by counsel. Looking at the right-hand margin, because the concordance is in text order, we can see episodes in the speech where the interviews are referred to in chunks at around 6, 9, 13, and 16 thousand words. Looking at the concordance, we can see recurrent patterns of reference to denial and distress. Counsel points the jury to Shipman's denial of the police hypotheses around the crime ("did not," line 1; "denied," line 7; "he wasn't told," line 8; "could not remember," line 10; "don't keep any controlled drugs," line 11; "cannot remember," line 19) and his distress while being interviewed about them ("distressed," lines 15, 21, 23), for their inference. Through repeated reference to lack of memory and use of the distancing verb "asserted" (lines 1, 9, 13, 18), in phrases such as in

Table 7.1 CONCORDANCE OF INSTANCES OF *INTERVIEW** IN PROSECUTION OPENING SPEECH

N	Concordance	Word No.
1	cases prescribing morphine to whom it was not administered. In **interview** by the police the defendant asserted that he did not keep	1,406
2	is very much in conflict with what he told the police later when **interviewed**, namely that he had gone there to take blood. At about	3,929
3	may well have been a rehearsal to what he was to tell the police in **interview**. He knew, of course, Mrs. Grundy's body had been	6,128
4	any trouble. Dr. Shipman was arrested on 7th September, he was **interviewed** at length at Ashton-Under-Lyne police station. He	6,404
5	point in the narrative where the defendant Dr. Shipman was being **interviewed** by police officers. Perhaps the most significant thing	6,826
6	the most significant thing that Dr. Shipman said to the police in **interview**, was that he suspected Mrs. Kathleen Grundy was	6,853
7	discovery of morphine in her body. Continuing Dr. Shipman's **interview** with the police, he denied any knowledge of the content of	9,455
8	if he was a beneficiary. Later, he told the police in a tape-recorded **interview**, he said, that he wasn't told it was a will nor did he ask.	9,686
9	wasn't told it was a will nor did he ask. Dr. Shipman was asked in **interview** about the typewriter, he asserted that Mrs. Grundy had	9,706
10	and in confidence leave her money to whoever she wanted. In **interview** Dr. Shipman could not remember when the typewriter was	9,820
11	real significance Members of the jury, Dr. Shipman said in this **interview**, "I don't keep any controlled drugs in my surgery, in my	9,882
12	and that is the only time I would touch them." He had earlier been **interviewed** on 14th August 1998, by Detective Constable Beard	9,949
13	have committed these murders. Unfortunately it was not true. In **interview** he again asserted as he had done on the death	10,116
14	toxicity. On 5th October 1998, the defendant was arrested and **interviewed** under caution, in the presence of his solicitor. During	13,357
15	under caution, in the presence of his solicitor. During the **interview**, he was too distressed to be interviewed further that day	13,368
16	of his solicitor. During the interview, he was too distressed to be **interviewed** further that day or indeed on 7th October whereupon he	13,375
17	5th October 1998, the arrest for his offense, the defendant was **interviewed** in relation to the death of Winifred Mellor. He faced	16,320
18	difficult questions, not least in relation to the computer entries. In **interview**, he asserted that he had seen Mrs. Mellor in the surgery,	16,343
19	remember visiting that day." He told police in a tape-recorded **interview**, "I reiterate, I cannot remember going to visit this lady at	16,385
20	the day after Mrs. Mellor's death, his solicitor asked for the **interviews** to be interrupted, so that she might have a conversation	16,639
21	of 5th October. On 7th October, it was proposed to resume the **interview**, but the defendant was found to be in a distressed	16,675
22	found to be in a distressed condition and not fit to be further **interviewed**. There are a number of similarities with the two previous	16,694
23	confirmed. After his arrest Dr. Shipman was too distressed to be **interviewed** in any detail concerning the death of Joan Melia and	17,610

line 1 of the concordance, the jury is given a view of an uncooperative intervie-wee and thus denial and distress equal guilt. The full context of the line 1 use of "asserted" is:

> In interview by the police the defendant *asserted* he did not keep morphine or diamor-phine or carry it and if he needed it for a patient he went to a pharmacist and obtained it by prescription. *That was a manifest lie* designed to avoid responsibility for these mur-ders. (Opening speech, Day 2, page 2, emphasis added)

The embedding of the defendant's speech, here, makes it an object for bold evalua-tion. It is metadiscursively labeled as: "a manifest lie [which was] designed to avoid responsibility for these murders." The heavy pre- and post-modification of the noun, "lie," packs maximum meaning into the noun phrase contained within the anaphoric evaluational frame: "That was X." The verb "asserted" is used by prosecuting counsel to signal a counter-assertion by the prosecution in a he-said-we-say routine that is an effective prosecution tactic. Counsel's use of the verb "assert" to report the defen-dant's speech makes Shipman tell the story, but his words are projected through the lawyer's power to assert it. Assertion by means of embedded speech makes strate-gic evaluation possible in the prosecution's outlining of the facts. This shift between "teller" and "knower" (Harris 2005) adds an additional layer of meaning to the reported indirect speech via intertextual reference. Time has added knowledge and meaning, and in its new context of the courtroom the symbolic value of the physical legal space and its textual position in the prosecution speech foregrounds its status as an important prosecution fact. It is recontextualized in its new institutional context, gaining new significance. Embedded in the prosecution speech these assertions— embedded quotations from police interviews and reference to interview material— become sites of power and persuasion for the jury to consume. "Assert*" is used 15 times in the prosecution speech and always to negatively evaluate, sometimes pre-modified itself with an evaluatory adjective or adverb: "false assertion," "a lamen-table assertion," "falsely asserting." We see too in this discussion of the examples how counsel moves between fact (quotation from interview) and argument (presenta-tion and evaluation of it) to make his narrative strategic.

Turning to the closing speech, we can observe a different function for prosecu-tion reference to interviews here and a different distribution of reference between the prosecution and defense closing speeches. Reference to "interview*" in the prosecution closing speech is primarily for the purpose of argument, seen in col-locates such as "terrible lie," "inference," "conclusion," "striking coincidence," "lost gamble," "pattern" (table 7.2). These discourse "labeling nouns" metalinguistically label (Francis 1994) previous stretches of discourse in strategic ways: to label prior talk as a "terrible lie" is to objectify and mark it for evaluation by the jury. Of note too in table 7.2 are the evaluative "boosters" (Holmes 1990), "of course," "full well," "proper," "all the more striking," "exactly," "only reasonable (conclusion)," and the use of interactive rhetorical questions. While the collocates of "interview*" in the

TABLE 7.2 CONCORDANCE OF *INTERVIEW** IN PROSECUTION CLOSING SPEECH, SHOWING COLLOCATES (ITALICIZED)

1	Never to keep controlled drugs. That was an *assertion* which he repeated in the police **interview**. Those are *lies* only if you conclude that he did keep morphine when he did not have a register.
2	*knew full well* what a *proper examination* involved when **interviewed**. He told the police what a *proper examination* involved. He also told the police: "It impressed the relatives if nothing else."
3	indeed at the time of his arrest, he had not *thought up that lie* about *the grand disclosure*, had he? But when **interviewed** by the police, he was specifically asked about each of the visits set out on the day of death
4	DS Wareing asked him: "Were all those visits to your surgery?" Answer: "Yes, yes." That is at page 251 of the **interview**. He *accepted* that on each date this lady presented with this problem.
5	He *now says exactly the opposite*. He had not *thought of the grand disclosure lie* when **interviewed** by the police.
6	When *confronted* with the audit trail, at a subsequent **interview** at page 313, *just before he was taken ill, he said three times*: "I have no recollection of me putting that on the machine."
7	*of course* he would remember putting that on the machine. *This defence has been fabricated* subsequent to police **interview**.
8	When he *pretended*, at page 228 of the **interview**, that he knew nothing about computers when he now says he was a member of a user group and he knows all about the audit trail
9	You may draw an inference from *the fact that he lied* on the 14th August to DC Beard and Mr. Calder, and later to police officers in **interview**, stating that he never kept drugs in his house, car or surgery. You may draw an *inference* that he said that he said that out of a sense of guilt
10	*renders the coincidence all the more striking*. When the same doctor *lies* both to the drug inspectorate and to **interviewing** officers, you may *well have reached your own conclusion*.
11	*What a terrible lie* to suggest, not only on the certificate of cause of death but to the police in **interview**, and even here in this court, that old age could have been a cause of death.
12	*Not only lies prepared in advance in his surgery but lies repeated* to the police in **interview**. He said this at page 128: "I wondered very seriously whether this lady was taking drugs."
13	but again *he has lost the gamble and changes his evidence*. He was asked in **interview**: "How often could samples go missing like this?" Page 66. Answer: "We thought about this and we would think perhaps possibly once every quarter or six months."
14	the defendant, prior to being taken ill, chose to answer questions in police **interview**. When *confronted* with the critical late entries, he was asked if all these were visits to the surgery.

(Continued)

TABLE 7.2 CONCORDANCE OF *INTERVIEW** IN PROSECUTION CLOSING SPEECH, SHOWING COLLOCATES (ITALICIZED)

15	*because a medical history was created; and because he answered questions in* **interview**, *we are able to see exactly what has occurred—the pattern*—and at every stage: the 3 o'clock to 3.20 visit; *diamorphine* administered; *return to surgery; medical history falsified*
16	You will remember that this is the case in which Angela Wagstaffe was hysterical. You will remember how, in **interview**, *when he realized how damaged he was by the audit trail, he broke down then,*
17	*when he realized how damaged he was by the audit trail, he broke down then,* and the **interview** could not be continued. *Again, we submit here that the only reasonable conclusion here is that the defendant murdered Mrs Wagstaffe.*
18	*We rely too upon the many lies told by the defendant, both in documentary form and in* **interview** with the police. You will, *of course, ask yourselves, why the false documents? Why the lies?*

opening speech build up a semantic picture of a guilty defendant in denial and distress, the collocates in the closing speech have a pragmatic function to signal and evoke decision-making in the jury in the light of the clear picture they now have. The embedded reference to interview fragments therefore has differing but complementary functions at the beginning and end of the prosecution task: first, who is this person and what did he say? and then, why did he say this and how does that affect your decision? In both cases the argument centers on associations of guilt, and explicit and implied evaluation provide certainty and persuasion.

There are 18 references to the police interviews, 17 times in the prosecution closing speech and once in the defense. This shows us that such mention is a prosecution resource. One sustained excerpt (5) of just under 200 words contains six of these occurrences (emphasis added), so it is useful to demonstrate what the prosecution is doing beyond the meanings created through collocation.

Excerpt 5: Prosecution Closing Speech, Day 40

You can picture him [Shipman] now, can you not, in the presence of Father Maher, standing behind Mrs. Mellor's seat, arms apart again, declaiming the fact that "only this afternoon your mother told me of angina, dating back to August of 1997. If only she had told me earlier, I would have been able to treat her." Not at that time, nor indeed at the time of his arrest, he had not thought up that lie about the grand disclosure, had he? *But when interviewed* by the police, he was specifically asked about each of the visits set out on the day of death, by the police. DS Wareing asked him: "Were all those visits to your surgery?" Answer: "Yes, yes." That is at page 251 of the *interview.* He accepted that on each date this lady presented with this problem. *He now says* exactly the opposite. He had not thought of the grand disclosure lie when *interviewed* by the police. *When confronted* with the audit trail, at a subsequent *interview* at page 313, just before he was taken ill, he said three times: "I have no recollection of me putting that on the machine." If this had been a grand disclosure, and the lady had died some two hours later, of course he would remember putting that on the machine. This defence has been fabricated subsequent to police *interview. When he pretended*, at page 228 of the *interview*, that *he knew* nothing about computers when *he now says* he was a member of a user group and *he knows* all about the audit trail, [Question] why to the police was he playing so dumb? [Answer] This feigned ignorance was at a time when the police had not disclosed to him their findings from the audit trail. Beware, members of the jury, of the argument that nobody who knew of the audit trail could possibly manufacture these four false medical histories and hope to get away with it. This defendant gambles on the authorities not checking up sufficiently upon him. *When he spoke* of the wet and windy night when Mrs. Quinn died and nobody attended the open surgery, he gambled that nobody would check up. *When he spoke* of Mrs. Nuttall's new home, he gambled that nobody would check up. *When he entered* on cremation certificates that neighbours and the warden were present at the time of death, he gambled that nobody would check up. *Here and now* he has lost that gamble, but for some time he had succeeded.

The last 10 lines of (excerpt 5) (from "Beware, members of the jury") show us more about the prosecution's use of embedding of interview fragments. The first aspect relates to the relevance of the Police Caution's words: "It may harm your defence if you do not mention when questioned something which you later rely on in court." This is emphasized rhetorically, though not explicitly mentioned, in the pattern: "when interviewed"; "when confronted"; "when he pretended … he now says"; and in the contrasting of "when" + past tense verb with "here and now." In addition, this rhetorical patterning, which first of all includes repetition and parallelism and then repetition with deviation from the pattern, creates an additional resource for conclusion-drawing. Past interview and present courtroom testimony (in cross-examination) talk are compared and inconsistencies are pointed out. Then/now patterning is also produced in tense contrasts with simple past tenses ("he spoke," "he gambled") and then the perfective aspect ("has lost"). Grammatical parallelism initially creates emphasis through similarity ("when he spoke … he gambled"). Then, as the deictic center moves back to the courtroom ("Here and now"), it is used to emphasize difference ("Here and now he has lost that gamble"). The past moves to present and the verb "gambled" is repeated three times and then as a noun ("that gamble"), a transformational process that seems to freeze action as a thing and rhetorically move the jury to silently agree.

EMBEDDING THE POLICE INTERVIEWS IN WITNESS APPEARANCES IN THE TRIAL

We now move from the monologic mode to the dialogic, as we move to day 23 of the trial, where the prosecution case focuses on the police interviews, which now become both textual and embodied courtroom objects rather than mentions. Having seen their diegetic and metadiegetic use in the opening and closing speeches, here we see them in the witness appearances, first of Detective Sergeant Walker and then DS Wareing, the interviewing officers, as they appear in the witness box to re-enact the interviews they conducted, in mimetic mode. In excerpt 6, we see the beginning of two entire days where prosecuting counsel and police sergeant re-enact the police interviews for the court. DS Walker reads his own turns and prosecuting counsel reads Shipman's. In spatial terms prosecuting counsel and police witness are in close proximity at the front of the court with the jury opposite, while Shipman is distant at the back of the court and not addressed. The prosecuting barrister has his back to Shipman and the police witness faces the jury while addressing them. Shipman's voice is therefore projected through the barrister from the front of the court and in the jury's line of view as they look at the witness box, while he remains silent and distant at the back. While this may seem an astonishing thing to do, when the tapes could simply be played, the effect is striking and powerful, bringing the defendant's words and evidence into the prosecution case. This strategy is not unusual in an English courtroom. The interviews become objects to be heard and handled by the jury as physically and immediately co-present in their current space: the trial in the courtroom. This is ultimately more powerful than what is the alternative: playing the tapes and experiencing them as an ethereal presence projected from another place and time. The jury's focus is on the real "actors" rather than a machine. Their performance "stands in" (Rock 2001) for the accused, who has yet to speak and for the other officer who was present but also watches from the courtroom.

Before the interview is re-enacted it is brought into the courtroom through deictic reference (emphasis added) (excerpt 6).

Excerpt 6: Witness Appearance of DS Walker, Day 23

MR WRIGHT: I am going to turn to *the interviews* now, …

MR WRIGHT: My Lord, with my learned friends' approval, with their consent, may I invite your Lordship to consider that the brother officer Detective Constable Denham, who was present at *these interviews*, may sit in court during examination-in-chief whilst *the interviews* are being read to the jury? …

MR. WRIGHT: Thank you. (To the witness) Sergeant, on the 7th September 1998 did you, together with Detective Constable Denham, conduct *a series of interviews* with the defendant Dr. Shipman?

A. Yes, I did.

Q. And were *those interviews* in the presence of his solicitor Miss Ball?

A. At all times, yes.

Q. Were *those interviews* tape-recorded?

A. Yes.

Q. And have *transcripts* been made *of the tape of the interviews themselves*?

A. Yes, they have.

Q. And in due course *those* have been prepared into *a file in edited form* for the ladies and gentlemen of the jury?

A. Yes.

Q. My Lord, *it* is still *a fairly substantial document* but I think *it* is now available for distribution. If I can just check one matter…. Yes, thank you. If *those* can be distributed to the ladies and gentlemen of the jury now. (Pause) …

MR. WRIGHT: … (To the witness) Now, sergeant, so that we familiarise ourselves with *the bundle itself, the first interview*, we see *the formal contents of this document* before us. *It* identifies the person *interviewed*, the place of *the interview*, the date of *it*, the time *it* commenced and the time *it* concluded, and then the duration of *that interview*, together with *a tape reference number* because *each interview* was, as indeed are *all interviews*, tape-recorded. Yes?

A. Correct.

Q. *This document* also identifies the orficers [*sic*] present and any other person present. We see that Miss Ball of Hempsons [*sic*] solicitors was present, as indeed she was present throughout.

A. Yes.

Q. As I say, *these interviews* are *a synopsis of that* that took place and so there are occasions when you will see within *the bundle of documents themselves* what appear to be gaps.... Officer, may we deal with *it* in this way, please? You ask the questions of each individual officer and I will give the replies that Dr. Shipman gave.

A. Yes. I began *the interview* by saying: "*This interview* is being tape-recorded. *It* may be given in evidence if your case is brought to court. As you can see there's a note explaining that *this interview* may be the subject of remote monitoring. When the red light above the machine's illuminated this means that *this interview* is being monitored by other officers to assist the investigation".

Q. ...If you could slow down a little, please, then we can all digest what you are saying.

A. "The time presently is 9.43 a.m. on Monday the 7th September 1998. I'm Detective Sergeant Walker and the other officer is Detective Constable Denham. We're in the interview room at Ashton-under-Lyne police station on interviewing [*sic*]. If you could state your full name, please." ...

Q. [*sic*] "Harold Frederick Shipman."

A chain of reference in this excerpt constitutes a continued focus on the same item—"the interview," "these interviews," "those interviews," "transcripts," "the interviews themselves," "those [transcripts]," "a file in edited form," "those," "the bundle itself," "it" [the interview], "a tape reference number," "this document," "these interviews," "this interview." This activity transforms the interviews from being distant and removed from the current time and space, though mentioned in it ("those interviews that the officer conducted") to being distant but present in the current time and space ("those documents or transcripts that are being distributed to the jury") to being near and present—"this document"—that the lawyer, police witness, judge, and jury are now holding and which now makes these interviews present, tangible, and a legally named and transformed object ("the bundle"; "formal contents"). Prosecuting counsel in performing these acts of deictic reference "take[s] up a position" in the deictic field, one which powerfully objectifies and appropriates the object from the past and another place, and positions it in the current location to be held, handled, viewed, and then heard and evaluated as it is re-enacted. At the same time Shipman, the second interviewing officer (Constable Denham), and Shipman's solicitor (Miss Ball) are all referred to and therefore "thrust into a position" in the court (Hanks 2005: 193). In this way deixis contributes to the process of embedding the interview in the courtroom activity.

This is further signaled by the change of tense "were" and "was" to "are" and "is" (Fludernik 2003) as we saw in the use of tense shifts in the closing speech.

When DS Walker begins to read the transcript of Shipman's interview—"this interview is being tape-recorded"—the deictic reference is simultaneously past and present. The temporal and spatial world becomes displaced and transferred to the courtroom through the projective power of the prosecution role. As Hanks (2005: 194) points out, when deictic expressions are used and embedded in a social setting they gain meaning: "embedding converts abstract positions like Speaker, Addressee, Object, and the lived space of utterances into sites to which power, conflict, controlled access and other features of the social fields attach." Embedded in the judicial field, the re-enacted interview transcript becomes an evidential object for scrutiny and evaluation by the jury. It makes the defendant speak for the prosecution while waiting to defend himself and while positioned as a silent spectator, though speaking through the mouth of the prosecution.

The context shifts constantly from the "primary reality" (Hale and Gibbons 1999; Gibbons 2003) of the courtroom to the other or "secondary reality" of the interview, which is one stage removed from the events. And the prosecution's repertoire of stances in relation to the case shifts from third-person narrator, in the opening statement, to impersonation, in the re-enactment of the interviews. These shifts of reality and stance (Jaffe 2009) are significant in the process of embedding. Gibbons (2003: 78) talks about how the primary reality of the courtroom refers to the secondary reality of the alleged criminal events and how the police interview also does this. When we have embedding of the police interview in the courtroom, the "layers of action" (Clark 1996, cited in Gibbons 2003: 78) become even thicker, making the events and the person who tells of the events further removed from the current reality. The verbatim interview brings Shipman into the central focus of the courtroom (through the mouth of the prosecution barrister) making him speak without speaking—truly ventriloquated. Planes of reality intersect in new ways and the primary event is seen through these institutional layers of talk and evaluation (as we saw in the embedding of these events in the news report).

EMBEDDING THE INTERVIEWS IN THE JUDGE'S SUMMING-UP

The final site of embedded reference is in the 10 days of judicial summing-up, as the judge condenses 40 days of evidence, before the jury retires to deliberate their verdicts on all 15 charges. His use of the interviews, which the jury now have in their "bundles" and have heard in re-enactment, is significant (80 occurrences of "interview*"), though there are large sections of the summing-up where the interviews are not mentioned at all (5 whole days). There are clusters of references in the other 5 days, from which we will examine two: from day 46 and 52. As in the prosecution closing speech, the judge's main use of reference is to contrast what Shipman said in cross-examination in court with what he said in interview, and the rhetorical effect of this, coupled with the selectivity which is also present here, serves to underline particular points of the prosecution evidence for the jury to consider in their deliberation. Both verbatim reading from the interviews in the bundles (with the jury invited to read along together) and summary of it in indirect speech is done. Verbatim reading is highlighted by examining a concordance of the 80 occurrences of "interview*" and finding numerous page references (18 in the 80 lines; nearly a quarter) in the immediate (80 word) context of the search word (e.g., "Dr. Shipman was then referred to page 161 of the interviews and it is the second question down from the top. Police officer: "You mentioned before regarding drugs that you don't keep in the surgery controlled drugs?" Dr. Shipman: "That's correct.") Directing the jury to particular pages and lines and engaging the jury in extended shared reading underlines both the importance of the words and the documents they hold for future reference.

In excerpt 7, near to the end of the tenth day of summing-up, we see the judge largely narrating in past tense the courtroom evidence given by Shipman in cross-examination, with occasional verbatim reference to the transcripts. When he gets to the part of the narrative that refers to the transcripts (emphasis added), the tense moves to present as the jury read along with the judge's reading of the questions and answers.

Excerpt 7: Judge's Summing-up, Day 52

> Dr. Shipman said that apart from the case of Mr. Arrandale he did not believe ·
> that he had handled any of the drugs referred to in the formal admissions,
> apart from those cases where he had taken the drugs to a patient or those
> cases where the drugs were destroyed by him. He was asked how [... a range
> of drugs found at his house are then listed]. Dr. Shipman was then asked to
> look at page 120 of the police interviews, if now turn to those [*sic*], page 120
> of the transcripts of the police interviews, and he was referred to the answer
> which he gave at the bottom of page 120. *The question put by the officer is,*
> *"Okay, just move on a little. Where do you keep dangerous drugs in your practice?"*
> *Dr. Shipman: ... "I don't have any DDAs on the premises, in my car. I don't have*
> *a dangerous drugs book."* Then he was referred to that answer and he said to
> you that with the exception of Mr. Arrandale he still stood by his statement
> that he would never take the drugs away after the patient had died.

The final sentence of excerpt 7 moves back to past tense narration and progresses to the point of the embedded verbatim interview extract: Shipman "still st[ands] by his statement." Present time and potential obstinacy in the face of contradictory evidence is indicated by "still," though the verb ("stood") is in the past tense. The jury is invited, by inference ("he said to you"), to consider whether this is truthful or a lie.

Comparing the final sentence of excerpt 7 with what was said 20 days earlier in cross-examination (excerpt 8), we can see how the judge transforms dialogue into monologue and in doing so incorporates both question and answer into his summary (italics indicates material that is repeated in 7 and bold indicates material that is paraphrased).

Excerpt 8: Cross-examination, Day 32

> MR. HENRIQUES: [reading from the police interview] "Question: Now what happens say **if one of your patients dies** from a terminal illness.... Answer: "…the patient's relatives are told to destroy the drugs. I would never take the drugs away." Now do you stand by that answer you gave to the police, "*I would never take the drugs away?*"
> A. *With the exception of Mr. Arundale* **I would stand** *by* **that** *statement.*

Institutional embedding repeats and transforms in favor of institutional meanings. The dialogue of the original interview read out in excerpt 8, and in particular question and answer dialogue, which is converted to monologue and summary in excerpt 7, clearly undergoes transformation through selection and omission. But more importantly embedding allows for ellipsis, which is built into answers in question and answer dialogue, to be built back in to monologue, thereby giving Shipman's statements a completeness they only had by implicit acceptance of the proposition—"I would never take the drugs away"—in the question.

CONCLUSION

We have seen how the police interview texts travel from the interview room to the tape to the court and how, through re-enactment, objectification in transcribed bundles of documents, shared reading between the judge and jury, and narrated in monologue, they are institutionally evaluated and transformed. They travel across time and place and are ventriloquized, summarized in monologue, read, and enacted as they are embedded in the prosecution case, and taken up by the judge in his summing up of the prosecution case. As they travel, we see how the interview narratives are "fragmented" (Harris 2001) and colored with new meaning as they are embedded and seen through the layers of prosecution courtroom activity. Important resources of embedding as a form of "style-shifting" (Hernandez-Campoy and Cutillas-Espinosa 2012) have been revealed: shifts of reality from the primary reality of the courtroom to the secondary reality of the interviews and back; shifts of stance from third-person narration to prosecution ventriloquizing and re-enactment, and judge and jury shared reading; shifts of audience as the police interviewers in the interview room are augmented by the judge, jury, public, and media; shifts of tense from "was" and "were" to "are" and "is," and of "then" to "now," which signal Shipman's contradictory evidence between interview and courtroom and a defense which is constructed after interview.

The effect of embedding the interviews at all stages of the prosecution case and in the judicial summing-up is stunning advocacy in action. The Crown's case is powerfully presented, none more so than in the re-enactment activity, which makes the defendant speak for the prosecution. As interview material is repeated over time in the trial—from the opening speech to the witness appearances of the Sergeants and their re-enactments of the interview to the closing speech and judge's summing-up—layers of meaning and significance are attached to Shipman's words. As they are evaluated in rhetorically patterned sequences by the prosecution, for the jury, and interpreted and reacted to by the jury, as the prosecution speak and as the judge sums up the prosecution case, they are weighed and reflected on. The embedded repetition achieves a sedimentary semantic effect and the repeated words and the word "interview" itself rings with a pragmatic sonority that provokes a response: the "decision-making" (Kerr 1982) that is the job of the jury and the target for the prosecution performance.

REFERENCES

Bakhtin, M. 1981. *The Dialogic Imagination: Four Essays*. Translated by C. Emerson and M. Holquist and edited by M. Holquist, Austin: University of Texas Press.

Bal, M. 1981. Notes on Narrative Embedding. *Poetics Today* 2(2): 41–59.

Bauman, R., and C. L. Briggs. 2003. *Voices of Modernity. Language Ideologies and the Politics of Inequality*. Cambridge: Cambridge University Press.

BBC. 1999. UK Doctor "Lied about Having Morphine." BBC News Online. 15 November. Available at: http://news.bbc.co.uk/1/hi/uk/521386.stm.

———. 2000. The Shipman Tapes I. BBC News Online. 31 January. Available at: http://news.bbc.co.uk/1/hi/in_depth/uk/2000/the_shipman_murders/the_shipman_files/613286.stm.

Blackledge, A. 2006. The racialization of language in British political discourse. *Critical Discourse Studies* 3(1): 61–79.

Briggs, C. L., and R. Bauman. 1992. Genre, intertextuality and social power. *Journal of Linguistic Anthropology* 2: 131–72. Reprinted in *Linguistic Anthropology: A Reader* (2d ed.), ed. A. Duranti, 214–44. Oxford: John Wiley.

Cotterill, J. 2003. *Language and Power in Court: A Linguistic Analysis of the O. J. Simpson Trial*. Basingstoke, UK: Palgrave.

Fludernik, M. 2003. Chronology, time, tense and experientiality in narrative. *Language and Literature* 12(2): 117–34.

Francis, G. 1994. Labelling discourse: An aspect of nominal-group lexical cohesion. In *Advances in Written Text Analysis*, ed. M. Coulthard, 83–101. London: Routledge.

Genette, G. 1980. *Narrative Discourse: An Essay in Method [Discours du récit, 1966]*. Ithaca, NY: Cornell University Press.

Gibbons, J. 2003. *Forensic Linguistics: An Introduction to Language in the Justice System*. Oxford: Blackwell.

Goffman, E. 1981. *Forms of Talk*. Oxford: Blackwell.

Gordon, C. 2006. Reshaping prior text, reshaping identities. *Text and Talk* 26(4/5): 545–47.

Hale, S., and J. Gibbons. 1999. Varying realities: Patterned changes in the interpreter's representation of courtroom and external realities. *Applied Linguistics* 20(2): 203–20.

Hanks, W. F. 2005. Explorations in the deictic field. *Current Anthropology* 46(2): 191–220.

Harris, S. 2001. Fragmented narratives and multiple tellers: Witness and defendant accounts in trials. *Discourse Studies* 3(1): 53–74.

———. 2005. Telling stories and giving evidence: The hybridisation of narrative and non-narrative modes of discourse in a sexual assault trial. In *The Sociolinguistics of Narrative*, ed. J. Thornborrow and J. Coates, 215–37. Amsterdam: John Benjamins.

Hernández-Campoy, J. M., and J. A. Cutillas-Espinosa, eds. 2012. *Style-Shifting in Public. New Perspectives on Stylistic Variation.* Amsterdam: John Benjamins.

Hodges, A. 2008. The politics of recontextualisation: Discursive competition over claims of Iranian involvement in Iraq. *Discourse and Society* 19(4): 483–505.

Holmes, J. 1990. Hedges and boosters in women's and men's speech. *Language and Communication* 10(3): 185–205.

Iedema, R. 1999. Formalizing organizational meaning. *Discourse and Society* 10(1): 49–65.

Iedema, R., and R. Wodak. 1999. Introduction: Organizational discourses and practices. *Discourse and Society* 10(1): 5–19.

Jaffe, A. 2009. The sociolinguistics of stance. In *Stance: Sociolinguistic Perspectives,* ed. A Jaffe, 3–28. New York: Oxford University Press.

Johnson, A. J. 2008. "From where we're sat…": Negotiating narrative transformation through questioning in police interviews with suspects. *Text and Talk* 28(3): 327–49.

Kerr, N. 1982. Trial participants' behaviors and jury verdicts: An exploratory study. In *The Criminal Justice System,* ed. V. J. Konecni and E. B. Ebbeson, 261–90. London: Freeman.

Kozin, A. V. 2008. Unsettled facts: On the transformational dynamism of evidence in legal discourse. *Text and Talk* 28(2): 219–38.

Lauerbach, G. 2006. Discourse representation in political interviews: The construction of identities and relations through voicing and ventriloquizing. *Journal of Pragmatics* 38: 196–215.

Linell, P. 1998. Discourse across boundaries: Recontextualisations and blending of voices in professional discourses. *Text* 18(2): 143–57.

Matoesian, G. 2000. Intertextual authority in reported speech: Production media in the William Kennedy Smith rape trial.' *Journal of Pragmatics* 33: 879–914.

Rock, F. 2001. The genesis of a witness statement. *Forensic Linguistics* 8(2): 44–72.

———. 2007. *Communicating Rights: The Language of Arrest and Detention.* Basingstoke, UK: Palgrave Macmillan.

Sarangi, S. 1998. Rethinking recontextualisation in professional discourse studies: An epilogue. *Text* 18(2): 301–16.

Sarangi, S., and L. Brookes-Howell. 2006. Recontextualising the familial lifeworld in genetic counselling casenotes. In *Advances in Medical Discourse Analysis: Oral and Written Contexts,* ed. M. Gotti and F. Salagar-Meyer, 197–225. Bern: Peter Lang.

Scott, M. 2008. *Wordsmith Tools, version 5.* Oxford: Oxford University Press.

Shipman Inquiry, The. 2001. Shipman Trial Transcript. Online. Available at: http://webarchive.nationalarchives.gov.uk/20090619142823/http://www.the-shipman-inquiry.org.uk/trialtrans.asp

Solin, A. 2004. Intertextuality as mediation: On the analysis of intertextual relations in public discourse. *Text* 24(2): 267–96.

Tannen, D. 2006. Intertextuality in interaction: Reframing family arguments in public and private. *Text and Talk* 26(4/5): 597–617.

Tannen, D. 2007. *Talking Voices: Repetition, Dialogue, and Imagery in Conversational Discourse.* 2d ed. Cambridge: Cambridge University Press.

Toolan, M. 2001. *Narrative: A Critical Linguistic Introduction.* 2d ed. London: Routledge.

Vincent, D., and L. Perrin 1999. On the narrative vs non-narrative functions of reported speech: A socio-pragmatic study. *Journal of Sociolinguistics* 3(3): 291–313.

Wodak, R. 2007. Discourses in European Union organizations: Aspects of access, participation and inclusion. *Text and Talk* 27(5/6): 655–80.

CHAPTER 8

Tracing Crime Narratives in the Palmer Trial (1856)

From the Lawyer's Opening Speeches to the Judge's Summing Up

DAWN ARCHER

INTRODUCTION

In 1856, William Palmer was found guilty of fatally poisoning John Parsons Cook for financial gain. Dubbed the "trial of the century" by Victorian newspapers, *Palmer*[1] is now said to mark the coming of age of the adversarial criminal trial, following the implementation of the Prisoners' Counsel Act (1836):

> [T]his trial, one of the great criminal trials in the history of English law, triumphantly realised the expectations of full defence by counsel [made possible by the 1836 Act]. A case of labyrinthine facts, involving a mass of circumstantial evidence, the conflicting recollections of dozens of witnesses, and questions of bewildering medical and toxilogical perplexity was reduced by the prosecution and defence to coherent alternative versions of events… [introduced in] the speeches of counsel… tested in examination and cross-examination… [and confirmed in] the prosecution reply. (Cairns 1998: 163)

Cairns's comments allude to one of the main themes of this collection: the way(s) in which legal actors knowingly draw on accounts of crime events originally produced by others (e.g., witnesses, police, coroners, experts) to create—via processes of entextualization and recontextualization (see, e.g., Bauman and Briggs 1990), intertextuality and interdiscursivity (see, e.g., Fairclough 1992, 2001)—crime narratives that account for relevant evidence and/or discount irrelevant information, depending on their macro perspective (i.e., the guilt/innocence of the accused).

In this chapter, I use the keyword/key domains facility of Wmatrix (Rayson 2003) to determine the extent—and effects—of such *textual travelling* in this important historical trial. In brief, I have automatically constructed word and semantic domain lists of various aspects of the trial, using the corpus analysis and comparison tool; specifically, word and domain lists relating to Attorney General Alexander Cockburn's addresses to the jury (for the prosecution) and Mr. Sergeant Shee's address to the jury (for the defense), their examinations-in-chief and their cross-examinations, and also word and domain lists relating to Lord Chief Justice John Campbell's summing up. Again using Wmatrix, I have then automatically compared these lists (let's call them *Palmer*) against a normative corpus—in my case, a larger collection of texts representative of more general (spoken) English, which for explanatory purposes, we will call Corpus B— as a means of identifying those lexical items within *Palmer* (e.g., words, multi-word-units, and semantic domains such as *medicines and medical treatment; health and disease; crime, law and order; evaluation*, etc.), which appear more frequently than chance (i.e., the normative corpus) would predict.[2] Because of the sheer number of items identified automatically by Wmatrix, I focus, below, on those key lexical items in *Palmer* which, when compared to Corpus B, have been assigned a statistical significance of < 5 percent; and, hence, provide us with the best insight into Cockburn, Shee, and Campbell's textual practices.[3]

As will become clear through the sections that follow, some of the textual practices discussed here share striking similarities with the modern courtroom. For example, Cockburn, Shee, and to some extent Campbell all referred to (while simultaneously filtering) pretrial documentation; their motivation, of course, was to establish the facts of the case and also (the lack of a) motive. Thus, all made much of the pretrial medical records that had been submitted and also the events surrounding Cook's (now infamous) autopsy. They also reanimated the "voices" of lay actors: Cockburn and Shee both utilized the deceased's voice in their opening speeches, for example—Cockburn, as a means of allowing the victim to identify his murderer, and Shee, as a means of urging the jury to not be influenced by the "voice of the blood of John Parsons Cook" and the subsequent public cries of "blood for blood" before "hearing the evidence on both sides"; Campbell, in contrast, opted to read from and/or summarize witness depositions in his summing up to the jury.

I begin my discussion of *Palmer* with a brief summary of the events surrounding Cook's death and Palmer's subsequent indictment. My analysis of the respective counsels' opening speeches and their entextualization/recontextualization of key (opening speech) items during the examination-in-chief and cross-examination phases of *Palmer* then form the basis of the mid-sections of this chapter. This is followed by an exploration of the key features of the prosecution reply and the Judge's reiteration of (what, for him, were some of) the key testimonies of the trial in his summing up, and my own summation of the extent of textual travel within *Palmer*, which includes the effect of that travel on the arguments, ideas, and voices presented therein.

On November 13, 1855, Cook's horse, Polestar, won at the Shrewsbury racecourse, earning his owner approximately £3,000. Cook collected some of his winnings on the day, leaving the remainder to be payable later—upon the presentation of his betting book in London. As Cook did not feel well following a celebration with friends (which included Palmer), he returned to Rugeley with Palmer and stayed at the Talbot Arms (an inn situated immediately opposite Palmer's house). By the 16th, Cook felt well enough to dine with Palmer and a mutual acquaintance, but was again taken ill the following morning, after drinking coffee that had been ordered for him by Palmer. As Palmer was a trained physician, he initially cared for Cook, but a second medical man—Bamford—was called in on November 18th. While Palmer was in London on the 19th, Cook displayed a marked improvement. However, his "illness" returned following Palmer's homecoming that evening. On the 20th, a third doctor—James— also arrived to attend to Cook. But he died sometime that evening/the following morning—after informing James that "that damned Palmer had dosed him."

Following his death, Cook's stepfather requested that Cook's body be exhumed and examined. A post-mortem examination was performed (November 26th), with Palmer present as a medical colleague. It was later claimed that Palmer tampered with a key piece of evidence during that autopsy—the contents of Cook's stomach—by bumping into one of the physicians as he was lifting out the stomach and tampering with the seal of the jar in which the stomach contents were placed. Dr. Alfred Swaine Taylor, a renowned Victorian authority on forensic medicine, was invited to test the stomach/stomach contents. He reported finding a small nonlethal amount of antimony, the active ingredient of tartar emetic (a common medicine at the time) but, on the basis of reported symptoms prior to death, concluded Cook had been poisoned by strychnine—and gave evidence to this effect at the coroner's inquest on December 14th. Palmer was indicted for Cook's murder and incarcerated (at Stafford). As news reports prior to the trial helped to arouse unprecedented levels of public interest in the Palmer case, a new Act of Parliament (19 Vict. Cap. 16) was rushed through so that the trial could be heard in the Old Bailey (as opposed to an Assize Court in Staffordshire). The Old Bailey trial began May 14, 1856, and lasted twelve days (making it the longest murder trial in England, at that time).[4]

THE OPENING SPEECH OF THE ATTORNEY GENERAL

After some courtroom preliminaries, Cockburn rose to make his opening speech to a packed courtroom—and immediately utilized the rhetorical strategy of repetition to stress the solemn "duty" that he and the jurors faced:

> Gentlemen of the jury, the duty you are called upon to discharge is the most solemn
> which a man can possibly have to perform—it is to sit in judgment and to decide an
> issue on which depends the life of a fellow human being.... Your duty—your bounden

duty—is to try this case according to the evidence which shall be brought before you, and according to that alone.... My duty, gentlemen, will be a simple one. It will be to lay before you the facts on which the prosecution is based.

Cockburn also chose to allude—albeit briefly—to the tremendous public interest that the case had aroused, and the extensive newspaper coverage given to it prior to coming to trial, so that he might emphasize the jury's need to assess the case on the evidence as it was presented to them in the courtroom:

> You must discard from your minds anything that you may have read or heard, or any opinion that you may have formed. If the evidence shall satisfy you of the prisoner's guilt, you will discharge your duty to society, to your consciences, and to the oaths which you have taken, by fearlessly pronouncing your verdict accordingly, but if the evidence fail to produce a reasonable conviction of guilt in your minds, God forbid that the scale of justice should be inclined against the prisoner by anything of prejudice or preconceived opinion.

As previously established, however, the lack of strychnine in Cook's remains meant that the prosecution's case against Palmer was actually based on circumstantial evidence—a factor that may explain Cockburn's infrequent use of "evidence," statistically speaking, when compared to Shee in his opening speech (i.e., 14 times as opposed to 118: see below, 'Shee's "Evidence"').

Cockburn's Crime Narrative

In spite of Cockburn's reliance on circumstantial evidence, he is nonetheless credited with weaving—in his opening—a comprehensive narrative that accounted for virtually every aspect of the crime, including the motive of the accused, the activities of the alleged accomplices, the suffering of the victim, and the perspective of the people who cared for Cook (see, e.g., Cairns 1998; Archer 2006). As Gergen (1999: 69) notes, such "criminal occurrence narratives" (i.e., narratives which are simultaneously informative *and* interpretative) are very common in the opening speeches of prosecution counsel today. A reminder of Kristeva's ([1966] 1986: 69) and Derrida's (1981: 26) notions of intertextuality might also be opportune here, for both understood a text to be a metaphorical "fabric" woven from other texts—but, in such a way that, while the original texts leave a trace or remnant, the ultimate creation is something new. Somewhat predictably, Cockburn's most statistically significant words (see emboldened items) and statistically significant semantic fields (see italicized items), when compared to Corpus B, included:

- *sickness* and the *treatment* of (e.g., **bilious, consciousness, Dr, fever, pills, sickness, strychnine**);
- (specific periods in) *time* (e.g., **o' clock, 1854, hours, the night before, year**);
- *crime* (e.g., **forged**);

- *money* (e.g., **bills, debt, cheques, insurance, liabilities, money, notes**);
- *gambling* (e.g., **bets**)
- *people* (e.g., **Palmer, (Dr) Bamford, Cheshire, Padwick, Bates, Hawkings, prisoner, Mr Stevens**);
- *places* (e.g., **Tattersall, Shrewsbury**).

(Adapted from Archer 2006: 57)

As we might expect, the interpretive element of Cockburn's narrative was at its most obvious when he attempted to account for the intention(s) of the accused. Keywords used to construct motive included **bets, turf, debt, liabilities, money, bills, commit, insurance, forged**, and **motives**. Cumulatively, they allowed Cockburn to propose that Palmer's gambling debts were such he initially forged his mother's name to secure a new gambling income. However, when that source of funding dried up, and his debts began to mount again, he resorted to murder:

> In the course of his pursuits connected with the turf, Palmer became intimate with [Cook]…being in desperate circumstances…he took advantage of [t]his intimacy…when Cook had become the winner of a considerable sum….Out of the circumstances of Palmer at that time arose… the motive which induced him to commit this crime.…Here is a man overwhelmed with pecuniary difficulties, obliged to resort to the desperate expedient of forging acceptances to raise money, hoping to meet them by the proceedings of the insurances he had effected upon a life.…You, gentlemen, must say whether he had not sufficient inducement to commit the crime.

"Cook's" Positioning of Cook and Palmer

A second crucial component of Cockburn's opening narrative was his appraisal of Palmer as a prolific criminal, who had been involved in multiple "transactions of fraud," as well as forgery. Cockburn still needed to establish that Palmer was capable of murder, of course, not least because—as he himself pointed out to the jury—"a man may be guilty of fraud and forgery" but not be prepared to take the life of another. Cockburn sought to do so, initially, by reanimating Cook's own exclamation of "Murder!" shortly before his death. He then went on to stress that the murder was undertaken in a calculated and clandestine fashion—such that Cook was initially inclined to question his own recollections of various events than believe his friend was poisoning him for his own financial gain: for example, when Dr. Bamford informed Cook that Palmer had "ascribed his illness to an excess of wine on the previous day," Cook had stated, "Well, I suppose I must have taken too much, but it's very odd, for I only took three glasses." As Cockburn explained to the jury, however, the "truth" was not that Cook had drunk too much wine, for "whenever he [Palmer] gave him [Cook] anything sickness invariably ensued":

Coffee was brought up to Cook at 4 o'clock when Palmer was there, and he vomited immediately. At 6 some barley-water was taken to him when Palmer was not there, and the barley-water did not produce vomiting. At 8 some arrowroot was given him, Palmer was present, and vomiting took place again.

Rather controversially, Cockburn also opted to introduce the jury to a *darker* Cook in his opening speech: he informed the jury that Cook had been involved, with Palmer, in persuading a mutual acquaintance—Bates (another of Cockburn's keywords)—to allow Palmer to take out a policy on Bates's life, with Palmer as beneficiary, and, by so doing, implied that Cook must have known about (and was perhaps involved in?) some of Palmer's fraudulent activities. The trial transcript does not make it clear as to whether Cook knew the full extent of Palmer's plans to benefit from insuring the life of Bates—and whether Cook knew that Palmer had previously insured his wife and brother, both of whom died in suspicious circumstances. Instead, Cockburn chose to emphasize that "knowing too much" actually equated to a second possible motive for Cook's "murder":

> The fact...that Cook was mixed up in the insurance of Bates may lead one to surmise that he was in possession of secrets [in] relation to the desperate expedients to which this man has resorted to obtain money. I will leave you to say whether this [in] combination [with other] motives may not have led to the crime with which [Palmer] is charged.

THE INTERACTION BETWEEN PROSECUTION COUNSEL AND WITNESSES

Predictably, the prosecution team (Cockburn, James, Welsby, Bodkin, and Huddleston) utilized the examination-in-chief phase of *Palmer* to consolidate their interpretation of events (as put forward by Cockburn). Specifically, they made much of *medicine and medical treatment, dangerous substances,* specific periods of/ moments in *time,* the *place* of the alleged crime, the main players in the crime event, the supporting cast, *money*—especially *debt*—and items relating to gambling and insurance fraud: statistically frequent words therefore included **antinomy, medicine, pills, examination, strychnine, 10 o'clock, 12 o'clock, 8 o'clock, evening, Friday, Monday, Saturday, Tuesday, Nov, Talbot Arms, Palmer, prisoner, Cook, deceased, Bamford, Gardner, James, Sarah Palmer, Thirlby, Thomas Pratt, Ward, Newton, account, betting book, cheque, letter(s), money, papers,** and **payment.**

In the cross-examination phase, the prosecution team sought to defend their interpretation of events while undermining the (counter) crime narrative put forward by the defense. As such, a number of the statistically frequent words/semantic fields related to: *medical illnesses/symptoms,* but in a way that suggested foul play and/or emphasized the victim's suffering (see, e.g., **convulsions, symptoms,** paroxysm, **twitching**, **irritation**); particular *investigations* (**Leeds**, **case**, **experiments**, **dog**, **cats**); and *negation*, *probability* and *likelihood* (**not**, **never may**, **might**, **doubt**, **likely**).

Cook's Betting Book

Length constraints prevent a detailed discussion of all relevant keywords/domains. As such, this subsection traces the prosecution's use (of the witnesses' recollections) of Cook's **betting book** from Cockburn's opening speech through to examination-in-chief. For example, Cockburn initially reported how:

> Scarcely was the breath out of [Cook's] body when Palmer...engages two women to lay out the corpse...on entering the room, [they] find him searching the pockets of a coat which, no doubt, belonged to Cook.... They saw some letters on the mantel-shelf, which, in all probability, had been taken out of the dead man's pocket; and...from that day to this, nothing has been seen or heard either of the betting-book or of any of the papers connected with Cook's money affairs.

Cockburn then summarized a conversation—about the book—between William Vernon Stevens (Cook's stepfather) and Palmer:

> On Friday Mr. Stevens...came down to Rugeley...[to view] the body of his relative.... After dinner, Mr. Stevens asked Jones to step upstairs and bring down all books and papers belonging to Cook. Jones left...to do so, and Palmer followed him...on their return Jones observed that they were unable to find the betting-book or any of the papers belonging to the deceased. Palmer added, "The betting-book would be of no use to you if you found it, for the bets are void by his death."

The initial mention of the betting book during examination-in-chief was rather innocuous: Ishmael Fisher (wine merchant) was actually asked whether "Cook [had] come into [Fisher's] bedroom after he had got up," but he opted to supply Mr. James (and, hence, the jury) nonsolicited information respect his seeing "Cook's betting book in his hand at Shrewsbury" on the day of Polestar's victory. Mr. James then waited until the fifth witness, Elizabeth Mills (chambermaid at the Talbot Arms, where Cook died), to ask about the betting book directly: he asked Mills whether she remembered seeing it "in Mr. Cook's room, during the time he was there." She affirmed she had seen it "in his room on the Monday night before his death" and had passed it to Cook (on his request). Like Fisher, she also supplied additional information: she (i) stated that, following Cook's death, she was asked "to search the room for it" but that, in spite of searching "everywhere," she "could not find it," and (ii) corroborated Cockburn's account (made in his opening) of seeing "Palmer searching the pockets of [the deceased's] coat." Lavinia Barnes (waitress) then confirmed that Mills had searched for the betting book, and William Henry Jones Jr. (surgeon), that he (like Mills) had seen Palmer "with Mr. Cook's coat in his hand...[but] could not find any betting book, or any papers." The fifth witness to mention Cook's betting book—Stevens—also corroborated aspects of Cockburn's criminal occurrence narrative, specifically, Jones being unable to find his son's betting book, and his conversation with Palmer:

I said, "How is this?"— Palmer said, "Oh, it is no manner of use if you find it," ... —I said, "No use, sir! I am the best judge of that"—he again said, "It is of no manner of use"—I said, "I am the best judge of that; I am told it is of use; I understand my son won a great deal of money at Shrewsbury." ... Palmer said, "It is no use, I assure you; when a man dies his bets are done with; " I think those were the words; "besides," he said, "Cook received the greater part of his money on the course at Shrewsbury"—I said, "Very well, sir, the book must be found ..." Palmer then, in a much quieter tone, said, "Oh, it will be found, no doubt"—I again said, "Sir, it shall be found"—I then went to the door of the sitting room, and...I desired [the housekeeper] that everything in the deceased's room might be locked up ...

As Stevens' account pointed to (but did not establish) Palmer's involvement, the prosecution sought to demonstrate how "Palmer had collected [Cook's] bets and applied the proceeds to his own purposes" (Cairns 1998: 155) in the examinations of a series of witnesses (e.g., Samuel Cheshire, Charles Weatherby, John Boycott, Captain Hatton, and George Herring). Samuel Cheshire, for example, confirmed seeing a bill "addressed to Messrs. Weatherby...[which stated] something to the effect of 'Please pay to Mr. William Palmer the sum of 300l.'" And Herring read out a document that Palmer had dictated to him, which supposedly "settled Cook's account" (during Cook's illness). However, Palmer also instructed Herring to pay some of his own bills (to Mr. Pratt and Mr. Padwick).

THE OPENING SPEECH OF SERGEANT SHEE

Shee gave his opening speech on behalf of the defense on day seven of the trial. Similar to Cockburn, his initial tactic involved reanimating the voice of both Cook and the "population" at large. Shee did so, however, so that he might allude to the infamy and prejudicial views against Palmer that the case had generated prior to coming to trial:

Gentlemen, it is useless for me to conceal what you know perfectly well, what...[you] cannot wholly have effaced from your recollection, that for six long months, under the sanction and upon the authority of science, an opinion has universally prevailed that the voice of the blood of John Parsons Cook was crying up unto us from the ground, and that that cry was met by the whole population under an impression and conviction of the prisoner's guilt in a delirium of horror and indignation by another cry of "blood for blood!" You cannot have failed to have...been to a great extent influenced by that cry; you could not know that it would be your duty to sit in that box...whatever that opinion may have been it is your duty [now] to discard it, at least until you have heard the evidence on both sides.

Shee's next tactic was to stress how, having had "no opinion upon the guilt or the innocence of the prisoner at the bar" prior to studying the papers that had come into his hands, he had been able to reach "the right judgement in this case"—that Palmer was innocent. As a means of emphasizing Palmer's innocence further, Shee also recontextualized Palmer's response to the murder charge by embedding it in a statement of his own opinion: "I believe that there never was a truer word pronounced than the words which he [Palmer] pronounced when he said "Not guilty" to the charge." Such behavior was so unusual that it provoked both Cockburn and the Lord Chief Justice Campbell to themselves recontextualize the incident in their final addresses to the jury. Interestingly, Cockburn utilized Shee's "unprecedented assurance of his conviction of his client's innocence" as a means of grouping him with "those advocates" who were prepared to "adopt a course" that was "more or less an insult to a jury, the endeavouring to intimidate them by the fear of their own consciences and the fear of the country's opinion." Campbell's concern, in contrast, was not the (potential) intimidation of the jury but, rather, the resultant merging of (what are meant to be) distinct functions (i.e., testimonial and defensive) "if...a jury [was] to believe...a prisoner [was] not guilty because his advocate express[ed] his perfect conviction of his innocence."

Shee's "Evidence"

It is difficult to ascertain whether Shee was uncertain in respect to how far lawyers could go in encouraging jurors to "discern the truth" or willing to (deliberately) introduce personal opinion in order to test the limits of forensic argument at this time (cf. Cairns 1998). What is clear, however, is that many of his statistically frequent words—**appear, Attorney General, because, convulsions, Crown, Elizabeth Mills, evidence, Fisher, friend, good, innocence, knew, knowledge, probably, not, supposed, suspicions, tetanic, theory, submit, Stevens, strychnia, think, thought, would**, and **could**—highlight Shee's attempt to show how "the case for the Crown" was reliant on "circumstantial evidence."

Shee also argued vociferously that, if one was to look at the "long correspondence...put in...and scrutinise it in every corner...this correspondence saves the prisoner, if there is common sense in man." Part of "this correspondence" related to letters that, according to the prosecution, proved Palmer was so in debt he was prepared to murder Cook. But Shee utilized those same letters to establish Palmer was helped by Cook, and helped his "friend" in return:

Can you doubt when you take all [this] together—the dining together...Cook writing that letter to Fisher, saying it was of the greatest importance to him as well as to Palmer that the 200 [Palmer owed] should be paid...can you doubt that...Cook was a most convenient friend to Palmer, and that [Palmer] could not by any possibility do without him...[and Palmer, in return, was] the dearest and best friend of Cook...who liked him and loved him well enough...[to] be ready to attend to him in case he wanted assistance during the night.

Shee's (Re-)positioning of Cook, Taylor, and Stevens

Shee also referred to a letter (dated December 4th) co-authored by Dr. Taylor—the man tasked with examining Cook's stomach contents—in his opening. The letter was important, as it revealed that Taylor (and his colleague, Dr. Rees) had failed to "find strychnia, prussic acid, or any trace of opium" in Cook's remains. Indeed, Shee relayed how Taylor himself had acknowledged that he only "came to the conclusion" that Cook was "poisoned" by **strychnia** (one of Shee's keywords) after attending Cook's:

inquest, and hear[ing] the evidence of Elizabeth Mills...Jones...[and also] Roberts, who spoke to the purchase of strychnia poison by Palmer on the morning of the Tuesday...[Yet, t]hat opinion...Instantly followed by the verdict of wilful murder...flew upon the wings of the Press into every house in the United Kingdom. It became known that, according to the opinion of a man whose life had been devoted to science, a gentleman of personal character perfectly unimpeachable...Cook's death had been caused by strychnia.

Shee further suggested Taylor's testimony (given during the prosecution's examination-in-chief) was "not...scientific, or well-informed, or consistent testimony, but...testimony ill-informed," for Taylor had not:

seen a single case of strychnia in the human subject; and yet he ha[d] been daring enough, knowing that the consequences would be disastrous to this man—knowing perfectly well that...the great majority of the world would take for granted that a medical man in his position would not give a hasty opinion—he ha[d] the incredible courage to declare, on his oath, that the pills that were given, as far as he knew, by Dr. Bamford, contained strychnia, and that Cook was poisoned by them!

Shee also chose to position Cook and Stevens (Cook's stepfather) in ways that were unfavorable to them but favorable to Palmer—and referred to Stevens' deposition to do so. For example, Shee recounted Stevens' own deposition in a way that suggested he was immediately resolved upon wrong-footing Palmer, following his stepson's death:

He [said that he] dined that day at Rugeley, and asked Palmer to dinner with him, and questioned him about the betting-book; got angry that it was not produced, dissembled with Palmer, cross-examined him, went up to town, met him afterwards at the station at Euston Square, afterwards at Rugby, afterwards at Wolverton, again at Rugeley, and at last threw off the mask, and…gave Palmer clearly to understand that he suspected him, and intended to probe the whole matter to the very core.

As previously established (in the "Cook's 'Sudden' Illness" section), Stevens had pushed for a postmortem, the results of which did not establish murder—according to Shee—but, rather, Cook's "course of life and his general [ill] health." Although Shee expressed "pity" at having to "say anything hard of" the deceased, he then went on to draw the jury's attention (albeit briefly) to Cook's "vices" and "the drinking, idle, racing company which he kept."

THE INTERACTION BETWEEN DEFENSE COUNSEL AND WITNESSES

The keywords/domains utilized by the defense counsel during cross-examination and examination-in-chief display a strong resemblance with one another and also (some of) the keywords of the prosecution during their examination-in-chief and cross-examination. What the defense team (Shee, Grove, Gray, Keaneley) did not do, perhaps predictably, was discuss Palmer's gambling problems/debt to any great extent, beyond pointing out Cook's willingness to help his friend, when necessary. But they did attempt to undermine the other aspects of the prosecution's criminal occurrence narrative. For example, in their cross-examinations, the defense team consistently utilized words/multi-word-units pertaining to (periods of/moments in) *time* (**10 o'clock, after, before**), the alleged *crime* (**poison, poisoning, strychnia, strychnine**), the victim, the accused, and other actors (**Cook, Dolly, Gardner, Jones, Palmer, Stevens**), significant *places* (**Rugeley, Shrewsbury, Stafford, Talbot Arms**), *sickness/symptoms* (and the *treatment* of) (**antinomy, convulsions, deceased, disease, dose/s, emetic, idiopathic, ill, irritation, patient, paroxysm, spasm/s, symptoms, tetanic, tetanus, vomited**), *death* (**death, died**), the *medical profession* and their *investigations* (**administered, animals, case/s, coroner, Dr(.), examination, examined, experiments, inquest, medical, grain/s, observed, effect**), *anatomy and physiology* (**blood, body, heart, limbs, spinal, stomach**), *food* (**broth**), *opinion* (**believe, opinion**), **knowledge** and *remembering* (**remember, recollect**). Their purpose? To remind the jury that the prosecution's case was based on circumstantial evidence and that the symptoms that Cook experienced were not as similar to those suffered by a recent victim of strychnia poisoning (Dove) as the prosecution were claiming. By way of illustration, under cross-examination by Grove, George Morley (the doctor who attended to Dove) admitted that he:

> discovered strychnia with all the tests [he] applied [on Dove's stomach and also animals] with more or less distinctness [adding that he had] detected strychnia in [a] stomach two months after death, and after decomposition had proceeded to a considerable extent.

The defense team's examination-in-chief sought to cast further doubt on the prosecution's criminal occurrence narrative, by reaffirming the lack of strychnine in Cook's remains, and the need to therefore find Palmer innocent. Specifically, they asked a group of medical experts (thirteen in total) to debate the validity of Taylor's "findings," as well as the extent to which Cook's symptoms and subsequent death could have been caused by tetanic convulsions (as opposed to tetanus)—which helps to explain the defense team's statistically frequent use of the following: the alleged *crime* (**poison/ed, strychnia**), *sickness/symptoms* (and the *treatment* of) (**administered, came on, consciousness, convulsion/s, convulsive, disease, dose, Dr., epilepsy, epileptic, paroxysm/s, patient, in a state, congested, rigidity, spasm/s, symptoms, tetaniform, tetanus, vomiting**), *death* (**death, decomposition, died**), the *medical* profession and their *investigations* (**animal/s, case/s, detect/ed, observed, post mortem examination, evidence, examination, examined, experimented, experiments, tests**), *anatomy and physiology* (**blood, body, brain, chemical, cord, muscles, stomach, contents, fluid, grain, granules, membranes, spinal, throat, vessels**), and *opinion* (**opinion, judgment**). By way of illustration, one of the defense team's expert witnesses, Dr. George Robinson, confirmed that he had:

> devoted considerable attention to pathology, and…published essays on it....[Yet] From the symptoms [he had heard] described [his] opinion [was] that Mr. Cook died from tetanic convulsions, by which [he] mean[t], not the disease of tetanus, but convulsions similar to those witnessed in tetanus [and which]…occasionally assume the nature of epilepsy.

Robinson went on to proclaim that he knew "of no department of pathology which [wa]s more obscure than that of convulsive disease" and thus pointed (albeit unknowingly) to a problem that the defense team was facing: how to convince the jury that tetanic convulsions had, in fact, killed Cook. The "problem" was not lost on Cockburn, however: he immediately asked Robinson to confirm whether he'd seen such "violent" symptoms (as Cook suffered) in other cases of death caused by tetanic convulsions, and Robinson had to concede that he had not (in his "own experience").

ADDRESSES TO THE JURY

Closing speeches are the ultimate examples of "transformational texts" as they enable prosecution counsel (in our case, Cockburn) and presiding judge (in our case, Campbell) to communicate their criminal occurrence narrative and instructions to lay jurors (immediately) prior to them giving their verdict. The defense counsel did not make a closing speech, however: while the Prisoners' Counsel Act (1836) ensured defense counsels could make opening speeches by the time of the

Palmer trial, they were not given the option of making closing addresses until 1856 (see Criminal Procedure Act: see also Hostettler 2006: 146).[5]

The Attorney General's Closing Speech to the Jury

As part of his re-presentation of prior events, Cockburn reiterated much of the criminal occurrence narrative he and his team had so carefully crafted and maintained throughout the trial. On this occasion, however, he enacted a pseudo-dialogue with the jury, in which he initially summarized the case for them as a choice between "a natural death" and a death "by the foul means of poison," adding "if the latter proposition be sanctioned by [their] approbation, then comes the important...question of whether the prisoner at the bar was the author of [Cook's] death."

As all the relevant evidence (of both sides) had now been submitted, Cockburn was able to use keywords denoting *cause and effect* (**cause, due** (to), **because**), *finding/showing* (**purpose, so, evidence, found, find, result, therefore, conclusion**), and *evaluation* (in respect to *truth/falsity* and *importance*: **fact/s, true, forged, important, great**) to emphasize that this was, indeed, a "case of tetanus from strychnia," administered to Cook by Palmer. He also emphasized how the prosecution case had been based on "the most abundant and conclusive evidence"—which "gentlemen" renowned for their expertise had confirmed—and that "experts" for "the other side," in contrast, had "misconceive[d] every fact which they could pervert to their purpose" "and prostituted [science] to the purposes of a particular cause in a Court of justice" "with the view of deceiving a jury."

Ironically, of course, Cockburn's own case was built upon circumstantial medical evidence as opposed to established medical "fact." Rather than avoid this issue in his closing, however, he returned to it. Initially, he pointed out that:

> If strychnia had been found...there would have been no difficulty, and we should have had none of the ingenious theories which...have been brought forward.

Cockburn then asked the jury to "consider" a "question" that seemed to be contrary to the prosecution's need to prove their case beyond all possible doubt: "whether the absence of its detection leads conclusively to the view that this death could not have been caused by the administration of that poison." As an apparent "answer," he also went on to spell out the state that Cook's stomach was in, when Drs Taylor and Rees came to examine it:

> They tell you that when the stomach of this man was brought to them for the purpose of analysis, it was presented to them under the most unfavourable circumstances. They say that its contents had been lost, and that they had no opportunity of experimenting upon them...[because] there appears (at all events, I will not put it higher than accident), by accident, to have been some spilling of the contents.

Aware that three of the medical experts introduced by "the other side" (i.e., Mr. Nunneley, Mr. Herepath, and Dr. Letheby) had stated that "no matter how contaminated or how mixed with impurities, they would have been able to ascertain the presence of strychnia in the stomach, *if strychnia had been there*" (my italics), Cockburn then set about proving that their "partiality and partisanship" effectively rendered them "discreditable and unworthy witness[es]." He was particularly scathing of Herepath in his closing speech, not least because (under cross-examination) Cockburn had forced him:

> to admit…a fact which had come to [Cockburn's] knowledge, that he has again and again asserted that this case was a case of poisoning by strychnia, but that Dr. Taylor had not known how to find it out—he admits that that is a statement he has again and again made.

Cockburn's re-contextualized comment prompted Shee to interrupt the closing speech at this point, so that he might correct him, for this was something that the newspapers had assigned to Herepath. Indeed, Herepath had actually answered Cockburn's cross-examination question by asserting:

> Judging from reports in newspapers, I have said in conversation that strychnia had been given, and that "If it was there, Professor Taylor ought to have found it."

What seems to be in question here, then, is Cockburn's literal *transformation* of Herepath's words so that they *meant* something different from what Herepath had apparently intended (cf. Kristeva 1980). And yet, Herepath's assertion was ambiguous enough to allow Cockburn to make an equally valid response to Shee during his closing speech. And it was one that intimated that the newspaper summations had captured Herepath's "real" opinion:

> He [Herepath] did not venture to say that the newspaper statement in any way differed from the fact which he admitted in this Court. I have seen that gentleman not merely contenting himself with coming forward, when called upon for the purposes of justice, to state that which he knew as a matter of science or of experiment, but I have seen him mixing himself up as a thoroughgoing partisan in this case, advising my learned friend, suggesting question upon question, and that in behalf of a man whom he has again and again asserted he believed to be a poisoner by strychnia. I do not say that alters the fact; but I do say that it induces one to look at the credit of those witnesses with a very great amount of suspicion….I ask you therefore to look at the statements of those witnesses with dispassionate consideration before you attach implicit credit to them. But let me assume that all they say is true, that it is the fact that they in their experiments have succeeded in discovering strychnia when mixed with other impurities, and contaminated, no matter by what cause—they say that no extent of putrefaction, no amount of decomposition, will alter the character of that vegetable matter, so that it may not be detected

if it is in the human stomach. Be it so. But then must it always be found in every case where death has ensued? Professor Taylor says no; and he says it would be a most dangerous and mischievous proposition to assert that that must necessarily be so—that it would enable many a guilty man to escape who, by administering the smallest quantity whereby life can be affected and destroyed, might by that means prevent the possibility of the detection of the poison in the stomach of the individual.

Cockburn's parting advice to the jury made reference to the "voice of the country"—and, by so doing, echoed Shee's earlier opening speech. That advice involved "pay[ing] no regard to the voice of the country, whether it be for condemnation or acquittal" and, instead, listening only to "the internal voice of [their] own consciences." However, as his very last utterance (and many of the utterances which preceded it) exposed, Cockburn actually sought a guilty "verdict, by which alone...the safety of society [could] be secured, and the demands...of public justice...satisfied."

Campbell's Address to the Jury

Cockburn's address was followed by that of the presiding judge, Lord Chief Justice Campbell. From the outset, Campbell made it clear that his role was to "guide" rather than "influence" the jury. However, his statistically frequent lexical items paint a different picture—namely, a speech characterized by *evaluation* (**evidence, facts, doubt, conclusion**), *importance* (**important/importance**), *cause/connection* (**cause, according** to, **regard** to), *finding/showing* (**found, find, appears, exhibited**), *thought/belief* (**opinion, believe, consider, think, consideration, seems**), *comparison* (**consistent, other, against**), modality (**will, would, may, must, should, ought, could, can, might, certainly**), and conditionals (**unless, if**). Rather than engage in a pseudo-dialogue, as Cockburn had done, Campbell opted to reanimate the (pre)trial speech of many of the lay actors: specifically, he read from and/or summarized their witness depositions. Of these lay actors, **Taylor**, **Newton**, **Rees**, and **Roberts** were utilized frequently enough by Campbell to be deemed key to his address (by Wmatrix). For example, Campbell drew the jury's attention to "Roberts swear[ing]...that he sold strychnia, among other drugs, to Palmer" so that he might emphasize (i) how Roberts's testimony had remained "undenied and unquestioned" throughout the trial, and (ii) that the jurors should therefore "consider" Palmer's reason(s) for buying the poison. Campbell then pointed out other "instances of [Palmer's] conduct" for the jurors to consider—but in a way that summarized (a large part of) the prosecution's criminal occurrence narrative:

He was eager to have the body fastened down in the coffin. Then, with regard to the betting book, there is certainly evidence from which you may infer that he did get possession of the betting book, that he abstracted it and concealed it. Then, gentlemen, you must not omit his conduct in trying to bribe the postboy to overturn the carriage in which the jar was being conveyed, to be analysed in London, and from which evidence might be obtained of his guilt. Again, you find him tampering with the postmaster, and procuring from the postmaster the opening of a letter from Dr. Taylor, who had been examining the contents of the jar, to Mr. Gardner, the attorney employed upon the part of Mr Stevens. And then, gentlemen, you have tampering with the coroner, and trying to induce him to procure a verdict from the coroner's jury which would amount to an acquittal. These are serious matters for your consideration, but you, and you alone, will say what inference is to be drawn from them. … Either you may be of opinion that the case on the part of the prosecution is insufficient, or you may be of opinion that the answer to it is satisfactory.

This similarity is even more apparent when we list Campbell's keywords relating to *crime, law and order* (i.e., **prisoner, witness/es, verdict, jury, court, trial, prosecution, advocate, bar, case/s, guilt/y, offence, conviction, motive**), *death* (i.e., **death, deceased**), *medical treatment* (i.e., **medical, disease, tetanus, epilepsy, symptoms, idiopathic, administered, given**), *dangerous substances* (i.e., **strychnia, antimony, poison**), and *investigations* (i.e., **examination, examined, experiments, animals, scientific**).

When summarizing the evidence for the defense, Campbell opted to also inform the jury of the defense witnesses' "reliability" (or lack of). For example, Dr. Nunneley was said to have given "his evidence in a manner not quite becoming a witness in a Court of Justice." Campbell did not offer any reasoning but did state that Nunneley's "general opinion" differed "very materially…from several of the witnesses who were examined on the part of the prosecution"—thereby implicitly suggesting to the jury that the prosecution witnesses had been more convincing than some of the defense witnesses, in his view. Campbell also alluded to the testimony of Herepath, as Cockburn had done. But he was less critical than the latter, describing Herepath as "a very skilful chemist," who "no doubt":

spoke sincerely what he thought…[in respect to] when there has been death by strychnia, strychnia ought to be discovered; but it seems he intimated an opinion on this very case of Cook there might have been strychnia, and that Dr. Taylor did not use the proper means to detect it.

The implication, of course, was that he shared Cockburn's view that Herepath believed strychnine to be present in Cook's body.

Shee's Last Stand

Before Campbell had finished his summing up, Shee complained that his question to the jury—"whether the evidence that ha[d] been brought forward [was] consistent with the death of Cook by strychnia"—was inappropriate and that the jurors should actually be asked to address "whether the medical evidence establishe[d] beyond all reasonable doubt the death of Cook by strychnia." At this point, Campbell turned to address the jury a second time:

> Gentleman of the jury, I did not submit to you that the question upon which your ver-
> dict alone was to turn was whether the symptoms of Cook were consistent with death
> by strychnia, but I said that that was a most material question for you; and I desired you
> to consider that question with a view to guide your judgment as to whether he died from
> natural disease, or whether he did not die by poison, by strychnia administered by the
> prisoner. Then I went on to say that if you were of the opinion that the symptoms were
> consistent with death from strychnia, you should go on to consider the other evidence
> given in the case, whether strychnia had been administered to him; and whether strych-
> nia had been administered by the prisoner at the bar; and those are the questions that I
> again put to you.... Do not find a verdict of guilty unless you believe that the strychnia
> was administered to the deceased by the prisoner at the bar. But if you belief that, it is
> your duty to God and man to find a verdict of guilty.

The jury returned a verdict of guilty after "an hour and eighteen minutes" of deliberation.

CONCLUSION

It is widely accepted that the modern courtroom is characterized by textual travel—in the sense that pretrial material is (re-)interpreted, (re-)visited, and (re-)created in ways that lead to "new" texts. As this chapter demonstrates, the nineteenth-century courtroom following the Prisoners' Counsel Act (1836) involved very similar (textual travel) practices, in many respects. For example, the respective counsels within *Palmer* alluded to and/or reanimated the voices of lay actors in both their addresses to the jury and their (cross-)examination of witnesses. They also referred (on numerous occasions) to pretrial documentation, some of which was directly related to the workings of the legal system (i.e., depositions, autopsy reports, etc.) and some of which became an important means by which respective counsel established (the lack of a) motive and thus innocence or guilt (see, e.g., their observations respecting Cook's betting book, Palmer's insurance claims, letters, bills, etc). In a very real sense, then, *Palmer* can be said to be a "heterogeneous constitution of [other] texts" (cf. Fairclough 1992: 85).

Such intertextuality comes at a price, of course, for the need to "reduce" a case of "labyrinthine facts" (Cairns 1998: 163) to a coherent crime narrative that can be successfully conveyed to a jury means that the testimony of some witnesses will become reshaped (at best) and (at worst) become backgrounded to the extent that it no longer reflects the original, *textually* speaking (cf. Harris 2001). Moreover, in reanimating the voice of murder victims, as is the case here, counsel may (sometimes wittingly) construct intention in a way that (i) does not reflect the actual ("criminal") event and/or (ii) cannot easily be (in)validated.

In this chapter, I have demonstrated how the keyness approach might be used to detect *traces* of texts (be they specific words, multi-word-units, or semantic domains), which have been (statistically) replicated and, in many cases, recontextualized, as a means of creating "new" meta-narratives (depicting guilt or innocence). In some instances, there is evidence to suggest the process of "re-using as a means of (re-)shaping" is undertaken deliberately, by the respective counsels: note, in particular, Cockburn's ability to weave scientific and circumstantial evidence together into a compelling criminal occurrence narrative that the jurors were willing to believe. In others, the keyness (i.e., statistical frequency) of particular words and/ or semantic domains (e.g., words relating to *dangerous substances*) probably relates more to the type of evidence presented in a case such as *Palmer*. As such, I recommend that statistical analysis be seen as a way of uncovering linguistic items that are (i) indicative of textual travel having taken place, and thus (ii) are likely to repay more detailed (qualitative) exploration (see Archer 2009: 4).

NOTES

1. I have utilized the Old Bailey account of *Palmer* (ref: t18560514–490) and *The Queen vs. Palmer*, both of which are available online (via the *Old Bailey Online* website and Google Books, respectively), and also Watson's (1952) revision of Knott's *Trial of William Palmer*, which is part of the renowned *Notable British Trials Series*.
2. For a more detailed explanation of the keyness approach, see Archer 2009: 1–4.
3. The types of statistical operations used to find these statistically (in)frequent words/ domains (i.e., cross-tabulation/chi-square significance test) can be undertaken manually, of course. However, Wmatrix can carry out these procedures very quickly/efficiently.
4. For useful accounts of Palmer's life and alleged crimes, see, e.g., Burney 2006, Davenport-Hines 2004, and Watson 1952.
5. Even in today's (English and Welsh) judicial system, counsel for the defense can only address the jury once. As a result, most opt to make a closing speech.

REFERENCES

Archer, D. 2006. Tracing the development of advocacy in two nineteenth-century English trials. In *Diachronic Perspectives on Domain-Specific English*, ed. Marina Dossena and Irma Taavitsainen, 43–67. Bern: Peter Lang.
———. 2009. Does frequency really matter? In *What's in a Word-list? Investigating Word Frequency and Keyword Extraction*, ed. Dawn Archer, 1–15. Surrey, UK: Ashgate.
Bauman, R., and C. L. Briggs. 1990. Poetics and performance as critical perspectives on language and social life. *Annual Review of Anthropology* 19: 59–88.
Burney, I. 2006. *Poison, Detection, and the Victorian Imagination*. Manchester/New York: Manchester University Press.

Cairns, D. J. A. 1998. *Advocacy and the Making of the Adversarial Criminal Trial 1800–1865.* Oxford: Clarendon Press.

Davenport-Hines, R. 2004. Palmer, William [the Rugeley Poisoner] (1824–1856). In *Oxford Dictionary of National Biography*. Oxford: Oxford University Press.

Derrida, J. [1972] 1981. *Positions*. London: Athlone Press.

Fairclough, N. 1992. *Discourse and Social Change*. Cambridge: Polity Press.

———. 2001. *Language and Power*. 2d ed. London: Longman.

Gergen, K. 1999. *An Invitation to Social Construction*. Thousand Oaks, CA: Sage Publications.

Harris, S. 2001. Fragmented narratives and multiple tellers: Witness and defendant accounts in trials. *Discourse Studies* 3(1): 53–74.

Hostettler, J. 2006. *Fighting for Justice: The History and Origins of Adversary Trial*. Hampshire, UK: Waterside Press.

Kristeva, J. [1966] 1986. Word, dialogue and novel. In *The Kristeva Reader*, ed. Toril Moi,, 34–61. Oxford: Blackwell.

Kristeva, J. 1980. *Desire in Language: A Semiotic Approach to Literature and Art*. New York: Columbia University Press.

Rayson, P. 2003. *Matrix: A statistical method and software tool for linguistic analysis through corpus comparison*. Ph.D. diss. Lancaster University.

Stephen, F. [1863] 1890. *A General View of the Criminal Law*. 2d ed. London: MacMillan and Co.

Watson, Eric R. 1952. *Trial of William Palmer*. Revised Edition. Edinburgh: William Hodge.

PART THREE

*Judicial Discourse as Legal
Recontextualization*

CHAPTER 9

Post-Penetration Rape and the Decontextualization of Witness Testimony

SUSAN EHRLICH

INTRODUCTION

As the theme of this volume suggests, a salient feature of communication within the legal system is the "travelling" of texts across contexts (Blommaert 2005)—what Bauman and Briggs (1990) have termed entextualization practices. Texts travel in the legal system, for instance, when trial testimony is represented in closing arguments, is discussed by juries, or is excerpted in the appellate decisions of judges.[1] For Bauman and Briggs (1990: 73–75), what is significant about these kinds of entextualization practices are their transformative effects (see also Silverstein and Urban 1996). That is, once a stretch of talk is "lifted out of its interactional setting" and turned into a "text" (what Bauman and Briggs define as "discourse rendered decontextualizable"), it may bring something from its earlier context, but may also take on different meanings as it is "recentered" in a new context. Indeed, when Blommaert (2005: 78) talks about "texts that do not travel well," he is referring to this transformational process, specifically, the recontextualization of texts within discursive spaces where the texts' original meanings and values are altered. Closely linked to Blommaert's idea of texts not travelling well is his notion of "voice." For Blommaert, when speakers' words are moved into contextualizing spaces where their original meanings are transformed, speakers can "lose voice." Voice, according to Blommaert (2005: 68), is the "capacity to generate an uptake of one's words as close as possible to one's desired contextualization." Using Blommaert's notions of textual travel and of voice, in this chapter I attempt to demonstrate how a lay litigant—a complainant in a rape trial—loses her "voice" as she engages with the legal system. More specifically, I show how excerpts from the complainant's testimony are entextualized, that is, they are extracted from their original speech event, the trial, and turned into texts. Once entextualized, they are transplanted into various other contexts within the legal system, and, crucially, when recontextualized in these other contexts, take on meanings that are quite different from the ones originally intended. In Blommaert's terms, the complainant's testimony does not receive an "uptake" during its textual travels that corresponds to its original contextualization.

POST-PENETRATION RAPE

In what follows, I examine a type of rape case that has appeared relatively recently in courts in the United States—what has been termed a post-penetration rape case. The first post-penetration rape case was heard in a US court almost 30 years ago and since that time post-penetration rape cases have increasingly been heard in US courts. Post-penetration rape is defined as a situation in which both parties initially consent to sexual intercourse, but at some time during the act of intercourse, one party, typically the woman, withdraws her consent; after this withdrawal of consent, the other party, typically the man, forces the woman to continue intercourse against her will (Davis 2005: 732–33). The question that has arisen in these cases is whether a rape can legally occur if a victim initially consents to intercourse but then withdraws her consent "post-penetration." The answer to this question has been different in different jurisdictions and courts. Some courts have found post-penetration rape to be a legal impossibility—that is, if a woman consents to sexual intercourse, that initial consent prevents the sexual act from ever legally becoming a rape. Other courts have held that a withdrawal of consent post-penetration negates any earlier consent and thereby subjects the defendant to rape charges if he continues what has become nonconsensual sexual intercourse.

The case that I analyze in this chapter, *Maouloud Baby v. the State of Maryland*, has a complex procedural history revolving around the issue I have just described. The accused, Baby, was convicted of first degree rape and some lesser offenses (i.e., one count of sexual offense and two counts of third degree sexual offense) in December 2004 and was sentenced to 15 years in jail, with all but five years suspended.[2] Baby appealed this decision and, upon appeal, the Maryland Court of Special Appeals (the second highest court in Maryland) reversed Baby's convictions in September 2006, arguing that the trial judge erred in failing to tell the jury of a 1980 case, *Battle v. Maryland*, which determined that if a woman "consents [to sexual intercourse] prior to penetration and withdraws the consent following penetration, there is no rape" (cited in *Maouloud Baby v. State of Maryland*, Court of Special Appeals of Maryland, 2005).[3] In other words, the Court of Special Appeals believed that Maryland was bound by the *Battle* decision—that post-penetration rape was a legal impossibility—and ordered a new trial to be conducted in light of this decision. In April 2008, after Baby and the State cross-appealed to the Maryland Court of Appeals (the highest court in Maryland), the Court of Appeals also determined that the trial judge erred in not responding to the jury's questions about the legal possibility of post-penetration rape. For this reason, like the Court of Special Appeals, it reversed Baby's convictions and ordered a new trial.[4] In contrast to the Court of Special Appeals, however, the Court of Appeals concluded that the crime of first degree rape in Maryland does include post-penetration rape: "the crime of first degree rape includes post-penetration vaginal intercourse ... without the consent of the victim, even if the victim consented to the initial penetration" (*State of Maryland v. Maouloud Baby*, Court of Appeals of Maryland, 2007.).[5] That is, the Court of Appeals clarified the Maryland rape statute, arguing that a woman may say "no" at any time during intercourse and a man can be subject to rape charges/convictions if he does not stop.

While the *Baby* case, as I have just described, came to be understood as a post-penetration rape case in its appellate decisions, the trial was not framed in this way, neither by the prosecution nor by the defense. Rather, the prosecution in the case argued that the complainant never consented to the sexual acts initiated by Baby (nor to the sexual acts initiated by another young man, Mike) while the defense argued that she did consent to these acts. Crucially, neither the prosecution nor the defense invoked categories of pre- vs. post-penetration consent or withdrawal of consent. So, how did the case become framed as a post-penetration rape case in the appellate decisions—a framing that is predicated on the assumption that the complainant at some point consented to sexual intercourse with Baby? These questions are particularly perplexing because, as I argue below, the audio-taped recordings of the trial show that what was represented as consent in the appellate decisions is more reasonably understood in the complainant's testimony as a strategy of resistance. Indeed, in what follows, I show how the complainant's trial testimony was reshaped and reinterpreted as it was entextualized and then recontextualized in different kinds of contextualizing frameworks within the legal system. Given the metaphor of "travelling texts," I organize the following sections chronologically, tracing the movement of the complainant's testimony from the trial context, into the jury discussions (to the extent that those can be known based on the jury's communication with the trial judge), and finally into the decisions of the appellate courts. (See Ehrlich 2007 for a comparable investigation within the context of a Canadian sexual assault trial.)

THE COMPLAINANT'S TESTIMONY: CONSENT OR A STRATEGY OF RESISTANCE?

The adversarial nature of trials within the Anglo-American legal system means that determining the "facts" of cases is often not a straightforward task. Nonetheless, there were a number of "facts" in the Baby trial that the prosecution and the defense agreed upon. The complainant, Jewel, and the accused, Baby, met at a McDonald's restaurant the night of the events in question—December 13, 2003.

Jewel was with her best friend, Lacey, and was introduced to Baby because he was both a friend of Lacey's younger brother and of Lacey's boyfriend. When Jewel and Lacey were about to leave McDonald's, Baby asked whether he and his friend, Mike, could get a ride in Jewel's car. They all drove to a community center where they believed there was a party. Upon discovering there was no party, Jewel drove to a clearing between two townhouses and the four passengers exited the car. Baby and Mike smoked marijuana and joked with the young women about getting a hotel room. The four then drove back to McDonald's in Jewel's car and Lacey left the group to join a friend. Jewel then agreed to drive Mike and Baby to a residential neighborhood where she parked her car and agreed to sit in the back seat of the car with the two young men. It was at this point in the testimonies of Jewel and Baby where their stories began to diverge, although it should be noted that the Court of Special Appeals remarked in its opinion that the accused's testimony "was surprisingly consistent" with the complainant's (*Maouloud Baby v. State of Maryland*, Court of Special Appeals of Maryland, 2005). Below I present an excerpt from Jewel's testimony in re-direct examination (following cross-examination); this testimony describes, from Jewel's point of view, the events that transpired once she agreed to sit in the back seat of the car with Baby and Mike.[6]

Excerpt 1

1	L:	Okay. Now, about the- when you said- when- when they started
2		to do these things and you said, "No, I'm not that kind
3		of person." Jewel, how many times did you say "No," when you
4		were in the backseat.
5	JL:	I don't know how many times. Every time I said, "No," or "I
6		have to go," or "My ten minutes are up," then they'd add uh-
7		add time or be like, "As soon as you get done with this, you can
8		leave."
9	L:	Well, was it- do you think it was- was it more than once that you
10		said [no.]
11	JL:	[Yes.]
12	L:	And I have to go? =
13	JL:	= Yes.
14	L:	More than five times?
15	JL:	Yes.
16	L:	More than ten times? (1.0) Too many to count? You're
17		nodding, is that yes?
18	JL:	Yes.
19	L:	Okay. Now uhm, uh- in those times when you were saying
20		"No," and "Stop," Where was Maouloud. (1.0) Was he in the
21		car?
22	JL:	Yes.

23	L:	(5.0) And when, uhm, M-Mike first tried to put his penis in
24		you and he said- "If I can't-" he wasn't able to do that, is that
25		what you said?
26	JL:	Yes.
27	L:	And he said, "If I can't fit, you can't fit," who was he talking to,
28		Jewel.
29	JL:	M-talking to Maouloud.
30	L:	And Maouloud was still in the car at the [time] that happened?
31	JL:	[Yes.]
32	L:	What was Maouloud doing at the time Mike was trying to put
33		his penis in you.
34	JL:	Uhm, he was sitting like, I mean he was kind of hunched over
35		like in- on the- like, in the back of Mike. And that's when he
36		opened my legs and stuck his fingers.
37	L:	When who opened his legs [and stuck his] fingers.
38	JL:	[Maouloud.]
39	L:	And this is after Mike said, "If I can't fit, you can't fit?"
40	JL:	Yes.
41	L:	((clears throat)) (4.0) Now you said that you said "No," and
42		"Stop" too many times to count.
43	JL:	Yes.
44	L:	Did you ever say, "It hurts?"
45	JL:	Yes.
46	L:	How many times did you say, "It hurts," Jewel.
47	JL:	Uhm, I know I kind of yelled a little bit when they put- when he
48		put his fingers in. [And then-]
49	L:	[When-] when who put his fingers in.
50	JL:	Maouloud. And uhm, I know I also said it hurt- when he tried to
51		put it in, I told him to stop.
52	L:	When Maouloud put it in?
53	JL:	Yes.
54	L:	And when Mike put his penis in your rectum?
55	JL:	Yes.
56	L:	You said, "It hurts?"
57	JL:	Yes.
		((some intervening turns))
58	L:	Now, you mentioned uhm, that they kept adding more time and
59		they said "As soon- as soon as you're finished, you can leave."
60	JL:	Yeah.
61	L:	Was it as soon as YOU'RE finished, or as soon as THEY'RE
62		finished?
63	JL:	As soon as THEY'RE finished.
64	L:	As soon- so they would say a-"As soon as we're finished-"

65		they would let you [leave.]
66	JL:	[Yeah .] Yes.
67	L:	Okay, and by the time Mike got out of the car and Maouloud got
68		in the car, you had been, correct me if I'm wrong, uhm, Mike
69		had put his fingers in your- in your vagina.
70	JL:	Yes. Uh- and Maouloud.
71	L:	And Maouloud. And Mike had tried to put his penis in your
72		mouth.
73	JL:	Yes.
74	L:	And Maouloud had uhm, grabbed your- your shirt and touched
75		you on the breast.
76	JL:	Yes.
77	L:	And Mike had put his penis in your rectum.
78	JL:	Yes.
79	L:	And Mike had put his penis in your vagina.
80	JL:	Yes.
81	L:	And that was all before Maouloud got out of the car.
82	JL:	Yes.
83	L:	And so by the time Maouloud got back in the car, and you said-
84		and- and he said to you, "Are you gonna let me have my turn."
85		(2.0) Did you think that if you allowed that to happen, then you
86		would be able to leave and go home?
87	DL:	Objection, your honour. Leading.
88	J:	Sustained as leading.
89	L:	What did you think, Jewel, would happen if you let him do it at
90		that point.
91	JL:	I just wanted to go home.
92	L:	(1.0) You just wanted to go home. (2.0) And you said, did you-
93		you said that you told him, "Okay, if I tell you to stop, will you
94		stop?" Did he say anything when you said that to him? =
95	JL:	= He
96	L:	And then he tried to put his penis in you. And what did you say,
97		Jewel?
98	JL:	I said, "Ow, it hurts." And I was pushing his knees. ((sniffles))
99		But he kept pushing. ((sniffles))
100	L:	Did you tell him to stop?
101	JL:	Yes.
102	L:	Did he stop?
103	JL:	No, after uh- he stopped after like, ten seconds or so. ((sniffles))
104	L:	After he continued to push his penis inside you?
105	JL:	Yes.

106	L:	(3.0) Jewel, at any point that night did you ever give either of
107		them permission to touch you?
108	JL:	No. (4.0) ((sniffles))
109	L:	Did you ever consent to any of this?
110	JL:	No.
111	L:	(4.0) Did you ever willingly engage in any sexual acts with
112		Maouloud or Mike?
113	JL:	No.
114	L:	That's all, your honour. Thank you.

What we see in this excerpt is that Jewel, after enduring much nonconsensual sex (i.e., Baby putting his fingers in her vagina (lines 34–38); Mike trying to put his penis into her mouth (lines 71–73); Baby grabbing and touching her breast (lines 74–76); Mike putting his penis into her rectum (lines 77–78); Mike putting his penis into her vagina (lines 79–80)), agrees to have intercourse with Baby as long as he stops when she tells him to stop (lines 91–96).[7] And it was this agreement that came to be understood as Jewel consenting to sexual intercourse with Baby, once the case became framed as a post-penetration rape case. As noted above, the issue for the courts *then* became whether this initial "consent" protected the sexual intercourse from legally becoming a rape or not.

The issue that I want to raise about Jewel's agreement concerns its status as a signal of consent. While it is true that, by her own admission, Jewel allows Baby "to take his turn," it is also significant that she reports saying "it hurts" (lines 44–51 and lines 56–57) and "no" multiple times (lines 9–18 and lines 41–43) in response to Baby's and Mike's previous sexual advances. That is, Jewel's agreement to have sexual intercourse with Baby occurs *after* she has experienced much unwanted sexual aggression from the two men. How, then, do we interpret agreement that occurs in such a context? I suggest, based on the violence against women literature, that Jewel's agreement was not a signal of consent but rather was a form of resistance, in particular, a way to prevent more prolonged and/or extreme instances of violence. Indeed, women's submission to sex has been shown, in many circumstances, to be a better strategy for surviving violence than physical resistance, given that physical resistance has the potential to escalate and intensify men's violence (Dobash and Dobash 1992). In particular, the literature on battered women has demonstrated that seemingly passive behavior on the part of women can be the result of carefully thought-out, creative strategies for dealing with the threat of domestic violence. Campbell et al. (1998), for example, based on interviews with approximately 100 battered women over a three-year period, found clear support for agency on the part of their subjects even when the women adopted compliant and submissive behaviors. For Campbell et al. (1998: 755), "subordinating the self" was one of these behaviors; it was characterized as a woman's "conscious decision to be as non-responsive as possible [in order] to stop the escalation of [her partner's] anger." That this kind of behavior was in fact the result of conscious decision making was evidenced by its selective use: women reported making choices as to when to resist in more active ways and when to adopt a subordinating posture. For example, one woman reported standing her ground in disagreements with her partner when her children were out of the house, thereby risking the possibility of a beating, but subordinated herself in other arguments in order to avoid being hit in the presence of her children. Campbell et al. (1998: 758) argue that, in the face of potential danger to both women and their children, the adoption of these seemingly subordinate stances was "clearly intelligent, courageous and healthy, rather than passive."

In a similar way, research conducted on rape victim impact statements in the United Kingdom (Woodhams 2008) demonstrated that there are a wide variety of ways that women "resist" the threat of rape that do not involve physical resistance. One set of strategies, what Woodhams (2008) refers to as "offender management strategies," involves women negotiating with their perpetrators in order to minimize the harm inflicted upon them. For example, women may agree to submit to "lesser" forms of sexual assault in exchange for being let go. Indeed, in the excerpt from Jewel's testimony above, we see Jewel adopting such a strategy. While Jewel reports that she told Baby that he could "take his turn" as long as he stopped when she said "stop," lines 89–91 reveal the rationale behind Jewel's compliance—"[she] just wanted to go home." In fact, we see in lines 58–66 the basis for this kind of reasoning: the young men had told Jewel a number of times that she could leave when they were "finished." Thus, one way of understanding Jewel's acquiescence to Baby's request/demand is as a strategy of resistance: Jewel agreed to have sex with Baby in order to end the unwanted sexual advances sooner rather than later, that is, in order to resist a prolonging and intensification of the sexual aggression she had already experienced. If Jewel's agreement to have sex with Baby was in fact not a signal of consent, but rather a strategy of resistance, why was it not understood in this way as Jewel's testimony traveled through the legal system? In what follows, I attempt to show how Jewel's testimony was shaped by both procedural and ideological constraints as it moved out of the trial and into other kinds of contexts within the legal system.

THE JURY'S COMMUNICATION WITH THE JUDGE

After the jury began its deliberations in the Baby trial, it submitted two questions to the judge. The first question read: "If a female consents to sex initially and, during the course of the sex act to which she consented, for whatever reason, she changes her mind and the man continues until climax, does the result constitute rape?" (*State of Maryland v. Maouloud Baby*, Court of Appeals of Maryland, 2007). The second question, submitted a day after the first note, read: "If at any time, the woman says stop, is that rape?" (*State of Maryland v. Maouloud Baby*, Court of Appeals of Maryland, 2007). Essentially, the judge did not answer these questions and instead directed the jurors to answer the questions for themselves based on the legal definitions of rape and of consent that she had provided during her jury instructions. While the jury ultimately convicted Baby of first-degree rape and of some lesser sexual offenses, what these questions suggest is that at least some of the jurors considered the idea that Jewel's qualified agreement to have sex with Baby *was* consent. And they did this in spite of the fact that the definition of consent provided by the judge stipulated that agreement to sex be freely given; that is, consent was defined by the judge as "actually agreeing to the sexual act rather than merely submitting as a result of force or threat of force" (*Maouloud Baby v. State of Maryland*, Court of Special Appeals of Maryland, 2005). Note that this definition of consent is consistent with the preceding discussion of women's resistance: agreement (like Jewel's) that comes about as a result of the threat of more extreme or prolonged instances of violence is not considered to be consent.

So, given the definition of consent provided by the judge, why might some of the jury members (at least, temporarily) have entertained the idea that Jewel's agreement was freely given and not motivated by a "threat of force"? In attempting to answer this question, it is useful to return to the preceding discussion of entextualization practices and the interpretive processes that accompany them. Linguistic anthropologists have argued that meta-level understandings of language, what have been termed linguistic ideologies, can have a profound influence on how speakers use and interpret language (see, e.g., Schieffelin, Woolard, and Kroskrity 1998 and Blommaert 1999). Indeed, a powerful ideology surrounding the interpretation of texts in the West is what has been called a "referentialist" or "textualist" ideology (Collins 1996)—a belief in stable, denotational, and context-free meaning. According to this idea, meaning resides exclusively in linguistic forms and, as a result, words, phrases, or sentences can be extracted from their original interactional and social context and moved to other contexts without any change in meaning. As Mertz (2007: 48) argues, the textualist or referentialist ideology focuses one's attention on "decontextualized aspects of meaning, to the exclusion of the more contextually dependent aspects of meaning." (This view of meaning is, of course, incompatible with the theories of meaning held by discourse analysts, pragmatists, sociolinguists, etc.) Thus, one way of accounting for (some of) the jurors' interpretation of Jewel's qualified agreement as consent is by reference to this linguistic ideology. During the jury's discussions, the qualified consent that Jewel reported giving Baby would have been "entextualized"; that is, it would have been lifted out of its interactional setting and segmented into a "text." During this process of entextualization, other portions of Jewel's testimony may have fallen away. In particular, the series of nonconsensual sexual acts that comprised the context for Jewel's qualified consent may have been erased. And, crucially, in line with the textualist or referentialist linguistic ideology, the meaning that would have been ascribed to Jewel's one, seemingly consensual, instance of agreement was its literal, context-independent meaning—"consent." In sum, the extraction of Jewel's words from the entirety of her testimony in combination with the referentialist or textualist ideology—the idea that meaning resides in the linguistic forms of words or sentences—may have facilitated a context-free reading of Jewel's "agreement."[8]

I am suggesting that a context-free interpretation of Jewel's agreement precluded or, at the least, made difficult certain ways of conceiving Jewel's responses to Mike's and Baby's sexual advances. First, as I have argued above, a context-free reading of Jewel's qualified agreement eliminates the series of nonconsensual sexual acts that preceded it and, thereby, makes difficult its interpretation as coerced agreement, that is, as submission or compliance motivated by a fear of more prolonged or extreme instances of violence. Second, a context-free reading of Jewel's agreement also prevents it from being understood as a weak agreement, implying refusal (Kitzinger and Frith 1999). In an insightful critique of date rape programs that emphasize women's direct and straightforward refusals to men's sexual advances (e.g., "No means No" date rape programs), Kitzinger and Frith (1999) argue that attention to the way refusals are actually performed in ordinary conversational interaction shows that they are anything but direct, clear, and straightforward. Rather, in the terms of conversational analysis, refusals are "dispreferred" responses; that is, they require much more conversational work than, for example, acceptances. Included among the interactional features that characterize refusals are delays (e.g., pauses and hesitations), hedges (e.g., expressions such as *well*, *uh*), palliatives (e.g., apologies, token agreements), and accounts (e.g., explanations, justifications). Furthermore, in ordinary, naturally occurring speech, even weak agreements (such as half-hearted *yeah*'s or *uh-huh*'s) are often heard and reacted to as if they imply disagreement or refusal. Indeed, there is some evidence that Baby may have understood Jewel's so-called consent as a weak agreement, implying refusal. Consider excerpts 2 and 3 below, from Jewel's cross-examination and from Baby's direct examination, respectively.

Excerpt 2

1	CE:	So Maouloud gets back in the car and he asks if it- if he could
2		have his turn. =
3	JL:	= Yes.
4	CE:	In effect? And what did you say.
5	JL:	Uhm, I said you have to- I said as long as you stop when I tell
6		you to.
7	CE:	(10.0) Did he also say something to the effect that he wanted to
8		have sex but that he did not want to rape you.
9	JL:	Uhm, yes, uhm, but a little bit before that they had both said that
10		whenever I'm done I can leave.
11	CE:	Well, I'm talking about when Maouloud came back in the car.
12	JL:	Yes.
13	CE:	He ASKED if he could have sex with you.

14	JL:	Yes.

14 JL: Yes.

15 CE: And you said, "You can have sex but when I say stop, you gotta
16   stop."

17 JL: Yes.

18 CE: (2.0) But didn't he also say something like, "I wanna have sex
19   with you but I do NOT (1.0) want to rape you."

20 JL: Yeah, he just said uhm, "I don't want to rape you."

Excerpt 3

1 MB: Then Mike got outta thuh car = in about five seven minutes = he
2   got out thuh car and came back in thuh car = I mean I came in
3   thuh car (.) and I asked her (.) can I have sex with you an she
4   said (.) fine as long as you stop when I say to (.) and I said I
5   don't wanna rape you (.) and then she s-uhm: (.) she said okay
6   an then she placed (.) I (place) myself in between her legs....

In both of these excerpts, we see Jewel and Baby recounting the events that occurred once Baby reentered the car: in particular, both of them report that Jewel's agreement to allow Baby to take his turn was followed by Baby's saying that he did not want to rape Jewel. (This can be seen in lines 7–8 and 18–20 of excerpt 2 and in lines 4–5 of excerpt 3.) If we adopt a basic analytic tool of conversation analysis—what is known as the next-turn proof procedure—we can assume that Baby's utterance displays his understanding of what Jewel's prior turn was doing (i.e., how it was functioning). That is, if we understand Baby's utterance as an attempt to reassure Jewel that he does not want to rape her, then this is perhaps some indication that Baby has understood Jewel as producing a weak agreement, implying refusal. Alternatively, if we understand Baby's utterance as a threat (i.e., I don't want to have to rape you, but if you don't comply I will), such a speech act is also consistent with Baby's understanding of Jewel's "agreement" as a weak agreement, implying refusal. While this discussion is not meant to arrive at a definitive determination of how Jewel's utterance, and her behavior more generally, should have been understood by the jury and/or the courts, it *is* meant to demonstrate the varying kinds of interpretations that are *not* allowed if Jewel's one "yes" is ascribed its context-free meaning.

BABY'S APPEAL AND THE APPELLATE OPINIONS

As the previous section has shown, it was the jurors who first introduced the notion of post-penetration rape into the *Baby* case by way of the questions they posed to the trial judge. And it was these questions that gave rise to Baby's appeal. More specifically, Baby appealed his convictions, arguing that the trial judge had erred in not answering the jurors' questions in the negative, given the precedential

Battle decision (1980), which, in the opinion of the appeal, ruled post-penetration rape to be a legal impossibility in Maryland. In other words, the legal status of post-penetration rape in Maryland was the basis of Baby's appeal, and, in turn, became the primary issue addressed by the appellate courts. In a discussion of how legal professionals understand the textual authority of legal cases, Mertz (2007) shows how the procedural history of a case is instrumental in determining what a case comes to "mean." In particular, appellate courts can only address issues in their opinions that have been invoked during appeals; "issues not raised at trial or on appeal may generally not be addressed by an appellate court" (Mertz 2007: 62). In Mertz's (2007: 62) words, "the semiotic frame imposed by ... litigants as they [choose] particular issues to appeal" constrains "the issues to which an appellate court may speak." In the *Baby* case, then, because Baby's appeal revolved around the issue of post-penetration rape, the case *became* a post-penetration rape case. That is, while the two appellate courts (the Court of Special Appeals and the Court of Appeals) disagreed about whether post-penetration rape was a legal possibility in Maryland, because of the procedural constraints alluded to above, they both treated post-penetration rape as the central issue in the case.

Although appellate courts are concerned with legal issues, and not factual ones, the selection of "facts" to be represented in appellate courts' opinions will be influenced by the legal issues under consideration in appeals (Mertz 2007). It is perhaps not surprising, then, that when the appellate courts represented the "facts" of the *Baby* case, they continued to decontextualize Jewel's one instance of agreement in keeping with their framing of the case as a post-penetration rape case. In particular, the opinions textually foregrounded Jewel's recounting of the series of events that occurred once Baby re-entered the car (i.e., Baby saying he wanted to take his turn; Jewel agreeing as long as he stopped when she said "stop," etc.) while textually backgrounding her representation of the series of nonconsensual sexual acts that preceded Baby's reentry into the car. Consider excerpt 4 below from the Court of Special Appeals opinion.

Excerpt 4

Upon their arrival at McDonald's, Lacey left the group to join a friend, after which the complainant agreed to drive appellant and Mike to a residential neighborhood where she parked her car. The complainant complied with the request of appellant and Mike to sit between them on the back seat of her car. Mike put her hand down in his pants and asked her "to lick it." Appellant then asked her to expose her breasts; when she did not comply, he fondled her breast with his hand.

After Jewel acquiesced to the boys' insistence that they stay ten more minutes, she found herself on her back with appellant removing her jeans and Mike sitting on her chest, attempting to place his penis in her mouth. After she told them to stop, the pair moved her around so that her body was up in appellant's lap as he held her arms and Mike tried to insert his penis in her, but briefly inserted it into her rectum by mistake. After Mike again tried to insert his penis in the complainant's vagina, appellant inserted his fingers in her vagina. After appellant exited the car, Mike inserted his finger, then his penis into her vagina.

Mike then got out of the car and appellant got in. Appellant told Jewel that it was his turn and, according to the complainant, the following transpired:

> Q. [ASSISTANT STATE'S ATTORNEY]: And what else did he say?
> A. He, after that we sat there for a couple seconds and he was like so are you going to let me hit it and I didn't really say anything and he was like I don't want to rape you.
>
> * * *
>
> Q. So when Maouloud said I don't want to rape you, did you respond?
> A. Yes. I said that as long as he stops when I tell him to, then -
> Q. Now, that he could?
> A. Yes.
>
> * * *
>
> Q. Did you feel like you had a choice?
> A. Not really. I don't know. Something just clicked off and I just did whatever they said.
>
> * * *
>
> Q. Now when you told [appellant] if I say stop, something like that, you have to stop. What did he do after you spoke those words?
> A. Well he got on top of me and he tried to put it in and it hurt. So I said stop and that's when he kept pushing it in and I was pushing his knees to get off me.
> Q. You were on your back and he was on top of you?
> A. Yes.
> Q. Did he stop pushing his penis into your vagina?
> A. Not right away.
> Q. About how long did he continue to put his penis into your vagina?
> A. About five or so seconds.
> Q. And then what happened?
> A. And that's when he just got off me and that's when Mike got in the car....
>
> (*Maouloud Baby v. State of Maryland,* Court of Special Appeals of Maryland, 2005)

What we see in this excerpt from the appellate court's opinion is a difference in the way that various parts of Jewel's testimony are represented: when the opinion represents the events following Baby's reentry into the car (i.e., Jewel's so-called consent), it directly quotes Jewel's trial testimony (and this is the only instance of direct quotes in the entire opinion); when the opinion represents the events preceding Baby's reentry (i.e., the series of nonconsensual activities that Jewel reports preceded her agreement to have sex with Baby), it represents her trial testimony indirectly. Previous research on the use of reported speech in legal contexts (e.g., Philips 1986; Rumsey 1990; Trinch 2010) has pointed to the greater authority and reliability that direct speech (i.e., direct quotes) is understood to convey (relative to indirect speech), given its (supposed) exactitude in the reporting of speech. Philips (1986: 169), for example, argues that the different ways of representing reported speech indicate to listeners or readers that the reported speech has different functions or meanings in the discourse. In particular, she shows, on the basis of transcripts from a criminal trial, that direct speech was used to represent evidence that was crucial to the case, while indirect speech was used to represent evidence that was less crucial to the case and/or information that provided the background to crucial evidence. In Philips's words (1986: 154), "quoting is reserved for information being presented as evidence directly related to proof of the elements of a criminal charge, to foreground this information, and to give it more fixedness and credibility as 'exact words' than other forms of reported speech are given." The differential use of reported speech in the excerpt above, then, functions to highlight the importance of the events related to Jewel's so-called agreement, while downgrading the significance of the events leading up to this so-called agreement. These backgrounded events, of course, are the ones that, I argue, provide contextualizing information that is *crucial* to understanding what Jewel is actually doing when she agrees to have sex with Baby. Rather than creating a sense of this contextualizing relationship, however, the textual foregrounding and backgrounding that we see in excerpt 4 has the effect of decontextualizing Jewel's agreement by creating a distinction or separation between the two sets of events. Thus, in spite of the fact that appellate courts are meant to address legal issues and not factual ones, I am suggesting that the appellate courts' means of representing the "facts" of the Baby case supported an interpretation of Jewel's agreement as consent, rather than as submission or acquiescence.[9]

CONCLUSIONS

I began this chapter by discussing Blommaert's notion of textual travel and his notion of voice. Using these concepts, I have tried to show how a complainant in a rape trial "lost her voice" as she engaged with the legal system. Specifically, as the complainant's testimony was entextualized and then recontextualized in various kinds of settings within that system, it underwent a fairly radical transformation: a strategy for resisting more extreme and prolonged instances of sexual violence became reconstructed as consensual sex. In Blommaert's terms, the complainant's testimony did not travel well; it did not receive an uptake in the appellate decisions (and perhaps in the jurors' discussions) that retained its original contextualization. Moreover, I have argued that the lack of uptake accorded to the complainant's testimony was a result of linguistic ideologies that operate in the legal system (and elsewhere) in combination with institutional conventions that constrain the kinds of legal issues appellate courts are empowered to address in their rulings.

While the decision of the highest court in Maryland to clarify the state's rape statute and to give women the right to retract consent after penetration is clearly positive to the extent that it supports women's autonomy in a very general way, I have tried to argue that this decision has little to do with the events under investigation in the Baby trial. Put somewhat differently, the framing of the *Baby* case as a post-penetration rape case did not resonate with the complainant's testimony and, arguably, had negative consequences for *her* autonomy as an *individual* woman.[10] Beyond its effects on particular individuals, however, I want to suggest that the problem with the framing of this case as a post-penetration rape case is more far-reaching. An important aspect of rape law reform in the United States has been the requirement in many states that consent be "affirmatively" and "freely given" (Schulhofer 1998). Indeed, the rape statute in Maryland, as we have seen, defines consent in precisely this way: consent is "actually agreeing to the act of intercourse" as opposed to "merely submitting as a result of force or threat of force." That is, agreement, like Jewel's, that is coerced as a result of force or the fear of force is not deemed to be consent in Maryland, nor in many other American states. One of the disturbing aspects of the *Baby* case, then, is the outdated notion of consent that underlies its framing as a post-penetration rape case. Gavey (2005) has argued that at least part of the struggle against rape involves the development of a new cultural terrain in which it would be completely implausible to read a woman's passivity and nonresponsiveness as sexual consent. Yet, the official narrative of the *Baby* case (i.e., that of post-penentration rape) does little to move us toward such a cultural terrain, given that it is predicated on the assumption that Jewel's attempts to end the sexual violence inflicted upon her were signals of consent.

ACKNOWLEDGMENTS

Previous versions of this chapter were presented at the International Gender and Language Conference (New Zealand, July 2008), the Cardiff Roundtable on Sociolinguistics (Cardiff, July 2008), the Women's Studies Lecture Series at the University of Western Ontario (March 2009), and the International Forensic Linguistics Association Conference (July 2009). I thank audience members at those talks for helpful comments. I also thank Alice Freed, Larry Solan, and Shonna Trinch for very useful conversations that helped me clarify many of the ideas presented here. All shortcomings are, of course, my own. De Gruyter Publishing Company has generously allowed me to reprint here portions of my article, "Text Trajectories, Legal Discourse, and Gendered Inequalities" from *Applied Linguistics Review* (2012), 3: 47–73.

NOTES

1. For other investigations of how texts travel in the legal system, see Matoesian 2001, Trinch 2003, Ehrlich 2007, Eades 2008, and Andrus 2011.

2. The first trial, also in 2004, was declared a mistrial because of a hung jury.
3. After the jury began its deliberations, it asked the judge: "If a woman consents to sex initially and then changes her mind during the sex act and the man continues until climax, does that constitute rape?" The trial judge responded by saying that the legal definition of rape had been provided and that the question was one for the jury to decide.
4. According to the state attorney (personal communication) who tried the original case, there will not be another trial because Jewel is unwilling to testify once again.
5. The Court of Appeals determined that the Court of Special Appeals had invoked a part of the *Battle* decision that was non-binding, that is, was not the "holding" of the case.
6. These are not the official trial transcripts, but rather ones that I transcribed based on the audio-taped recording of the trial. L = Examining Lawyer, JL = Jewel.
7. Mike pled guilty to all of his charges.
8. See also Eades (2008: 320–22) for a discussion of the lack of significance attached to the decontextualization of propositions within the legal system.
9. It should be noted that the Maryland Court of Appeals, the highest court in the state of Maryland, represents these events in exactly the same way as the Maryland Special Court of Appeals. That is, when the opinion represents the events following Baby's reentry into the car (i.e., Jewel's so-called consent), it directly quotes Jewel's trial testimony; when the opinion represents the events preceding Baby's reentry (i.e., the series of nonconsensual activities that Jewel reports preceded her agreement to have sex with Baby), it represents her trial testimony indirectly.
10. The fact that Jewel is unwilling to testify in another trial is perhaps testimony to the ability of rape trials to re-victimize rape victims/survivors. Lees (1996: 36), for example, calls the rape trial "judicial rape," arguing that it can be more damaging than an actual rape, "masquerading" as it does "under the name of justice."

CASES CITED

Maouloud Baby v. State of Maryland, Court of Special Appeals of Maryland, 2005. 172 Md. App. 588, 916 A.2d 410; 2007 Md. App. LEXIS 60.
State of Maryland v. Maouloud Baby, Court of Appeals of Maryland, 2007. 404 Md. 220, 946 A.2d 463; 2008 Md. LEXIS 190.

REFERENCES

Andrus, Jennifer. 2011. Beyond texts in context: Recontextualization and the co-production of texts and contexts in the legal discourse, excited utterance exception to hearsay. *Discourse and Society* 22(2): 115–36.
Bauman, Richard, and Charles L. Briggs. 1990. Poetics and performance as critical perspectives on language and social life. *Annual Review of Anthropology* 19: 59–88.
Blommaert, Jan. ed. 1999. *Language Ideological Debates.* Berlin: Mouton de Gruyter.
———. 2005. *Discourse.* Cambridge: Cambridge University Press.
Campbell, Jacquelyn, Linda Rose, Joan Kub, and Daphne Nedd. 1998. Voices of strength and resistance: A contextual and longitudinal analysis of women's responses to battering. *Journal of Interpersonal Violence* 13: 743–62.

Collins, James. 1996. Socialization to text: Structure and contradiction in schooled literacy. In *Natural Histories of Discourse*, ed. M. Silverstein and G. Urban, 203–28. Chicago: University of Chicago Press.

Davis, Amanda. 2005. Clarifying the issue of consent: The evolution of post-penetration rape law. *Stetson Law Review* 34: 729–66.

Dobash, R. Emerson, and Russell P. Dobash. 1992. *Women, Violence and Social Change*. London: Routledge.

Eades, Diana. 2008. *Courtroom Talk and Neocolonial Control*. Berlin: Mouton de Gruyter.

Ehrlich, Susan. 2007. Legal discourse and the cultural intelligibility of gendered meanings. *Journal of Sociolinguistics* 11: 452–77.

Gavey, Nicola. 2005. *Just Sex?: The Cultural Scaffolding of Rape*. London: Routledge.

Kitzinger, Celia, and Hannah Frith. 1999. Just say no? The use of conversation analysis in developing a feminist perspective on sexual refusal. *Discourse & Society* 10: 293–316.

Lees, Sue. 1996. *Carnal Knowledge: Rape on Trial*. London: Hamish Hamilton.

Matoesian, Gregory 2001. *Law and the Language of Identity: Discourse in the William Kennedy Smith Rape Trial*. New York: Oxford University Press.

Mertz, Elizabeth. 2007. *The Language of Law School: Learning to Think Like a Lawyer*. Oxford: Oxford University Press.

Philips, Susan. 1986. Reported speech as evidence in an American trial. In *Georgetown University Roundtable '85 Languages and Linguistics: The Interdependence of Theory, Data and Application*, ed. Deborah Tannen and James Alatis, 154–70. Washington, DC: Georgetown University Press.

Rumsey, Alan. 1990. Wording, meaning and linguistic ideology. *American Anthropologist*: 92: 346–61.

Schieffelin, Bambi, Kathryn Woolard, and Paul Kroskrity, eds. 1998. *Language Ideologies: Practice and Theory*. Oxford: Oxford University Press.

Schulhofer, Stephen J. 1998. *Unwanted Sex: The Culture of Intimidation and the Failure of Law*. Cambridge, MA: Harvard University Press.

Silverstein, Michael, and Greg Urban, eds. 1996. *Natural Histories of Discourse*. Chicago: University of Chicago Press.

Trinch, Shonna. 2003. *Latinas' Narratives of Domestic Abuse: Discrepant Versions of Violence*. Amsterdam: John Publishing Company.

———. 2010. Disappearing discourse: Performative texts and identity in legal contexts. *Critical Inquiry in Language Studies* 7(2–3): 207–29.

Woodhams, Jessica. 2008. How victims behave during stranger sexual assaults. Unpublished manuscript.

CHAPTER 10

Communication and Magic

Authorized Voice, Legal-Linguistic Habitus, and the
Recontextualization of "Beyond Reasonable Doubt"

CHRIS HEFFER

> Once, in simpler times, there was perhaps a thorough belief that what the judge said
> about the law had marked effect on the jury. But today, although that belief has atro-
> phied, the elaborate ceremony continues, just as, we hear, religious or magical rites, once
> performed with entire conviction as to their power, often degenerate into formalism
> until "right" or "wrong" come to mean merely the exact execution or neglect of all the
> details of a prescribed ritual. So the judicially intoned formulas are now like debased or
> devitalized magic incantations, which "depend for their efficacy on being uttered rather
> than being heard."[1]
>
> (Frank 1930: 195–96)

INTRODUCTION

The underlying assumption in most work informed by Saussurian synchronic linguistics or Gricean pragmatics is that speakers intend to communicate (whether
directly or deceptively) with their hearers. This is all the more so with speech acts
labeled as 'instruction' or 'direction', which appear to incorporate hearer uptake in
the label. Yet as a given speech act undergoes the diachronic process of continual
recontextualization (Bauman and Briggs 1990), it may become a prescribed and
consecrated form of linguistic behavior, or ritual, in which what is considered
institutionally to be at stake is the proper performance of words (Kuipers 1990)
rather than the negotiation of meaning or the consequent performance of action.
This chapter provides a theoretical account of how textual travel can lead to an act
of instructional communication becoming an act of ritual magic. The account is

more optimistic than the structural pessimism of the legal realists and their talk, as in Frank above, of "atrophy," "degeneration," "debasement," and "devitalization." Viewing textual travel in terms of acts of recontextualization (the placing of texts in new contexts) enables us to ascribe much greater significance to individual agency without denying structural constraints and effects. According to the theory of legal textual travel I develop here, a few individuals, invested with the highest institutional authority, can use their powerful agency, or *authorized voice*, in legal metadiscourse to establish a privileged reading of a text that resounds through time. The structural processes of legal socialization and iterative normative practice can then lead legal professionals to internalize the authorized voice as "authoritative discourse" to the point where it becomes part of their legal-linguistic habitus—their accumulated, normalized, and unquestioned experience of discursive practice in legal settings. Where this legal-linguistic habitus is, or becomes, incommensurable with lay discursive practice, the result can be a total breakdown in communication. The capacity of the legal professional to *hear* the lay voice becomes impaired and the tendency will be to defend the authoritative discourse and to question the competence of the lay person. Where lay participants in the legal process are responsible for determining guilt (as in juries), communication breakdown can be highly consequential and may result in miscarriages of justice. Nevertheless, if the problem is acknowledged, there is scope for a remedy. Powerful legal agents with authorized voice retain the capacity to change the trajectory the legal text has taken, to realign it with lay expectations and thus improve communication between legal professionals and lay participants in the legal process.

The thesis I put forward here is wide-ranging. In theory, it should apply to any legal text habitually used in legal–lay communication. Here, though, I explore it through judges' instructions to juries on the "beyond reasonable doubt" standard of proof in criminal trials (Solan 1999; Heffer 2006, 2007; Whitman 2008). This particular object of study is motivated both socially and methodologically. Socially, it matters significantly for the democratic credentials of a society retaining trial by jury. Since the standard sets the evidential threshold at which a criminal defendant may be convicted, if a jury understands that standard to be significantly higher or lower than intended, defendants will be convicted or acquitted unfairly, with significant consequences for justice. Unfortunately, there is ample empirical evidence demonstrating that jurors do misunderstand and misapply "beyond reasonable doubt" (Horowitz and Kirkpatrick 1996; Saxton 1998; Solan 1999). There is a social imperative, then, to inform legal authorities of the need to reform instruction in this area (Heffer 2009).

Methodologically, a number of key variables are kept relatively stable. In terms of form, the legal standard fossilized a couple of centuries ago into a fairly invariable formula—"beyond (a/any/all) reasonable doubt" (Whitman 2008). Semantically, there is general consensus (at least at the highest legal levels) on the intended meaning of the legal concept: that the "fact-finder" must be firmly convinced of guilt before convicting a defendant (Solan 1999). Pragmatically, it is agreed that the primary function in instructing juries on the standard of proof should be to enable them to apply it to the case at hand—jury instruction is intended as an act of communication, even if this is all too often forgotten (Heffer 2006). These stable elements are useful for a study of textual travel in legal–lay communication (the theme of this book), since the different types of transformation (formal, semantic, pragmatic) do not reach the point where the travelling text can merge into the contextual crowd; that is, where it ceases to be distinguishable from other texts and other discourses.

Given the comparative stability of form, conceptual meaning, and function, one might expect interpretation and delivery of the standard, whether as communication or magic, to be fairly uniform across those legal jurisdictions that use it. Yet the term is construed as either "legal" or "ordinary" language according to jurisdiction and is thus interpreted by judges as either clearly needing to be defined for the jury or as obviously understood by the jury, as either a paraphrasable message or as an untouchable ritual formula. These readings directly affect the way the standard is conveyed to juries and the likelihood of jurors actually understanding the instruction.

I begin by showing how a phrase ("beyond reasonable doubt"), and the underlying concept it is intended to convey (being firmly convinced about guilt), can follow different trajectories over the centuries. I then provide an account, through the notion of "authorized voice," of how such divergent legal readings of the phrase as "legal" and "ordinary" language can come about. Next I explore the clash of incommensurable discursive practices that occurs when jurors ask for explanation of the term in a jurisdiction that has followed the "ordinary language" trajectory. Finally, I consider the implications of this study for legal–lay communication in general.

TEXTUAL TRAVAILS: THE TRAVELS OF "BEYOND REASONABLE DOUBT"

As texts travel through time and space, they might be seen to undergo transformation in two main ways: the texts can be formally adapted to the new environment and take on a new linguistic shape, as in the police reconstruction of a witness statement (Rock, this volume) or the various editions of the *Highway Code* (Davies, this volume), or they can remain more or less the "same" in terms of formal expression but take on a new meaning, as in the reconstrual in court of a rape victim's final abandonment of resistance as a simple act of consent (Ehrlich, this volume) or in Western readings of English texts produced in the periphery of the world system, where the texts "travel across the globe . . . but their value, meaning or function do not often travel along" (Blommaert 2005: 72). The case of "beyond reasonable doubt" might appear, on the face of it, to be similar to Blommaert's retained-shape-but-changed-meaning case of textual travel. Its shape has certainly remained broadly the same, with minor variation on the determiner of doubt (*beyond a/ø/any/all reasonable doubt*), since it was first rendered into text, or "entextualized" (Bauman and Briggs 1990), in the late seventeenth century. It is also clear that the meaning of its components has changed. Wierzbicka (2003) notes, for example, that in twentieth-century usage the term "reasonable doubt" shifted from a personal to an impersonal grammatical frame, from "if *you have* a reasonable doubt" to "if *there is* a reasonable doubt." However, unlike in Blommaert's case, where the non-Western values may simply be lost in the new context, in the present case, the legal authorities may *reassert* the intended legal values through their legal metadiscourse.

We need to distinguish, then, between the normative *legal standard* of proof and the *linguistic expression* commonly used to convey that standard. Quite simply, in its travels through time and space, the linguistic expression may cease to convey adequately the standard of proof it was intended to convey. That does not mean, though, that the normative legal standard itself must change. The criminal standard of proof is one of a set of "proof principles" intended to incorporate fundamental democratic "due process" values: the prosecution must ("burden of proof") firmly convince the jury ("standard of proof") that the defendant is guilty (thus overcoming the initial "presumption of innocence"). If we hold those values dear, then it is rather odd to make them subject to the vicissitudes of linguistic travel. Yet this is what happens if you prioritize linguistic description over normative legal intent. For example, Wierzbicka concludes from her above analysis of "reasonable doubt" that "the question is whether a 'reasonable case' can be made" not whether the jurors are firmly convinced (2003: 16). But to talk of jurors looking for a "reasonable case" for the defense (which Laudan 2006 also does) is to reinstate two common biases that the proof principles attempt to overcome: a presumption of guilt and a consequent burden on the defense to prove innocence.

We need to trace separately, then, the development of the legal standard and the historical vicissitudes of the linguistic expression.

The Development of the Standard

The *legal standard* of criminal proof *has* undergone change over the centuries. Whitman (2008) argues convincingly that the standard arose not as a way of setting a high threshold for conviction, as previously thought (Shapiro 1991; Heffer 2007), but as a means of providing moral comfort to jurors who were terrified of the theological imperative not to make false judgment—according to one Norman oath, if you judge wrongly, "your souls will be damned in perpetuity, and your bodies will be exposed to shameful abuses in a gaping Hell" (cited in Whitman 2008: 45). In a religious world in which jurors were extremely reluctant to convict, the reasonable doubt standard was designed to persuade them that they *only* had to be "convinced in reason." As Morano (1975: 515) points out, it represented a reduction from "beyond *any* doubt," to "beyond *reasonable* doubt." By the mid-nineteenth century, though, "beyond reasonable doubt" was indeed construed by the legal community as an evidential standard corresponding to the highest level of theological certainty: moral certainty. Rather than the type of *formal* certainty discussed by scientists and mathematicians (corresponding to an impossible *absolute* knowledge), moral certainty was a form of subjectively based *functional* certainty (Heffer 2007).

The highest legal authorities across the common law world still show a clear consensus in identifying the evidential threshold of the standard as one of "subjective certainty" (e.g., *Victor v. Nebraska*). These authorities (such as the US Supreme Court) eschew more objective assessments, such as the existence of "concrete" doubts or the identification of an alternative hypothesis (Laudan 2006). The focus on a subjective mental state of conviction is evidenced by paraphrases of the standard recommended to trial judges by national judicial advisory boards. The US Federal Judicial Center recommends "Proof beyond a reasonable doubt is proof that *leaves you firmly convinced* of the defendant's guilt" (FJC 1988, emphasis added), while the Judicial Studies Board for England and Wales talks of the prosecution "*making you sure*" that the defendant is guilty (JSB 2005). Despite its origins as a salve to the religious conscience, then, "beyond reasonable doubt" became an evidential standard designed to convey the highest practical threshold of proof, and this legal standard has remained relatively stable through time and across jurisdictions.

The Vicissitudes of the Linguistic Expression

The same cannot be said of the *linguistic expression*, since the normative legal meaning became lost through successive recontextualizations in both lay and legal contexts. With respect to *lay contexts* of use, there are two semantic directions the phrase could have taken that would have preserved the link between legal standard and linguistic expression in everyday language: the components of the phrase could have retained their meaning both individually and together; or the phrase could have become unanalyzable but retained its meaning as a whole. Neither happened. Whitman (2008) points out that when the term "beyond reasonable doubt" became popular in the Christian eighteenth century, most jurors, prepared in sermons and Sunday School, would have been used to searching their souls for "reasonable" (i.e., rational) doubts. But with the dissipation of the theological context, this idea is now quite alien to lay people. "Reasonable doubt" very rarely occurs today as a collocation outside the legal use: we talk of absence of doubt (*no, without*), degrees of doubt (*little, some, considerable*), and its gravity (*grave, serious*), but we do not identify substantial categories of doubt (Heffer 2006: 168–70). Nor do we talk of a "reasonable conviction" or "reasonable certainty" in the sense of being "quite certain" (Wierzbicka 2003: 13–14). There has been a significant semantic shift in the everyday meaning of "reasonable." While dictionaries based on historical principles, such as the *OED*, still give "rational" as a primary sense of "reasonable," those based solely on analysis of contemporary contexts of use as found in large corpora (namely, learners' dictionaries) provide a quite different picture. The British English *Longman Dictionary of Contemporary English* (LDCE 1995) gives the following senses of "reasonable": "**1** fair and sensible ... **2** fairly good ... **3** ... not too much ... **4** [of prices] fair ... not too high." The American English *Merriam-Webster's Advanced Learner's Dictionary* has: "**1** fair and sensible ... **2** fairly or moderately good ... **3** not too expensive" (MWALD 2008). There is no mention in these dictionaries of the etymological "pertaining to reason" or "rational." If a jury, then, is to compose the meaning of "beyond reasonable doubt" from the sum of the contemporary meanings of its parts, it is likely to construe it as something like "beyond a fair amount of doubt." This might well explain why research in the United States has shown a lay perception of the term as requiring a fairly low threshold for conviction (Horowitz and Kirkpatrick 1996).

The second direction that could have been taken in lay contexts was if the phrase had become unanalyzable but retained its overall meaning. This is a very common phenomenon at both morphemic and lexical levels (Wray 2002). For example, the polymorphemic legal term "mortgage" is understood in (more or less) the intended legal sense by lay people without having to analyze the Old French morphemes *mort* (death) and *gage* (security). However, phrases need to be commonly used in everyday language to retain ordinary meaning. An idiom like "by and large" may have lost its original compositional nautical meaning "to the wind and off it" but its everyday meaning "in general" has survived the winds of time. "Beyond reasonable doubt," on the other hand, is well known metalinguistically as a term that is used to convey the level of proof needed to convict, but its prescribed legal meaning (and thus how to apply it) is poorly understood by the general public (as well as many lawyers). Corpus evidence suggests both that the term is not as frequent as many legal observers seem to think (Heffer 2006: 168), and that, where it is used outside legal contexts, it tends to be synonymous with the "beyond doubt" standard that "beyond reasonable doubt" was meant to replace: "You say that something is **beyond doubt** or **beyond reasonable doubt** when you are certain that it is true and it cannot be contradicted and disproved" (COBUILD 2001).

Accordingly, lay construals of "beyond reasonable doubt" now appear to set the standard of proof either too low or too high. Either the phrase is decomposed and the semantic shift in the meaning of "reasonable" (from "rational" to "fair") leads to too low a standard, or it is left unanalyzed and "reasonable" is bleached out of the meaning, potentially leading to the impossible standard of formal certainty.

With respect to *legal contexts* of use, both judges' legal instructions to juries and trial lawyers' opening and closing speeches to juries militate against preservation of the legal standard. Judges, like all lawyers, are trained to atomize legal concepts; they will take an abstract concept, define it, and then define the words within the definition (Mertz 2007). Accordingly, when the concept of reasonable doubt ceased to be transparent to lay jurors (roughly in the late nineteenth century), judges began defining "reasonable doubt" rather than explaining "beyond reasonable doubt" in the context of the prosecution proving their case (Solan 1999). "Reasonable" thus became a class of doubt, contrasted with a range of other possible types of doubt (fanciful, speculative, imaginary, etc.). This took the focus away from the juror's process of decision making and reified doubt as a category. Use of the phrase in lawyers' opening and closing speeches also did not help matters. These are highly rhetorical forms of discourse in which counsel will stretch language to their persuasive ends. Thus defense lawyers will highlight any concrete doubt as showing that the case is not proved while prosecutors will stress that not any doubt is sufficient to overturn their case (Heffer 2007: 25). It is dangerous, then, to rely on such speeches as evidence of the normative legal meaning of the phrase. One of the roles of the judge in summing-up is precisely to correct such misleading impressions provided by the parties during their speeches.

Given the semantic shift or bleaching of "reasonable" in the everyday understanding of "beyond reasonable doubt," and the confusion that has been engendered in the use of the term by legal professionals, the phrase would appear to have outlived its usefulness as a way of conveying the criminal standard of proof. How could it come about, then, that the judge's instruction on the standard of proof could take certain trajectories that would either clearly distort the intended meaning of the standard or that would refuse to explain it for jurors despite clear evidence that they have difficulty understanding it (as in Australian and some US jurisdictions)? My argument is that the answer lies in the notion of *authorized voice*.

INSTRUCTIONAL TRAJECTORIES: AUTHORIZED VOICE AND LEGAL/LAY CATEGORIZATION

Drawing on Hymes, who considered voice central to linguistic agency ("freedom to have one's voice heard, freedom to develop a voice worth hearing"—1996: 64), Blommaert defines voice critically as "the capacity to make oneself understood...a capacity to generate an uptake of one's words as close as possible to one's desired contextualization" (2005: 68). Ehrlich (this volume), for example, demonstrates how a complainant in a rape trial loses her voice as her original interaction with her attacker is entextualized in courtroom testimony and then recontextualized to the point where the uptake of her words is quite distinct from her desired contextualization. However, Blommaert and Ehrlich are considering voice from an emancipatory perspective rather than an institutional one. What is striking about voice in institutional genres such as jury instruction is that those with the power of the institution behind them do not necessarily care about the uptake of their words: their efficacy lies in the performative ritual of their being uttered rather than being heard.

As Bourdieu makes clear, authority comes to language not from within but from outside. This is symbolized in Homer by the *skeptron*, which is passed to the nominated orator to give him the power of authority to speak (Bourdieu 1991: 109). Authorization comes from the social field, in this case the law, and the performative power of an institutional speaker's utterances derives not from the linguistic forms used (as in Austin 1962) but from the fact that "his speech concentrates within it the accumulated symbolic capital of the group which has delegated him and of which he is the *authorized representative*" (Bourdieu 1991: 109–11). For example, however a police officer words a "request" to a suspect, it is likely be taken as a command (Solan and Tiersma 2005: 38–46); the command is not conveyed through the imperative mood but through the police officer's status as an authorized representative of the police. Bourdieu notes that it is neither necessary nor sufficient for the "discourse of authority" to be understood, but it only obtains its "authorizing effect" if it is recognized by its receivers as legitimate. The "legitimacy conditions" are that it must be uttered by the "legitimately licensed" person, in a legitimate situation in front of legitimate receivers, and "it must be enunciated according to the legitimate forms" (Bourdieu 1991: 113). Malinowski (1935) similarly observed that magical incantations, if properly enacted, were efficacious in themselves.

Drawing on Bourdieu, we can say that judges, in delivering their instructions to the jury, draw on the social field of the law for their authority. To maintain that authority, it is neither necessary nor sufficient for the jury to *understand* those instructions. The words will be recognized by the jury (the legitimate receivers) as having authority because the spokesperson (the judge) and the situation (jury instruction) are both legitimate. This is typical of religious ritual, which, from Latin Mass to Thai chants in Pali, is often performed in a language that most of the congregation does not understand (Tambiah 1987). However, the judge has a second potential audience—the court of appeal—and knows that, for them, the key legitimacy condition is that the instruction "must be enunciated according to the legitimate forms" as regulated by those higher courts. Furthermore, in producing authorized versions of the instructions, judges are then, in turn, reinforcing those versions as authoritative.

We should make a distinction, at this point, between *authorized voice* and *authoritative discourse* based on agency. An *authorized voice* is empowered to effect change. Judges, for example, are empowered to "make law" by producing judgments that diverge from previous authoritative discourse in the form of earlier judgments. *Authoritative discourse*, on the other hand, is perceived as a structural constraint, as a set of normative rules constraining one's own voice: "it binds us, quite independent of any power it might have to persuade us internally; we encounter it with its authority already fused to it" (Bakhtin 1981: 342). Law students are socialized into attributing extreme importance to the authoritative discourse of precedential judgments made by senior judges with authorized voice (Mertz 2007).

The way "beyond reasonable doubt" is handled in jury instruction depends on its authorized categorization as "legal" or "ordinary language" and on the symbolic capital, or accumulated prestige, associated with the metadiscourse accompanying the term in a given jurisdiction. With regard to lexical categorization, "legal" terms are considered to derive their authority from the legal field while "ordinary language" terms are said to derive their authority from the community (Hutton 2009). More specifically, terms construed as "legal" are considered to derive their semantic legitimacy from explicitly stipulated definition in legal texts (statutes or judgments) drafted by legal professionals invested with high authority (the degree of authority invested in the authors of judgments depends on their overall status in the judicial hierarchy). Accordingly, authorized legal definitions might be quite different from an understanding of the same term used in everyday contexts. For example, in ordinary usage, "if someone commits a burglary, they enter a building by force and steal things" (COBUILD 2001), but in legal usage, the burglary might include entering a ship or inhabited caravan, not necessarily by force, and with merely the *intent* not necessarily to steal but also to inflict grievous bodily harm or cause criminal damage (UK Theft Act 1968). Terms construed by the law as "ordinary language," on the other hand, are claimed to derive their semantic legitimacy and authority from the speech community. In judicial discourse, they are often referred to as "common," "everyday," and "known to jurors." This perceived distinction has a marked effect on the way terms are handled by the judge in jury instruction. Where terms such as "burglary" or "murder" are authorized as "legal," judges will provide explicit (though not necessarily comprehensible) stipulative definitions in their instructions. Where terms are considered "ordinary language," on the other hand, and are thus said to be "shared" by the community, it is generally considered a trespass on the juror's province to attempt to define them: the "meaning of an ordinary word of the English language is not a question of law" (*Brutus v. Cozens*, at 861).

Within legal metadiscourse, the power dynamics of both authorized voice and authoritative discourse are extremely hierarchical. At the top of the legal food chain, Supreme Court Justices and Lord Chief Justices wield extreme power as authorized voices. As such, the opinions they express are likely to become authoritative discourse which then binds judges at lower levels in the judicial hierarchy. In the case of the criminal standard of proof, as awkward definitions of "reasonable doubt" increasingly became grounds for appeal, two Chief Justices came to diametrically opposed solutions to the problem, and thereby set the formula in their jurisdictions on opposing trajectories. Note that in neither case was the solution based on empirical evidence but merely on the extremely powerful voice of the highest legal figure in a jurisdiction.

In England and Wales, Lord Chief Justice Goddard, in *R v. Summers* in 1952, suggested that "reasonable doubt" should be replaced altogether in instructions:

> I have never yet heard a court give a real definition of what is a "reasonable doubt," and it would be very much better if that expression was not used. Whenever a court attempts to explain what is meant by it, the explanation tends to result in confusion rather than clarity.... The jury should be told that it is not for the prisoner to prove his innocence, but for the prosecution to prove his guilt, and that it is their duty to regard the evidence and see if it satisfies them so that they can feel sure, when they give their verdict, that it is a right one.

This radical solution of replacing the formula with a plain English paraphrase in jury instruction, though still resisted fiercely in some quarters (see Heffer 2007), became well established, as can be seen in the England and Wales judicial advisory board's former recommended direction: "How does the prosecution succeed in proving the defendant's guilt? The answer is—by making you sure of it. Nothing less than that will do" (JSB 2005).[2]

In Australia, on the other hand, Chief Justice Dixon strongly opposed this move and, in a landmark judgment a decade later (*Dawson v. R*), held that the formula itself need not be defined or paraphrased because it could be understood well enough by ordinary people:

> In my view it is a mistake to depart from the time-honoured formula. It is, I think, used by ordinary people and is understood well enough by the average man in the community. The attempts to substitute other expressions, of which there have been many

examples not only here but in England, have never prospered. It is wise as well as proper to avoid such expressions.

Despite recognition by the New South Wales Law Reform Commission that it "commonly occurs in criminal trials [that] the jury asks for some further explanation of the expression" (NSWLRC 2008: 69), the evidence of lack of understanding was and is still trumped by the authoritative voice of a man often described as "Australia's greatest jurist":

> Since 1961, when Chief Justice Dixon referred to the formula "beyond reasonable doubt" as "time honoured," appellate courts in Australia have consistently held that it is an expression well understood by ordinary people. (NSWLRC 2008: 67)

Yet the appellate courts hold that the expression is "well understood by ordinary people" precisely by referring to Chief Justice Dixon's authoritative word. The subjective hedging of CJ Dixon's opinion ("I think") on the matter does not weaken its status as authoritative discourse; indeed, it appears to strengthen it given the power of CJ Dixon as an authorized voice.

The "ordinary language" trajectory effectively puts "beyond reasonable doubt" in a state of apparent textual stasis. It is easy to see how the idea of fixing a text indelibly to a given meaning is enticing: "if a text has a despatialized and detemporalized meaning…then that meaning can be clearly transmitted across social boundaries such as generations, without regard for the kinds of recontextualizations it might undergo" (Silverstein and Urban 1996: 1). Yet we have seen that the many recontextualizations of "beyond reasonable doubt" have taken their toll on the original form-meaning pair. While, at the time of Dixon's comments, there was no empirical evidence beyond jury requests for clarification that the jury may not understand the term, we now have ample evidence from a variety of sources that this is the case.[3] While such evidence itself is unlikely to be known by many trial judges, it suggests that the problem of clarification must come up frequently in court. In fact, it probably does not come up as frequently as it should given the general reluctance to challenge an authorized and expert voice, particularly where the power differential is as great as that between judge and jury.

If a linguistic expression has travelled so far from the legal standard it is intended to convey, how is it possible to maintain the fiction that the two are still united? It is possible that some trial judges "on the ground" are simply responding to the authorized voice and authoritative discourse unthinkingly. They are following rules and rituals and abrogating personal responsibility. However, all judges are trained to think rationally and to carefully weigh up the various aspects of an issue. Justices in the higher courts are called on precisely to provide a very careful weighing of the issues. One is reluctant, then, to dismiss senior judges as nothing more than petty rule followers.

One rational possibility is that the metadiscursive commentaries of judges, their preferred readings, reflect their linguistic ideologies, their sets of "beliefs about language articulated by users as a rationalization or justification of perceived language structure and use" (Silverstein 1979: 103). Judges certainly hold sets of beliefs about language (Philips 1998; Mertz 2007), and they are articulating such beliefs when they claim, for example, that "beyond reasonable doubt" must be understood by ordinary people because it is "time-honoured" or a "familiar" expression. However, it is difficult to see how judges could arrive at a rational argument that jurors understand "beyond reasonable doubt" perfectly well even though juries frequently (and face-threateningly) ask for clarification of its meaning. It seems more credible, then, that judges' approach to language in such cases is below the surface of conscious reflection and articulation and belongs to their *legal-linguistic habitus*, their accumulated and naturalized experience of linguistic action in legal contexts.

TEXTUAL APORIA: LEGAL-LINGUISTIC HABITUS AND A DIFFERENT PRACTICE DANCE

It is not easy to show the workings of habitus rather than conscious ideology or rhetoric. Observation of discursive patterns across large numbers of text can show routinization, which may well be an index to linguistic habitus. However, unlike the taking of guilty pleas in the United States (Philips 1998) or the delivery of the standard of proof in England and Wales (Heffer 2005), judges in "ordinary language" jurisdictions have little or no discretion in the way they convey "beyond reasonable doubt" to the jury. In this case, then, what we are interested in is what happens when the discursive routine breaks down: when the unexplained delivery of "beyond reasonable doubt" is met with puzzlement by the jury and eventually requests for clarification.

For illustration, I turn to the State of Victoria case, *R v. Chatzidimitriou*.[4] The case was appealed primarily on the grounds that the trial judge had granted the jury's request for a dictionary after the jurors had failed to be satisfied by either his original direction or their requested re-direction on the criminal standard of proof. We are not interested here in the legal debate at appeal over the granting of the dictionary but in the communication breakdown that occurred at trial and how the trial judge and the three appeal justices explain what occurred. Methodologically, judgments certainly do not constitute ethnographic data, but they are intertextually complex heteroglossic documents with intricate embedding of texts from other judgments and trial transcripts. They accordingly provide access to a variety of texts and voices relevant to the case, as well as a legal-professional perspective on trial discourse.

We can trace five key moves in the communication breakdown over "beyond reasonable doubt" during the trial. I set these out in figure 10.1 below, attempting to separate the judicial and jury perspectives on the breakdown. The reactions of the trial judge, as evidenced in legal discussion with counsel, and of the appeal justices, as evidenced in the legal metadiscourse of their judgments, are summarized in *italics*. I also indicate possible reactions (in *italics* and <angled brackets>) of the jury, though these are clearly speculative as I had no access to the jury deliberations.

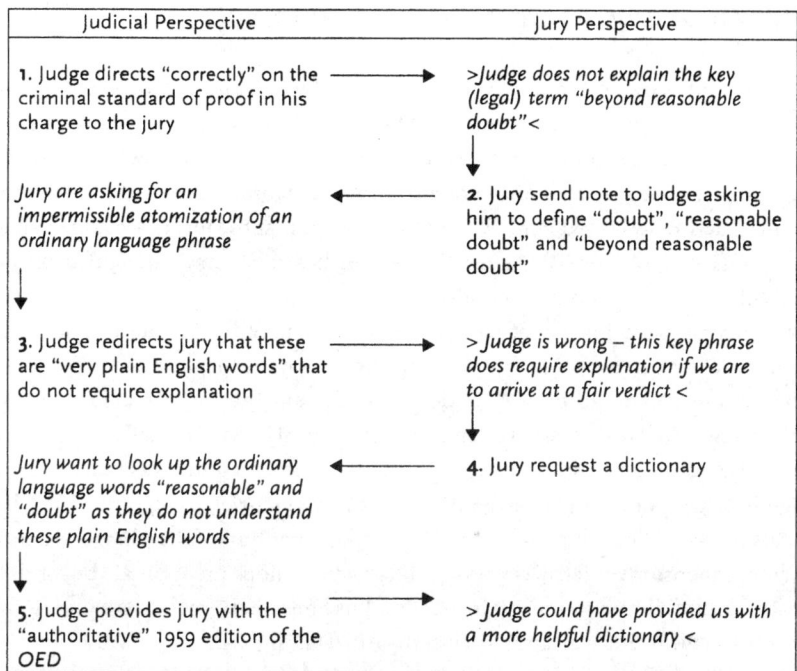

Judicial Perspective	Jury Perspective
1. Judge directs "correctly" on the criminal standard of proof in his charge to the jury ⟶	>*Judge does not explain the key (legal) term "beyond reasonable doubt"*<
Jury are asking for an impermissible atomization of an ordinary language phrase ⟵	**2.** Jury send note to judge asking him to define "doubt", "reasonable doubt" and "beyond reasonable doubt"
3. Judge redirects jury that these are "very plain English words" that do not require explanation ⟶	>*Judge is wrong – this key phrase does require explanation if we are to arrive at a fair verdict* <
Jury want to look up the ordinary language words "reasonable" and "doubt" as they do not understand these plain English words ⟵	**4.** Jury request a dictionary
5. Judge provides jury with the "authoritative" 1959 edition of the OED ⟶	> *Judge could have provided us with a more helpful dictionary* <

Figure 10.1 Incommensurable practices in explaining "beyond reasonable doubt".

What we see in this encounter is strangely analogous to Scollon's (1997) observation of embodied social practices in a pedestrian walkway in Hong Kong of China. Scollon notes how Hong Kong and North American pedestrians often bump into each other. Doing what comes naturally to them, People of Hong Kong give way by bearing to the left, while North Americans bear to the right. With no unwritten rules to go by, the pedestrians can then lurch one way or the other in accidental unison and end up performing an embarrassing street dance as they try to negotiate a way past. Scollon (2001:23) notes that this awkward dance results from a "fundamental incommen- surability of practice in which giving way is operationalized in opposite directions." These incommensurable practices are rooted precisely in what Bourdieu describes as "non-homologous habitus," distinctly different accumulations of experience of social action (Bourdieu 1990). The communication breakdown here is similar to this "different practice dance": coming face-to-face with the judge and his legal instructions, the lay jurors bear one way, seeking an explanation of a (legal) term ("beyond reasonable doubt") they do not understand, while the judge bears the other, appealing to the authoritative discourse that this "time-honoured formula" is expressed in "ordinary language" that can be understood by jurors.

Referring to this brief sketch of the breakdown, I would now like to consider in more detail a potentially general pragmatic index that the authorized voice, in this case on "beyond reasonable doubt," has been internalized to the point where it is part of the (judges') unquestioned (legal-)linguistic habitus. That pragmatic index is an impaired ability to hear others' voices.

When an authorized voice comes to be perceived by institutional players as "authoritative discourse" and becomes part of their linguistic habitus, it arguably begins to affect their capacity to hear and evaluate other voices. Scollon (2001) notes that negative imputations of identity are a common outcome of the type of "different practice" dance described here. Rather than accept that the jurors are adhering to a "foreign" (i.e., nonlegal) habitus, the judges, mishearing them, impute that they are ignorant, stupid, or simply misconceived.

In the first place, instead of recognizing that it might be difficult to understand this instruction (at move 1 in figure 10.1) when it is not explained and is embedded within a four-and-a-half hour monologue setting out the law and evidence applicable to the case, the justices note simply that the trial judge "correctly directed" the jury at the outset and end of the charge and that "no exception was taken ... to the judge's charge—nor could it have been" (*R v Chatzidimitriou*, paragraph [2]).[5] They mistakenly (see Pintrich and Sinatra 2003) take repetition of the phrase as a proxy for comprehension: defense counsel claims that the judge mentioned "beyond reasonable doubt" eleven times and Justice Phillips notes that "[w]hen the jury retired, they must have been very familiar with the expression" [2].

Second, when the jury appears to accommodate to legal-linguistic norms of explanation by breaking down the components of the phrase (figure 10.1, move 2), this is misheard as an impermissible construal of the term. Yet the very fact that the jurors are decomposing the term is clear evidence that they have not understood it. Wray (2002: 12) notes that we break down phrases on a "needs-only" basis, which is why British people are often surprised to learn that Rice Krispies (a common brand of cereal) are made of rice (2002: 3). Louisianans hear *coon ass* as a harmless slang term referring to Cajuns (white settlers of French descent) but when a "Coon Ass Certificate" was accidentally sent to an African American woman in Washington, DC, she received it with "shock, outrage and fury," since, not being aware of this dialect term, she (along with the prosecution expert and probably the jury, who found in her favor) naturally decomposed it and heard the racist *coon* combined with the degrading *ass* (Wray and Staczek 2005). Similarly, a judge does not need to decompose "beyond reasonable doubt" to understand its meaning, but a juror, probably faced for the first time with actually having to apply a term otherwise known only metalinguistically, will have an additional need to break the phrase down into its more comprehensible parts. The jurors in this case, however, hedged their bets and showed that they understood perfectly well the difference between compositional and idiomatic meaning by not asking for definitions of the individual words but for definitions of the grammatically meaningful units: the noun head ("doubt"), the noun phrase ("reasonable doubt"), and the prepositional phrase as a whole ("beyond reasonable doubt"). Furthermore, such analysis is perfectly in keeping with definitional practice throughout the summing-up, in which the judge would have defined with great legal precision ordinary-sounding terms such as "murder," along with more technical-sounding terms such as "circumstantial evidence." The justices, though, only appear to hear the request for analysis in the first two imperatives ("Define doubt. Define reasonable doubt.") and not the request for synthesis in the final imperative "Define 'beyond reasonable doubt'":

> The form of the question showed that the jury had not appreciated that "beyond reasonable doubt" was a composite expression, not *intended to* be broken into its component parts or analyzed, but *designed to* convey an accurate impression of the high standard of proof that the Crown was required to satisfy. ([20], emphasis added)

Curiously, the justices cite various precedents which "establish" that it is not possible to define each word individually and that the phrase "obviously means more in this context than the mere sum of its parts" [20], yet the use of "intended to" and "designed to" above suggests a stipulative legal construction of the term rather than an ordinary language phrase.

The judges also fail to hear clearly the jury's request for a dictionary (at move 4). Neither the trial judge nor the appeal justices entertain the possibility that the jurors are requesting a definition of the idiomatic phrase rather than its component parts or that they might be hoping to find an answer to two of their three questions: "Define 'reasonable doubt'" and "Define 'beyond reasonable doubt.'" Yet if, as the judges claim, the phrase is (a) part of the ordinary language, and (b) nonanalyzable and therefore idiomatic, it would be perfectly reasonable (rational *and* fair) to expect to find it listed as a headword or at least as a sense in a contemporary general dictionary. Indeed, it *is* listed in many contemporary general dictionaries but either in a lay sense that would make Australian judges shudder (as in the "beyond doubt" of the COBUILD entry above) or marked up as a legal term, as in the Australian *Macquarie Dictionary*'s definition of "reasonable doubt" as "*noun law* sufficient evidence to lead an ordinary person to believe that the defendant may not have committed the offence" (Macquarie 2010). The judges have internalized the authoritative discourse about the term being "ordinary language" to such an extent that they do not even consider the possibility of a dictionary providing a specialized legal definition of "reasonable doubt" or "beyond reasonable doubt," even if "reasonable doubt," "beyond reasonable doubt," or "proof beyond reasonable doubt" are invariably listed in legal dictionaries (e.g., Garner 2009; Law and Martin 2009). Instead, judge and justices all take as absolutely given that the jurors want to look up the individual words "reasonable" and "doubt" in a general dictionary because, as the trial judge indicates, they somehow do not understand these common words: "when one tells lay people that it is a matter of plain language and they want to understand the language better, why should they not have recourse to an authorised dictionary? It's not a matter of law they're looking at, it's a matter of language" [34].

Finally, despite maintaining consistently that we are dealing with a matter of contemporary language ("plain English words") rather than historically established law (the definition of a legal term), the judges fail to actually hear a request for help with the language of the day. Justice Cummins's rationale for the trial judge's choice of the particular edition of the *OED* is revealing:

> Responsible citizens have been consulting the Oxford English Dictionary since 1933 (and the New English Dictionary on Historical Principles since 1884), if not the dictionary of Dr. Samuel Johnson (A Dictionary of the English Language) since 1755 or that of Robert Cawdrey (A Table Alphabetical) since 1604. The two volume Shorter Oxford English Dictionary held in the Bendigo Court and provided to this jury was published in 1959 under the general editorship of the distinguished C. T. Onions. It is an authoritative work. [42]

As a discourse of authority, the dictionary, like judicial instruction, only exercises its specific effect when it is "recognized" as such. Cummins effectively establishes the legitimacy conditions that grant recognition to this 1959 edition of the *OED*: it is edited by "the distinguished C. T. Onions" (legitimately licensed animator); it is consulted by "responsible citizens" belonging to a long line of responsible users dating back to the early seventeenth century (legitimate receivers); and, implicitly, it describes/prescribes British English forms and does so on historical/etymological principles (legitimate forms). The fact that the jurors in the case (responsible or not) probably spoke 1990s Australian English rather than 1950s (and much earlier historical forms of) British English appears to be irrelevant. What is important is that the 1959 *OED* is "an authoritative work."

The authorized voice of CJ Dixon, then, echoed over the years by other senior judges and subsumed into trial judges' legal-linguistic habitus, appears to prevent judges in Victoria from hearing the jury's request for a simple explanation of a key term they need to apply in their deliberations. Instead they ascribe negative identity to the jurors in the form of misunderstanding or general ignorance, as in Justice Phillips's colorful imputation:

> If the jury is to be directed still in terms of "reasonable doubt," it cannot be error, in my view, for the jurors to consider, for themselves, what is "reasonable." And to give them a dictionary is, on one view, to let the jurors do by reading what any competent English teacher might be able to do by recollection. [13]

Such negative ascriptions preserve the judges' own professional identity and defend them the awful realization that current practice might be leading to unsafe convictions based on an inadequate understanding of the standard of proof. It is much safer to ascribe the problem to the inadequacies of the immediate jury than to accept that there might be a more systemic problem.

We can arguably see here, then, a move from communication to magic incantation. Justice Cummins sums up the case for appeal as follows:

> The risk inherent in the jury having recourse to a dictionary is that the jury having atomised the expression "beyond reasonable doubt" might fail to proceed to consider and apply it holistically. As Keats wrote, "philosophy will clip an angel's wings." [41]

The poetic reference here is to "Lamia," in which Keats attacks Newton, whose "philosophy" (the investigation of natural phenomena) had destroyed the beauty of nature by analyzing light with a prism and splitting it into different colors. Justice Cummins appears to be suggesting not just that "beyond reasonable doubt" needs to be considered holistically, but that there is something magical about the term which is debased by attempts to define or explain it. Uttering the phrase in its ritual form has a quasi-magical performative power that casts a decision-making spell over jurors.

CONCLUSION: COMMUNICATION, MAGIC, AND MAJESTY

This chapter has argued that the communicational conduct of courts in relation to lay participants needs to be understood in the historically contingent and normative context of the law. By tracing the trajectories of a legal text through time, we can see just how contingent current legal-linguistic practices and beliefs can be and how much they are shaped by normative legal pronouncements. From a synchronic linguistic perspective, one might read in the *Chatzidimitriou* case layers of assumption on the part of the legal profession regarding the meaning of expressions with which they are familiar, the undesirability of attempting to unpack the expressions word by word, and the absence of any necessity for jurors to do so, as speakers of the language. From the historically contingent and normative perspective I have argued for here, though, the way "beyond reasonable doubt" is conveyed to juries across jurisdictions is *not* dependent on linguistic assumptions or ideologies shared by the legal profession. Otherwise we might expect fairly common practice across common law jurisdictions. Instead, I have argued that legal practices with regard to language are contingent on the *authorized voice* of a few key legal players in a given jurisdiction, which then becomes *authoritative discourse* that is eventually absorbed into the *legal-linguistic habitus* of the trial judges "on the ground." While in Australian jurisdictions it is "obvious" (i.e., beyond the need for conscious reflection) that "beyond reasonable doubt" can only be construed holistically and without explanation, in many US jurisdictions it is equally "obvious" that the term needs to be carefully defined, while in England and Wales it is "obvious" that the term needs to be paraphrased. Authority on language in the law does not come from professional formation but from the authorized voice. It is a question not so much of profession but of power.

It is quite possible that I am overemphasizing the lack of agency of judges with respect to authoritative discourse about language in a given jurisdiction. The justices in the *Chatzidimitriou* judgment, for example, might have been making very conscious strategic choices in their metalinguistic comments. The primary function of an appeal is to determine whether the original conviction was "safe" and the fact that this was a "strong" hired-killer murder case would have provided significant motivation for the justices to find a means to dismiss the appeal, as they did, despite the trial judge's highly controversial ruling about the dictionary.[6] Yet the ritual incantation of the formula is taken for granted even by the trial judge (who suggests that jurors might *not* understand it) and by the dissenting Justice Phillips, who would have upheld the appeal. Delivering the standard as a ritual formula does, then, appear to have become part of the legal-linguistic habitus of judges in that particular jurisdictional nexus of practice.

The thesis presented here has wider implications for the survival of a jury system of criminal justice. The *Chatzidimitriou* case provides just one of many possible examples of how judicial instructions that are originally communicative can become, in Frank's words, "devitalized magic incantations," and Tiersma (2001), in particular, has done much to demonstrate the impenetrability of many devitalized US pattern jury instructions. Frank believed that more effective communication with juries would be pointless because "Juries are notoriously gullible and impressionable" (Frank 1930: 192), and are "hopelessly incompetent as fact-finders" (194). He was writing, though, long before Plain English campaigns had demonstrably improved lay comprehension of legal texts in many areas of the law (Butt and Castle 2001) and before more than 50 years of extensive empirical research into the jury had convincingly shown that jurors (though susceptible to the same psychological biases as legal professionals) are neither "notoriously gullible" nor "hopelessly incompetent" (Lieberman and Sales 1997). They *are* worth communicating with effectively.

I promised a remedy and the remedy is simple. It is perfectly possible to revitalize not the magic but the "majesty" (*maestas*, or "greatness") of the due process values of the criminal standard by translating it into contemporary lay terms such as "proof that leaves you firmly convinced." For the law gives judges authority not only over legal language but also over the liminal zones where the legal fades into the lay. It simply requires those with the greatest authoritative voice in the legal field of a given jurisdiction to take stock of empirical linguistic reality and to declare with the trial judge in *Chatzidimitriou* that the "courts might be wrong." In doing so, legal–lay interaction will continue to move away from the magic of incantation and toward the majesty of communication.

POSTSCRIPT

As this book reached proof stage, the New South Wales Law Reform Commission finally released their Report on jury instructions (NSW LRC 2012). My submission to the Commission's consultation (Heffer 2009) referred to an early draft of this paper. The item in the Report that made the headlines (Patty and Davies 2013) is its conclusion that "there is a strong case for providing additional guidance to juries on the standard of proof" and that "the current law severely limits the directions that can be given to juries and leaves them with insufficient assistance" (NSW LRC 2012: 72). While recognizing that the phrase "beyond reasonable doubt" is "deeply ingrained in our collective common law tradition," it concludes not that it therefore cannot be changed but that "it would be essential for reform to occur at a national level, with the aim of enacting uniform legislation on the point" (idem 72). This supports the thesis that authorised voice can override accumulated authoritative discourse, though it remains to be seen whether legislation will indeed be enacted.

ACKNOWLEDGMENTS

I am very grateful to Alison Wray for her astute and invaluable comments on various drafts of this chapter, and to John Conley, Cristina Marinetti, and Ron Carter, who provided perspicacious commentary on specific drafts. Justice Peter Gray kindly offered expert assistance with the technical aspects of Australian legal reports. Various elements of this chapter were presented at the 6th Cardiff Roundtable in Sociolinguistics in July 2008 and in the Linguistics Department, Auckland University, in April 2010. My thanks go to the participants at those events.

NOTES

1. The inverted commas in the original are for emphasis only but, recontextualized in a contemporary context, appear to be self-selected sound bites.
2. In 2010, the Judicial Studies Board replaced its "Specimen Directions" with more contextual "illustrations" of summing-up, which show an increased tendency toward a process of "narrativization" observed in Heffer (2002, 2005). As hypothesized, narrativization has been shown to significantly improve comprehension of instructions on the burden and standard of proof (Nelson 2013).
3. See, for example, Solan (1999) for an overview of US experimental evidence, Young et al. (1999) for a survey of New Zealand jurors, and Trimboli (2008) for a questionnaire study of New South Wales jurors.
4. I refer here to the authorized report of the case published in the Victorian Reports (1 VR 493) and available through LexisNexis. It is interesting to note that although there appears to be no significant textual difference between this authorized version and one that "does not purport to be the official or authorized version" but is made freely available by the Australian Legal Institute (AustLII 2010), the unauthorized one is considered less "legitimate" within the legal field.
5. All subsequent numbers in square brackets indicate the paragraph number in the judgment.
6. It might be of note in this respect that Justice Cummins was known as a particularly fervent proponent of "victims' rights" and that, in his retirement speech, he argued that judges had "fallen short on sentence" in cases involving violence (Wilkinson et al. 2010).

LIST OF CASES

Brutus v. Cozens [1973] AC 854.
Dawson v. R (1961) 106 CLR 1.
R v. Chatzidimitriou (2000) 1 VR 493.
R v. Summers [1952] 1 All ER 1059.
Victor v. Nebraska, 511 US 1 (1994).

REFERENCES

Austin, John. 1962. *How to Do Things with Words*. Oxford: Clarendon.
AustLII. 2010. *Supreme Court of Victoria—Court of Appeal*. Australian Legal Institute. Available at: http://www.austlii.edu.au/au/cases/vic/VSCA/2000/91.html.

Bakhtin, Mikhail. [1934–35] 1981. *The Dialogic Imagination*. Austin: University of Texas Press.

Bauman, Richard, and Charles L. Briggs. 1990. Poetics and performance as critical perspectives on language and social life. *Annual Review of Anthropology* 19:59–88.

Blommaert, Jan. 2005. *Discourse*. Cambridge: Cambridge University Press.

Bourdieu, Pierre. 1990. *The Logic of Practice*. Cambridge: Polity.

———. 1991. *Language and Symbolic Power*. Cambridge: Polity.

Butt, Peter, and Richard W. Castle. 2001. *Modern Legal Drafting*. Cambridge: Cambridge University Press.

COBUILD. 2001. *Collins COBUILD English Dictionary for Advanced Learners*. 3d ed. Glasgow: HarperCollins.

FJC. 1988. *Federal Judicial Center Pattern Criminal Jury Instructions*. Washington, DC: Federal Judicial Center.

Frank, Jerome. 1930. *Law and the Modern Mind*. New York: Brentano's.

Garner, Bryan, ed. 2009. *Black's Law Dictionary*. 9th ed. St. Paul, MN: West.

Heffer, Chris. 2002. 'If you were standing in Marks and Spencers': Narrativisation and comprehension in the English summing-up. In *Language in the Legal Process*, ed. Janet Cotterill, 228–45. Basingstoke: Palgrave Macmillan.

———. 2005. *The Language of Jury Trial*. Basingstoke, UK: Palgrave Macmillan.

———. 2006. Beyond 'reasonable doubt': The criminal standard of proof instruction as communicative act. *International Journal of Speech, Language and the Law* 13(2): 159–88.

———. 2007. The language of conviction and the convictions of certainty: Is 'sure' an impossible standard of proof? *International Commentary on Evidence* 5(1): Art. 5.

———. 2009. Directing on the Burden and Standard of Proof: A Submission on the NSW Law Reform Commission Consultation Paper 4 on Jury Directions.

Horowitz, Irwin A., and Laird C. Kirkpatrick. 1996. A concept in search of a definition: The effects of reasonable doubt instructions on certainty of guilt standards and jury verdicts. *Law and Human Behavior* 20(6): 655–70.

Hutton, Chris. 2009. *Language, Meaning and the Law*. Edinburgh: Edinburgh University Press.

Hymes, Dell. 1996. *Ethnography, Linguistics, Narrative Inequality: Towards an Understanding of Voice*. London: Taylor and Frances.

JCNSW. 1990–2008. *Criminal Trial Courts Bench Book*. Judicial Commission of New South Wales. Available at: http://www.judcom.nsw.gov.au/publications/benchbks.

JSB. 2005. *Crown Court Benchbook: Specimen Directions*. London: Judicial Studies Board.

Kuipers, Joel. 1990. *Power in Performance: The Creation of Textual Authority in Weyewa Ritual Speech*. Philadelphia: University of Pennsylvania Press.

Laudan, Larry. 2006. *Truth, Error, and Criminal Law*. Cambridge: Cambridge University Press.

Law, Jonathan, and Elizabeth A. Martin. 2009. *Oxford Dictionary of Law*. 7th ed. Oxford: Oxford University Press.

LDCE. 1995. *Longman Dictionary of Contemporary English*. Harlow, UK: Longman.

Lieberman, Joel D., and Bruce Sales. 1997. What social science teaches us about the jury instruction process. *Psychology, Public Policy and Law* 3(4): 589–644.

Macquarie. 2010. *The Macquarie Dictionary Online*. Sydney: Macquarie Dictionary. http://www.macquariedictionary.com.au.

Malinowski, Bronislaw. 1935. *Coral Gardens and their Magic*. Volume 2: *The Language of Magic and Gardening*. New York: American Book Company.

Mertz, Elizabeth. 2007. *The Language of Law School*. Oxford: Oxford University Press.

Morano, Anthony A. 1975. A re-examination of the reasonable doubt rule. *Boston University Law Review* 55: 507–28.

MWALD. 2008. *Merriam-Webster's Advanced Learner's Dictionary*. Springfield, MA: Merriam-Webster.

Nelson, Sally. 2013. Directing jurors in England and Wales: The effect of narrativization on comprehension. Ph.D. diss. Cardiff: Cardiff University.

NSWLRC. 2008. *Consultation Paper 4—Jury Instructions*. Sydney: New South Wales Law Reform Commission.

NSWLRC 2012. *Jury Direction*. New South Wales Law Reform Commission Report 136. Sydney: NSW Law Reform Commission. Available at HYPERLINK "http://www.lawlink.nsw.gov.au/lrc" www.lawlink.nsw.gov.au/lrc.

Patty, Anna and Davies, Lisa. 2013. Jurors need more direction – report. *The Sydney Morning Herald*. 26 March. Available at http://www.smh.com.au/nsw/jurors-need-more-direction-report-20130325-2gq7q.html.

Philips, Susan. 1998. *Ideology in the Language of Judges*. Oxford: Oxford University Press.

Pintrich, Paul R., and Gale M. Sinatra, eds. 2003. *Intentional Conceptual Change*. Mahwah, NJ: Erlbaum.

Saxton, Bradley. 1998. How well do jurors understand jury instructions? A field test using real juries and real trials in Wyoming. *Land and Water Law Review* 33: 59–190.

Scollon, Ron. 1997. Handbills, tissues and condoms: A site of engagement for the construction of identity in public discourse. *Journal of Sociolinguistics* 1(1): 39–61.

———. 2001. *Mediated Discourse: The Nexus of Practice*. London: Routledge.

Shapiro, Barbara. 1991. *Beyond Reasonable Doubt and Probable Cause: Historical Perspectives on the Anglo-American Law of Evidence*. Berkeley: University of California Press.

Silverstein, Michael. 1979. Language structure and linguistic ideology. In *The Elements: A Parasession on Linguistic Units and Levels, ed.* Paul R. Clyne, William F. Hanks, and Carol L. Hofbauer, 193–247. Chicago: Chicago Linguistic Society.

Silverstein, Michael, and Greg Urban. 1996. The natural history of discourse. In *Natural Histories of Discourse*, ed. Michael Silverstein and Greg Urban, 1–17. Chicago: Chicago University Press.

Solan, Lawrence M. 1999. Refocusing the burden of proof in criminal cases: Some doubt about reasonable doubt. *Texas Law Review* 78(1): 105–47.

Solan, Lawrence M., and Peter M. Tiersma. 2005. *Speaking of Crime: The Language of Criminal Justice*. Chicago: Chicago University Press.

Tambiah, Stanley J. 1985. *Culture, Thought, and Social Action: An Anthropological Perspective*. Cambridge, MA: Harvard University Press.

Tiersma, Peter M. 2001. The rocky road to legal reform: Improving the language of jury instructions. *Brooklyn Law Review* 66(4): 1081–1118.

Trimboli, Lily. 2008. Juror understanding of judicial instructions in criminal trials. *Contemporary Issues in Crime and Justice* 119:1–16.

Whitman, James. 2008. *The Origins of Reasonable Doubt*. New Haven: Yale University Press.

Wierzbicka, Anna. 2003. "Reasonable man" and "reasonable doubt": The English language, Anglo culture and Anglo-American law. *International Journal of Speech, Language and the Law* 10(1): 1–22.

Wilkinson, Geoff, Norrie Ross, and Wayne Flower. 2010. Criminals get it too easy, Victoria's Justice Philip Cummins says. *The Sun Herald*, 24 February.

Wray, Alison. 2002. *Formulaic Language and the Lexicon*. Cambridge: Cambridge University Press.

Wray, Alison, and John J. Staczek. 2005. One word or two? Psycholinguistic and sociolinguistic interpretations of meaning in a civil court case. *International Journal of Speech, Language and the Law* 12(1): 1–18.

Young, Warren, Neil Cameron, and Yvette Tinsley. 1999. *Juries in Criminal Trials*. New Zealand Law Commission Preliminary Paper No. 37. Vol. 2, Part II.

CHAPTER 11

Troubling the Legal–Lay Distinction

Litigant Briefs, Oral Argument, and a Public Hearing about Same-Sex Marriage

KAREN TRACY AND ERICA L. DELGADILLO

INTRODUCTION

In the opening chapter of *Order in Court*, the early and influential study of inter-action in judicial settings, Atkinson and Drew (1979: 9) asserted that "although there may in principle be no clear or absolute solution to the problem of how and where a precise line is to be drawn between legal and other styles of talking, there can be little doubt that in practice members are well able to identify and use such a contrast." We agree with this assessment, although we would inflect it differently and say: precise line drawing between legal and nonlegal discourse is difficult, even though in many settings it is easy. The ease (or difficulty) of distinc-tion making will tie to the particular configuration of setting, participants, act sequences, and ends, to borrow from Hymes (1974) for names of contributing factors. When the setting is a legal institution (i.e., a court) and key players are legal categories of persons (attorneys, judges, magistrates) involved in a recogniz-able genre of legal talk, then the distinction is almost always straightforward. But if the setting is not centrally a legal one, as is the case with a public hearing about law-linked matters, then the legal–lay discourse distinction becomes fuzzy. It is the setting more than anything else that makes it easy to distinguish legal and nonlegal discourse.

In this chapter we challenge the claim that legal texts are decontextualized principle-based forms whereas lay texts are narrative-based. The picture of discourse genres, we will show, is more complicated. Drawing on three sequentially linked texts about the legality of one US state's marriage law—written litigant briefs in the New

Jersey Supreme Court, oral argument in that same court, and a public hearing of the judicial committee of the New Jersey legislature—we show that the argumentative position of the two parties (pro and con same-sex marriage) explains the distinctive discourse features as much or more than the arguer's status as legal or lay. We begin by providing background on the case and the discourse materials. Then we overview the legal–lay concept and contrast it with relevant other discourse categorization systems. The analytic center of the chapter is a description of the textual features that travelled (and those that did not) from litigant briefs prepared for the Court to the attorney-judge oral argument to the public hearing about how the Court's ruling was to be implemented. We conclude by reflecting about the features of texts that travelled and how differences among the genres relate to the legal–lay distinction.

BACKGROUND ON *LEWIS V. HARRIS* AND THE DISCOURSE MATERIALS

In June 2002 Lambda Legal, a national organization pursuing civil rights legislation and advocacy for gay and lesbians, filed a lawsuit against the state of New Jersey on behalf of seven same-sex couples who were denied marriage licenses. The plaintiff's legal team claimed that the denial of a marriage license violated the couples' fundamental rights, grounding their argument in Article I of the New Jersey Constitution, which provides for due process and equal protection. The trial court judge had disagreed with Lambda Legal's claim, and following an appeal the advocacy group lost in an intermediate appellate court, Lambda Legal appealed to the state supreme court. In Fall 2006, seven months after oral argument, the New Jersey Supreme Court decided in favor of the plaintiffs. All seven justices believed that same-sex couples were entitled to the rights *of* marriage, but only three justices felt that anything less than full marriage, including its name, was unconstitutional. The Court gave the legislature 180 days to either amend the marriage laws to include same-sex couples or create "appropriate statutory structure[s]" with the same rights as marriage. Soon after the court ruling, the Assembly's Judiciary Committee held a public hearing to seek input on a bill, the Civil Union Act, that would extend the rights of marriage to same-sex couples but without the name "marriage." Following legislative debate and a positive vote, the bill was signed into law in 2007. Soon after, couples began to get civil-unioned.

To select discursive events for study, language and law scholars have tended either to focus on particular memorable cases, such as the trials of O.J. Simpson (Schuetz and Lilly 1999; Cotterill 2002) or the officers accused of beating Rodney King (Goodwin and Goodwin 1997), or have examined multiple instances across a single genre, such as small claims testimony (Conley and O'Barr 1990) or judges' plea taking (Philips 1998). What has *not* received attention is to look at the communication of multiple key players on the same legal issue/case across different genres. We think such a juxtaposition of genres may generate new insights into how talk and text travel, how a text is initially decontextualized and then recontextualized to do other kinds of interactional work (Hanks 1989; Bauman and Briggs 1990).

The focal materials for the analysis, in chronological order, are (1) the plaintiff's written brief submitted in the New Jersey *Lewis v. Harris* case, (2) the 65-minute oral argument by the two attorneys before the seven justices, and (3) the 3 hour+ public hearing held by the Assembly Judiciary Committee. Video- or audio-streaming of the oral argument and public hearing are available on the web pages of these government bodies,[1] and we transcribed the talk of these two occasions. Words, repairs, vocalized sounds (uh), and overlapping speech were recorded, but no attention was given to prosody or timing. In essence, we transcribed in a less detailed style than conversation analysis (Drew and Heritage 1992) but a more detailed fashion than is used in most court-prepared transcripts (Heffer 2005).

THE USEFULNESS OF THE "LEGAL-LAY DISCOURSE" DISTINCTION

There are several ways to conceptualize "legal versus lay." One way is to see the distinction as pointing to clearly defined vocabularies where a term is either a legal or ordinary one (see Heffer, this volume). Another way of conceptualizing "legal–lay discourse" is as a handy phrase for pointing to a variety of communicative activities that involve law-linked practitioners (attorneys, judges, and possibly police) writing or speaking for or to nonlegal others. In this, admittedly vague, domain-cueing sense, the term is helpful, demarcating some institutions (courts, police) and activities (trials, expression in legal documents, suspect interrogations) and not others (medical rounds, a therapy session, a public meeting about climate policy); distinguishing one community of language and discourse analysts—those with interests in justice sites—from others. For this simple deictic purpose, the term is useful, allowing communicators to invoke a relevant context with limited effort and, therein, give their attention to what is their main concern. If this kind of general domain-cueing is *legal–lay discourse*'s key purpose, then there is no problem.

But if a term is expected to do intellectual work, what it defines or implies is in (or outside) the category becomes important. Any linguistic concept, whether it is a natural category or a socially created one, privileges certain things as, for example, "bird" privileges "robin" and marginalizes "turkey" (Rosch et al. 1976).

Consider just a few questions about the legal–lay term: (1) Is legal a category of person (i.e., someone who possesses a law degree) or is it meant to include other law-related professions such as policing, court reporters, and interpreters? (2) Is "legal–lay" a descriptor for the talk that occurs in particular institutional sites, or is it better thought of as a style of thinking, speaking, and writing? (3) Why is legal the first part of the pair? Isn't this order privileging such settings as jury trials over small claims court where lay people do much of the speaking? (4) If "legal" is a style, in what sense is it what individuals do and in what sense does it point to a community of practice? (5) Does "lay" mean anything more than the absence of whatever legal is defined to be? Is it the case that all of the variations in speaking are best captured by these two labels? (6) Do both legal and lay parties have to be present for the discourse to count as legal–lay? What does "present" mean? What about exchanges that are between two legal players for the benefit of a lay person, such as plea bargaining or oral argument in appeals proceedings?

The robin-like instance of legal–lay discourse is undoubtedly the communication that occurs in courtrooms between attorneys or judges and witnesses and jurors. Heffer (2005: 3) characterizes legal–lay discourse as involving "a complex dialogue between two broad ways of making sense of the world; one based on the subjective reconstruction of personal experience; the other on detached analysis following legal principles." The claim that legal communicators favor and use a categorical, principle-based style more than lay reasoner-speakers, and that the reverse holds for narrative, is a reasonable *general* claim. But as our analysis of the appellate-linked discourse genres will evince, other distinctions are consequential.

Categorizing and defining are essential to sense-making, whether it be by scholars or ordinary people (Lakoff and Johnson 1980; Dey 2007). For language and discourse scholars, this leads to the need to create distinctions among styles of talking, communicative occasions, or speakers. In describing discourse categorization systems (DCS), we are creating an analogy to Sacks's (1992) membership categorization device. When a membership category (e.g., an occupation or family term) is applied to a person, it implies what kinds of attributes the party has, the kinds of activities the person is likely to do, and expected obligations and entitlements (Francis and Hester 2004). Similarly, a DCS directs attention toward (or away from) features of the language-discourse world. DCSs are inference-rich; to use one is not simply doing description. At a disciplinary level, the particular DCS that is most prominent will shape what topics/sites/issues will be widely investigated and which ones will be ignored. Table 11.1 compares legal–lay to three other categorization systems that could frame the three same-sex marriage texts that will be analyzed. For each we provide a description of the DCS and suggest the textual questions it would foreground for studies of litigant briefs, oral argument, and public hearings.

A discourse categorization system, like a city's subway lines, reflects its architect's philosophy of travellers' likely purposes and destinations. Travellers are not restricted to the most frequented destinations, but going other places is likely to require additional time and perhaps taxi rides. In the sections that follow, we move across the different discourse categorization systems and analyze the advocacy discourse in the *Lewis v. Harris* case. We trace the language about the same-sex marriage dispute as it travelled from litigant briefs to oral argument in the court to the public hearing run by the state's judicial committee.

GENRE 1: THE LITIGANT BRIEF

A discourse genre is a kind of talk or writing that possesses identifiable parts (or argument moves) that are sequenced in a particular order (Swales 1990). Genres also involve distinct styles of expression that bring together kinds of vocabularies,

TABLE 11.1 LEGAL–LAY VERSUS OTHER DISCOURSE CATEGORIZATION SYSTEMS

Discourse Categorization Systems	(a) Tradition (b) Key Idea-Focus (c) A Source	Implications of Discourse Categorization Systems for Same-Sex Marriage Texts
Institutional interaction vs. ordinary conversation	(a) Conversation analysis (b) Conversation is the bedrock of social life and structure. How do particular institutional interactions build on and modify basic conversational processes? (c) Drew and Heritage (1992)	• All of the texts are clearly institutional, but conversation analysis makes a sharp distinction between oral and written and hence would be unlikely to examine the plaintiff brief. • The public hearing is also likely to be ignored as an object of study because it is monologic in its turn format. • Limited interest in what makes legal talk legal.
Expert–lay knowledge/ discourse	(a) Sociology of science (b) What are distinctive features of expert scientific knowledge that separate it from ordinary knowing? Distinguishes experience-based and interactional, language-using expertises from full-fledged, credentialed and embodied expertise. (c) Collins and Evans (2007)	• More interested in cognitive abilities than discourse expression. • Draws attention to whose expertise should be given weight and degrees of expertise. • The expert–lay distinction assumes expertise includes embodied skills. This works for science, but less well for law which is so fundamentally a language-rooted expertise.
Technical vs. public vs. personal argument spheres	(a) Rhetorical studies in communication (b) Focuses on the content, style, and organization of arguments in different spheres. (c) Goodnight (1999)	• The plaintiff brief and the oral argument are clear cases of technical argument; the committee hearing is a clear case of a public argument context where technical (legal) arguments may enter. • Tends to favor written and public texts so oral argument is less likely to be studied; generally inattentive to linguistic specifics.
Legal–lay discourse	(a) Discourse analysts in linguistics (b) Focuses on the distinctive language/discourse features of talk between legal or legal-affiliated persons and nonlegal parties, especially in the courtroom, but also written texts for nonlegal consumers. (c) Heffer (2005)	• Equally interested in oral and written texts. • As the category is defined by what is legal, both the plaintiff brief and oral argument would be of interest; the public hearing is less likely to receive attention. • Takes the law for granted as a discourse container without examining discourses that give it its particular shape.

argumentative strategies, and preferred utterance or sentence formats. Becher (1989) distinguishes academic disciplines in terms of the degree to which their knowledge is tightly versus loosely organized. This tight–loose distinction is equally applicable to discourse genres. Some have tight constraints; others are more varied. At the tight end of the continuum of legal genres is the litigant brief prepared for an appeals hearing.

The appellant's 65-page brief in *Lewis v. Harris* begins with a table of contents listing six main sections. The first section is a table of authorities identifying the sources, dividing the sources into previous cases (e.g., "*Hernandez v. Robles*, 794 N.Y.S. 2d 579 (Sup Ct. N.Y. Cty 2005")), constitutional provisions, state statutes and regulations, and miscellaneous other authorities. It is the extensive citing of previous cases and statutes throughout the document that gives the text its distinctive legal feel; this brief cites 68 cases and 15 statutes.

The preliminary statement, or second section, provides a multipage summary of the arguments to be developed. An opening reference to the New Jersey constitutional guarantee to all citizens of liberty and equality explains why the lower level appeal court's decision was in error. It then announces its intent to show that "this is really a very simple case in constitutional terms. Plaintiffs ask to be given what their friends, relatives, coworkers and neighbors already enjoy—participation with the one person each loves in the central rite of passage in American family life" (Preliminary Statement, p. 3).

The third section, the procedural history, supplies a brief overview of the legal events that led up to the case's appearance at the Supreme Court, including the initial trial court decision and the appellate court's decision and split vote.

The statement-of-facts section provides information about the plaintiffs and the harms inflicted by the state on the seven couples. As discourse scholars (Drew 1992; Edwards and Potter 1992) repeatedly have noted, description is often evaluative. What is stylistically noticeable about this statement of facts is the degree to which it works to be neutral. The prose uses only the mildest of forms to convey emotion and evaluation of wrongdoing (Besnier 1990). The first paragraph, for instance, begins by asserting that the plaintiff couples have been in committed relationships for a long time, followed by statements about the genesis and length of each couple's relationship: "Chris Lodewyks and Craig Hutchinson, who met in college and are now in their early fifties, have been in a committed relationship for 34 years" (p. 5). A style of limited emotional expressiveness, so different from ordinary talk, is particularly evidenced in the section describing harms.

"Exclusion from marriage has caused plaintiffs substantial harm" (Statements of Facts, p. 7) asserts the document. Karen and Marcye Nicholson-McFadden have had "to pay for expensive cross-adoptions of their children that would not have been necessary had they been married" (Statement of Facts, pp. 7–8). The brief lists three other harms with the most feeling-rich expression created by an extreme case formulation (Pomerantz 1986) describing one partner's difficulty accessing the hospital during her partner's birthing of their daughter: "Karen's role needed to be established *over and over again.*" For the most part, emotions are named and reported ("painful sadness") rather than enacted though vivid details and intense language choices.

The fifth and longest section of the brief is the argument. For the plaintiffs, this section details why the stated harm deserves to be remedied by allowing same-sex couples to marry. The main argument and its sub-points are included in the table of contents and each point then becomes a section heading in the document, reflecting the preferred formal legal format. The plantiffs' arguments center on equality. The brief argues that the plaintiffs "have extremely weighty interests in exercising the fundamental right to marry their irreplaceable loved one." This argument section contains citations of prior cases and statutes with a frequency sure to intimidate even the most intrepid nonlegal reader.

Excerpt 1 (Last paragraph, End of Argument Section IIC, 2b, p. 44)

> Plaintiffs have strong interests in being freed of the stigma of being defined by the State as "unmarriageable" because they are lesbian and gay and are not drawn to opposite-sex partners. Constitutional doctrine "neither knows nor tolerates classes among citizens." *Romer, supra* 517 U.S. (quoting *Plessy v. Ferguson*, 163 U.S. 537, 559 (Harlan, dissenting)). The state's intrusion on plaintiffs' substantial dignitary, social, tangible, and intangible interests "works a deep and scarring hardship on a very real segment of the community." *Goodridge, supra*, 798 N.E.2d at 968, and should be accorded maximum weight in the balancing test.

With extensive quotes from US Supreme Court opinions and those of relevant state cases, precedent is marshaled to persuade that no other conclusion is warrantable save granting the action argued for by the litigant.[2]

Occasionally speech is reported to evidence a particular claim. Under the argument that asserts plaintiffs and their families have substantial interests in the dignitary and intangible benefits of marriage, the brief develops the current difficulty for lesbian and gay parents who want to be role models for their children. For instance, the couple Karen and Marcye are quoted saying, "We want Kasey and Maya to get the right messages. We want to tell them that their parents are married just like grandmom and grandpop" (p. 42). Similar to the way reported speech is used in everyday contexts (Holt 1996; Buttny 1997), the reasonableness of the author's view and the unreasonableness of the opposed other is indirectly but powerfully built by using quotes that present themselves as actual speech.

The sixth and final section of the brief, "Conclusion" offers a short restatement of what the plaintiffs are seeking, along with a listing of the attorneys submitting the document with a signature from the lead attorney.

In summary, a litigant brief is a tightly organized written genre that is persuasive in thrust. As a text genre, litigant briefs are designed by a legal specialist (the attorney) for fellow legal specialists (the judges) who make a final decision. Although one could describe the litigant briefs as legal–legal communication, the lay parties never entirely disappear despite their limited role and inability to speak directly for themselves. The lay parties' actions, sentiments, and actual words are represented and reported by the attorney in a document that is principle-based and drawing on abstract, historically defined legal terms. But while largely a narrative-less genre, some of the person-linked examples, such as those reported for Karen and Marcye, could be thought of as small stories (Bamberg and Georgakopoulo 2008), what we would call narrative seeds, brief remarks about persons and events that evidence a potential to flower into full-blown stories.

The defendant brief was equally long (70 pages) and similarly organized in terms of sections and argumentative structures. The brief drew upon slightly more prior cases (76) and New Jersey statutes (44).[3] The most notable difference between the two briefs was the absence in the defendant brief of any discourse segments that could be described as narrative seeds.

GENRE 2: ORAL ARGUMENT

Most political scientists and some judges believe that oral argument is a relatively unimportant activity. Although he changed his mind later, before he became a Supreme Court Justice, Justice Scalia characterized oral argument as a ritualistic "dog and pony show" (Johnson 2004). Examining the influence of litigant and amicus curiae (friend of the court) briefs, and oral argument on US Supreme Court opinions over a 15-year period, Johnson (2004: 91) concluded a multipronged quantitative study noting, "oral arguments clearly provide unique information about the court's policy options that the justices deem important enough to discuss as they bargain with one another about how to substantively decide a case." Among discourse scholars, legal briefs have received some attention (Stratman 1994), as have judicial opinions (Ehrlich 2007; Hobbs 2007), but with the exception of a handful of analyses focused on the US Supreme Court (e.g., Wasby, D'Amato, and Metrailer 1976; Benoit 1989; Wrightsman 2008), oral argument has been an ignored genre of legal discourse.

In the oral argument stage of the *Lewis v. Harris* case, both the appellants' attorney (Buckel) and the defending state attorney (DeAlmeida) had approximately 30 minutes of presentation and question-and-answer time. Each attorney began by greeting the court and introducing self and the party he was representing. In introductions, each speaker used a bit of legal-speak that, while not particularly technical does mark the occasion: from the plaintiff: "Good morning your Honors. And *may it please the court*, my name is David Buckel"; from the defense: "*May it please the court*, I'm Patrick DeAlmeida. I'm the assistant attorney general"). Similar to trial attorneys' usage of "I put it to you" during cross-examination (Heffer 2005) or Koresh's King-James-Bible inflected style (e.g., "I swear by God unto you") used in negotiations with FBI agents at Waco (Agne and Tracy 2001), particular phrases such as these cue a speaker's affiliation and identities.

Following the introduction, each attorney began to present a summary of the arguments he had advanced in the written brief. Presentations were carried out using a planned oral style (Ochs 1979) that reflected a unique set of similarities/differences with the written briefs and the conversational Q-and-A period that followed. The oral argument of each attorney closed with a several sentence summary of the side's position and a round of thanks.

Compared to the written briefs, case references during oral argument were far fewer in number and those that occurred were more allusive (e.g., in speaking about anti-miscegenation, "From 1948...until nearly 20 years later when the Supreme Court struck down") or used a shorthand (e.g., "in Tomarchio"). Only three times in the 65 minutes was a case referenced using its full name (e.g., "Dale v. Boy Scouts"). The difference between the written briefs and oral argument is similar to Bernstein's (1966) distinction between elaborated and restricted codes. While not easy reading, the briefs are explicit about defining terms, listing evidence for a claim, and explaining the author's inferencing procedures. Given the limited use of technical terms, oral argument initially feels more accessible. A close look at the discourse, though, makes clear that the attorney and judges are having a highly coded discussion where their full meanings cannot be ascertained without extensive background knowledge of legal precedent, state laws, and acceptable legal reasoning practices.

The distinctive feature of oral argument is that it rather quickly changes from a presentation into a question-and-answer event where judges probe and challenge each attorney's assertions. In the *Lewis v. Harris* case, not only did judges frequently interrupt the attorneys, but they also interrupted each other. The conversationally formatted structure was similar for both attorneys, but the questioning that the judges directed to the defense was tougher. Judges gave the defense attorney a shorter time before they began questioning, interrupted more, and asked more

TABLE 11.2 OVERVIEW OF *LEWIS V. HARRIS* ORAL ARGUMENT

	Plaintiff (Buckel)	Defense (DeAlmeida)
Time	36 mins	29 mins
Uninterrupted presentation time[a]	6 mins.	3 mins
Number of questions[b]	32	46
Questions per non-presentational time	1.07 per min.	1.77 per min.
Judge interruptions of attorney[c]	14	27
Usage of term "fundamental"	15	10

[a] Times were rounded to the nearest 15-second interval.
[b] Questioning turns were computed using the same procedures explained in Tracy (2009).
[c] If several judges began speaking at once, this was counted as a single attorney interruption. The assessment of when a piece of overlapping speech is an interruption and who is interrupting whom are complicated social judgments (James and Clark 1993). One of the ways attorneys display deference to judges is to stop speaking quickly when there is overlapping talk. It was not always easy to tell if a partial word overlap was a transition relevance point with minor latching on the last syllable or a turn being cut off. Judgments were made taking account of the content of the turn and whether it seemed a likely juncture for ending a claim.

questions (see table 11.2). In addition, although the plaintiff's attorney received nonchallenging questions that simply checked understanding (e.g., "Your argument basically is that there are public interests that would undergird ah ah a prohibition against polygamy that are absent in this case"), such questions were not directed to the defense.

In oral argument in the New York Supreme Court (*Hernandez v. Robles*) in which the Court reached an opposite decision from New Jersey's Court—denying gay couples access to marriage rights, tougher more frequent questioning was directed to the plaintiffs' attorneys (Tracy 2009). It might be that the party with whom the judges use the more adversarial style of questioning cues a Court's likely opinion direction. Such a relationship was evidenced in the New York and the New Jersey same-sex marriage cases. Whether this relationship would hold more broadly deserves investigation.

We would draw attention to two final features of the oral arguments in *Lewis v. Harris*. A first is the way a single term functioned as a morally loaded symbol to advance opposing sides of the argument. Each attorney repeatedly used the term "fundamental" in an effort to accrue rightness to his side of the debate. Weaver (1953) uses the name "god" and "devil terms" to identify symbols that are treated as unarguable, self-evident good or bads within a particular social scene. In a court setting where constitutionality is at stake, "fundamental" functions as a god term. What is fundamental deserves to be upheld, and whatever threatens that which is fundamental deserves to be resisted. Excerpts 2 and 3 illustrate a use by each of the attorneys. For the plaintiff, what fundamental modified was the right of gay couples to be able to marry. For the defense, however, fundamental modified the institution of marriage.

Excerpt 2 (Line 34, Plaintiff)

> In terms of how the balancing test operates for these two claims, boils down to how the court would weigh the plantiffs' interests in the balancing test. With a *fundamental* right there's a requirement that the maximal weight be assigned because the court has determined that the underlying liberty interests warrant the protection of the ah *fundamental* right.

Excerpt 3 (Line 632, Defense)

> Because it is such a *fundamental* institution in our society that it is a reasonable thing for the legislature not to change it radically. That is- there are some things that make up our society that are so *fundamental* that a change in them is something that belongs to the elected representatives of the people.

Second, similar to the written briefs, narrative seeds were absent from the defense attorney's comments but were present in plaintiff attorney Buckel's comments. Excerpt 4 illustrates one such segment.

Excerpt 4 (Line 22)

> Plaintiff Karen Nicholson McFadden explained that without being married, in everyday conversations she feels like her dignity is always on the line, quote open for anyone to question rather than assume. And that the battle is not to feel that our commitment and our family is pretend. Her dignity remains open to question if she calls her relationship a domestic partnership. Because the message is still there. Not marriage. How do plaintiffs answer their children's questions about why they are not married? The only answer is that the state does not believe the parents' relationship is worthwhile enough.

GENRE 3: THE PUBLIC HEARING DISCOURSE

The public hearing on Bill A3787, overseen by the six-person Assembly Judiciary Committee, was modeled after one in another US state. The bill proposed extending to same-sex couples all the legal rights of marriage but using the name "civil union." The hearing began with brief comments by the committee chair and the bill's sponsor. After 54 people testified, the committee voted to move the bill to the Assembly floor. Of note, before listening to a single word of testimony, the chair indicated her intention to vote for the bill and also acknowledged her hope to see gay marriage approved in future bills.

Excerpt 5 (Line 12, Chair Greenstein)

> I know that the issue of legal recognition for same-sex relationships is one that sparks emotional responses from both sides of the debate. Hopefully this morning we'll all be able to harness that emotion to have an honest, civil, and meaningful discussion. It would have been my personal wish to also be able to hear a bill granting full rights of marriage to same-sex couples today, um but as chair of this committee …

In the beginning of the public commentary the chair instructed speakers to keep their remarks to three minutes. Few did. The first speaker, in fact, spoke for more than 12 minutes. The hearing was punctuated recurrently with the chair's request for speakers to finish up (e.g., "Could I- could I just ask if you wrap up. A few more seconds"). In an attempt to insure that all people who wanted to testify had an opportunity, the chair requested during the last hour that speakers limit remarks to one minute. As more anti-gay marriage speakers spoke later, there was grumbling about inequitable time-keeping. One speaker explicitly chastised the Chair for her unfairness to the traditional marriage side; another commented sarcastically, "Okay Madam Chair I understand I'm down to five seconds. Right?"

A first distinctive characteristic of the public hearing was the fragility and contested quality of its participation format: rules about speaker time changed across participants, speakers violated time restrictions, the chair frequently interjected to ask speakers to stop, which they often did not do with any alacrity, and several speakers straightforwardly challenged the chair's procedural fairness. The public hearing possessed a disorderliness not seen in the courtroom oral argument.

The discourse of public testimony has been examined in a number of settings, including hearings about genetically modified foods (Hausendorf and Bora 2006), a university board of regents examining its affirmative action policies (West and Fensternmaker 2002), and school boards. Drawing on analysis of 100+ speeches given by citizens at one education governance meeting, Tracy and Durfy (2007) describe the genre of public commentary as including: (a) an introduction with the person's name and self-categorization related to the speaker's occupation, school, or town, and relationship to or investment in the school district; (b) the body of the speech which involved specific school or district-related issues; and (c) saying "thanks" to mark the speaker was concluding. Public commentaries were usually read rather than spoken extemporaneously and rarely did speeches involve exchanges with officials. With recognition of the topical difference, the public testimony at the judiciary committee hearing was strikingly similar in text structure; style (mostly read); and the official response (almost none other than an acknowledging thanks).

Table 11.3 offers an overview of the categories of participants giving public testimony.

The public that attended the hearing, as can be seen in table 11.3, was attitudinally tilted toward the pro-gay position that advocated that the name "marriage," as well as the rights of marriage, be extended to same-sex couples. It was apparent through committee members' remarks, though, that the committee did not take

TABLE 11.3 A PORTRAIT OF PARTICIPANTS IN THE PUBLIC HEARING

	Pro Same-Sex marriage	Against Same-Sex Marriage
Number of Speakers (Total)	41	13
Religious Speakers	10	9

	Speaker Identifications		
With gays	Self is gay	Close other is gay	No connection
	23	4	27
With the legal case	Attorneys	Plaintiffs	No connection
	2	4	48

Note: Speakers were coded into categories based on the content of their argument; the assignment to pro- and anti-gay positions was an easy judgment to make. The determination of whether someone was a religious, legal, or plaintiff speaker was based on how the speaker identified self (e.g., "My name is Reverend Mark Bird from Christ the Liberator Metropolitan Community Church"). Identification as gay was inferred when speakers referenced significant others as "partners" or referenced another by name in narrating life events where the name was typical for others of the speaker's sex. "Connected to gay others" indicated an explicit mention of a connection, such as "My daughter and her partner June." Drew (1992) shows how descriptions imply what is maximal. Thus, in speaking about a lesbian daughter positively with no reference to his own sexual orientation, listeners will infer that the speaker is pro-gay but not himself gay.

what speakers said to be representative of public sentiment in New Jersey. In opening the Chair said:

Excerpt 6 (Line 22)

> I would close by noting the results released this morning of a Quinnipiac University poll asking New Jerseyians their thoughts on this topic. Sixty percent of New Jersey's residents support civil unions. Thankfully, an overwhelming majority, 58%, oppose amending the state constitution to outright ban same-sex marriage.

And in the final discussion before the positive vote to move the bill forward was taken, a committee member commented "I've sat through 13 years of hearings on a lot of touchy subjects but never have I sat through one where we heard only from the extremes on both sides of an issue. We have heard from no one in the middle." The ambiguous relationship between opinion distribution in a larger public and the distribution of opinions expressed in a particular hearing means that committees must exercise judgment. In this case, the committee voted to move the bill forward even though almost all speakers opposed it.

If we look at Attorney Buckel's speech of advocacy in this hearing and consider the similarities it has to the two legal genres, as well as to other speakers in the same hearing, three features deserve comment. First, unlike the plaintiff brief and oral argument in which Buckel makes clear his spokesperson role for the plaintiffs, in the hearing he spoke for himself albeit seeking to credential his role in the case.

Excerpt 7 (Line 769)

> My name is David Buckel. I am senior counsel at Lambda Legal and the lead attorney in the New Jersey Supreme Court case, *Lewis v. Harris*. It is the decision in that case and the lives and needs of our plaintiffs and of New Jersey's 20,000 same-sex couples and their 12,000 children that bring us all here today.

Second, no mention is made of legal cases. Rather, Buckel seeks to persuade the committee to advance a bill that gives same-sex couples the right to call their unions marriage by praising the legislature for its "proud history" of protecting civil rights and describing the hardships experienced by New Jersey couples:

Excerpt 8 (Line 801)

> The need to talk about their relationships comes up as often as it does for married couples. By the water cooler at work, with the human resources department, in the neighborhood, at their children's schools, for the forms at the doctor's and the dentist's office, and when it sometimes counts the most. In

the hospital. They cannot use the word everyone immediately understands. Married.

Third, Attorney Buckel's testimony is treated by the committee in a fashion similar to most others. He, like the attorney for the American Civil Liberties Union, was interrupted, asked to stop speaking, and ushered away from the lectern with perfunctory thanks. Of the 54 people testifying, only one speaker was treated by the committee as an expert. This speaker, one of three attorneys, the only one not involved in the appeal, referenced sections of the debated bill by letter and numbers. Following this attorney's testimony, a committee member asked him to examine a soon-to-be-released revised bill to see if it met his concerns.

During the hearing many gay speakers told moving stories about the effects of not having their relationships recognized. Consider one instance from one of the Nicholson-McFadden plaintiffs.

Excerpt 9 (Line 1040)

When Kasey says to us, "Mommy, Momma, why won't the la- government let you get married?" There's only one answer. The government thinks it's okay to treat us differently because we're gay. There's no other reason.... How do we talk to them [our children] about their future? What life should look like in marriage? "Cause marriage is a good thing. And I- an" I was thinking about this and saying, we'd love to give them the easy, sensible answer, which is "Honey one day you're gonna meet a wonderful person. You're gonna fall in love and you're gonna get married." But if you choose- ((laughter)) It will happen. If you choose civil unions, it gets really murky. Because now I have to say to my son and daughter, who I would do anything for, Well actually you'll only be able to get married if you fall in love with someone of the opposite sex.

The Nicholson-McFadden testimony offers a developed story version of the narrative seeds that we saw in Attorney Buckel's plaintiff brief and oral argument. In the public testimony, speakers offered stories filled with reported speech of actual and hypothetical persons. Other speakers, while not technically telling stories (Labov 1997; Schiffrin 1994) disclosed intimate personal feelings and reactions. A pro-gay speaker who followed his partner was asked by the committee if he had anything to add. He commented: "*Only that I love this man. I um, have known him for 15 years. I want to be married to him.* I do not believe that a civil union is the adequate way to refer to anyone's relationship." An anti-gay marriage speaker said:

Excerpt 10 (Line 1895)

And my biggest burden is my horror for my grandchildren. Because I have two granddaughters that I really do not want them to grow up in a society where they're confused.... Are we gonna redefine what a woman is? Are we going to redefine what a man is?... We're redefining something that's been from the beginning of time. *And in my heart, my heart is that I don't want my grandchildren to grow up with a confused society.* Thank you.

When we consider who made personal disclosures or told stories the pattern is striking. Only one of the 13 anti-gay speakers engaged in personal disclosure (above), whereas 30 of 41 pro-gay speakers told stories or made personal disclosures.

The arguments about same-sex marriage in the public testimony had one striking difference and one marked similarity to the Court arguments. In the hearing, arguments based on religious authority were front and center-stage. A full 35 percent of speakers legitimated their opinions by identifying religious affiliations as pastors, rabbis, or ministers. Although there were clear differences in how each side used its religious grounding, both pro- and anti-gay speakers quoted scripture and announced what God wanted or endorsed. In the Supreme Court briefs and oral arguments religion was noticeably absent. Only one time did use of a religious word (God/religio*/Jesus/Christ/church) occur. During oral argument one of the Justices asked the defense Attorney DeAlmeida if "tradition" was a code word for moral disapproval. Consider how the exchange unfolded.

Excerpt 11 (Line 603)

JBTA:	Now is th- this- it's a traditional view on which the state asserts the marriage laws should maintain their present structure based upon moral disapproval. Is that part of it?
MrD:	It's based on the existing institution and the desire not to change it.
JBTA:	But is that based on moral disapproval?
MrD:	There are some who uh f- for them this is a moral question, there are others that [it's a religious question
JBT:	[but is that the state's position?
MrD:	Uh it's the state's position that there are numerous competing interests with respect to changing who may marry...

In the public hearing, religious talk was prominent, but in the legal sphere it stayed below the surface, buried in the discussion of tradition. To state it baldly, religious arguments are "bad travellers." They may be central to public discussion, but they will be stopped at legal borders. In contrast, rights-based arguments, and especially the "separate is not equal" argument, were good travellers. This argument easily travelled from initial public/media texts to plaintiff appeals briefs and oral arguments and then back to the public hearing. To be sure, the argument's linguistic garb differed in the two contexts, but it was the same argument. The principle-based argument of "separate is not equal" was equally used and equally at home in both legal and public

TABLE 11.4 FEATURES OF DISCOURSE GENRES

Genre	Litigant Brief	Oral Argument	Public Testimony
Format	Written	Oral	Oral
	Monologic	Dialogic	Monologic
Message designer(s)	Attorneys	Attorneys and judge	Public testifiers (interested parties including plaintiffs, attorneys, and other citizens)
Focal audience	Judges	Judges	Legislators
Role for nonlegal parties	Spoken-for Parties	Spoken-for Parties	Same as attorneys and other testifiers
		Overhearing audience	
Distinctive features	• Narrow issue of dispute	• Narrow issue of dispute	• Broadly focused issue of dispute
	• Tightly structured arguments	• Time-constrained question-answer argumentation	• Read-aloud arguments, stories, and personal disclosures
	• Prior case references		
	• Rights arguments were common	• Rights arguments were common	• Rights and religious arguments were common
Outcome	Court Opinion	Court Opinion	Policy and State Law

spheres. Table 11.4 summarizes differences among the advocacy discourse of the three genres.

CONCLUSIONS

Currently in the United States, public, legislative, and legal battles are occurring regarding whether same-sex couples should have marriage rights extended to them, be barred from the institution, or have some intermediate format for recognizing their committed relationships. These battles are occurring in oral and written texts of a variety of genres as each US state debates what its marriage and partnership laws should be. In this analysis of same-sex marriage discourse genres, an important distinction was whether a party was pro- or anti-gay marriage. Pro-gay marriage speakers, whether they were legal or lay parties, regularly used the principle-based "separate is not equal" argument. At the same time, storytelling and experience-grounded emotional reactions, almost entirely, were the purview of pro-gay speakers (and not anti-gay ones). In the public hearing, anti-gay speakers advanced mostly principle-grounded religious arguments; whereas, many pro-gay speakers used narratives alongside of the rights-based argument. Of note, it was on the plaintiff's side (and not the defense) where both written and oral texts included narrative seeds.

As discourse-rhetorical scholars in the field of Communication, we have been drawn to the study of different texts than what the legal–lay discourse categorization system foregrounds and promotes. As a result of the particular legal issue we studied, same-sex marriage in the United States, and the discourse genres selected, we have observed different patterns of contextualization and recontextualization than have been observed elsewhere. Our analysis showed that legal communicators do not necessarily stick to a principle-based style nor do lay speakers unilaterally prefer narrative. Rather both legal and lay communicators use principle-grounded and narrative styles.

When a legal issue involves how a category of person ought to be treated, stories become a particularly useful tool for "overcoming otherness." In a review article that argued for legitimating narratives in law settings, Delgado (1988: 2412) notes that storytelling is for oppositionists. It is "outgroups, groups whose marginality define the boundaries of the mainstream, whose voice and perspective—whose consciousness—has been suppressed, devalued and abnormalized" that like stories. In sum, whether a party is marginalized or mainstream is a better predictor of narrative use than whether they are a legal or lay speaker.

NOTES

1. To access the Court opinion, see *Lewis v. Harris*, 188 N.J. 415; 908 A.2d 196 (N.J. 2006); for the appellant brief, see http://www.lambdalegal.org/sites/default/files/legal-docs/downloads/lewis_nj_20051021_brief-of-appellants.pdf; for the New Jersey Court's oral argument, see http://njlegallib.rutgers.edu/supct/args/A_68_05.php; and for the Assembly Judiciary Committee Hearing click on the Thursday, December 07, 2006, hearing at http://www.njleg.state.nj.us/media/archive_audio2.asp?KEY=AJU&SESSION=2006.
2. In a study of multiple appeals briefs, Stratman (1994) found that appellants used more explicit strategies of advocacy. Defendants were more likely to adopt a "scholarly," here-are-the-pros-and-cons style.
3. Since the state's position was upheld at trial and appeal, the Brief for the Defendant-Respondents was the same as the one submitted for the lower court.

REFERENCES

Agne, Robert R., and Karen Tracy. 2001. "Bible babble": Naming the interactional trouble at Waco. *Discourse Studies* 3: 269–94.

Atkinson, J. Maxwell, and Drew, Paul. 1979. *Order in Court: The Organization of Verbal Interaction in Judicial Settings*. Atlantic Highlands, NJ: Humanities Press.

Bamberg, Michael, and Alessandra Georgakopoulou. 2008. Small stories as a new perspective in narrative and identity analysis. *Text & Talk* 28: 377–96.

Bauman, Richard, and Charles L. Briggs. 1990. Poetics and performance as critical perspective on language and social life. *Annual Review of Anthropology* 19: 59–88.

Becher, Tony. 1989. *Academic Tribes and Territories: Intellectual Inquiry and the Culture of Disciplines*. Milton Keynes, UK: Open University Press.

Benoit, William L. 1989. Attorney argumentation and Supreme Court opinions. *Argumentation and Advocacy* 26: 22–38.

Bernstein, Basil. 1966. Elaborated and restricted codes: An outline. *Sociological Inquiry* 36: 254–61.

Besnier, Niko. 1990. Language and affect. *Annual Review of Anthropology* 19: 419–51.

Buttny, Richard. 1997. Reported speech in talking race on campus. *Human Communication Research* 23: 477–506.

Collins, Harry, and Robert Evans. 2007. *Rethinking Expertise*. Chicago: University of Chicago Press.

Conley, John M., and William M. O'Barr. 1990. *Rules Versus Relationships*. Chicago: University of Chicago Press.

Cotterill, Janet, ed. 2002. *Language in the Legal Process*. Brunel, UK: Palgrave.

Delgado, Richard. 1988–89. Storytelling for oppositionists and others: A plea for narrative. *Michigan Law Review* 87: 2411–41.

Dey, Ian. 2007. Grounding categories. In *The Sage Handbook of Grounded Theory*, ed. A. Bryant and K. Charmaz, 167–190. Los Angeles: Sage.

Drew, Paul. 1992. Contested evidence in courtroom cross-examination: The case of a trial for rape. In *Talk at Work*, ed. Paul Drew and John Heritage, 470–520. Cambridge: Cambridge University Press.

Drew, Paul, and John Heritage, eds. 1992. *Talk at Work: Interaction in Institutional Settings*. Cambridge: Cambridge University Press.

Edwards, Derek, and Jonathan Potter. 1992. *Discursive Psychology*. London: Sage.

Ehrlich, Susan. 2007. Legal discourse and the cultural intelligibility of gendered meanings. *Journal of Sociolinguistics* 11: 452–77.

Francis, David, and Stephen Hester. 2004. *An Invitation to Ethnomethodology: Language, Society and Interaction*. London: Sage.

Goodnight, G. Thomas. 1999. The personal, technical, and public spheres of argument: A speculative inquiry into the art of public deliberation. In *Contemporary Rhetorical Theory: A Reader*, ed. John L. Lucaites, Celeste M. Condit, and Sally Caudill, 251–64. New York: Guilford Press.

Goodwin, Charles, and Marjorie H. Goodwin. 1997. Contested vision: The discursive constitution of Rodney King. In *The Construction of Professional Discourse*, ed. Britt-Louise Gunnarsson, Per Linell, and Bringt Nordberg, 292–316. London: Longman.

Hanks, William F. 1989. Text and textuality. *Annual Review of Anthropology* 18: 95–127.

Hausendorf, Heiko, and Alfons Bora, eds. 2006. *Analysing Citizenship Talk: Social Positioning in Political and Legal Decision-Making Processes*. Amsterdam: John Benjamins.

Heffer, Chris. 2005. *The Language of Jury Trial: A Corpus-aided Analysis of Legal–Lay Discourse*. Basingstoke: Palgrave Macmillan.

Hobbs, Pamela. 2007. Extraterritoriality and extralegality: The United States Supreme Court and Guantánamo Bay. *Text & Talk* 27(2): 171–200.

Holt, Elizabeth. 1996. Reporting on talk: The use of direct reported speech in conversation. *Research on Language and Social Interaction* 29: 219–45.

Hymes, Dell. 1974. *Foundations in Sociolinguistics: An Ethnographic Approach*. Philadelphia: University of Pennsylvania Press.

James, Deborah, and Sandra Clarke. 1993. Women, men and interruptions: A critical review. In *Gender and Conversational Interaction*, ed. D. Tannen, 231–80. Oxford: Oxford University Press.

Johnson, Timothy R. 2004. *Oral Arguments and Decision Making on the United States Supreme Court*. Albany, NY: State University of New York.

Labov, W., and J. Waletsky. 1997. Narrative analysis: Oral versions of personal experience. *Journal of Narrative and Life History* 7: 3–38.

Lakoff, George, and Mark Johnson. 1980. *Metaphors We Live By*. Chicago: University of Chicago Press.

Ochs, Elinor. 1979. Planned and unplanned discourse. In *Syntax and Semantics: Discourse and Syntax*, ed. Talmy Givon, 51–80. New York: Academic Press.

Philips, Susan U. 1998. *Ideology in the Language of Judges: How Judges Practice Law, Politics, and Courtroom Control*. New York: Oxford University Press.

Rosch, Eleanor, Carolyn B. Mervis, Wayne D. Gray, David M. Johnson, and Penny Boyce-Braem. 1976. Basic objects in natural categories. *Cognitive Psychology* 8: 382–439.

Sacks, Harvey. 1992. *Lectures on Conversation*. Vol. 1. Cambridge, MA: Blackwell.

Schiffrin, Deborah. 1994. *Approaches to Discourse*. Oxford, UK: Blackwell.

Schuetz, Janice, and Lin S. Lilley, eds. 1999. *The O. J. Simpson Trials: Rhetoric, Media and the Law*. Carbondale: Southern Illinois Press.

Stratman, John F. (1994). Investigating persuasive processes in legal discourse in real time: Cognitive biases and rhetorical strategies in appeal court briefs. *Discourse Processes*, 17: 1–57.

Swales, John M. 1990. *Genre Analysis: English in Academic and Research Settings*. Cambridge: Cambridge University Press.

Tracy, Karen. 2009. How questioning constructs appellate judge identities: The case of a hearing about same-sex marriage. *Discourse Studies* 11: 199–221.

Tracy, Karen, and Margaret Durfy. 2007. Speaking out in public: Citizen participation in contentious school board meetings. *Discourse and Communication* 1: 223–49.

Wasby, Stephen L., Anthony A. D'Amato, and Rosemary Metrailer. 1976. The functions of oral argument in the U.S. Supreme Court. *Quarterly Journal of Speech* 62: 410–24.

Weaver, Richard M. 1953. *The Ethics of Rhetoric*. Chicago: Henry Regnery Company.

West, Candice, and Sarah Fenstermaker. 2002. Accountability in action: The accomplishment of gender, race and class in a meeting of the University of California Board of Regents. *Discourse & Society* 13: 537–63.

Wrightsman, Lawrence S. (2008). *Oral Arguments before the Supreme Court: An Empirical Approach*. Oxford: Oxford University Press.

PART FOUR

Crossing Cultural and Ideological Categories in Lay–Legal Communication

CHAPTER 12

The Discourse of DNA

Giving Informed Consent to Genetic Research

JOHN M. CONLEY, R. JEAN CADIGAN, ARLENE M. DAVIS,
ALLISON W. DOBSON, ERIN EDWARDS, WENDELL FORTSON,
AND ROBERT MITCHELL

INTRODUCTION

This chapter analyzes the travels of texts in an environment where the lay, legal, and scientific worlds intersect: the highly regulated domain of genetic research. Specifically, it reports the results of a linguistic analysis of interviews with persons who were asked to contribute DNA samples to a genomic biobank—a repository of human DNA and/or associated data, collected and maintained for biomedical research. DNA research presents medical ethics with challenges that are qualitatively unique and quantitatively unprecedented. Throughout the developed world, informed consent by individual research subjects has been a core requirement since the 1947 Nuremburg Declaration. Medical research has traditionally involved single researchers or existing groups of researchers obtaining and using tissue samples for defined purposes, with appropriate disclosures to and the specific consent of the participants (Rothstein 2005). With genomic biobanks, by contrast, the entity holding the samples may not even be involved in the research, the uses of the samples may be unknown at the time of collection, and, accordingly, traditional informed consent may be illusory if not impossible. Moreover, a series of recent scientific papers argues that advances in DNA technology have rendered the customary guarantees of confidentiality and/or anonymity all but meaningless (Greely 2007; Jacobs et al. 2009; Lunshof et al. 2008).

These papers are part of a substantial and growing literature that seeks both to articulate and to develop strategies for dealing with these challenges. This literature and the medical research practices that both inform and motivate it comprise *expert* discourses. The rules, practices, and writings of medical and ethical experts embody and give voice to concerns that they think subjects have or, at least, ought to have.

In the project from which this chapter is drawn we investigate the *folk* discourse of genetic research. That is, what do the subjects themselves say when allowed to voice their own concerns, fears, and agendas? This chapter focuses particularly on the way that subjects draw on texts from a broad range of sources—including science and law, as they understand them; popular media; conversations with friends and relatives; interior dialogs with themselves; and the interaction with the interviewer—to construct and explain what their participation means to them.

The solicitation of informed consent to research is a significant if somewhat unusual form of lay-legal communication. The lay subject's direct communication is with a representative of the scientific world, typically a research coordinator. But the requirement of informed consent, usually memorialized in a signed document, is prescribed by law—in the United States, by federal regulations that are a condition of government funding for research, as interpreted and applied by Institutional Review Boards at universities and hospitals. The communications with prospective subjects thus take place in the shadow of the law, and the research coordinator who seeks to obtain consent is, at a minimum, the law's indirect agent. Moreover, as our data will illustrate, there is frequently conflict between the expert legal understandings of subjects' consent and participation and those expressed by lay subjects themselves.

Our project's most significant finding concerns the sociolinguistic nature of informed consent: whereas medical practice treats it as an event, our subjects talk about it as a discursive process—that is, a process that unfolds over the course of multiple communicative interactions. Like many such processes, that which our subjects describe is open-ended, unstable, and sometimes unsettling. Our subjects import, recontextualize, and reanimate texts from many sources as they talk about consent with the interviewer; recount (and often perform) conversations with friends, families, and even themselves; and describe their exposure to various public discourses. As the subjects talk, new meanings constantly emerge that cause them to challenge their prior understandings.

METHODS

We analyzed 29 semi-structured interviews of people from a university campus (which includes a major medical center) who were invited to contribute DNA samples to a large-scale, long-term, government-funded biobank. Information on the biobank was broadly available to potential subjects and others via a website. We recruited individuals by sending a mass email to the same university faculty, staff, and students who had recently received a recruitment email from the biobank.

Demographic information collected from this subject population revealed that most were well-educated and many had experience working in the healthcare or scientific fields. A separate research group that includes two of the co-authors interviewed 15 people who joined the biobank ("joiners") and 14 people who chose not to join ("decliners") for reasons other than convenience or logistics. Interviews lasted approximately 60 minutes and covered a variety of topics including reasons for accepting or declining participation; perceptions of personal benefits and risks, as well as benefits or risks for families, special groups, or society; understanding of key features of the biobank; and perceptions of genetic information. All interviews were transcribed and the transcripts were verified during the course of our analysis. Our analytic approach has followed the model of conversation analysis (Garfinkel 1967; Atkinson and Drew 1979), with all of the co-authors participating in the analysis sessions.

In tracing the travels of texts, we adopt the basic definition of "text" as a "unit of language in use" (Halliday and Hasan 1976: 2), "a unit.... that can be lifted out of its interactional setting" (Bauman and Briggs 1990: 72), a stretch of oral or written linguistic production that, standing alone, seems sensible to the members of a linguistic community and can thus be analyzed as a unit. We also take the linguistic anthropological view that, since language production is cultural, texts are also and, importantly, "the precipitates of continuous cultural processes" (Silverstein and Urban 1996: 1). Whereas earlier views treated texts as static and distinguishable from their "surround" or context (Silverstein and Urban 1996: 1), more recent work is less concerned with defining the boundaries of a text than in analyzing what can be done with it, by the original author, as well as subsequent recipients and users. Indeed, in the contemporary view the boundary between a text and its context is illusory, a contestable interstitial zone rather than a bright line. Our consideration of texts and their travels focuses on how texts are made—entextualization, or "the process of rendering discourse extractable" (Bauman and Briggs 1990: 72)—and the interesting lives that they lead, what Blommaert (2005: 255) has called "textual trajectories." Among other things, the extracted text can be placed into a new interactive setting, or recontextualized; it can be performed or "reanimated"; and it can take on meaning at many levels, from the denotational analysis of words on a page to the consideration of what the text "does" socially (Mertz 2007: 45).

THE LINGUISTIC LITERATURE ON BIOBANKS

There is a small but interesting literature on various linguistic aspects of biobanking, including informed consent. Most similar to this project in its method is Wade and colleagues' (Wade et al. 2009) study of "the 'black box' of informed consent appointments"—what some medical scholars have characterized as the "ceremony" (Allen and McNamara 2009; Lipworth et al. 2009). Applying techniques of thematic, content, and conversation analysis to transcripts of 23 consent interviews with recruits for a randomized British cancer research study, Wade and colleagues focused on the interviewers' strategic use of question form, pauses, and turn-taking. They suggest (Wade et al. 2009: 2026) that "the current focus on what information should be provided must be broadened to include consideration of how information is best conveyed and how it is interpreted" by subjects, toward the end of better understanding "whether consent for randomization was truly informed."

Most relevant in substance are recent papers by Lipworth and colleagues (Lipworth et al. 2009) and Allen and McNamara (2009). Lipworth and colleagues analyzed semi-structured interviews of 12 "stakeholders" (including patient/donors, parents of child patients, and health advocates) in an Australian biobank to examine the concept of public trust in research. They find that securing consent functions "as a means not only of allowing [donors] to exercise their autonomy but also as a 'ceremony' that can help to 'secure trust'" (Lipworth et al. 2009: 130). They further argue that this trust "needs to be seen as an emergent property of good social relationships that are built up over time" (Lipworth et al. 2009: 130, quoting Levitt and Weldon 2005: 320).

In a similar study also done in Australia, Allen and McNamara (2009: 8) find that research participants "express a degree of autonomy that moves beyond its association with a self-sufficient and self-realizing individual to encompass a relational framework based on inter-subjectivity." They, too, focus on the formal consent ceremony, finding that (Allen and McNamara 2009: 9) "the actual act of giving consent through the signing of a document ritualizes the process, thus allowing the participants to declare themselves as moral beings." We also focus on this ritual act, but our subjects suggest a different and more problematic interpretation of its significance.

INFORMED CONSENT AS A DISCURSIVE PROCESS

Informed consent emerges from our interviews as an elaborately discursive process. On a practical level, medical researchers treat consent as an event. Linguistically, they use *consent* as a transitive verb, routinely speaking of *consenting* subjects, and, when the scope or purpose of the research changes, *reconsenting* them. Medical ethicists are aware that the event model is flawed and have often discussed consent as a process; for example, Barton and Eggly (2009) have analyzed offers to participate in clinical trials as persuasive processes, while Allen and McNamara (2009) have described the giving of consent to participate in a biobank as a decision-making process with ongoing social significance. There is also a growing body of empirical literature that argues that subjects often do not read consent forms and in fact choose whether to participate in genetic studies and biobanks for a wide assortment of reasons that have little or nothing to do with the information contained in a consent form (Barr 2006; Hoeyer 2003).

No prior work, however, has treated informed consent as a discursive production. As often happens with open-ended discourse analysis, our subjects have forced such a perspective on us. They repeatedly reveal informed consent to be the evolving product of an open-ended and multilayered discourse. Some subjects recall the event, or "ceremony," at which the legal requirement of informed consent was satisfied, sometimes focusing on signing a document of unrecalled contents. But they tend to divorce the ceremony from the emotional, cognitive, and social process of consent that medical scholarship presumes that the ceremony consummates or "ritualizes" (Allen and McNamara 2009: 9).

Instead, our subjects comment on the relative emptiness of the signing ceremony, emphasizing what they did not apprehend, or even think about, at that time. They detail the ways in which the meaning of both *informed* and *consent* has changed over time as they have interacted with the interviewer, families and friends, public media, and even themselves. Many describe that process explicitly—sometimes expressing retrospective surprise—making clear that new meanings have been contingent on these interactions. As subjects learn more, they question their initial state of information; by the same token, they become increasingly dubious about the quality of their consent. Indeed, they challenge the very possibility of informed consent having a fixed, pre-existing, or stable meaning for its presumed beneficiaries, thus providing a vivid illustration of the concept of emergent meaning.

The Consent Ceremony

Some subjects recall that the informed consent ceremony centered on a particular expert text: the legally mandated informed consent document. In the succinct words of one subject who joined:

Excerpt 1 (101/joiner/male)[1]

> And, he handed us a brochure. We read over it. Signed it. Filled it out. Gave it back to him. He gave us our money. Then, we went and waited for the phlebotomist to take our blood.

The subject in excerpt 2 below gives a more elaborate account of the consent ceremony. He presumes that the signing of the consent form text must have produced an understanding of the transaction. But his recollection does not extend to the contents of that text nor to what, precisely, he presumes that he must have understood in the past:

Excerpt 2 (102/joiner/male)

> I: And, after joining did you talk to anyone from the registry such as when you went to donate your blood sample?

R: I just talked to the people that were there. That were drawing the blood. And, there's certain things that they had to read off. Even whether I'd heard it before or whatever. I think that I signed something. But, I don't remember. I must have signed some sort of a consent form that I understood. And, that this was—I understood that I was going to be paid twenty dollars for doing this or whatever. I seem to remember signing something.

A third joiner gives a parallel but even more analytical account of the ceremony and the text it produced:

Excerpt 3 (103/joiner/female)

[Questions about how important it is that subjects understand the terms of the consent form.]

R: ...But, like I said, it was so easy. It was "Oh, come on down. We're doing this. And, this is what it's about. All done. Just a little bit of blood. And, you can be on your way." I mean like I said, they did put everything in the release form. But, I think you're just not—you don't have time to process everything. And, like I did. I have copies of it. And, I know I can find it. Sooner or later. If I get in my junk room and mess around. But, I don't know. And, maybe—I don't know. I was going to say maybe release forms need to be more—I don't know. Shorter or something. Or, not so many large paragraphs. Sometimes it just seems a little complicated. I know that it's—because, you're reading it. You're like "Okay. Yeah. I understand that. I understand that. I understand that." You understand it. Then, to process it or whatever is slightly different.

Here too, the event was easy and quick. It was "so easy," a point that is dramatically underscored by the subject's reanimation of the researcher coordinator's breezy pitch ("come on down" is an iconic line from American television's *The Price Is Right*). And it was so quick that "you don't have time to process everything." The subject characterizes the written text as a "release form," an interesting folk-legal conclusion that the expert legal and research communities would vigorously contest. The form carries some kind of lasting power, perhaps as evidence of what was "released." Indeed, such is its significance that the subject might be motivated to search for it in her "junk room." Most interesting, perhaps, is the distinction she draws between the consent ceremony and the ability to "process"—a verb she introduces twice—the contents of the consent document. She vividly performs the ceremony, with the generic "you" serving to generalize the description—that is, "you" in the sense of "one," or an average person in the same situation: "You're reading" the document. As "you" do so, "you're like" (that is, you say to yourself) "I understand that"—three times. If that were not clear enough, she summarizes with a final "You understand it." Except that you don't, because "to process it or whatever is slightly different."

The Unfolding Discourse of Consent

Some subjects describe explicitly what it means to "process" consent. For them, it has involved discourse, at various times, at multiple levels, and with multiple interlocutors. Some of the interlocutors were concrete people; whereas others were disembodied voices vaguely recalled. Several subjects comment explicitly on the way that our interview itself produced different understandings of informed consent. In excerpt 4, the joiner just quoted in excerpt 3, makes the point through an elaborate exercise in reported speech. Reanimating an unusual text—her thought process——as a lecture that she is giving to herself, she carefully distinguishes "what you knew then" from "what you know now."

Excerpt 4 (103/joiner/female)

> I: And, I just have a couple of questions for, to get some feedback from you. Were any of our questions difficult to answer?
>
> R: The only reason they were difficult is because you were asking me things about what I had thought at the time. And so, I'm like "Think about it. No. Don't consider what you're thinking now. You have to think about that. And, remember what you knew then. Not what you know now." So, that's the main difficulty.

But the interview is not the only kind of discourse that can prompt a change in thinking and cause new meaning to emerge. At another point in her interview, the same subject distinguishes again between "thinking at the time" and "thinking later." She initially describes the triggering discourse in vague terms—she had "heard something." She then fixes the time ("even just yesterday") although the source remains unspecified ("I think I heard"). (Comparable references occur throughout the interviews: one subject reported that her understanding evolved as "I discussed it with my fiancé," while another talked with a "paranoid" boyfriend.) And as in excerpt 4, the subject describes the process of rethinking her participation in the research in extraordinary and dramatic detail.

Excerpt 5 (103/joiner/female)

> I: When you were deciding, did you think you might benefit personally from being in the [biobank]?
>
> R: Yes.
>
> I: And, how so?

R:	This may be kind of not even true. But, you think things. I thought "Well, if I have something, maybe I'll find out about it." If I have some kind of genetic pre-disposition to a certain kind of disease or something like that. Or, "Maybe I could have—I don't know." That's not what I was thinking at the time. That's what I started thinking later. Because, I'd heard something. Well, even just yesterday I think I heard about some women who had been—had a pre-disposition not to get breast cancer from a certain gene or something like that. So, I thought "Wow. That would be great, too." It's like I wasn't thinking about that at the time. Because, I'd never considered the possibility that they would find certain genes that indicated these people are less likely to get this.

DNA AND SUBJECTS' FEARS

When asked to express their concerns about participating in DNA research, some subjects draw on texts—often in the form of narratives, or micro-narratives (Cotterill 2003)—from personal experience and family history. In this instance, a question about "an occasion in your life that has caused you to think about your own DNA" leads a decliner into a long narrative about genes and family history. The question triggers a particularized memory—"*the* mental illness." The subject expresses a specific folk-scientific theory ("environmental factors *let out* these bad genetics"), describes an "odd" relative, and concludes with some concrete and personal observations about genetics and marriage. When dating prospective mates, he "needed to understand their [genetic] background"; having met his future wife, "bad genes" were something he "had to consider" and that they "had to talk about."

Excerpt 6 (120/decliner/male)

Yeah. The mental illness. In fact more specifically schizophrenia....My mom has two brothers with schizophrenia. And, it's unclear how it occurred. It seemed like a combination of bad genetics and very poor living conditions. They were poor farmers. And, didn't have a lot of nutrition. So, somehow environmental factors let out these bad genetics. There was a pre-disposition genetically. And, the environment was bad enough to let it come out....And so, on my dad's side of the family about two or three generations ago there was someone who was "odd." And, that's the term for someone who was probably crazy. And so, when I was dating and finding someone that I was interested in marrying, it was very important to me to find someone who—I at least needed to understand their background. Did they have a lot of mental illness in the family? Because, these things while they're genetic—if you take two people with bad genes and pair them together, the outcome might not be very good. And so, that's something I had to consider when I was dating my wife. And, we had to talk about it....

Other discussions of subjects' fears center on misuse of DNA and the information it encodes by the government and insurance companies. Two metaphors are especially prominent in their commentary: *out there* and *hands. Out there* repeatedly appears as a dangerous space where bad things may happen to DNA, especially in the unknown future. The ominous and ubiquitous *hands*—sometimes *the wrong hands*—most often belong to the government or an insurance company.

In a narrative response to a question about "concerns you might have had as you were making the decision," a joiner introduces many of these themes. The subject, whose interview evidences substantial knowledge of DNA and medical research, begins with a specific worry about insurance, then moves into the realm of vaguer concerns. Note the serial (and unsolicited) elaborations on his original statement about insurance, each introduced by "or" and marked with such indicators of vagueness as "something like," "somehow," and "sort of." But he finishes on a specific note, seemingly defining "information getting *out*" as its movement into a space "outside of like a research focus."

Excerpt 7 (101/joiner/male)

I guess I was worried when I found out I had to give all this personal information. It would remain linked however securely to my identity. So, you always have the nightmare scenarios where insurance companies deny you coverage based on something they find twenty years down the line. Or, something like that. Or, somehow that information gets out. Just the sort of general data security. Or, that the government gets its hands on it somehow. Outside of like a research focus.

Another decliner offers some variations on these themes. For her, *out there* is a place that may be of interest to future law enforcement authorities. Interestingly, while this subject elsewhere identified herself as someone "in the sciences," and used such insider terminology as "data point" and "manipulating the sample," she identifies a television show as the source of her concerns. Popular culture is in fact a recurrent theme throughout the interviews; other subjects make reference to television and two, a joiner and a decliner, cite the movie *Gattaca* as a basis for their concerns.

Excerpt 8 (117/decliner/female)

I: Is there anything in particular...that influenced your decision not to join?

R: Yeah. I don't think I have criminal tendencies. But, for any reason my DNA would be out there, I wouldn't want it to be—just I guess I don't want it out there. I mean not that it would be associated with my name in a study like this. But.

I: Can you say more about criminal tendencies?

R: I guess just from watching *Law and Order* and things like that. And, they all talk about DNA evidence. And so, I don't expect that to ever be the case for me. But, that kind of was in the back of my head. Like they say that I'm not going to be connected to this test tube with a number and my name. But, who's to say that's not going to be the case in the future?

As this subject's reference to "the future" illustrates, the passage of time is a recurrent concern. Several subjects note that bad things can happen when tissue samples are stored for a long time, perhaps as a result of changing technology. Another joiner speculates that over time *out there* might become even more dangerous than it is now: "you might weigh your options differently in five years with regards to having that information out there based on how things have changed." In a couple of other instances, subjects, like this decliner, worry that information that is *out there* could end up *on file*:

Excerpt 9 (116/decliner/female)

It's such a personal thing. Like it's your genetics. It's who you are. And, like having that on file is just like having—more invasive than having your fingerprint on file or having your photo on file or something.... It's like an unsettling feeling I guess.

In summary, the concerns expressed by our subjects are not surprising—they are the same privacy issues that dominate the expert and popular literatures. They speak of vague threats that are likely to get worse in an uncertain technological future and repeatedly attribute their worries to popular culture sources. Their dominant metaphors—about DNA being *out there* and getting into untrustworthy *hands*—lend an ominous, conspiracy-theory tone to their narratives. Despite the fact that our interviewees are themselves employed at a (state) government institution, "the government" nevertheless functions in these interviews as an elusive yet powerful agent and one with suspect motives. Finally, their personal experience with science, far from comforting them, frequently exacerbates their fears.

SUBJECTS' THEORIES OF THE TRANSACTION

Expert legal discourse on ownership of genetic specimens reflects no consensus on the appropriate legal framework for characterizing the event by which a specimen is obtained or the subsequent uses of that specimen (O'Brien 2009; USSHHS Advisory Committee on Heritable Disorders in Newborns and Children Work Group White Paper 2009; Charo 2006). The few American legal cases involving specimen ownership favor institutions or researchers over the individuals from whom the specimens were obtained (Rao 2007; Andrews 2006).[2] Legal scholars often import models from property, contract, or privacy law to frame the transaction and subsequent specimen uses (Rao 2007; Nelkin and Andrews 1998). One novel approach adopts the model of the charitable trust, conceiving of the donor as a settlor (the party who sets up a trust) who formally transfers an interest in the specimen to a trust and appoints the recipient as trustee. The trustee, a legal fiduciary, must keep and use the property to benefit the beneficiary—in the case of charitable trusts, the general public (Winickoff and Winickoff 2003). Other scholars look outside legal models. For instance, some promote "stewardship," where researchers or their institutions are seen as stewards (rather than owners) of specimens and thus obliged to balance the interests of all research stakeholders, including subjects (Dressler 2007). "Benefit-sharing" models replace what some view as the artifice of "altruistic" participation with a promise that subjects will share in the benefits that accrue to other participants in a profitable research enterprise––researchers, companies, and universities (Hayden 2007).

During the interviews, subjects were asked directly about who would "own" their DNA samples, as well as about the ownership of the entire biobank. In response to those questions and elsewhere in the interviews, many subjects reveal their folk-legal theories of the transfer. They address the legal nature of the original transfer and the rights that they and others would have in the samples in the future. Many espouse theories of ownership similar to those found in the expert legal discourse, invoking such concepts (with or without the specific legal terms) as gift, sale, and trust. In the sections that follow we review examples of discourse that evidence several of these theories of the transfer.

A Straightforward Transfer: Gift or Sale

Some subjects analyze the transfer in language that suggests a straightforward and unconditional gift or a sale. One joiner (106), for example, speaks of the ease of "*giving up* my DNA," while a decliner (120) notes how easy it would be "to go and *give* them a blood sample." In excerpt 10, another joiner, in talking about his comfort level with future studies of his DNA, makes it clear that the transfer was an unconditional sale—"Somebody else owns it" because "They bought it":

Excerpt 10 (110/joiner/male)

I: ...Would you be comfortable in having your DNA studied in any way? Or, do some kinds of tests make you feel more uneasy than others?

R: Any kind probably.

I: And, why is that?

R: Well, I'm thinking if they're just doing tests on the sample they took, it has really nothing to do with me. I mean if you're asking me like what kind of tests do I want to have performed on me? That's different.

I:	But, once it comes out of your body.

R:	Yeah. Right. It's like it's over there somewhere. Somebody else owns it. . . . I don't own it any more. They bought it from me actually.

I:	For twenty dollars.

R:	For twenty dollars they got a little thing of blood.

Another subject, a decliner, uses the word "give" to describe the transfer, but also speaks of compensation—using the legal-sounding "remuneration"—which suggests a sale. She then expresses surprise at the number of unenlightened sellers in the market:

Excerpt 11 (122/decliner/female)

I:	And, is there anything about the content of the [recruitment] e-mail that you can remember?

R:	No. Nothing unusual. They were asking for a blood sample. A teaspoon full of blood. I think the remuneration was twenty dollars. And, I was astonished at the number of grad students and staff in my office who went over to give their teaspoon full of blood. Without actually thinking about the registry. . . . It just didn't sit well with me. I'm not that desperate for twenty bucks.

She returns to "compensation" later, making her view of the transaction as a sale even more apparent:

Excerpt 12 (122/decliner/female)

I:	. . . If you had a friend or family member that might be interested in joining it, how would you describe the registry and what someone has to do to be a participant?

R:	I would say that they're doing a study at [the university]. Where they are drawing I think it's a teaspoon full of blood from volunteers. To bank the blood for testing at a later date perhaps. And, as compensation for giving up your teaspoon full of blood, you would receive twenty dollars.

The irrevocable quality of the transaction is underscored by the same decliner's subsequent use of the term "surrender" to describe the transfer of her blood to the researchers:

Excerpt 13 (122/decliner/female)

I:	Now, can you drop out of the registry if you want to?

R:	I don't know the answer to that. I just assumed not. Once you surrender your sample, I assume you've surrendered your sample.

I: And, how important do you think that is for people to understand?

R: I think that's critical.

A More Complex Transaction

For others, the transaction is more complex. Several subjects share their lingering doubts or unease about the kind of transaction that has occurred. In excerpt 14, one of the joiners ruminates at length on the ambiguities and implications of the concept of ownership, thus reinforcing the discursive nature of informed consent. After a reference to her interaction with popular culture (television), she gives a vivid performance of the thought process that a generic "you" might go through in reading the consent form, then shifts to a set of questions she is apparently asking herself now, concluding with the telling observation that she is "only thinking about these things now since we're talking about it":

Excerpt 14 (103/joiner/female)

I: Who owns the DNA sample that someone gives?

R: I think it's the—I don't know if it's the hospital. It's whoever—because, I know that it was a combined thing. It was not just [the university]. And, isn't it even national? I don't know. And so, I don't know. I don't know who owns it.

I: And, how important do you think it is that people know who owns it?

R: I think that's pretty important. Very important to know.

I: How come?

R: Because. Once again going back to television. Whoever owns it, you, except for abiding by the rules, you would think could do perhaps whatever with it they wanted to. I mean I know there are standards in place and everything. And, I guess even if there are standards in place. And, I'm worried that whoever can do with it whatever they want to. Then, it doesn't really matter whether there are standards in place or not. But, I still think it's important that a person knows. So, that they can make a more informed decision. And, maybe when you read it, you're like "Yeah. Okay. Well, I see this is the owner. And, okay." It seems a little odd though, doesn't it? It's like "I own my DNA. Don't I own my own DNA?" Like "Do I?" Who does own it? So, I'm only thinking about these things now since we're talking about it.

Moments later, this same joiner makes a sweeping general pronouncement regarding the legalities of ownership. The subject's doubts about this "pretty heavy legal stuff" encompass not only who owns "this information of everybody" but also what the implications of ownership are. Note that, having been moved to think about these issues for the first time "now" (excerpt 14)—during the interview—the subject has elevated the question of ownership to "the most important thing."

Excerpt 15 (103/joiner/female)

I: And, what do you think is the most important thing for someone to understand about being in the registry?

R: Probably who owns it. Who owns this information of everybody. Because, ownership is pretty heavy legal stuff. If you own it, well it's yours. Isn't it? I don't know.

While this joiner struggles with ownership interests that may not include her, the decliner in excerpt 16 describes a complicated multiparty ownership and custody arrangement that is evocative of the lack of certainty in the expert legal literature. Individuals own their samples, the funding agency "manages" them—perhaps as a trustee, in the way that a bank might manage a trust fund?—while either "the public" or "the research community" seems to own the whole collection:

Excerpt 16 (123/decliner/female)

I: And, who owns the entire [biobank]?

R: [The government agency that funds it]. I mean that's a hard question. The ownership issue.

I: It is.

R: Because, I really feel like individuals own the samples. And, the [government funding agency] sort of manages the samples. You could say the public owned it. Because, you're giving different investigators access to data that comes from it. So, they're not limiting it and saying "No. Only our small group is using it." They're making it available to other researchers. You could say the research community owns it. I mean it's sort of—there are a lot of ways to look at that.

One of the joiners is equally confused about multiple rights in the sample. Although he does not know who owns the DNA samples (perhaps, he suggests, because he failed to pay attention during the consent process), he does know that ownership is important. He expresses this proposition as an if-then conditional: "If you technically still own it, then you have more say in what [the researchers] can and can't do with it." Technical ownership, whatever that might be, gives subjects important rights against "them," particularly the right to be contacted to give—or, presumably, withhold—their "okay" for future research. And, in fact, this particular biobank does require researchers to obtain consent from subjects prior to using their samples in studies, a point that this joiner only remembers during the course of the interview discussion:

Excerpt 17 (102/joiner/male)

I: Who owns the DNA sample that someone gives?

R: That's a good question. I don't know. That's something it seems like I would have paid more attention to. But, I didn't.

I: So, how important do you think it is that participants understand who owns the DNA sample?

R: I think it's important. Because, like if since it's your DNA. If you technically still own it, then you have more say in what they can and can't do with it. I think I remember now they said since they were just building up a data base essentially that if someone does want to use your DNA in a study, they will contact you again to make sure it's okay for you to participate in that study. So, I think if they still have to contact you in order to be able to use it, I guess in a sense you still own it. And, it's certainly important for the participants to understand that. But, that's something I just remembered.

A decliner puts a legal label on this complexity, referring to "joint ownership between the scientific community involved in the research and the individual." But this is not joint ownership as the law recognizes it, with each owner having an undivided interest in the entire property. The subject apparently has limited rights, which do not include taking the sample back:

Excerpt 18 (120/decliner/male)

I: Who owns the DNA sample that someone gives?

R: That's a hard question.... I would say it no longer owns—I think that there is a joint ownership between the scientific community involved in the research and the individual.

I: And, how important do you think it is that participants know who owns the sample they give?

R: I think it's very important. That way so if it is what how I described it, then I think it's important they understand that. So, that they can't choose later on to try to take the sample back. That they understand once they've given it, it becomes property that's shared by other people for other purposes.

He later adds that the subject is "not going to have access to any information regarding their sample once they give ownership to the institution," and then acknowledges, with evident irony, just how "hard" the ownership question is in his response to a question about who owns the entire sample collection: "I have no idea. The man."

CONCLUSIONS

The solicitation of informed consent to research is especially complex because it takes place at the intersection of three disparate worlds: the lay (the research subjects), the scientific (the researchers), and the legal (the regulatory framework within which the research takes place). Although the medical ethics literature is increasingly sensitive to the reality that the giving of informed consent is a process, research practice continues to treat it as a ceremonial event that centers on a written text, the informed consent document. Some of our subjects attribute great power to the written text that they signed, suggesting that it must define their participation, and even contemplating trying to find it. But their overriding focus is on the subsequent trajectory (Blommaert 2005) that that text follows. After the ceremony, their initial understanding of informed consent—such as it was, since many go out of their way to emphasize that they did not pay attention to the form when they signed it and cannot remember its contents now—is continually reshaped by subsequent discourse.

Over and over, the interview subjects express regret about not thinking *then*—at the time they joined—about issues that have subsequently come to concern them. In their comments, they not only confirm that informed consent is indeed a process, but they reveal it to be a specifically discursive process. The expert medical and legal literature seeks to ascribe a fixed, exogenous meaning to informed consent. For our subjects, however, its meaning evolves over time as the subjects engage in discourse about the research—with families and friends, the public media, the interviewer, and even themselves. In ethnomethodological terms, the meanings of both *informed* and *consent* are "emergent from the use of language in context" (Mertz 2007: 21) and, consequently, unstable.

This discourse often involves texts that travel from a variety of sources, including popular culture, folk conceptions of law and science, and remembered personal and family histories. The ensuing intertextual encounters destabilize and reshape the original text. The intertextuality seen here is thus a vivid illustration of Fairclough's (1992: 84) definition of the term: "the property texts have of being full of snatches of other texts which may be explicitly demarcated or merged in, and which the text may assimilate, contradict, ironically echo, and so forth." As the discourse of informed consent unfolds, subjects perceive and reveal new understandings of what it means to be informed and, derivatively, the ramifications of giving consent. One cannot say it any better than the subject who said, "Everything seems important now. It's like, 'Man, I really should have been paying attention.'"

Beyond the informed consent process, our interviews also reveal a great deal about the substance of subjects' concerns. Some of these issues are consistent with the concerns expressed on their behalf in expert discourses, while others are surprising. Here again, it is important to emphasize that our sample is an unusual one, with all of the subjects recruited at a research university. Perhaps predictably, this group seems especially aware that things can go wrong even in well-intentioned and well-designed research projects, with the possibility of data leaks. They thus fear, quite reasonably, that insurance companies could acquire and misuse their genetic information. Yet even among this science-savvy group, less rational fears abound: that future law enforcement technologies might entrap them, or that an omnipotent and sinister government will somehow victimize them. Several subjects cite television and movies as the sources of these fears.

Two metaphors dominate this discourse of fear: *out there* and *hands*, as in "the hands of the government" or "the wrong hands." If metaphors are, as Lakoff and Johnson (1980) suggest, links between the material and discursive worlds, then these are especially powerful expressions of fear. *Out there* is a vast and dangerous domain, encompassing the entire discursive universe beyond the individual's direct control. It is so dangerous in large part because of the presence of grasping hands that do the work of entities whose motives cannot be trusted. It is difficult to imagine how such fears could be overcome, but overcome they often are—by a payment of $20.

In addition, our subjects offer a rich array of folk-legal theories of the transaction. Some are straightforward, invoking the legal concepts of gift and sale that have been widely discussed in the expert literature. Others are more complex, producing ambiguous conclusions. Much of the subjects' theorizing involves the importation of labels and larger texts from the folk-legal realm.

On a practical level, these findings further complicate an already daunting problem for medical researchers and ethicists. Many of them have recognized that conventional models of consent may be inadequate in a scientific regime where it is simply impossible to predict the future uses of a donor's sample, or to guarantee that confidentiality and anonymity will survive the onslaught of future technology. Our findings add a new level of worries: the behavioral process of informed consent seems almost designed to fail. And recall that our subjects are insiders, university employees, many of whom have worked in medical research—if they do not understand informed consent, who would?

Our final point is a general one: those who design policy should listen in great detail to those for whose benefit they presume to act. Virtually all the empirical research and normative work on informed consent in the genetic context begins with a set of assumptions about the issues that subjects ought to be worried about. Perhaps they should be, but are we sure that they are? The power of linguistic analysis is that it gives subjects a chance to speak for themselves, to work out their concerns discursively as we listen. The research policy community should attend to what they are telling us.

ACKNOWLEDGMENTS

Gail E. Henderson and Michele M. Easter are fellow investigators on this project. The project was supported by Grant Number P50HG004488 from the United States National Human Genome Research Institute. The content is solely our responsibility and does not necessarily represent the official views of the National Human Genome Research Institute or the National Institutes of Health.

NOTES

1. Because we quote some individual subjects more than once, we have included an arbitrary identification number for the speaker in the heading for each text in case readers want to track individual speakers across the body of texts. We have also noted the subject's gender in response to requests for that information by early readers of this chapter.
2. The principal US cases are *Moore v. Regents of the University of California*, 793 P.2d 479 (Cal. 1990) (denying a research subject a property interest in his tissue samples); *Greenberg v. Miami Children's Hospital*, 264 F. Supp. 2d 1064 (S.D. Fla. 2003) (denying plaintiffs a property interest not only in the tissues they supplied, but in the gene isolated and patented from those tissues); and *Washington University v. Catalona*, 437 F. Supp. 2d 985 (E.D. Missouri 2006) (denying subjects a property right that would permit them to withdraw their specimens from university biobank and give them to a specific researcher).

CASES CITED

Greenberg v. Miami Children's Hospital, 264 F. Supp. 2d 1064 (S.D. Fla. 2003).
Moore v. Regents of the University of California, 793 P.2d 479 (Cal. 1990).
Washington University v. Catalona, 437 F. Supp. 2d 985 (E.D. Missouri 2006).

REFERENCES

Allen, Judy, and Beverley McNamara. 2009. *Reconsidering the Value of Consent in Biobank Research, Bioethics*. Online. Available at: http://www3.interscience.wiley.com/cgi-Bin/fulltext/122525569/HTMLSTART.
Andrews, L. B. 2006. Who owns your body? A patient's perspective on Washington University v. Catalona. *J. Law Med. Ethics* 34: 398–407.
Atkinson, J. Maxwell, and Paul Drew. 1979. *Order in Court: The Organization of Verbal Interaction in Judicial Settings*. Atlantic Highlands, NJ: Humanities Press.
Barr, Michael. 2006. "I'm not really read up on genetics": Biobanks and the social context of informed consent. *BioSocieties* 1: 251–62.
Barton, Ellen, and Susan Eggly. 2009. Ethical or unethical persuasion?: The rhetoric of offers to participate in clinical trials. *Written Communications* 26: 295–319.

Bauman, Richard, and Charles L. Briggs. 1990. Poetics and performance as critical perspectives on language and social life. *Annual Review of Anthropology* 19: 59–88.

Blommaert, J. 2005. *Discourse*. Cambridge: Cambridge University Press.

Charo, R. A. 2006. Body of research: Ownership and use of human tissue. *New England J. Med.* 355: 1517–19.

Cotterill, Janet. 2003. *Language and Power in Court: A Linguistic Analysis of the O. J. Simpson Trial*. London: Palgrave Macmillan.

Dressler, L. G. 2007. Biospecimen "ownership": Counterpoint. *Cancer, Epidemiology, Biomarkers & Prevention* 16: 190–91.

Fairclough, N. 1992. *Discourse and Social Change*. Cambridge: Polity Press.

Garfinkel, Harold. 1967. *Studies in Ethnomethodology*. Englewood Cliffs, NJ: Prentice-Hall.

Greely, Henry T. 2007. The uneasy ethical and legal underpinnings of large-scale genomic biobanks. *Annual Rev. of Human Genetics* 8: 343–64.

Halliday, Michael A. K., and Ruqaiya Hasan. 1976. *Cohesion in English*. London: Longman.

Hayden, C. 2007. Taking as giving: Bioscience, exchange, and the politics of benefit-sharing. *Social Studies of Science* 37: 729–58.

Hoeyer, Klaus. 2003. "Science is really needed—that's all I know": Informed consent and the non-verbal practices of collecting blood for genetic research in Northern Sweden. *New Genetics and Society* 22: 229–44.

Jacobs, Kevin B., et al. 2009. *A New Statistic and Its Power to Infer Membership in a Genome-Wide Association Study Using Genotype Frequencies, Nature Genetics*. Online. Available at: http://www.nature.com/ng/journal/v41/n11/abs/ng.455.html?lang=en.

Lakoff, George, and Mark Johnson. 1980. *Metaphors We Live By*. Chicago: University of Chicago Press.

Levitt, Mairi, and Sue Weldon. 2005. A well placed trust? Public perceptions of the governance of DNA databases. *Critical Public Health* 15: 311–21.

Lipworth, Wendy, et al. 2009. An empirical reappraisal of public trust in biobanking research: Rethinking restrictive consent requirements. *J. of Law & Medicine* 17: 119–32.

Lunshof, Jeantine E., et al. 2008. *From Genetic Privacy to Open Consent, Nature Reviews Genetics*. Online. Available at: doi:10.1038/nrg2360.

Mertz, Elizabeth. 2007. *The Language of Law School: Learning to "Think Like a Lawyer."* Oxford: Oxford University Press.

Nelkin, Dorothy, and Lori Andrews. 1998. Homo economicus: Commercialization of body tissue in the age of biotechnology. *Hastings Center Report* 28(Sept.-Oct.): 30–39.

O'Brien, S. J. 2009. Stewardship of human biospecimens, DNA, genotype, and clinical data in the GWAS era. *Annual Rev. of Genomics Human Genetics* 10: 193–209.

Rao, Radhika. 2007. Genes and spleens: Property, contract, or privacy rights in the human body? *J. Law Medicine & Ethics* 35: 371–82.

Rothstein, Mark A. 2005. Expanding the ethical analysis of biobanks. *J. Law Medicine & Ethics* 33: 89–101.

Silverstein, Michael, and Greg Urban. 1996. The natural history of discourse. In *Natural Histories of Discourse*, ed. Michael Silverstein and Greg Urban, 1–17. Chicago: Chicago University Press.

Wade, Julia, et al. 2009. It's not just what you say, it's how you say IT: Opening the "black box" of informed consent appointments in randomized clinical trials. *Social Science & Medicine* 68: 2018–28.

Winickoff, D. E., and R. Winickoff. 2003. Charitable trust as a model for genomic biobanks. *New England J. Medicine* 349: 1180–84.

CHAPTER 13

Travelling Texts

The Legal–Lay Interface in The Highway Code

BETHAN L. DAVIES

INTRODUCTION

This chapter will focus on the text lives of a particular official document in the United Kingdom. *The Highway Code* is published by the Department for Transport on behalf of the Driving Standards Agency, both of which are UK government organizations. Its most obvious role is as the "rules of the road" for the British road user; it contains advice about using the road, legal requirements for road users, and explanations of all road signs and markings. However, this is not its only function. It can also act as an operative document in a court of law as it "may be used in evidence in any court proceedings under the Traffic Acts…to establish liability" (*Highway Code* 2007: 4). Unlike most text trajectories (Blommaert 2005), *The Highway Code* hasn't gradually shifted its role over time; rather, these functions are performed simultaneously on a daily basis. Thus, this is a text which is continually travelling.

For this text to be successful, lay readers of *The Highway Code* would need to be able to both recognize its multiple purposes and understand the text as a legal document. In order to investigate whether this is the case, the public consultation process surrounding the most recent revision of *The Highway Code* is examined for evidence of lay readers' understanding of its legal status and attendant implications. The linguistic focus of this chapter will be on the use of modality: the use of modal (or modal-like) verbs and/or adverbs to indicate the author's degree of commitment to the necessity, obligation, or truth of some act of reference or predication. These are utilized in the text both to indicate distinctions between advisory and mandatory rules and to suggest the relative strength of advisory rules (through modal-like adverbs like *where practicable* or *wherever possible*, which we will consider here). It was this use of modality which seemed to create the most issues within the consultation process.

The Highway Code is explicitly addressed to *all* road users "including drivers, motorcyclists, cyclists, horse riders and pedestrians" (Highway Code 2007: back cover) and when a new edition is being prepared the government consultation process involves representation from all of these groups. However, during this process in 2006 two particular rules relating to the use of cycle facilities dominated the debate. Special attention will be paid to these rules as the issues raised embodied the features of legal language that lay readers found problematic, and they also provided examples of engagement from both specialist user groups and the government itself.

Before considering the consultation process, I will first look in detail at the different roles of *The Highway Code*, discuss its use of modality, and introduce some background to the cycling facility rules which form the basis for the analysis that follows. I will argue that there are a number of different ways in which the ability of *The Highway Code* to function successfully as an operative document is compromised. Some of these are textual matters—issues which arise in many legal documents—but in this case there are also circumstances outwith the text that affect its interpretability. One of the key points is that not all *The Highway Code*'s user groups are likely to be affected equally.

THE MULTIPLE IDENTITIES OF *THE HIGHWAY CODE*

The problem for users of *The Highway Code* is that it has roles associated with multiple contexts. In Bernstein's (1990) terms, it functions in two primary contexts and one secondary context (see table 13.1 below). Most people in the United Kingdom first encounter *The Highway Code* in its primary context of "advisory manual" as part of the process of learning to drive a car or ride a motorcycle. However, it also has two other roles. Most road users would not read road traffic law and are largely not expected to do so. The means by which the road user is expected to learn about road traffic law is via *The Highway Code*. Thus, it also acts in a *secondary context* as a recontextualization of road traffic law—a different, but key primary context. Finally, it is also a legal document in its own right: it is deemed to be a statement of what constitutes taking "due care" on the roads, and thus has a role in the judgment of liability (Primary Context 2). In contrast to Bernstein's approach, I am not overly concerned here with the recontextualization process involved in delocating and relocating a text from a primary to a secondary context,[1] rather, my interest is in the parallel contexts in which this text is required to function simultaneously. Bernstein's categories are used here simply as a way to enumerate and tease out these relationships.

Table 13.1 THE DIFFERENT CONTEXTS OF *THE HIGHWAY CODE*

Primary Context 1	Primary Context 2	Primary Context 3
Highway Code Advisory manual of "best practice" (from 1931)	**Highway Code** Operative document (can be used to establish liability) (from 1931)	Road Traffic law
Secondary Context 1	**Secondary Context 2**	**Secondary Context 1**
Driving manuals, DVLA written tests, driving instructors	Legal proceedings	**Highway Code** Mediator of Road Traffic law (separate section, from 1935; fully integrated, from 1998)
Recontextualizing Context 1	**Recontextualizing Context 2**	**Recontextualizing Context 3**
• Authoring process of manuals • Authoring process of multiple choice tests • Discussions between driving instructors • Discussions between driving instructors and learners	• Consulting process for successive editions of the *Code* (involves interested organizations and general public) • Discussions between members of the public about legal interpretation	• Government process: decisions made about how traffic law is indexed in *The Highway Code* and differentiated from optional advice (e.g., using modality to signal legal requirements)

In legal terms, then, it has three different statuses:

- As an advice manual (**PC1**), it has no legal status—it is up to the individual how they interpret and act on advice
- As an intermediary between the road user and traffic law (**SC1**), it has no legal status in itself, but plays an important role in the *mediation* of traffic law to road users
- As an operative document (**PC2**), it has a legal status—although it can only be used to determine civil liability, not as a basis for criminal prosecution

These multiple identities mean that this text is constantly travelling between lay and legal contexts: at one moment it is being consumed by a learner driver who wishes to find out the recommended procedure for traversing a roundabout (traffic circle), at the next by a road user checking who has legal right of way at a particular type of junction, and at another by a legal team using it as a potential resource in building a case. The question is whether such different purposes can be conveyed successfully by the same text: do lay readers understand the relationship between *The Highway Code* and traffic law, and are they able to interpret *The Highway Code* as a legal document in its own right?

MODALITY IN *THE HIGHWAY CODE*

From a legal perspective, the key function that modals and other similar items perform is the indexing of obligation, permission, and the degree of choice that obtains in a particular circumstance. Maley (1994: 20–21) lists three modals which are used in statutes to distinguish between mandatory/directory rules and discretionary/permissive rules:

- *must/shall*—mandatory
- *may*—discretionary/permissive

In comparison to the complex system recognized in linguistics (e.g., Coates 1983), this is a very limited set of modal items. There is no conventionalized legal use of *should*, nor is the status of a categorical assertion explicitly codified. Maley suggests that the use of the modal *shall/must* increases the degree of compulsion in comparison with a categorical construction. This reverses the scalar relationship assumed in linguistic theory, where it is argued that *any* use of modality introduces some degree of choice: even the use of a strong deontic modal such as *must* weakens the speaker's commitment to the necessity of action. Therefore, it is not entirely clear how general readers will interpret this scale: as legal language perceives it, as linguistic theory perceives it, or as something else entirely.

There are also other lexical items which are used in a legal context to encode some element of discretion. Such terms include *possible, practicable,* and *reasonably practicable.* If we take a broad definition of modality—that is, as any lexical item or construction that affects "the 'pure' reference-and-predication content of an utterance" (Verschueren 1999: 129)—then these too would come within its remit. These particular terms do not seem to have attracted much attention within the legal language literature but are equally important to the lay reader's ability to understand the precise meaning of a legal text. Both modal verbs and words or phrases acting as modal adverbs occur in *The Highway Code*.

The most explicit use of modality in this text is the use of the modal construction *must/must not* to index rules that are mandatory: those rules that are based on legal statutes. This is further emphasized in the text of *The Highway Code* through the use of capitalization and bolded red font, in contrast to the standard black type.

The reader of the text is informed of this usage on the first (content) page of *The Highway Code*:

> Many of the rules in the Code are legal requirements, and if you disobey these rules you are committing a criminal offence. You may be fined, given penalty points on your license or be disqualified from driving. In the most serious cases you may be sent to prison. Such rules are identified by the use of the words "MUST/MUST NOT"....
>
> Although failure to comply with the other rules of the Code will not, in itself, cause a person to be prosecuted, *The Highway Code* may be used in evidence in any court proceedings under the Traffic Acts...to establish liability.
>
> (Introduction, *The Highway Code* 2004: 4 / *The Highway Code* 2007: 4)

In 2007, a further explanation was added to show how language choices were being used to formally distinguish between mandatory and optional requirements. The following sentence relating to the status of rules including *should* and *do* was added as a continuation to the text above:

> This includes rules which use advisory wording such as "should/should not" or "do/
> do not."

(Introduction, The Highway Code 2007: 4)

It should be noted that, in general, the words *should* and *do* were not added to particular rules in the 2007 edition—they were already there. Rather, the sentence quoted above was added in an attempt to clarify the status of particular rules. Following the public consultation on the draft *Highway Code* in 2006, a report was published which summarized the public's responses and justified the intended changes. The authors of this document highlight an apparent misunderstanding of the relationship between *The Highway Code* and traffic law:

> There appeared to be confusion among many road users, about the use of the phrases "MUST/MUST NOT" and "should/should not." Many respondents asked for instances of "MUST" to be changed to "should" and vice versa, within a variety of rules. However, the use of "MUST/MUST NOT" identifies rules where legislation is in force, with an abbreviation of the relevant law listed below the rule. Therefore, it would be inappropriate to use this phrasing where rules are advisory only. Taking these issues into consideration, it has been decided to further expand the explanation of the differences between mandatory and advisory rules within the introduction to help alleviate the confusion.

(A Response to Consultation Report: the Highway Code 2007: 5)

This seems to be clear evidence that the reentextualization of legal statutes within *The Highway Code* has not been entirely successful: many lay readers simply have not recognized the indexing function of modal verbs. Even at this very basic level, it would appear that *The Highway Code* is failing to travel successfully between two of its contexts—*mediating road traffic law* and *advisory manual*. In the following sections, we will see more evidence of this failure to travel between its multiple roles.

A CASE STUDY: THE BACKGROUND TO THE CYCLING FACILITIES DEBATE

Even if the road user shows awareness of the differentiated legal roles of *The Highway Code*, there is still the issue that as an operative document *The Highway Code* has to be interpreted as legal language. As has been frequently pointed out (e.g., Gibbons 2003), legal language is often difficult for lay readers to understand—or, at least, to reach the *same understanding* as those in the legal profession. Those training to be lawyers need to be taught to read like lawyers; this applies not only to lexical items such as those included in "the terms of art" (Tiersma 1999) but also to a wider range of terms which have particular technical legal interpretations that may not be evident to lay readers. While these interpretations are often based on dictionary definitions, the appearance of words like *reasonable, practicable,* and *possible* in legal dictionaries tells us that their interpretation is evidently not so straightforward. This issue is further magnified by the fact that the language generally used in *The Highway Code* does not immediately invoke the genre of legal language:

> Rule 111
> Never assume that flashing headlights is a signal inviting you to proceed. Use your own judgment and proceed carefully.
>
> (*The Highway Code* 2007)

This might be compared to other pieces of legal language that lay people might encounter in their day to day lives. These two examples are taken from my filing cabinet:

> SIGNED by the above-named Testatrix as and for her last Will and Testament in the presence of us both being present at the same time who at her request in her presence and in the presence of each other have hereunto subscribed our names as Witnesses.
>
> (taken from a family member's will)

> This is to certify that a charge for the moneys within mentioned has been registered at H.M Land Registry against the Title number endorsed hereon. The charge together with an office copy of the entries in the register relating thereto, and a plan of the land affected by the registration are within.
>
> (taken from house ownership documentation)

These texts both use easily recognizable features of legal language such as repetition (*Will and Testament*), archaic language (*hereon, hereunto*), and careful use of reference, including the avoidance of ambiguous deixis like *you*. The first example also employs the kind of sentence length only associated with formal genres. In contrast, the rule from *The Highway Code* uses short sentences, deictic *you*, and modern English, albeit including the more formal lexis *invite* and *proceed*. Thus, there is nothing to signal to the reader that this text needs to be interpreted in any way other than as *advice*—how best to act in these circumstances. Readers are not encouraged in any way to consider the legal implications of not following this "advice," even if they are using their own judgment in making that decision.

It is this uneasy relationship between the contexts of advice manual and operative document that has led to a long-running dissatisfaction in the cycling community about the wording of rules pertaining to the use of cycle paths. The point

Table 13.2 THE CYCLE PATH RULE (EMPHASIS ADDED)

Edition	Wording of "The Cycle Path Rule"
1946	If there is a cycle track—use it.
1954, 1959	If there is an *adequate* cycle track, use it.
1968	If there is an *adequate* cycle track beside the road, ride on it.
1978, 1967	If there is a *suitable* cycle path, ride on it.
1993	Use cycle lanes and tracks *wherever possible*. They can make your journey safer and quicker.
1998, 2004	Use cycle routes *where practicable*. They can make your journey safer.

Table 13.3 THE CYCLE LANE RULE (EMPHASIS ADDED)

Edition	Wording of "The Cycle Lane Rule"
1993	Cycle lanes are marked by either an unbroken or broken white line along the carriageway. Keep within the lane and watch out for traffic emerging from side turnings.
1998, 2004	**Cycle Lanes**. These are marked by a white line (which may be broken) along the carriageway (see Rule 119). Keep within the lane *wherever possible*.

at issue has been the degree to which the use of cycle routes and other cycle facilities is perceived to be optional or mandatory by road users in general and by the legal system in particular. This can be illustrated by the way in which the "cycle path rule" has changed since its first entry into *The Highway Code* in 1946 (table 13.2). A related rule concerning cycle lanes was introduced in 1993 (table 13.3).[2]

I would argue that the continual alterations to the formulation of these particular rules show evidence of an ongoing discursive struggle in relation to the perception of cycling as a mode of transport. Changes in formulation could be seen as a related process to that of relexicalization, which Fairclough describes in his notion of "overwording" (Fairclough 2001: 96).

Changes to *The Highway Code* have largely happened through a process of consultation, where the government has released a draft *Highway Code* and interested organizations have been invited to comment on that draft before the new edition is finalized. This involves groups concerned with the interests of all types of road users: motorists, pedestrians, cyclists, horse riders, professional drivers. But, of course, the government always has the final say on the precise wording of the *Code*.

In the most recent consultation process in 2006, individuals could also respond to a draft *Highway Code* which was made available via the Internet. In addition, the whole process was made more accessible to the public at large because discussions about the draft were disseminated via the websites of various campaigning organizations. Here we can see individuals—members of the public and politicians—engaging with language on the cusp of the legal-lay divide.

THE CONSULTATION PROCESS FOR *THE HIGHWAY CODE* 2007

According to the government (A Response to Consultation Report: the Highway Code 2007), the draft of the 2007 *Highway Code* elicited 27,000 comments. Seventy percent of these comments could be attributed to cyclists, cycling organizations, or MPs writing on behalf of cycling constituents; by far the majority of these comments from cyclists related to the two rules introduced above:

Rule 58
Use cycle routes *when practicable* and cycling facilities such as advanced stop lines *where they are provided* as they can make your journey safer.

Rule 60
Cycle Lanes. These are marked by a white line (which may be broken) along the carriageway. Keep within the lane *wherever possible*.
(Draft *Highway Code* 2006, emphasis added)

The Problem of "Legal Definitions"

The main concern expressed was the degree to which compulsion to use facilities was encoded by these rules, and thus its implications for legal proceedings. In particular, the discussions focused on the modifying phrases highlighted here in italics. In this case, the cycling campaigners were showing a clear understanding of the legal status of *The Highway Code* in its own right. A member of one local cycling campaign group undertook his own research into legal precedent in the interpretation of *practicable*:

Excerpt 1

The definition of 'practicable' was tested in "Richmond upon Thames London Borough Council v. Express Ltd (2003)."
Under the Greater London (Restriction of Goods Vehicles) Traffic Order 1985, it is required that "the vehicle minimises the use of restricted roads. To this end, the applicant and driver of the vehicle shall ensure that the vehicle ... (b) takes the shortest practicable route ..."
The case against Express Ltd for breach of this condition went to appeal on the interpretation of the word 'practicable.'

It was contended that "The justices should consider the word 'practicable' and the Oxford English Dictionary definitions: (i) able to put into practice; able to be effected; accomplished; or done; feasible; (ii) of a road, passage, etc; able to be used or traversed."

In judgment it was held that "The word 'practicable' in context, it is clear, means 'physically practicable.'" The judges found themselves unable to consider other 'practical' matters (such as the additional congestion, noise and pollution caused by taking the alternative route) for the purposes of the condition.

(Cambridge Cycling Campaign 2007)

This definition confines the accepted meaning of the term to physical possibility. However, the general concept of "practicality" would involve exactly the kind of cost-benefit analysis which the ruling in excerpt 1 excludes. The legal definition can be contrasted to the rather broader definition given in another dictionary, *Collins COBUILD English Language Dictionary* (1987: 1124), which includes a sense that is glossed as having a synonymous relationship with *practical*:

Something that is **practicable** is suitable to be used for a particular purpose. EG *A dark fabric is easily the most practicable for upholstery*

The *COBUILD* dictionary was one of the first to use a corpus to inform its lexicography, arguably giving a better representation of actual usage; these corpora now include spoken, as well as written language. This can be contrasted with the *Oxford English Dictionary* (as cited in excerpt 1), which has traditionally relied on written language only, and privileged forms of written language at that.[3] Thus, not all dictionaries will give the same range of meanings or necessarily represent native speakers' daily use of language. Solan (2005) identifies another related issue with the reliance on dictionaries. He makes the point that the idea of plain meaning "asks only whether the disputed events fit clearly within the outer boundary of the disputed word's meaning" (2005: 2038); it takes no account of the prototypical meanings of words. In addition, dictionary entries rarely comment on a word's frequency. Yet psycholinguistic research has long shown that both prototypicality and word frequency affect lexical access and understanding (see Harley 2007 for a review). It is interesting to note in this particular case that a word frequency program based on the British National Corpus (Harris 2004) rates the relative frequencies of *practical* and *practicable* as 1,329 and 10,231, respectively.[4] For all these reasons, equating dictionary definitions with "plain and ordinary" language is problematic. The type of textualist ruling (Tiersma 1999) given in excerpt 1 above might purport to reflect general usage, but it can have no guarantee of doing so. Given these demands on readers, it already seems unlikely that *The Highway Code* is a text that will be able to travel effectively between its competing roles.

If we consider the other two formulations which were raised as issues by cyclists in the consultation process (*where they are provided, wherever possible*), then from the lay person's perspective a slightly different issue arises. Here it is not so much understanding the lexis that is the issue as being able to interpret what this would mean in a legal context. Even for the lay reader, neither of these two apparent modifiers seems to weaken the requirement for the action at all. *Collins COBUILD English Language Dictionary* (1987: 1118) defines *wherever possible* as:

If you do something **where possible, wherever possible, whenever possible**, etc, you do it on every occasion that you have the opportunity to do it. EG *We traded with the British wherever possible*

Essentially, this seems to equate to the definition of "physically possible," which forms part of the definitions of *practicable* given above. Even more extremely, *where they are provided* seems only to allow for the nonexistence of facilities as a reason not to use them; even the notion of physical traversability is not taken into account. What, then, is the likely legal interpretation of these constructions?

The Problem of Grammar: Using Categorical and Modal Constructions

The use of categorical formulations in the rules above also does not help matters, since *The Highway Code* gives no explicit guidance about the status of this type of construction. As discussed above, the reader is informed on the first content page that MUST/MUST NOT encodes the requirements of traffic law, and *should/should not* and *do/do not* indicate "advisory wording" (*The Highway Code* 2007: 4). While a categorical instruction without MUST/MUST NOT evidently does not encode a legal requirement, it is not clear whether it is supposed to be a stronger or weaker formulation than one using *should/should not* or *do/do not*. One might argue that the listing of these alternative constructions gives them greater status as advice (following the legal principle of *expression unius est exclusion alterius*, Tiersma 1999: 85). Yet this goes against linguistic theory, which would rate categorical formulations as stronger than *should/should not* (and also stronger than MUST/MUST NOT). The following illustrates this problem, using an example from the part of *The Highway Code* predominantly addressed to pedestrians:

Rule 17

At night. Wear something reflective to make it easier for others to see you.... If there is no pedestrian crossing nearby, cross near a street light so that traffic can see you more easily. (*The Highway Code* 2007)

It is clear there is no legal compulsion on pedestrian behavior here, but the use of categorical constructions would appear to increase the strength of the advice. There would certainly seem to be the possibility that this rule could be used in ascription of liability in a civil case. Indeed, a cursory search on the Internet shows many law firms willing to take on liability cases in respect of pedestrians involved in road traffic incidents. However, one such law firm highlights the complexities involved in ascribing liability as illustrated in the extract below. Note that it explicitly names clothing and the choice of crossing point as key factors in liability—issues which are items of "advice" in rule 17 above and never appear in rules using MUST/MUST NOT:

> Many people are involved in road traffic accidents as pedestrians. It is not unusual for there to be disputes on liability, or responsibility for the accident, in such cases. Often the injuries can be severe, despite the improvements in vehicle safety technology of recent years.
>
> It is essential to seek expert legal advice if you are injured as a result of an accident as a pedestrian. The liability arguments can be complex, and may involve the type of clothing being worn, the time of day, the type of road, what the crossing facilities were in the area and whether the pedestrian was taking all suitable care in crossing where and when they did. Guidance through the various stances taken by insurers and experience of previous case law in such circumstances is vital. (My Claim, n.d.)

It is questionable whether many pedestrians in the United Kingdom would be aware of the possible implications of choosing not to wear reflective items when crossing a road at night. Indeed, when I have given talks on this research area, I have shown the pictures which were used in the previous edition of *The Highway Code* (2004) to illustrate the recommended use of reflective items[5] (see figure 13.1). These have never yet failed to raise a laugh—the implication seeming to be that no one could reasonably be expected to dress in such a way just for the purpose of walking on the street at night. Special equipment is perceived to be for vulnerable groups such as children or the elderly, or for specialist activities such as cycling or motorcycling (the equivalent pictures for these last two user groups rarely evoke a response). This issue of societal expectations will be returned to below.

The Problem of the Government Response

So far in this section, I have concentrated on the interpretation of *The Highway Code* by its eventual readers and their ability to understand the legal implications of the text. At this point I would like to return to the consultation process and consider what was said about the key issue of *choice* with respect to the use of cycle paths by those ultimately responsible for the new edition of *The Highway Code*: the then Minister for Transport and his parliamentary undersecretary (Stephen Ladyman and Tom Harris, respectively).

In the first case, we see interaction from within a small government committee whose sole purpose is to discuss the current revision of *The Highway Code*. In his opening statement, Stephen Ladyman states:

Figure 13.1
Picture illustrating Rule 3: Help yourself be seen (*The Highway Code* 2004).

Excerpt 2

> **Dr Ladyman:** One of the most obvious areas of discussion in the consultation was about matters on which there is legislative provision—where people on the roads must or must not do something. Those are marked as "must" or "must not." There are also parts of the code in which there is no prohibition or compulsory statement, and the words "should" or "should not" are used to indicate that people have some choice about those matters and should exercise their personal judgment when using the road. Most of the debate prior to tabling this version of the code was about the difference between those two areas of activity.
>
> (Alterations in the Provisions of *The Highway Code*, June 26, 2007)

The reference to "personal judgment" seems to invoke the concept of free choice: a matter for personal consideration in which road users are invited to weigh up different factors that they perceive to be relevant. Yet, as we have seen above, this is not the likely legal interpretation. Further comment is made on the issue of road users' discretion in relation to a rule on horse-riding, which exhorts riders that they should "never ride more than two abreast, and ride in single file on narrow or busy roads and when riding round bends" (Rule 53, *The Highway Code* 2007):

Excerpt 3

> **Mr. Brazier:**[6] The [British Horse Society] believes that if those words remain in rule 53, they could have serious legal consequences for riders who are

riding two abreast on a narrow or busy road or around a bend when they are involved in an accident.

Dr. Ladyman: The hon. Gentleman is right that the Highway Code can be used in court for the purpose of establish liability, but, in making its decision, the court would have to take account of the fact that it was considering advisory rather than compulsory statements.

(Alterations in the Provisions of *The Highway Code,* June 26, 2007)

This statement continues to reinforce Ladyman's original representation of the situation, that advice can be taken or refused, providing the latter is done for good reason. Tom Harris, Parliamentary Under-Secretary for Transport, maintains this stance in the more public domain of an open parliamentary debate. In this case he is commenting directly on the rule relating to the use of cycling facilities:

Excerpt 4

May I take this opportunity to emphasize that the advice on using cycle facilities in both the current and the proposed revised version of "The Highway Code" is not a legal requirement? It places no compulsion on cyclists to use cycle facilities, and it remains their decision whether or not to follow this advice. The distinction between legal requirements and advisory rules is made clear in the introduction to the code.

(Cycling, Westminster Hall Debates, May 23, 2007)

While what Harris says is strictly accurate, it does not engage with the key point at issue: that the limits to the ways in which these advisory rules can be used in a court of law are not clear to the lay road user. And it is this that makes *The Highway Code* problematic for them, and thus a text that does not travel well. While in law there is an absolute difference between criminal law (the mandatory rules) and civil law (the use of *The Highway* Code to determine if any party were negligent), to lay road users that distinction is not so obvious. To them, it seems counterintuitive that one can be not at fault in terms of traffic law, yet still be judged negligent and thus liable in terms of civil law. I will return to this issue in the discussion.

In the latter stages of the consultation process in a parliamentary web chat, Stephen Ladyman does show some awareness that this concept of "personal judgment" is an apparent rather than real choice for the cyclist:

Excerpt 5

[**question from member of the public**]: Is there any plan to target cycling measures more effectively? Millions have been spent particularly on short cycle lanes with many give ways at side turnings and driveways. Now we are to be told we have to use these deathtraps. I don't have to use the motorway in my car, so why force cyclists to use these lanes, however badly designed or maintained?

Stephen [*sic*] **replies:**

No-one has told you that you have to use these facilities. The Highway Code uses the terms MUST and MUST NOT when you have to do something—and advice about cycle lanes did not use these terms. But after consulting we tried to make this distinction clearer and this week after more representations from cyclists we've announced changes to make it clearer still.

Cycle lanes can make your journey safer but whether you use them is up to you—if you don't then be aware of the needs of other road users and the extra risks you may be taking.

(Web chat with Dr. Stephen Ladyman, Transport Minister, June 6, 2007)

While Ladyman repeats the status of the cycle path rule in traffic law (or its lack thereof), his final comment constitutes a warning: not using a cycle lane puts you at risk. This is quite a shift from the emphasis on personal choice seen in the previous examples. From the perspective of the lay road user (pedestrian, cyclist, or horse rider) who is seeking guidance on what these formulations might mean in a legal context, these comments seem to muddy the waters further. They largely play down the issue of liability and foreground the compulsory elements that are determined by road traffic law. In turn, this highlights *The Highway Code*'s secondary context as a mediator of traffic law at the expense of one of its primary contexts, as an operative document in its own right. By doing this, Ladyman and Harris circumvent the issue of *The Highway Code* as a text trying to negotiate multiple roles. Certainly, their comments do not engage with the very real concerns raised through the consultation process which shows road users struggling with exactly this problem.

It is also interesting to note the way in which Ladyman frames his warning in the final excerpt above. First, cyclists are asked to take into account "the needs of other road users." What this means is not made explicit. However, given that cyclists using roads rather than cycle routes is likely to have little impact on pedestrians, the only plausible inference is that the presence of cyclists on the road is perceived to have a negative impact on motorized traffic. This point will be returned to below. Second, not using cycle routes is deemed to be risky behavior, a view that is not shared by all parties interested in road safety as we will see in the next section.

The Problem of Conflicting "Advice"

Aside from *The Highway Code*, the only other government-endorsed source of advice about cycling in general and road skills in particular is John Franklin's book, *Cyclecraft* (Franklin 2007). Like *The Highway Code*, this is published by the Stationery Office and thus has some status as an official publication. It also forms the basis for *Bikeability*, the National Cycle Training Standard, which according to the Department for Transport is "'Cycling Proficiency' for the 21st century designed to give children the skills and confidence to cycle safely in and around today's modern roads and environment" (Department for Transport, n.d.). However, the advice given about the use of cycle tracks and cycle lanes in Franklin (2007) is somewhat at odds with the view expressed by Ladyman in the excerpt above and also with *The Highway Code* in general. In particular, Franklin challenges the idea that cycle lanes and tracks are likely to be safer for the cyclist. In the case of tracks separated from the road, he points out issues of poor design, poor maintenance, and increased points of conflict with motorized vehicles (where cycle tracks give way at every side road, for example). Paths shared between pedestrians and cyclists are seen as particularly problematic because of their different expectations—for cyclists it is a "road," for pedestrians it is not. Franklin (2007: 194) concludes by saying: "If you can cycle competently on the road, you should avoid the inherently less safe environment of the shared-use footway."

His views on the relative safety of cycle lanes marked as part of the road are no less critical. For Franklin (2007: 91), safety is determined by being maximally visible to other traffic and this is not aided by being in a lane which at best will only be in the driver's peripheral vision, and at worst will be entirely occluded by the vehicle's blind spot:

> Safe cycling requires cyclists to keep close to the moving traffic lane where they are easily seen by other drivers. Cycle lanes, however, remain inflexibly fixed adjacent to the kerb irrespective of traffic conditions. Cyclists who keep within them can easily escape the notice of drivers from both behind and ahead....
>
> In the UK, there is no legal obligation on cyclists to use cycle lanes and you should do so only where it is safe and to your advantage. As far as you can, ignore the presence of a cycle lane in determining the best position to ride on the road, but be extra careful, as some other drivers may not expect you to ride outside the line.

In all cases, then, this government-endorsed publication advises cyclists to make their own judgments and not to assume that structures labeled as "cycling facilities" are necessarily usable, safe, or useful.[7] Indeed, some of its comments on *The Highway Code* itself caution the reader to be aware of the *Code*'s limitations as a source of guidance:

> The Highway Code is a generalist guide, dominated by consideration of motor traffic, and it does not always reflect a good understanding about cycling. As a result, its advice for cyclists is sometimes simplistic, impractical or controversial. You should bear this in mind and not regard it as a definitive summary of best practice. (Franklin 2007: 40)

While it does state that advice in *The Highway Code* may be used in a court to establish blame (2007: 40), it doesn't say that the courts *are* likely to view *The Highway*

Code as "a definitive summary of best practice," to the degree that precise word-ings will have an impact on its interpretation in a court of law. Thus, the existence of conflicting government-endorsed advice serves to compound the difficulties for cyclists in interpreting *The Highway Code*, as they are encouraged toward a lay reading—where their judgment is key in deciding whether to adhere to optional rules—rather than being guided to the necessity for a legal interpretation of the precise wording.

The Problem of Societal Standards

As was intimated in Stephen Ladyman's web chat above (excerpt 5), changes were made to the two rules under discussion as a result of the consultation process:

Rule 61

Cycle Routes and Other Facilities. Use cycle routes, advanced stop lines, cycle boxes and toucan crossings *unless at the time it is unsafe to do so. Use of these facilities is not compul-sory and will depend on your experience and skills, but they can make your journey safer.*

Rule 63

Cycle Lanes. These are marked by a white line (which may be broken) along the carriageway. When using a cycle lane, keep within the lane *when practicable.* When leav-ing a cycle lane check before pulling out that it is safe to do so and signal your intention clearly to other road users. *Use of these facilities is not compulsory and will depend on your experience and skills, but they can make your journey safer.*

(*The Highway Code* 2007, emphasis added)

In terms of the liability issue, there is now a clear statement that the use of cycling facilities is not compulsory, but this would seem to be in apposition to a categorical instruction which—like the previous version—is modified by a word or phrase with the potential for problematic interpretation. *Practicable* replaces *wherever possible* in Rule 63, which arguably makes it more of an issue for a lay reader than previously, both because it replaces a more frequently used word[8] and because of the potential for confusing the concepts of *practical* and *prac-ticable* as argued in above. *Practicable* and *where they are provided* are replaced in Rule 61 by *unless at the time it is unsafe to do so.* This phrase brings to the fore a different issue in legal interpretation—what Gibbons (2003: 70) terms "applying societal standards." In essence, Gibbons argues that this approach to legal interpretation means applying the default assumptions of the hegemonic group in that society at that time. In other words, what is at stake here is not the literal understanding of a word—*safe* is a fairly basic concept—but rather what it would mean to act safely in a particular context. In terms of liability, then, it is likely to be the court's judgment of whether it was unsafe to use a particular facility at a particular time. This becomes a problem for a text travelling across the legal-lay divide if the assessment of the target group (cyclists in this case, but perhaps pedestrians or horse riders in others) does not necessarily coincide with that of the judiciary.

The fact that there is already conflicting advice available to this particular user group suggests that this is a site of societal struggle. Indeed, the Cyclists' Touring Club (the largest national cycling organization in the United Kingdom) points out this lack of agreement between the government and cycling organizations when commenting on the draft versions of the two rules relating to cycling facilities and the ensuing consultation process:

> CTC felt that [the wording of the rules] would reinforce the erroneous belief that cycle facilities are essentially safety features. In CTC's experience, far too many cycle facilities are far from safe, so expecting people to use them as a matter of course and in the interests of their own 'safety,' is ill-advised. . . .
>
> Unfortunately, the concept that many experienced cyclists regard the road as the safest place for them was counter-intuitive to some officials and Ministers, so CTC's battle over this proposed wording was far from straightforward.
>
> (Cyclists' Touring Club 2007)

Cycling in the United Kingdom is generally perceived as a minority activity, particularly when it is for commuting rather than leisure purposes: high-profile public figures that choose to cycle to work gain media coverage on the basis of this fact.[9] This activity would not be newsworthy if it were common—thus it can probably be inferred that cyclists are not overrepresented in the higher echelons of government. This perception of cycling as a leisure activity rather than as a mode of transport represents a general societal shift in the last 50 years or so. Cycling to work has traditionally been associated with those who earn lower incomes. As the standard of living has grown in the United Kingdom, so car ownership and commuting have increased and the number of cycle commuters has decreased. Indeed, if one has a professional job, car ownership is largely assumed. While increases in traffic congestion are starting to alter this simple relationship between earnings and car ownership/use, it can still be suggested that those in professions with high salaries are likely to be car users. This begins to explain why cycle use by high-ranking MPs is considered newsworthy. Also, it suggests that other well paid professions (such as the law and particularly the judiciary) are not very likely to have an unrepresentatively large number of cycle commuters within their ranks.

It is thus likely that many of the people responsible for the composition of *The Highway Code* and many of those interpreting it in a legal context will not be experienced cyclists and are likely to take for granted the hegemonic position of the car in *The Highway Code* (Horton 2007; Davies 2006). Indeed, as was indicated in the discussion of excerpt 5 above, even the then Minister for Transport seemed to assume the "common sense" position that cyclists would necessarily be safer if they used cycling facilities and that this was also preferable for other road users.

These hegemonic assumptions can also still persist even when challenged by experts. Julian Brazier raises this issue in his discussion of whether non-mandatory rules could truly be considered optional, given the role of *The Highway Code* in establishing liability. Excerpt 6 is his response to Stephen Ladyman's assurances relating to the existence of choice in excerpt 3 above:

Excerpt 6

Mr. Brazier: The Minister knows that I have a particular interest in the issue of risk and the courts' attitudes to it. I am the co-chairman of an all-party group on the subject and tried to introduce a private Member's Bill on the issue. The problem is that the courts have had a steady history of overriding professional views over the past 15 years.

Let me take one example from outside the world of horse riding, which neatly illustrates the point. It involves a mountaineering case—I can write to the Minister afterwards with the details—in which a climber was killed when travelling with a professional guide. What really shocked the professional mountaineering community was that there was no dispute whatever in the court about the facts of the case. Everybody fully accepted them, but the judge's view simply went against that of almost all the mountaineering community and he disagreed with the mountaineering instructor's split-second decision. If that can happen in such a case, one can imagine how easily it could happen in the much more commonplace situation of riders getting into difficulty on a road.

(Alterations in the Provisions of *The Highway Code*, June 26, 2007)

While this isn't an example from *The Highway Code*, the point made would generalize. Members of non-hegemonic groups have to be aware that their "common sense" may not be the "common sense" of those writing the operative documents or interpreting them in a legal context. Thus, *The Highway Code* becomes even more potentially problematic as a legal text when interpreting it as a cyclist, pedestrian, horse rider, or motorcyclist because the wording—and any legal implications—becomes even more critical. While I have already argued that *The Highway Code* is a text that does not travel well between its multiple contexts, the impact of this may disproportionately affect more marginalized road users than its hegemonic user group: the car driver.

DISCUSSION

For a text to travel well, the distinction between its different purposes has to be understood by its readers. It's questionable whether *The Highway Code* is equally well recognized as an advisory text, a mediator of traffic law, and an operative document. Indeed, I would argue that it is not. There is certainly evidence in Stephen Ladyman's written response to the consultation (Department for Transport 2007) that a number of respondents did not understand the significance of MUST/MUST NOT in signaling a relationship to road traffic law. This suggests that these readers do not appreciate either the distinction between traffic law and advice, or the distinction between traffic law and the role of *The Highway Code* in establishing liability (as an operative document). Presumably, modality for them only works within the primary context of advice, where stronger modals do no more than indicate stronger advice. Such a basic failure in the recognition of the different contexts of *The Highway Code* must be a concern.

Once readers have recognized the different functions of *The Highway Code*—and in this case have understood its function as an operative document—then the question is whether they can successfully interpret its contents as legal language. This issue has two different aspects: the problem of understanding particular lexical items or grammatical constructions, and the problem of the *Code's* relationship to other texts and discourses.

Most readers of *The Highway Code* are not going to use a dictionary to check the precise meanings of lexical items: they will largely rely on their intuitive knowledge of the language. This in itself could lead them to an incorrect interpretation as the textualist approach to the interpretation of legal language relies heavily on this resource. Even where readers do recognize the potential import of particular terms or particular constructions, there is no straightforward way for them to find out what the most likely interpretation would be in the legal context. In excerpt 1 from the Cambridge Cycling Campaign website (2007) we saw evidence of nonlawyers researching legal decisions to try to gain access to this understanding. However, when it comes to the use of categorical instructions or the use of strong deontic modality like *should* it becomes much more difficult to undertake this type of research. Individual lexical items can form the basis of searches, but grammatical constructions cannot easily do so.

The questions being raised in the consultation process showed that members of the public were uncertain of the likely interpretation of rules in *The Highway Code*. This uncertainty seemed to be further compounded by the way in which those in the government responsible for the consultation process seemed to sidestep the whole issue of the impact of wording in *The Highway Code*: they downplayed the role of *The Highway Code* as an operative document by continually emphasizing "personal choice" and the distinction between mandatory and optional rules. This is further demonstrated below:

Excerpt 7

I should clarify that the purpose of the code is to give sound advice and guidance to all road users on safe use of the roads, as well as to explain where the law applies. The code is intended as general guidance only, and cannot provide road users with detailed instructions or cover every eventuality. More detailed guidance can be found elsewhere—for example, through the driving test and supporting materials for car drivers, and through Bikeability for cyclists.

(Tom Harris, Parliamentary Under-Secretary, Dept. for Transport, Cycling, Westminster Hall Debates, May 23, 2007)

All of this seems to exploit a distinction in the law which itself does not travel well across the legal-lay divide. While criminal prosecutions can only be on the basis of traffic law (the rules which are indicated via MUST/MUST NOT in *The Highway Code*), individuals can be found partly or wholly responsible (liable) for civil damages on the basis of *The Highway Code*. Thus, a party who was not at fault in terms of traffic law could find themselves denied financial compensation on the basis of being judged to be negligent—to not have exercised due care. To a lay person, that distinction may not seem valid. Being denied compensation due to "advice" that they are told is optional may seem as much like losing the case as being found criminally at fault. This is especially the case given that what is construed as "negligence" in *The Highway Code* may not accord with their judgment, or the judgment of specialists in that field. At this point, the whole of *The Highway Code* effectively becomes mandatory from the lay perspective: the distinction between the contexts of *mediator of traffic law* and *operative document for negligence on the road* breaks down.

A further confusion is created by the existence of government-endorsed expert advice which conflicts with *The Highway Code*. Texts exist within a societal context and are read within the context of other texts. *The Highway Code* and *Cyclecraft* become competing advice manuals, not a legal document and a lay text: the qualitative difference between them is not self-evident to the lay reader.

The legal-lay divide is also at issue when current cultural assumptions are brought into the interpretation process (what Gibbons 2003 terms "applying societal standards"). The problem can be that such assumptions reflect hegemonic discourses which may not encompass different types of expertise. In the case of *The Highway Code*, the hegemonic discourse is that of the motorized road user, most particularly the car driver, and the majority of rules are written from their perspective (Davies 2006). This does reflect the discourse of transport in current British society, and these assumptions will inevitably affect interpretation in the courtroom. Thus, what is considered "safe" or "unsafe" is likely to be assessed from the perspective of that dominant road user rather than from the perspective of the (expert) cyclist or horse rider. For a minority road user to interpret the legal implications of *The Highway Code* accurately, this is yet another issue of which they have to be aware.

In sum, then, *The Highway Code* is not a text that travels well. Most crucially, it is questionable whether it is reliably recognized as a travelling text at all—it is not clear whether the population at large see it as anything more than the document on which they are tested as part of the process of gaining a vehicle license. Those who do recognize its legal status may also be aware of further potential issues, such as the likely interpretation of specific grammatical constructions or possible conflicts between expert knowledge and hegemonic assumptions. However, this awareness does not automatically confer the ability to assess probable outcomes accurately. In the case of *The Highway Code*, the situation is made worse by the confusion between criminal law and the civil law of liability; this distinction is clear to lawyers but does not travel well over the legal-lay divide. It is also certainly the case that the responses given by the Department for Transport during the recent consultation process did little to clarify these difficulties for lay readers of this legal text even when specific issues were identified. Texts are not entities in a vacuum: their ability to function effectively is not solely about the way that they are written but can also be affected by the web of texts and discourses that surround them.

NOTES

1. However, some limited attention is paid to the way in which the demands of traffic law are explicitly signaled in *The Highway Code*.
2. Cycle paths and cycle tracks are cycle facilities that are separated from the road. Cycle lanes are cycle facilities that are part of the road itself.
3. It should be noted that work on the current edition uses a wider range of written material.
4. These frequencies are out of 86,800 words which occur twice or more in the overall corpus of 100 million words.
5. There is a similar picture in the current edition (2007), but this is now a photograph rather than a schematic figure and is thus less likely to be reproduced effectively in this context. It can be seen at
   http://www.direct.gov.uk/en/TravelAndTransport/Highwaycode/DG_070108, which is part of the official online site for *The Highway Code*.
6. Then Conservative MP for Canterbury, Kent.
7. One UK regional cycling organization, Warrington Cycle Campaign, has collected images of problematic cycle routes and cycle facilities which can be viewed at http://homepage.ntlworld.com/pete.meg/wcc/facility-of-the-month/book.htm. It provides an excellent illustration of the reasons why cyclists do not wish cycle facilities to be made (effectively) mandatory.
8. *Possible* is ranked 254/86,800 and *wherever* 3,896/86,800 in Harris's (2004) word frequency program which uses the British National Corpus as source material. *Practicable* is ranked as 10,321/86,800.
9. For example, Boris Johnson (the current mayor of London and a former MP) and David Cameron (the current leader of the Conservative Party) have both been subject to much media reporting on the basis of their cycling to Parliament.

REFERENCES

Bernstein, Basil. 1990. *Class, Codes and Control*. Volume 4: *The Structuring of Pedagogic Discourse*. London/New York: Routledge.

Blommaert, Jan. 2005. *Discourse*. Cambridge: Cambridge University Press.

Coates, Jennifer. 1983. *The Semantics of the Modal Auxiliaries*. London: Croom Helm.

Collins COBUILD English Language Dictionary (1987).

Davies, Bethan L. (2006). Representations of different road users in *The Highway Code*: Discourses of "safety." Sociolinguistics Symposium 16, July 2006, University of Limerick, Eire.

Fairclough, Norman. 2001. *Language and Power*. 2d ed. London: Longman.

Gibbons, John. 2003. *Forensic Linguistics: An Introduction to Language in the Justice System*. Oxford: Blackwell.

Harley, Trevor. 2007. *The Psychology of Language: From Data to Theory*. 3d ed. Hove: Psychology Press.

Harris, Jonathan. 2004. *Wordcount*. Online. Available at: http://www.wordcount.org/about. html.

Horton, Dave. 2007. Fear of cycling. In *Cycling and Society*, ed. Dave Horton, Paul Rosen, and Peter Cox, 133–52. Aldershot, UK: Ashgate.

Maley, Yon. 1994. The language of the law. In *Language and the Law*, ed. John Gibbons, 11–50. London: Longman.

Solan, Laurence M. 2005. The new textualists' new text. *Loyola of Los Angeles Law Review* 38: 2027–62.

Tiersma, Peter M. 1999. *Legal Language*. Chicago: University of Chicago Press.

Verschueren, Jef. 1999. *Understanding Pragmatics*. London: Arnold.

OFFICIAL PUBLICATIONS

A Response to Consultation Report. *The Highway Code*. 2007. Driving Standards Agency. Available at: http://www.dsa.gov.uk/Documents/consult/Responses/Response_to_ Highway_Code_Consultation_report.pdf. December 17, 2009.

Alterations in the Provisions of *The Highway Code*. House of Commons General Committee on Delegated Legislation (26/06/2007). Available at: http://www.publications.parliament. uk/pa/cm200607/cmgeneral/deleg3/070626/70626s01.htm. December 17, 2009.

Cycling. Westminster Hall Debates (May 23, 2007). Available at: http://www.theyworkforyou. com/whall/?id=2007-05-23b.491.0.

Cycling Policy: An Overview. Accessed December 17, 2009 (no longer available): http://www. dft.gov.uk/pgr/sustainable/cycling/cyclingpolicyoverview?page=8.

Franklin, John. 2007. *Cyclecraft*. 4th ed. London: The Stationery Office.

The Highway Code. 2004. London: The Stationery Office.

The Highway Code. 2007. London: The Stationery Office.

Web chat with Dr. Stephen Ladyman, Transport Minister (June 6, 2007). Accessed December 17, 2009 (no longer available): http://www.number10.gov.uk/Page11866.

INTERNET SOURCES

Cambridge Cycling Campaign. 2007. "*Highway Code*—the term 'practicable.'" Available at: http://www.camcycle.org.uk/campaigning/issues/highwaycode/practicable.html. December 17, 2009.

Cyclists' Touring Club. 2007. Rules 61 and 63 of *The Highway Code*. Available at: http://www. ctc.org.uk/blog/roger-geffen/why-ctc-challenged-latest-version-highway-code. January 31, 2013.

My Claim. n.d. Pedestrian accident compensation claims. Available at: http://www.mycompensa-tionclaim.co.uk/content/pedestrian-accident-compensation-claims. December 17, 2009.

CHAPTER 14

Recalling Rape

Moving Beyond What We Know

SHONNA TRINCH

> I have never allowed anyone to refer to me as a "rape victim." Certainly for the time that buddy held a knife to my throat I was his victim and I cannot deny that. But every time that term is used to define me, I feel I am returned to that moment, that night of terror and helplessness. Nor am I fond of "survivor." Like everyone else, I was already surviving the normal pain and hardships of life before I was raped, thank you very much. "Okay. So what do we call you?" you ask? Call me a woman. Call me a woman that has been raped. Call me a woman that has been raped by a man. (From *The Story of Jane Doe*, Doe 2003: 120)

INTRODUCTION

From the United States (Ponterotto 2007) and Canada (Ehrlich 2007a) to Israel (Bogoch 2007) and Scotland (Mooney 2007), we find that not only does rape persist as a social problem, but that victim-blaming, male privilege, and stereotypical interpretations of rape continue unabated in legal systems. Some scholars even argue that anti-rape work has further entrenched rape myths. This chapter employs the textual analyses of narrative and discourse to examine representations of sexual abuse put forth by women who resist rape—physically and/or discursively—and whose narratives seem to resist the "rape victim" label. The data suggest that texts women themselves create to represent rape can be mined for the resources we need in the criminal justice system to understand more fully how women deal with rape. Thus, rather than treating the travel of texts, this chapter will illustrate how texts could be used as the vehicles that can take us from our stereotypical and conventional wisdom to a new place where we might comprehend broader and more complicated representations of rape.

Specifically, this chapter will explore what might lie beyond the terms *victim* and *survivor* as they get conceptualized in talk-in-interaction that takes place between women and legal professionals in the US criminal and civil justice systems. Over the last decade sociolinguistic and discourse analytic research on the social act of reporting rape in legal settings has shown how language conspires with culture to reproduce rape (Matoesian 1993, 2001), to represent rape as consensual sex (Ehrlich 2001), and to manage euphemistic meanings of rape (Trinch 2001, 2003). These sociolinguistic approaches to studying discourse about violence against women have underscored that when women seek justice, they encounter different gender entitlements regarding sex that privilege a man's right to rape a woman.

The road to categorizing "rape" as a crime and making "raped women" into legitimate victims of crime has proven to be long and arduous, requiring its pioneers to forge new paths by overcoming obstacles and roadblocks along the way. Still, critics argue that the last 30 years of work about and against rape has made little progress to erode the mythology that continues to surround rape and even less to eradicate it. Some faultfinders claim that anti-rape work has further entrenched and even exacerbated certain rape myths.

In the pages that follow, I will investigate how one ideological vehicle of anti-rape work, namely the "trauma of rape" narrative, has been a double-edged sword in the feminist and psychological counseling movement against rape. While this dominant "trauma of rape" narrative has perhaps succeeded in gaining public attention, fostering outrage, and even securing assistance for women who have experienced rape, I argue that it has also taken us to a place that may silence those women who do not consistently represent their rape experience in terms of trauma. By problematizing the "victim-survivor" binaries in legal and lay language-in-interaction, I explore where we might travel if we consider the sociolinguistic and discursive possibilities inspired by Lamb's (1999) and Gavey's (2005) proposal to demystify rape by examining women's narratives of resistance as opposed to making arguments that women are either *victims* or *survivors* of rape.

Many women who experience a particular type of "real rape" give accounts of their victimization that fall short of their listeners' expectations to hear about trauma.[1] When this is the case, these women tend to get pushed off the path to justice that other presumed "deserving victims" get to take because they present their account and themselves as having suffered psychologically from the event. For this reason, the purpose of this chapter is threefold. First, this work will point out how the dominant "trauma of rape" narrative may overemphasize women's pain, suffering, and victimization at the expense of understanding rape when it is reported in the absence of any perceived psychological damage. Second, this chapter seeks to reveal textual representations of sexual abuse put forth by women who resist rape—either physically or discursively—and who narrate events and ideas that refute the "rape victim" label and many of its connotations.

And third, the analysis also attempts to contribute to a conversation about how victims act in the aftermath of rape, by listening to how some women quite pragmatically need and/or choose to perform aspects of themselves—such as power, resilience, and resistance—with which the cultural identity of "rape victim" is incongruent.

Situated in a larger cultural and political context yet created locally within a particular speech setting, narratives serve "to show our interlocutors the salience of particular aspects of our identities" (Schiffrin 1996: 199). Here, I will examine three women's narrative reports of rape in protective order interviews with legal professionals. I will show that some women represent rape as violence that does not get in the way of what they need to do in their everyday life. As they talk about what they do and what they need to do, they seem not to allow rape to define them as living "sadly ever after." These women's texts suggest that they do not let rape obliterate their lives. A singular focus on the damage rape causes may conceal the full spectrum of ways in which women represent, report, and perhaps even experience rape. By adding women's non-trauma narratives of sexual violence to our representations of rape, we might make progress in resisting rape's power to silence.

MOVING BEYOND VICTIM IDEOLOGIES

Beliefs and theories about how victims would or should act are well-studied in the literature on rape. Such ideas have often been referred to as rape myths, and they seem to take hold of Americans' minds in such a way that makes it nearly impossible in conversations, whether casual or classroom, for people to ask, "Why do men rape?" instead of the more commonly heard question, "Why was that woman in that situation (whatever it might be) if she did not want to be raped?" This epistemology of rape reveals the societal and cultural practices that uphold male privilege, male aggression against women, and women's lack of autonomy over their sexual selves. Cole (2007) links prevailing stereotypes about raped women with historical facts. She writes that, historically, the "victim" of rape was the man responsible for the woman raped, either her father or her husband, and that even today, "the rape victim's legal standing as a 'victim' continues to be greatly disputed" (Cole 2007: 122). Today, for example, rape of a woman who survives in the absence of physical bruises, cuts, lacerations, bleeding, and/or broken bones is still often conceptualized as sex. Furthermore, women who have experienced such rapes have been forced, through leading questions, to answer "no" in court when asked, "Was the man that raped you violent?," even though the perpetrator had held a knife to the woman's throat (Doe 2003).

As an antidote to this understanding of rape, feminists like Holmstrom and Burgess (1974) introduced the world to symptoms of what they called Rape Trauma Syndrome (RTS).

Later, Judith Herman (1992) introduced ground-breaking work on both trauma and recovery for people victimized by violence. Cole (2007: 122) states, "Diagnosing and publicizing RTS was a vital step in advancing the public's understanding of the psychological impact of rape as well as in helping victims recover from the experience." But feminists from the beginning of their work in the anti-rape movement were ambivalent about using victim discourse to further women's rights and status. And indeed, their nascent fears have proven prophetic as the "trauma of rape" narrative seems to be overdetermining how legal authorities, jurors, and judges expect to hear about rape. For instance, some Canadian judges have treated "post-traumatic stress disorder" as necessary evidence to rule in favor of a woman claiming to have been raped by a man (Des Rosiers, Feldthusen, and Hankivsky 1998). Along these lines, other researchers complain that psychology's rape trauma syndrome is essentializing because sexual violence is seen as "a totalizing experience itself, a singular event that fixes the victim on the trajectory of others who are defenseless and seeking rescue" (Haag 1996, cited in Gavey 2005).

Thus, the prevalent "trauma of rape" narrative may overemphasize women's victimization at the expense of really understanding rape. "Victims" get taken seriously when their actions prior to, during, and after a rape are consistent with the public's expectations.[2] Any action seen as incongruent with what the ideal "innocent victim" would do is cause for disbelief, concern, and derision. Before a rape occurs, less than ideal victims are blamed for putting themselves in the wrong place, drinking too much alcohol, or doing drugs, for example. During a rape, women are blamed because they did not fight hard enough, they did not say "no" explicitly enough, and they did not make a clear enough plea for help (see Ehrlich 2001; Matoesian 2001). And after a rape, less than ideal victims do not appear to have suffered enough trauma. Sometimes they go out with friends, they return to the place where they were raped, they even might have sex with their rapist or with someone else for that matter. When teaching excerpts of Peggy Sanday's (1990) *Fraternity Gang Rape* along with Philipe Bourgois's (2004) "The Everyday Violence of Gang Rape," I hear comments from students such as, "I mean, come on, was she really raped? If I were raped, I would not go back to the house where I was raped to get a pair of sunglasses." Or, "Who would get raped and then go back to the fraternity/crack house the next night?"

Along the same lines, when I tell some people what I study, they either shy away from me or they ask me, "How can you work on such a depressing and awful topic?" An acquaintance once asked me if it was hard for me to understand the women who participated in my studies because she assumed that they were crying while they were reporting what happened to them. Gavey (2005: 175) suggests that this rape myth about victims being incapable of life after rape comes from the way public rhetoric privileges "[rape's] power to cause severe and irrevocable psychological harm to the victim."

Suggesting that women are doing many things at once when talking about rape may appear to turn the idea of rape as a social, cultural, and linguistic taboo on its head. However, in the data that I present below, Latinas' stories of rape suggest sociolinguistic taboos about rape can and do co-occur with accounts of agency and resilience. These women are far from resigned to the social fact of having been raped, or to the limitations imposed by cultural norms for acting, speaking, and being in rape's wake. Instead, their narratives can be read for elements that show how women strongly oppose both the act of rape and the way rape has been constructed as an absolute and totalizing trauma. Rather than looking at rape disclosures in terms of the sociolinguistic system that constrains what speakers can say about it, these rape narratives will be examined for political strategies that could function in a larger cultural and linguistic field. With such a reading, women themselves might show us how to undermine the ways in which culture mystifies and maintains rape's unique power to horrify.

METHODOLOGY AND DATA ANALYSIS

The data I will discuss now come from Latina women's narrative reports of rape in protective order interviews. Protective orders are also known as restraining orders, protection from abuse orders, and orders of protection. They are issued by judges in civil proceedings, and they require that the respondent stay away from the complaining party for a specified period of time. Two different settings in two US cities in the Southwest provide the contexts for these interviews. One is a district attorney's office where paralegals interview women seeking protective orders and the other is a pro bono law clinic where volunteers—most of whom are attorneys and law students—do the interviewing. Elsewhere (Trinch 2003), I have detailed how these narratives are co-constructed between interviewer and interviewee in these legal contexts. Undoubtedly, the context is particular, as all contexts are. The women recounting their experiences in these settings are not in counseling sessions, talking to their close friends, in a courtroom, in a police department, or speaking to family. That said, as my prior work has demonstrated, women who have experienced both rape and domestic violence travel through social and legal settings and often need to or choose to tell their stories in these varied places. From sociolinguistics, we know that there is no essential way to tell the story. The context of any telling will inevitably contribute to the way an account is retold.[3]

In order to see what might lie beyond the categories of "rape victim" or "rape survivor," I want to explore situations in these protective order interviews in which women themselves indicate their resistance to rape and their resilience in the aftermath of a rape. In two prior, complementary studies about how Latina women report sexual violence in protective order interviews in the US Southwest (Trinch 2001, 2003), I hypothesized—based on theories of cultural taboo and euphemism (Ullman 1966)—that the topic of rape would be marked in the speech of both interviewers and victims as either prohibited or somehow restricted in the discourse. I also found a rich social science literature that portrayed Latina women as unwilling or reluctant to speak about rape directly (Larrain and Rodriguez 1993; Lefley et al. 1993; Michael et al. 1994; Williams and Holmes 1981).

From my analyses of disclosures of sexual violence from within a corpus of over 300 interviews, I found several patterns. First, contrary to generalizations made in the literature about Latina women's cultural sensibilities about reporting rape, they actually showed great variation in disclosing sexual violence. Second, topics that refer to sexual violence, and rape, *are marked* in many of these women's speech as taboo—usually through euphemism. At the same time, the use of euphemism is contextually determined, where women who use euphemistic speech in one context might not use it in another. Likewise, complete reporting of sexual violence sometimes depends on whether interviewers are willing to disambiguate meaning when clients' terms for sexual violence are euphemistic and vague. Finally, some interviewers also seemed to be constrained by the taboos associated with sexual assault. For example, when writing affidavits, interviewers sometimes select more euphemistic lexical items than their clients.

Beyond these linguistic aspects of the data corpus, other interesting observations also emerged, such as the fact that these women, who all came forward to tell their stories, did not show outward signs of shame, stigma, fear of speaking, or a need to suffer alone in silence. All the women in the corpus signed consent forms for me, and many of them stated that they would be happy if their story helped someone else in some way. They were well-dressed, composed, and few cried at all while speaking about what happened to them. Moreover, their coming to speak about their situations in search of a solution was only ONE of the things they had on their "to do" list for the day. In other words, they had jobs and made plans—both long term and short term. They discussed their own safety and talked about sexual violence openly. They never suggested that they deserved to be sexually, physically, or emotionally abused. Nor did their narratives in any way suggest that because they were some man's wife they were required by culture to submit to his will. Many had children, whom they took care of, and many had already separated from their abusers. Some of the women already had new boyfriends.

In short, these women, referred to sometimes in my work and in that of many other scholars as *victims*, looked and acted like women. I offer this ostensibly obvious observation in order to provide comparisons with stereotypes of rape victims that leave little room for women's diverse expressions of the sexual violence they suffer.

Aspects of these women's rape stories are marked sociolinguistically for being unexpectedly mundane, quite matter-of-fact, and even decidedly unemotional, and thus discordant with cultural expectations of victimization. Focusing on three examples from this corpus, I will show how women answer questions regarding sexual violence, how they create the topical coherence between sexual violence and domestic life, and how they include or omit evaluations of their assault. From these accounts emerge very multifaceted representations of rape in place of the more familiar, monolithic narrative of "rape trauma."

In excerpt 1[4] below, the client reports to the paralegal that her husband forced her to have sex with him and that this incident was physically rough enough to make her wrists swell and hurt. The rape incident she reports is decidedly violent, but she reports that her response to it was mundane. Namely, she went to work the next day. Although the rape trauma narrative would suggest that women need to convalesce physically and emotionally after rape, for many women, taking time off from work simply is not practical. This client also situates this rape squarely within domestic life. It takes place within her marriage, in the context of her home, and with the threat of her children seeing their father raping their mother. The rape she narrates in a matter-of-fact manner occurred a month and a half before the interview, and it is not the incident that brought her into the DA's office. She offers it at as mere evidence of the larger abuse problem that she faces regularly.

Excerpt 1: Victim returns to work after rape even though her arms hurt[5]

P: ¿Usted, ha, ha sostenido algún moretón o ah, golpes?

C: *Hace, la última vez que tuvo relaciones sexuales conmigo, hace como un mes y medio. Fue a fuerzas. Regresé al trabajo toda la semana, no podía ni trabajar (.02). Pero eso no le quiero decir a los niños (.03).*

P: ¿ Además del alcohol, él usa alguna otra droga? ...

P: O.K., durante un incidente, dice usted que había sexualmente, la, la

C:[Sí

P: se aprovechó de usted. Y eso, ¿cuándo sucedió señora, más o menos?

C: Hará, como un mes y medio también.

P: So más o menos también en ((month)).

C: Mhmh, y yo pensé de que lo vuelva a intentar, y ahora sí lo reporto porque pos no, eso no debe ser a fuerzas. Y fui al trabajo con todas las manos a adoloridas y todo. (.04)

P: So la agarró fuerte sus ah, ...

C: [Sí eso que se ((showing her wrists and forearms)) me (haya) hinchado me dolía.

P: Y, y hizo alguna amenaza si acaso, usted no (.)

C: [Mhmh

P: [lo *hacía.* ¿Que le dijo?

C: Que iba a hacer escándalo pa' que los niños miraran todo. ((.21 seconds of silence while paralegal types)) ...

Translation of Excerpt 1

P: Have you sustained any bruises?

C: **It was, the last time he had sexual relations with me, about a month and a half ago. He forced me. I returned to work all**

that week, I couldn't even work (.02). But I don't want to tell the children that. ((.03))

P: Besides alcohol, does he use any other drugs?   ...

P: O.K., during an incident you said that there was sexually, the, the

C: Yes

P: He took advantage of you. And that, when did that happen ma'am, approximately.

C: That would be about a month and a half ago also.

P: So more or less also ((month)).

C: Mhmh, and so I thought that in case he tried to do it again, and now I am reporting it because well, that should not be forced. And I went to work with sore hands and everything. ((.04))

P: So he grabbed on hard to your ah,

C: [Yes that ((showing her wrists and forearms)) was swollen, it was painful.

P: And did he happen to threaten you if you didn't do it?

C: Mhmh

P: What did he say to you?

C: That he was going to make a scandal so that the children watch ((.02)) And all the time he asked me why I didn't want to have relations with him, he said, um, he asked if I had someone else and I told him no, "It's the situation that we live in, what do you want?" ((.07)).

P: So did you fill out a police report on this, for that, on this occasion?

C: No.

P: And, and during the incident that happened, when, um, but whenever he tried um...

C: I just told him that so he wouldn't do it again.

In Excerpt 2 we find a client who is unique in that she sobs uncontrollably through parts of the interview. My ethnography of reporting rape in intimate-partner violence, following Hymes (1974), shows that women's crying and sobbing are the exception rather than the rule. Most clients do not cry when reporting in these contexts. However, the discourse context suggests that this client, though having been a victim of both domestic violence and rape, is not crying because of either battery or sexual assault. By reinserting the rape disclosure back into the original interview context, we learn that the sexual assault incident that this client discloses was the reason why she left her abusive husband some time prior to the interview. And this client, like most women who are raped, did not report her husband to authorities in order to accuse him of rape. Space constraints and issues of confidentiality keep me from including the entire interview, which shows that the client starts to cry at the beginning of the interview when she mentions the fact that her husband took their daughter from her and refuses to give her back. So, with her rape narrative we are able to see how a client juxtaposes representations of sexual violence and coercion with what, at the moment of her telling, she seems to deem "real terror": her estranged husband's abduction of their daughter. The woman starts weeping aloud at the beginning of the interview when she recounts the abduction of her child and she continues throughout.

If we isolate the retelling of sexual assault for analysis, then it appears to be a difficult topic for the client to speak about. She uses no direct referents to refer to rape, she cries and she admits that she acquiesced and had sex she did not want to have to avoid a fight.[6] But if we situate the rape narrative in the longer story, we could also conclude that the rape is of little importance to her, at least at the moment. While it might be true that at this instant this client does not want to talk about rape, her reluctance might actually have little to do with the fact that it is a taboo topic. The source of her horror and the focus of her attention are likely to be her daughter's abduction, and therefore, it may be that she does not want to talk about rape because she wants the interviewer to help her get her daughter back.

Excerpt 2: Client starts to cry again when reporting sexual assault

First reference to sexual assault

> P: O.K., on ((date)) could you tell me what happened during that, that incident and ( )
> C: [He was, he wasn't there
> P: o.k.
> C: He went to work, actually it happened Saturday the night before that *he forced himself on me.* And um, I have had, I have been bleeding for three months
> P: [*So he raped you.*
> C: *Um, he didn't get to. O.K. he didn't get to.* Um, ((starts to cry again)) then, "because I'm his wife" he kept telling me, "because I'm his wife" be supposed to, you know, "that's what wives are for."
> P: Mhmh
> C: And I told him, I said "Look ((alleged abuser's name)), I've been bleeding, I'm going through a doctor, and I have my surgery on ((date))" as a matter of fact,
> P: Mhmh
> C: And he knew, he knew my problem, medical problem.
> P: [Mhmh
> C: But because I'm his wife, I'm supposed to
> P: [O.K.
> C: [you know…
> P: [O.K., When did that occur?
> C: On ((date)).

P: ((repeats date))?

C: Uhuh.

P: About what time?

C: Umm, about eleven o'clock at night, I, I

P: Was he drunk?

C: Yes.

P: And so you got home and he

C: [he was just home, yeah, he was home drinking when I got there, and…

P: (types for 18 seconds) *So you said, he didn't really rape you, so he*

C: [*Yeah, I didn't,* I just, I finally, *other times I'll just, this is, this is awful and disgusting, and disgusting, but I'll just lay there, other times.* But I got, I, I was hurting, I was bleeding, I ((stops and sniffling)).

P: (typing for 12 seconds) O.K. And, ah, anything else that happened during that incident?

C: Um, no, he just um, where I kicked him, um, he just got upset and um

P: [Where did you kick him?

C: Right in his, like in his

P: [Groin?

C: Groin area.

P: O.K., and ah, that's it? Anything else?

C: No, and uh, he went to to the other bedroom and and passed out, and then the next morning, he works, on Saturdays,

P: [Mhmh.

C: [so, I could, I didn't sleep that night, so I had it already, planned, I, I, you know, that was enough and that I was gonna leave him that, that morning. And I did.

This client shows she used a number of strategies to deal with unwanted sexual aggression: (1) she acquiesced, (2) she had her 13-year-old son sleep with her for protection, (3) she used her physical strength to fight off her abuser off, (4) she left her abuser, and (5) she tried to move on with her life. For this client, the repeated rapes are not, it seems, nearly as threatening and/or violent as her estranged husband's having taken their child away from her.

Later on in the interview, the paralegal returns to the topic of sexual assault. She asks:

Excerpt 2 (continued):

Second reference to sexual assault:

P: O.K. Any other incident besid-, that has occurred during the past few months, whether he threatened to harm you, *or maybe attempted to, rape you, or force you to do something?*

C: No, that was, that was, like I said.

P: That's been the only time *that that has happened*?

C: *Well no. It occurred other times but, I can't recall.*

P: O.K.

C: *I mean it happened frequent.* And um, I even had my thirteen year-old son come over and stay with me to sleep with me cause I knew that if my son was there, he wouldn't come in the bedroom and

P: [*force himself?*

C: [*try anything.*

P: O.K. *So he has forced you to have sex several times during, during your marriage?*

C: [Yeah

The third excerpt stands in stark contrast to the two prior excerpts. The client in excerpt 3 has undoubtedly come to discuss a rape. In fact, she depicts it in painstaking detail, while remaining completely unflappable, even stoic. The narrative fragment included begins at this point where the client is recounting her response to her abuser's pleading with her to revive their relationship.

Excerpt 3: Can a woman let someone rape her?

C: Um, at that time, he was on top of me and I told him, um, **"You better finish this 'cause it's not gonna happen."** I had, I had, like I said, I had been telling him during past arguments, **"you need to either grow up, or kill me."** And that's what I meant by **"you need to finish this."**

P: Uhuh

C: Um, he started ripping at my clothes. He never said a word, but he started ripping at my clothes. Um, he ripped, I had three shirts on and he ripped my outer shirt. But uh, I started fighting with him, I started punching him with a closed fist and I was scratching at him. And I kicked him. When he didn't have my leg restrained, I was able to kick him. Um, but, on the floor, he was able to take off my pants, my underwear and my shoes. And during the struggle, I know at least twice, I was able to like sit up, or like, to try to like turn away from him, my upper body, and I did tell him that I was out of breath. I couldn't catch my breath. Um, but he continued. He finally got the pants, the underwear and the shoes off and then I was able to get up off the floor, and I went to open the front door and as I opened it and hit my rocking chair, he, he got to that point and he closed it.

P: O.K., so you opened the front door?

C: I opened the front door. My intentions were to yell, but that, since I was out of breath, I couldn't yell. But since he reached the door, I moved over to my sofa and um, he followed me there and he started trying to pull off my jacket and um, I had on three shirts. I struggled with him with the jacket and my long sleeved shirt, and during that course, I managed to um, kick him in the groin also. Um, I think I was still scratching at him at that point too. Um, and I was, by then I was tired with, with all the fighting so I didn't struggle as much and so he was able to take off my other t-shirts that I had on at that time.

P: Mhmh

C: Um, at that point, I did tell him um, (.03) uh (.01), I told him, **"What do you think, just 'cause I have no clothes on, I'm not gonna walk out the door?"** Now I don't know if he was like stopped because he was tired of the struggle too, but I, at that point, I ...

In retelling the sexual assault, the client says that she fought off her abuser, was not particularly afraid of him, mocked him, stiffened her body to make it difficult for him to manipulate her, called 911, and tried to yell out the front door. In her account of what happened after the rape (not reproduced for reasons of privacy and space), she tells her interviewer that she was active, thinking, and competent. That is, she was worrying about her children and about having enough time to take a shower to prepare for their coming home from school. She even reports having realized that she should not have been in the shower because she had been raped and should not have been washing away evidence. She talks of how she arranged for a friend to keep her children so she could go to the police. And she tells the interviewer that after speaking to the police, she followed their advice to take the necessary steps so that the police would be able to charge her abuser with the crime.

One interpretation of this woman's narrative of resistance is that her telling demonstrates her resolve to resist further domestic abuse. If we compare the rape narratives of the clients in excerpts 2 and 3, something interesting happens. The client in excerpt 2 stated that it was the night that she fought against her husband's sexual advances and that she had decided that the next morning she would leave him. She also, however, admitted "other times I'll just, this is, this is awful and disgusting, and disgusting, but I'll just lay there, other times." The client in excerpt 2 then suggests that sometimes, even when she did not want to engage in sexual activity, she let her husband have sex with her. So is it possible that the client in excerpt 3 is representing an instance of having let her husband rape her? Is she being strategic by physically resisting her abusers' unwanted sexual advances, in order to gain something substantive to report to authorities so that she can permanently make a break from her abuser? There is linguistic evidence in excerpt 3 to indicate that the client sees herself clearly as both witness and victim. She is able to speak from both of these discourse frames (Tannen 1993). In an extraordinary way, this client speaks from a witness frame while recounting the particulars of the rape. She is not crying as she gives meticulous details that include: when clothes came off, how clothes came off, how she struggled to resist both physically and intellectually, and how she spoke to the abuser in stern, humiliating, and threatening terms.

From her witness frame, she uses legalistic words and phrases as she describes what happened in utterances such as:

1. "When he didn't' have *my leg restrained*, I was able to kick him,"
2. "he did *penetrate* at that time, and then..."

Additionally she attempts to be precise in her description of actions with the following types of statements:

1. "...he kept putting his, *his left arm* to spread my, my legs."
2. "I started punching him *with a closed fist* and I was scratching him."

Her narrative flows on its own trajectory with very few interruptions from the paralegal, so these courtroom-like linguistic elements come from the client herself without elicitation or questioning from the interviewer.

Additionally, from the witness reporting frame, the client also includes direct quotes of her own prior language. Use of direct quotation is often interpreted by people, the press, and the courts as a technique of narrative precision, or a representation of teller fidelity to events as they really happened (Rumsey 1990; Matoesian 1999; Trinch 2010). While, on the one hand, the quotes make the client look like a faithful narrator on a quest for exactitude, on the other hand, the quotations also show a side of her that was not necessarily terrified by the rape experience. In other words, the quotes make her somewhat hard to interpret as a victim because they readily admit that she taunted her rapist, had a plan for survival, and was not shocked into submission. Moreover, in her narrative, she employs the following utterances that seem to indicate both that she resisted victimization and that in order to be a good reporter or witness, she has to be more than "just" a rape victim:

1. "What do you think, just 'cause I have no clothes on, I'm not going to walk out the door?"
2. "What's the matter big man, you can't get it up now?"
3. "What do you plan on doing now?"

Also from the witness-reporting frame, the client takes care to point out, again unprompted, that the abuser was saying nothing while he was raping her. Her linguistic choice to include this information seems to adhere to what is expected of her in these interviews. Apparently, she presumes that the interviewer would ask her, "What was he saying while he was raping you?" and indeed, interviewers regularly ask this type of question. And, most importantly, she confirms her witness frame by saying that during the rape she told her abuser:

4. (4) "You better enjoy this because I'm gonna report it."

This client's narrative includes all of the answers for which interviewers normally have to ask. Furthermore, her words do not construct her as having been emotionally distraught or terrified throughout the rape experience. Rather, her representation of rape makes her seem as though she had been in control of her own emotions and maybe of the situation in general. During the interview, she mentions having cried the next morning when her abuser was trying to reconcile with her. She says, "I *finally* blew up, I was crying during that time and I wouldn't face him." Here, she represents herself as having tried to hold it together during the incident. Her use of the word "finally" to introduce the loss of her own control shows a certain adherence to the rape trauma narrative. That is, she suggests that her crying is the last inevitable element in the succession of events she narrates.

But notice how differently she frames herself in the excerpt below:

Excerpt 4: Client changes her frame from witness to victim

> Um, so I called my girlfriend if she could take care of the kids. She asked me what was wrong and I told her that uh, he was there when I got home, that we had argued and that I, that I was tired of it. That I wanted to put a stop to it, and that I was gonna go talk to his parole officer. But, I had been calling and nobody had ever been answering at the parole offices, so I took my children to leave them with her. **And she came outside with me and she asked me what had happened. And I broke down at that time and I told her, "He raped me." And I said, "And I can't get a hold of the parole officer so I'm going to the police station." She asked me about, if I wanted her to accompany me and I told her no, but I continued crying, I broke down even more. And um, I told her no and I started walking away to get in my vehicle and she ran to let her husband know that she was gonna go with me. And she came with me and she took me to the [[police]] station, um, I gave the officer the report. He advised me to go to the ((name of)) hospital to be checked, um, then to go back to my home because he was gonna go with an investigator to take pictures and pick up evidence.** And uh, we did that, we stopped on the way for my friend's purse and her husband accompanied us. And, um, we went back to the house and um, the officer went back to the house and the officer had already advised me, **"You need to get some clothes and stay away from the home for a few days since you don't know how he is going to react."**

P: Mhmh

From this victim frame, the client shows herself to be very upset because of and as a result of the rape. First, she narrates that her friend noticed that something was wrong with her. In this way, the client suggests that she does appear to look different, if not from "any other woman," then definitely she does not look like herself. In her narrative, the client even has her friend asking her two times what was wrong.

Curiously, the client says she refused her girlfriend's help verbally, but she suggests, again from a victim frame, that her emotions spoke for her and told another story. The client goes from taking herself to see her alleged abuser's parole officer to being taken to the police station by her understanding and perceptive friend. At the police station, the officer to whom she makes the report, advises, informs, and protects her. The abuser is made out to be violent, even when the victim did not seem to be afraid of him in her account of the rape.

Perhaps it is too provocative to suggest that this client let her estranged husband rape her. And indeed, such a sentence—at some level—barely seems to make sense within a conventional cultural intelligibility of rape (Ehrlich 2007b). But as we look for agency in women's rape stories, we note and accept that women strategically allow their partners to have unwanted sex with them to avoid rape.[7] So, we should ask then, is it possible that some women might allow their partners to rape them—especially if they are seeking strategies to end an abusive marriage or relationship? In other words, did this woman fight back this time in order to bring her abuser's presumed entitlement to her body into question? Admittedly, it is dangerous to suggest that women are being pragmatic about being raped. Culturally, it is still quite a contentious belief that rape exists at all. Defense attorneys continue to get away with arguments in court that adult women wanted to have sex with the men they allege raped them. And they continue to suggest that these women, through their lies, managed to convince police, rape crisis advocates, and prosecutors to press charges against and bring to a rape trial a man that they willingly had sex with but then later decided to accuse of rape, because they got mad at him. Because this absurd defense of rape is such a prominent narrative that continues to resonate with judges and juries, it is probably time to realize that keeping silent about women's power and ability to resist rape is also very risky.

Gavey (2005: 215) argues that we need to "unsettle rigid gendered binaries around...representations of victimization." And as early as 1974, feminists, Medea and Thompson (1974: 6–7) stated that one condition necessary to end rape was to make all women learn "how to cope with the idea of rape." They maintained, "Until [rape] is reduced from an overwhelming, darkly evil prospect, the individual woman will not be able to deal with it." So, while we should not abandon rape narratives that speak of pain, suffering, and serious, long-term psychological damage, perhaps we should see if there is any value in adding more mundane representations of rape to the spectrum of gender-related violence. "Mundane" is used here in the sense that these rapes themselves are common, everyday occurrences, especially since these are the types of rapes—acquaintance, date, and marital rape that most often occur. And "mundane" is used to refer to the ways that some women actually represent rape sometimes.

CONCLUSION

McCaughey (1997: 17) suggests that the "broken body" narrative has been used repeatedly throughout the years to claim that "a set of social arrangements is objectively wrong." As a consequence, the rape trauma narrative has become the truth standard to which individual rape accounts are often held to for judgment and scrutiny. Lamb (1999: 133–34) proposes we change our focus from rape's ability to victimize women to women's ability to resist rape. She claims that such an approach would unite women by making them realize their sameness.[8]

Because Lamb and Gavey are quite certain that current status quo understandings of rape victimization are unlikely to end rape, they are committed to creating new understandings of victims. Yet they recognize the risk inherent in their proposals. The question of how much tolerance society will have for women claiming both victimization and resistance remains to be seen. For this reason, I cautiously propose that we maintain the category "victim," but that we try to re-humanize women who have been victimized by presenting them as complicated, competent, rational, thoughtful, strategic, and smart members of their families, workplaces, and communities. Pointing out resistance in rape narratives can help us show students of law, criminology, and criminal justice the complexities involved in the phenomenon of sexual victimization. This strategy may aid in striking an appropriate balance between demystifying rape and not trivializing it, as Gavey implores us to do. By adding these readings to our already existing representations of rape and by highlighting those nonvictim aspects of some women's rape narratives, we might find new and productive ways to treat women, to include them in the criminal justice system and ultimately even to stop rape.

By studying how women report rape, we cannot make claims about how women experience rape. However, we can see how rape narratives involve more than the idea that rape may cause its victims severe and irrevocable damage. With their texts in tow, we can, in a way, travel with women who have been sexually assaulted to new discursive territories where we can develop a richer understanding of the experience of rape—an understanding that can dispel existing stereotypes that box women in and limit their resilience. One strategy for getting to a place beyond "just" considering rape to be a crime might require travelling through existing texts of rape to see, in women's words, what they do afterwards, and how they themselves move forward after rape.

ACKNOWLEDGEMENTS

I am grateful for the National Science Foundation's Law and Social Science Program, the Social Science Research Council's Sexuality Research Fellowship Program, and the PSC-CUNY for funding data collection and data analysis for this chapter. I thank Susan Ehrlich, Greg Matoesian, Susan Hirsch, Norma

Mendoza-Denton, and John Conley for talking with me about this work. And finally, I would like to thank my parents, Sam and Angel Trinch for taking care of my then 3-year-old daughter and 5-year old son, so that their father could work while I went off to Cardiff, Wales, to participate in the Roundtable.

NOTES

1. I use the term "real rape" here ironically because what the public considers to be "real rape" (i.e., by a stranger that physically injures or that threatens great physical injury) occurs far less often than the majority of rapes (which are also quite "real") but for which the circumstances seem less violent to the public because the men that rape in these cases tend to know the women they rape.

2. Gavey (2005:172) states, "By the mid-1990s, the concept of victimization was arguably in crisis.... Representations of victims have always been double-edged, and there is some danger that understandings that invoke sympathy and support may again be overshadowed by those that invite disbelief and derision." As I mentioned earlier, I am not arguing that we do away with the terms "victim/survivor." Rather, my aim is to represent more fully the experiences of women who have endured some type of gendered violence like domestic abuse or sexual victimization/coercion so that we can demystify rape and stop reifying the idea that "women" experience rape in a certain way.

3. Frankly, this fact is precisely the point of the chapter. Some critics, both sociolinguists and other social scientists, of this notion that women do not always represent rape with trauma have tried to suggest that there is an essential trauma narrative that indeed would occur if only the conditions were right. They have said that the context of the narratives I examine (i.e., the protective order interview) does not allow for this narrative to emerge. While I do not deny this possibility, as an anti-essentialist, my point is that humans are flexible. And the data suggest that they are often flexible and adaptive to context after rape as well.

4. All names, dates, and other identifying characteristics have been changed.

5. Transcription conventions should be understood in the following way:
P refers to the paralegal-interviewer

C refers to the client

Bold type is meant to call the readers' attention to those parts of the dialogue that refer to the points I am making in the text.
[single left-hand brackets denote an overlap

((.05)) Double parentheses with decimals refer to pauses and silences in seconds

...refers to omitted text, irrelevant to the analysis

((month)) Words inside double parenthesis are author insertions and notes

( ) Empty parentheses refer to inaudible utterances.

6. In studies on battered women, it is remarkable how many women report having had sex they did not want to have. Campbell et al. (1998) and Woodham (2008) show that women acquiesce to unwanted sex as a means of managing and trying to control their abusers' and

rapists' violence toward them. In Ehrlich's data (2012 and in this volume), one of the rapists actually coerces the woman to have sex with him by threatening rape, as if there were a difference.

7. Terry A. Kupers ([2001] 2007) suggests that some men in prison may also utilize this strategy to avoid being raped and brutalized repeatedly. He interviewed a man that he described as heterosexual, yet effeminate, that decided to become another prisoner's "woman." While he considered the sexual acts that he engaged in to be coerced, rather than consensual, he saw his "relationship" with a physically dominant man to be a protection against other prisoners' raping him.

8. "This is an approach that could unite women, that sees victimization as a public health and safety issue and puts responsibility for change on the party most likely to cause the problem: men. The focus on difference—victim, survivor, battered woman, sexually abused, those who can remember, those who cannot...eclipses the fact that these are, we are, women who have a lot more in common than men and the media would have us believe" (Lamb 1999: 134).

REFERENCES

Bogoch, Bryna. 2007. The victim as "other": Analysis of the language of acquittal decisions in sexual offences in the Israeli Supreme Court. In *The Language of Sexual Crime*, ed. Janet Cotterill, 159–179. New York: Palgrave Macmillan.

Bourgois, Philippe. 2004. The every day violence of gang rape. In *Violence in War and Peace: An Anthology*, ed. Nancy Scheper-Hughes and Philippe Bourgois, 343–47. Oxford: Blackwell Publishing.

Campbell, Jacquelyn, Linda Rose, Joan Kub, and Daphne Nedd. 1998. Voices of strength and resistance: A contextual and longitudinal analysis of women's responses to battering. *Journal of Interpersonal Violence* 13: 743–62.

Cole, Alyson. 2007. *The Cult of True Victimhood: From the War of Welfare to the War on Terrorism.* Stanford, CA: Stanford University Press.

Des Rosiers, N., Feldthusen, B., and Hankivsky, O. A. R. 1998. Legal compensation for sexual violence: Therapeutic consequences and consequences for the judicial system. *Psychology, Public Policy and Law* 4: 433–51.

Doe, Jane. 2003. *The Story of Jane Doe.* Toronto: Vintage Canada of Random House.

Ehrlich, Susan. 2001. *Representing Rape: Language and Sexual Consent.* London: Routledge.

———. 2007a. Normative discourses and representations of coerced sex. In *The Language of Sexual Crime*, ed. Janet Cotterill, 126–38. New York: Palgrave Macmillan.

———. 2007b. Legal discourse and the cultural intelligibility of gendered meanings. *Journal of Sociolinguistics* 11(4): 452–77.

———. 2012. Text trajectories, legal discourse and gendered inequalities. *Applied Linguistics Review* 3(1): 47–73.

Gavey, Nicola. 2005. *Just Sex?: The Cultural Scaffolding of Rape.* London and New York: Routledge.

Haag, P. 1996. "Putting your body on the line": The question of violence, victims, and the legacies of second-wave feminism. *Differences: A Journal of Feminist Cultural Studies* 8(2): 23–67.

Herman, Judith L. 1992. *Trauma and Recovery: The Aftermath of Violence—from Domestic Abuse to Political Terror.* New York: Basic Books.

Holmstrom, Lynda, and Ann Burgess. 1974. Rape trauma syndrome. *American Journal of Psychiatry* 131(9): 981–86.

Hymes, Dell. 1974. *Foundations of Sociolinguistics: An Ethnographic Approach*. Philadelphia: University of Pennsylvania Press.

Kupers, Terry A. 2007. Rape and the prison code. In *Men's Lives* (7th ed.), ed. Michael S. Kimmel and Michale A. Messner, 348–53. New York: Pearson. Reprinted from *Prison Masculinities* (2001), ed. Dan Sabo. Philadelphia: Temple University Press.

Lamb, Sharon. 1999. Constructing the victim: Popular images and lasting labels. In *New Versions of Victims: Feminists Struggle with the Concept*, ed. Sharon Lamb, 108–38. New York and London: New York University Press.

Larrain, S., and T. Rodriguez. 1993. The origins of control and domestic violence against women. In *Gender, Women and Health in the Americas*, ed. E. Gómez-Gómez, 184–91. Washington, DC: Pan American Health Organization.

Lefley, H., C. Scott, M. Llabre, and D. Hicks. 1993. Cultural beliefs about rape and victims' responses in three ethnic groups. *American Journal of Orthopsychiatry* 63: 623–31.

Matoesian, Gregory M. 1993. *Reproducing Rape: Domination through Talk in the Courtroom*. Cambridge: Polity Press.

———. 1999. Intertextuality, affect, and ideology in legal discourse. *Text* 19(1): 73–109.

———. 2001. *Law and the Language of Identity: Discourse in the William Kennedy Smith Rape Trial*. New York: Oxford University Press.

McCaughey, M. 1997. *Real Knockouts: The Physical Feminism of Women's Self-Defense*. New York and London: New York University Press.

Medea, A., and K. Thompson. 1974. *Against Rape: A Survival Manual for Women: How to Avoid Entrapment and How to Cope with Rape Physically and Emotionally*. New York: Farrar, Straus & Giroux.

Michael, R., J. Gagnon, E. Laumann, and G. Kolata. 1994. *Sex in America: A Definitive Survey*. New York: Little Brown and Company.

Mooney, Annabelle. 2007. When rape is (not quite) rape. In *The Language of Sexual Crime*, ed. Janet Cotterill, 198–216. New York: Palgrave Macmillan.

Ponterotto, Diane. 2007. The repertoire of *complicity vs. coercion*: The discursive trap of the rape trial protocol. In *The Language of Sexual Crime*, ed. Janet Cotterill, 104–25. New York: Palgrave Macmillan.

Rumsey, Alan. 1990. Wording, meaning, and linguistic ideology. *American Anthropologist* 92: 346–61.

Sanday, Peggy Reeves. 1990. *Fraternity Gang Rape: Sex, Brotherhood and Privilege on Campus*. New York: New York University Press.

Schiffrin, Deborah. 1996. Narrative as self-portrait: Sociolinguistic constructions of identity. *Language in Society* 25: 167–203.

Tannen, Deborah. 1993. *Framing in Discourse*. New York: Oxford University Press.

Tiersma, Peter. 2007. The language of consent in rape law. In *The Language of Sexual Crime*, ed. Janet Cotterill, 104–25. New York: Palgrave Macmillan.

Trinch, Shonna. 2001. Managing euphemism and transcending taboos: Negotiating the meaning of sexual assault in Latinas' narratives of domestic violence. *Text* 21(4): 567–610.

———. 2003. *Latinas' Narratives of Domestic Abuse: Discrepant Versions of Violence*. Philadelphia and Amsterdam: John Benjamins Publishing.

———. 2010. Disappearing discourse: Performative texts and identity in legal contexts. *Critical Inquiry in Language Studies* 7(2): 207–29.

Ullman, Stephen. 1966. Semantic universals. In *Universals in Language*, ed. J. Greenberg, 217–63. Cambridge, MA: MIT Press.

Williams, J. E., and K. E. Holmes. 1981. *The Second Assault: Rape and Public Attitudes*. Westport, CT: Greenwood Press.

Woodhams, Jessica. 2008. How victims behave during stranger sexual assaults. Unpublished manuscript.

INDEX

Note: Page numbers followed by *f* and *t* indicate figures and tables, respectively.

in Belgian Assize Court, 110
intertextual practices of, 21
re-performance of pretrial dialogue, in
  Belgian Assize trials, 112–113
Deference structure, in information-
  gathering part of police interview,
  71–72
Definition(s). *See also* Dictionary(ies)
  authorized legal, 213–214
  dictionary, *vs.* plain and ordinary meaning,
    274, 284
  legal, and *The Highway Code* (U.K.),
    273–275, 284
Deictic expressions, 148, 160, 161–162
Deixis, and embedding of police interviews
  in courtroom activity, 162–163
Delgadillo, Erica, 5, 8, 22
Delgado, Richard, 25, 242
Delmas-Marty, M., 120
Delocation, 4
Denial, defendant's, reference to, in Shipman
  trial, 154–156, 159
Derrida, Jacques, 9, 171
Description, evaluative character of, 231
Deserving victims, 289
Des Rosiers, N., 291
"Devil" terms, 235
Dey, Ian, 229
D'hondt, S., 109, 119, 122
Dialogical principle, 9
Dialogic mode, in criminal trial, 160–163
Dialogue
  intertextuality and, 99
  transformation to monologue, 127,
    164–165
Dictation, mediation and, 10
Dictionary(ies)
  and definition of "reasonable," 210–211
  definitions in, *vs.* plain and ordinary
    meaning, 274
  as discourse of authority, 220
  jury's request for, 24, 216, 219
Digital radio, effects on communication, 49
Di Luzio, Aldo, 9
Diminutive(s), in Dutch, 131, 144n7
Direct quotes
  and narrative precision, 300
  and teller fidelity, 300
Direct speech, 202, 204n9
  in Belgian Assize trials, 111, 119–120
Discoursavization, 107

Discourse. *See also* Legal discourse; Legal-lay
    discourse; Metadiscourse
  authoritative. *See* Authoritative discourse
  of authority, 212
  categorization systems for, 8, 229, 230t
  co-narrated, in Belgian Assize trials,
    114–116
  educational, 11–12, 25
  event-level, transformation of, 16
  expert, 248
  expert-lay knowledge, 230t
  folk, 248
  genres of, 24, 226, 229–231, 241, 241t
  institutional, 6, 37
  interprofessional, 6
  intraprofessional, 6
  judicial, 22–25, 214
  legal and nonlegal, differentiation of, 226
  legal-lay distinction and, 226, 228–229
  professional-lay, 6
  reflexive capacity of, 10
  self-othering, 119
  triangular travel of, 120–121
Discourse analysis, 38, 60
  of rape reporting, 289
Discourse categorization systems (DCS),
    8, 229, 230t
Discourse frames, of raped woman,
    299–302
Discourse style, *legal-lay* distinction and, 24
Discretionary/permissive rules, modals
    in, 269
Discretionary power of the chair, 110
Discrimination, in witness interviews, 81
Discursive practices, definition of, 4–5
Discursive trajectory(ies)
  collision of, in police work, 17, 55–56, 74
  of lay-suspect discourse, 56
  of legal-police discourse, 55–56
Dispatcher, role in police call handling, 47,
    48–50, 51
Dispreferred responses, 198
Distress, defendant's, reference to, in
    Shipman trial, 154–156, 159
Dixon (Chief Justice, Australia), 220
  on "reasonable doubt," 214–215
DNA, research collection of
  as complex transaction, 259–262
  folk-legal theories of, 257–262, 263
  as gift by subject, 257–259
  misuse of, subjects' fears of, 255

DNA, research collection of (*Cont.*)
 and ownership of specimens, 256–257,
  259–262, 264n2
 and privacy issues, subjects' fears about,
  254–256
 as sale by subject, 257–259
 subject population, 248–249, 264n1
 subjects' consent and, 26, 247–248
 and subjects' fears, 254–256, 262–263
 subjects' theories of the transaction for,
  256–262
Dobash, R. Emerson, 195
Dobash, Russell P., 195
Dobson, Allison W., 5, 8
Doe, Jane, 288, 290
Domain cueing, legal-lay discourse and, 228
Domestic violence. *See also* Battered women
 case reports of, 87–88
 women's strategies for dealing with, 195
Doubt. *See also* Beyond reasonable doubt;
  Reasonable doubt
 absence of, 210
 categories of, 210
 degrees of, 210
 gravity of, 210
Dove (strychnia poisoning victim), 178
Dressler, L. G., 257
Drew, Paul, 7, 56, 129, 226, 228, 230, 231,
  237, 249
Duranti, A., 127
Duration, in police interviews, 93
Durfy, Margaret, 237
Dutch criminal law system, 126

Eades, Diana, 14, 81, 82, 98, 140,
  203n1, 203n8
Education, entextualization of talk in, 82
Educational discourse, 11–12, 25
Edwards, Derek, 130, 231
Edwards, Erin, 5, 8
Eggly, Susan, 250
Ehrlich, Susan, 4, 13–14, 22–23, 28, 107,
  191, 203n1, 208, 212, 233, 288,
  289, 291, 302
Elias, Norbert, 38
Embedding
 definition of, 148
 Genette's theory of, 148
 of narrative in narrative, 154
 in narrative theory, 149

in news coverage, 149–151
of police interviews in prosecution case
  (Shipman trial), 148
of speech within speech, 148
Emergency call handling (Britain), 35–38
Emergent meaning, of informed consent,
  251, 262
Entextualization, 4, 9–10, 107, 120–121,
  124n2, 126, 141–143, 168, 189–190,
  197, 249
 and authority, 94
 in Belgian Assize procedure, 108–109
 definition of, 80, 126
 in Palmer trial, 169
 and police call handling, 37–38
 and power relations, 94
 of suspect's statement, 141
Essential trauma narrative, 304n3
Euphemism(s), and rape, 289, 292–293
Evaluation, description and, 231
Evaluative boosters, 156
Evans, Robert, 8, 230
Everyday conversational mechanisms, 120,
  121, 122, 123
"The Everyday Violence of Gang Rape"
  (Bourgois), 291
Evidence
 admissibility of, 55, 57–58
 improperly obtained, 55
 from investigative interviews, 55
 in Palmer trial, 176–177
Examination-in-chief, in Palmer trial, 169,
  173–175, 178–179
Excited utterance exception to hearsay, 13
Expert, *vs.* lay, 8
Expert detainee, 6
Expert discourse(s), of genetic
  research, 248
Expertise
 contributory, 8
 interactional, 8
Expert-lay knowledge/discourse, 230t
Expert witness(es), 6
 institutional *vs.* lay role of, 7
Eyewitness accounts, 73

Fact(s)
 in *Baby* case, 191–192, 200
 determination of, in adversarial
  system, 191

and problem of government response, 276–279

and problem of grammar, 275–276

and problem of "legal definitions," 273–275

and problem of societal standards, 281–283, 285

public consultation about revision of, 266–267, 270, 272–283, 276–279, 281, 284, 286

public perception of, 285–286

recommended use of reflective items by pedestrians, 275–276, 277f, 286n5

reentextualization of legal statutes in, 270

as "rules of the road," 266

secondary context of, 267–268, 268t, 279

"should/should not" in, 270, 275

simultaneous functions of, 266

and societal expectations, 276, 281–283

and traffic law, public misunderstanding of, 270

Hobbs, Pamela, 233

Hodges, A., 148

Hoeyer, Klaus, 250

Holmes, J., 156

Holmes, K. E., 293

Holmstrom, Lynda, 290

Holquist, Michael, 70

Holt, Elizabeth, 232

Home Office Communications Directorate, 36

Horowitz, Irwin A., 207, 211

Horse riding rules, in *The Highway Code* (U.K.), 277–278

Horton, Dave, 282

Hostettler, J., 180

Hutton, Chris, 213

Hymes, Dell, 22, 212, 226, 295

Hypodiegesis, 148

Identity, of defendant, production of, by defense counsel, in Belgian Assize trials, 113

Ideology(ies)

language and, 8–9

in lay-legal communication, 25–27

linguistic, 197, 202

referentialist linguistic, 22–23, 197

textualist linguistic, 22–23, 197–198

victim, and raped women, 290–292

Iedema, R., 148, 149

Imbens-Bailey, Alison, 37

Incommensurable practices, 217, 217f

Inconsistency(ies)

in police interviewees' accounts, 82

vs. lies, 14, 82

Indexical meaning, 107, 109

Indictment, in Dutch criminal cases, 139, 144n13

Indirect speech, 164, 202, 204n9

in Belgian Assize trials, 111

Inference, in police interviews, 85

Information-flow model, 39–40, 52

Informed consent. *See also* Consent ceremony; Consent interviews

behavioral process of, failure of, 263

as discursive process, 26, 248, 250–254, 259, 262

emergent meaning of, 251, 262

in genetic context, and research policy, 263

and intertextuality, 262

as legal-lay communication, 248

to research, solicitation of, 262

from research subjects, 26, 247, 248

sociolinguistic nature of, 248

unfolding discourse of, 253–254

Insanity argument, in Belgian Assize trials, 116–119, 122

Institution(s), long intertextual chains in, 82

Institutional discourse, 6

police call handling and, 37

Institutional interaction

legal-lay as, 7

vs. ordinary discourse, 230t

Institutional memory, police call handling and, 52

Institutional record, entextualization of talk in, 82

Interaction(s)

communicative, 38–39, 51

context and, 148

institutional, 7, 148

with jury, 7

legally defined, in police interview, 62

police interrogation and, 135

of police officers and persons attending incident, 51

professional, 148

three-level approach to, 38–39

in trials, 6–7

Mandatory rules
  The Highway Code (U.K.) as, 266–267,
    269–270, 278, 284–285
  modals in, 269
Manifest intertextuality
  definition of, 16
  and interdiscursivity, 16
Manzo, John, 19
Maouloud Baby v. the State of Maryland, 22,
    190–195, 197, 204n2
  appeal of, and appellate opinions,
    199–202
  and complainant's (Jewel's)
    unwillingness to undergo another trial,
    204n4, 204n10
Marginality, and recontextualization,
    24–25, 242
Marks, Monique, 57
Martin, Elizabeth A., 220
Martinez, Esther, 12
Maryns, Katrijn, 19, 25, 108, 109
Matoesian, Gregory M., 6, 13, 107, 109, 140,
    148, 203n1, 289, 291, 300
Matthews, David, 39, 50
Maybin, Janet, 14
Maynard, Douglas, 19
McCabe, Allyssa, 37
McCaughey, M., 303
McNamara, Beverley, 249, 250, 251
Meaning. *See also* Emergent meaning
  compositional *vs.* idiomatic, 218
  of disputed words, 274
  institutional, embedding and, 165
  plain/ordinary, 211, 274
  prototypical, of words, 274
  socio-historical relevance and significance
    of, 149
  stable (context-free), 22, 197–199
  textual, 249
Meaning-making, 149
  intertextuality and, in police interview, 86
Medea, A., 302
Mediation
  and delivery of legal information, 14–15
  and information gathering, 14–15
  as interactional process, 17
  and lay people's access to police assistance,
    14–15
  in police settings, 14–18
  processes of, 10, 14

Mediational means, 10–11, 14
  appropriation of, 15
  individuals acting with, 14–15
  and police interview, 17
Mediational routines, and social distance, 15
Mediational tools, 10, 14
Medical counseling, entextualization of
    talk in, 82
Medical encounters, 6
  consent-taking in, 8
Medical ethics
  and consent process, 250, 262
  and DNA research, 247
Medical expert(s), in Palmer trial, 180–181
Medical research, ethical and legal
    considerations in, 247
Mehan, Hugh, 82, 89, 90, 93, 94
Melai, A. L., 144n13
Membership category, 229
Memon, Amina, 57
Men, in prison, acquiescence to unwanted
    sex, 305n7
*Merriam-Webster's Advanced Learner's
    Dictionary,* 210
Mertz, Elizabeth, 6, 18, 82, 107, 109, 197,
    200, 211, 213, 216, 249, 262
Mervis, Carolyn B., 228
Metadiegesis, 148
Metadiscourse, 4, 10
  authorized voice and, 207, 209
  in Belgian Assize trials, 111
  hierarchical power dynamics of, 214
  judges', and linguistic ideologies, 214–215
  legal, 23–24, 213–214
Metadiscursive devices, in Belgian Assize
    trials, 118
Metaphor(s), 115
  for subjects' fears about genetic research,
    255–256, 263
Metrailer, Rosemary, 233
Michael, R., 293
Michaud, Shari L., 62
Microformation, textual, 12–13
Mills, Elizabeth (chambermaid, witness in
    Palmer trial), 174, 177
Milne, Rebecca, 57, 63
Miranda warning, 12
Miscommunication. *See also* Communication
    breakdown
  of fingerprinting caution, 64–67, 72

Post-traumatic stress disorder, as necessary
evidence of rape, 291
Potter, Jonathan, 231
Power, of raped women, 290
Powesland, Peter, 12
Precedent
legal, 4, 18
legal-linguistic, 23
Precontextualization, 141
Pretrial dialogue
in Belgian Assize trials, 120–121
re-performance of, in Belgian Assize trials,
111–116
Pretrial documentation, referrals to, in
Palmer, 169, 184
Pretrial investigation, in Belgian Assize
procedure, 108, 110
Principal, role of, 121–122, 144n15
in analysis of police interviews, 61, 69–70
of confessional or informative talk, 61
professional voice and, 17, 56
Prisoners' Counsel Act (1836), 21, 168,
179–180, 184
Privacy, DNA research and, subjects' fears
about, 254–256
Procès-verbal, 120–121
Professional, *vs.* lay, 8
Professional-lay discourse, 6
Professionals, as lay persons, 6
Professional voice, 17
of oncologists, 56
of police, 56–57, 63
and role of principal, 56
Proof, beyond reasonable doubt, 11, 23–24,
72, 207. *See also* Beyond reasonable
doubt; Standard of proof, legal
Proof principles, 209
Prosecution
in Belgian Assize Court, 110
discursive trajectories and, 17
Prosecutors, intertextual practices of, 20–21
Protection from abuse orders. *See* Protective
order(s)
Protective order(s), 292
Protective order interviews, women's
narrative reports of rape in, 292–293
Public hearing(s), 24
categories of participants, before
New Jersey AssemblyJudiciary
Committee, 237, 237t

on same-sex marriage law, by New Jersey
AssemblyJudiciary Committee,
227–228, 236–241
Public testimony
discourse of, 237
features of, 241t
Public transcript, witness statement as, 17

Question(s)
in adjacency pairs, 129
conversational operation of, 129
Question and answer
dialogue, conversion to monologue,
164–165
re same-sex marriage, before New Jersey
Supreme Court, 234–235, 234t
Question-answer chains, 62
in police interview, 70–71
Question-answer pair(s), in police
interview, 70–71
Questioning. *See also* Cross-examination;
Examination-in-chief; Police
interrogation; Police interview(s)
adversarial, and appellate court's likely
opinion, 235
Quotation(s). *See also* Reported speech;
Verbatim quotes
in Belgian Assize trials, 111
from case file, in Belgian Assize procedure,
108–109
in police interview, 83–84
prosecution's use of, in Shipman trial, 21

Radio communication, Airwavespeak
for, 49–50
Rao, Radhika, 257
Rape
acquiescence to, as strategy to avoid
violence, 296, 302, 304n6, 305n7
aftermath of, 290, 291, 303
and consent, 289, 302
as crime, 289
defense of, 302
demystifying, vs trivializing, 303, 304n2
disclosure of, by Latina women, 27
in domestic life, 294
epistemology of, 290
and euphemisms, 289, 292–293
as everyday violence, 27, 293, 302
in intimate partner violence, 295

misconception about, and investigative
interviewing, 74
negative practices in, 14
in Palmer trial, 169, 176
and police interviews, 12, 56, 60, 70,
72–74, 86–87, 89–91, 94–95, 97–98
resources for, in police interview,
99–100, 99f
of road traffic law, in *The Highway Code*
(U.K.), 267–268, 268t, 286n1
in suspect's statement, 135
textual travel as, 206–207
in witness-interviewer dialogue, 82
Recontextualization phrases, 144n6
Recontextualizing agents, 12
police officers as, 72–74
Recontextualizing context, 12, 156
Recontextualizing space, police interview as,
99–100, 99f
Recovery, of people victimized by
violence, 291
Reddy, Margaret, 40
Reenactment, in Shipman trial, 21
Re-enactment, 165–166
in Belgian Assize trials, 111
of oral dialogue, in Belgian Assize
procedure, 109
of police interviews, in Shipman trial,
160–163
of trial performance, in Belgian Assize
trials, 114–118
Reentextualization, 4
and police call handling, 37–38
in police interview, 85
Rees (witness, Palmer trial), 177, 180, 182
Referentialist linguistic ideology,
22–23, 197
Reflexive capacity, of discourse, 10
Reflexivity
of context, 137
of language, 80–81
of talk and context, 127
Refusal(s)
interactional features characterizing, 198
weak agreement implying, 198–199
Relational orientation, of legal
discourse, 7–8
Release form, research subjects' perceptions
of, 252
Relexicalization, 272

Religious affiliations, of public speakers
before New Jersey Assembly Judiciary
Committee, 240
Religious ritual, and language, 213
Relocation, 4
Renkema, Jan, 38, 80
Repetition, 13, 160, 170–171
embedded, 165–166
as folk-linguistic category, 13
as legal category, 13
Reported speech
in Belgian Assize trials, 111, 121
in legal contexts, 202
in litigant brief for *Lewis v. Harris,* 232
in public testimony before New Jersey
Assembly Judiciary Committee, 239
in unfolding understanding of informed
consent, by research subject, 253–254
Research
benefit-sharing model for, 257
charitable trust model for, 257
public trust in, 250
stewardship model for, 257
Resilience, of raped women, 290, 292
Resistance
by abused women, 196
consent as strategy of, for raped woman,
191–196
of raped women, 196, 290, 292,
298–299, 303
Resistance narrative, of raped women, 289
Restraining order(s). *See* Protective order(s)
Rights, suspect's, 55. *See also* Police caution
communication of, by police, 56
Right to contact friend/relative, 55, 58
informing suspect about, 58–59
Right to legal advice, 55, 58
Right to silence, 55. *See also* Police caution
Ritual, linguistic behavior as, 206
Roberts (witness, Palmer trial), 177, 182
Robinson, George (medical expert,
Palmer trial), 179
Rock, Frances, 5, 6, 12, 14–17, 18, 21, 27, 56,
64, 69–70, 73, 81, 83, 91, 92, 100, 109,
147, 161, 208
Rodriguez, T., 293
Rosch, Eleanor, 228
Rose, Linda, 195, 196, 304n6
Ross, Norrie, 223n6
Rothstein, Mark A., 247

Text(s) (*Cont.*)
connections between, 9
and context, 9, 126–127, 148, 249
cultural processes and, 249
definition of, 4, 126, 189, 249
dialogicality of, 149
dialogue among, 9
extractability of, 107
as fabric, 9
intertextuality as "property" of, 9
as mosaic, 19
not travelling well, 189
primary, police interview and, 85
production of, from police interview,
83–84, 97
stable and fluid elements of, 11
successive, as functions of position in
sequence, 94–95
as tapestry, 17
as tool for social action, 18
Text trajectory(ies), 4, 11, 249
in Belgian Assize trials, 121
intersection of, in witness interview, 79
Textual chains, 9, 80, 82–87
from regulatory frames, 87–90
Textualism, and legal interpretation,
274, 284
Textualist linguistic ideology, 22–23,
197–198
Textuality, *vs.* orality, 19–20
Textual microformation, 12–13
Textual trajectories. *See* Text trajectory(ies)
Textual travel, 3, 8–14
and authority, 94
from institutional to noninstitutional,
11–12
in legal system, 189, 203n1
perspectives on, 3–4
related usages, 4
retained shape but changed meaning
in, 208
trajectories. *See* Text trajectory(ies)
variables of, in police interview,
99–100, 99*f*
Thomas, J. A., 71
Thompson, K., 302
Thought presentation, in police interview,
83–84
Tiersma, Peter M., 80, 212, 222, 271,
274, 275

Time
and subjects' fears about genetic
research, 256
textual travel in, 148
Timing, in police interviews, 93
Tinsley, Yyette, 223n3
Toolan, Michael, 13, 153
Topic initiations and transitions, 62
in police interviews, 71
Tracy, Karen, 5, 8, 22, 41, 233, 234, 235, 237
Trajectory(ies). *See* Discursive
trajectory(ies); Text trajectory(ies)
Transfer-and-transformation, 80
Transformation, 208
and entextualization, 189
in legal settings, 81
in police interviews, 89–93
of rape into consensual sex, 202
Transformational text(s), closing
speeches as, 179
Transmodality, in witness interviews, 79
Trauma, of people victimized by
violence, 291
Trauma narrative, 304n3
Trauma of rape narrative, 289, 291
Trial(s). *See also* Rape trial; *specific trial*
interactions in, 6–7
as professional-lay discourse, 6
Trial performance
in Belgian Assize trials, 119–120, 121
re-enactment of, in Belgian Assize trials,
114–118
Triangular travel of discourse, 120–121
Trimboli, Lily, 223n3
Trinch, Shonna, 12, 13, 27, 202, 203n1, 289,
292, 300
Trust
as emergent property, 250
public, in research, 250
Tsohatzidis, Savas L., 38
Turn-taking structure, and analysis of police
interviews, 69–73

Ullman, Stephen, 292
Uptake
of instruction/direction, 206
voice and, 189, 212
Urban, Greg, 4, 9–10, 107, 108, 124n2, 189,
215, 249
USSHHS, 256

Wodak, R., 148

Women. *See also* Battered women; Latina women; Raped women
  commonality of, 303, 305n8
  diverse expression of sexual violence they suffered, 293

Woodhams, Jessica, 196, 304n6

Woolard, Kathryn, 197

Word frequency
  in British National Corpus, 274, 281, 286n4, 286n8
  and lexical access, 274, 281

Worton, Michael, 79

Wray, Alison, 211, 218, 219

Wrightsman, Lawrence S., 233

Writing, of police interview, 83–84

Written briefs, 18, 234
  and oral arguments, comparison of, 234

Written statements, in Belgian Assize trials, 120

Written text
  call handler construction of, 43–46
  talk as means to, 82, 97

Wyeth, M., 36

Young, Warren, 223n3

Zimmerman, Don H., 16, 37, 41